The Catskills

THE CATSKILLS

*An Illustrated Historical Guide
with Gazetteer*

by

Arthur G. Adams

FORDHAM UNIVERSITY PRESS

NEW YORK

© Copyright 1977 and 1990 by Arthur G. Adams
All rights reserved
LC 90-82351
ISBN 0-8232-1300-5 (clothbound)
ISBN 0-8232-1301-3 (paperback)
Second edition, revised.
Fordham paperback, 1993
Second paperback printing, 1995

First published as *Guide to the Catskills and the Region Around* by Sun Publishing Company, Albuquerque, NM., 1977.

Library of Congress Cataloging-in-Publication Data

Adams, Arthur G.
   The Catskills : an illustrated historical guide with gazetteer / by Arthur G. Adams.—2nd rev. ed.
       p.   cm.
   Rev. ed. of: Guide to the Catskills, with trail guide and maps / by Arthur G. Adams . . . [et al.]. 1975.
   ISBN 0-8232-1300-5 (cloth).—ISBN 0-8232-1301-3 (paper)
   1. Catskill Mountains (N.Y.)—Guidebooks. 2. Trails—New York (State)—Catskill Mountains. 3. Hiking—New York (State)—Catskill Mountains. I. Guide to the Catskills, with trail guide and maps. II. Title.
F127.C3A33   1990
917.47′380443—dc20   90-82351
                                                      CIP

Printed in the United States of America

Dedicated to my wife and my mother,
whose encouragement and help
made this book possible.

Contents

Acknowledgments

No work of this scope is written without the aid of many people. Of necessity the author is dependent upon the goodwill and interest of many private citizens who are willing to share their own knowledge and family memories.

I would particularly like to acknowledge the kind help of Alf Evers, noted Catskill historian and author of *The Catskills: From Wilderness to Woodstock*, for his encouragement and informative comments; Roland Van Zandt, author of *The Catskill Mountain House*, for his well-wishes and whose earlier book served as an important source of information; Edward G. West, former Superintendent of Land Acquisition, New York State Conservation Department, whose editing of the topographical information in the author's earlier book, *Guide to the Catskills with Trail Guide and Maps*, has continuing benefit in the present book; Professor Dale Stein of the State University of New York at New Paltz, coordinator of an important lecture series on the Catskills who gave early and continuing encouragement; he introduced the author to Dr. Alfred H. Marks, Coordinator of the New Paltz Center for Catskill Mountain and Hudson River Studies, who ultimately collaborated in the illustration of this book; James E. Lawrence of Outdoor Publications, Ithaca, N. Y., and Charles E. Dornbusch of the Hope Farm Press and Bookshop, Cornwallville, N. Y., who helped obtain valuable information and gave encouragement.

Thanks are also owing to Esther Dunn of Twilight Park and New York City and Justine L. Hommel, Librarian of the Haines Falls Free Library, who gave information on Twilight Park, as did Mr. John P. Adriance of Poughkeepsie.

Further thanks are due to John N. Watt, General Manager of the Otesaga Hotel and Cooper Inn at Cooperstown, who made it clear to the author that it was of utmost importance to include his area in this book; Keith and Daniel Smiley of Lake Mohonk and Kenneth B. Phillips, both Senior and Junior, for information on Mohonk and Minnewaska and also for personal assistance; Harris Gordon of the Catskill Mountain Transportation Co.; Walter C. Fitzpatrick, Deputy Chief Engineer, Board of Water Supply, City of New York; Mrs. Grace Wilner of the Suffern Public Library and also the staffs of the Mahwah and Ramsey, N. J., Public Libraries; Leon and Harriet Greenman, collaborators in the author's earlier book and editors and publisher of Walking News; and finally, many people in the public relations departments of the former Erie and New York Central Railroads and the late New York State Historian, Albert B. Corey.

It is also fitting to give thanks and ackowledgment to my wife, Daryl, my mother, Mrs. Arthur G. Adams, Sr., and Mrs. Alfred Marks, who all put up with several years of early breakfasts, late suppers and poor accommodations and who put up innumerable picnic lunches and took reams of field notes, and last, but not least, gave unfailing encouragement in what seemed an endless work.

Preface

The Catskill Mountain Region, situated near the nation's largest cities and within one hundred miles of the Eastern Megalopolis, has attracted many visitors since the early 19th century. Ever since James Kirke Paulding's *New Mirror For Travellers* was published in 1828, there has been no shortage of tourist guidebooks—until about thirty years ago when Eric Posselt's *The Rip Van Winkle Trail* went out of publication. While some very fine books have been written about the area by Alf Evers, Arthur Mack and Roland Van Zandt, none of them have been comprehensive tourist guidebooks in the traditional sense. The present author has also collaborated in writing a book entitled *Guide to the Catskills with Trail Guide and Maps*, but this was designed to meet the special needs of the hiker and outdoorsman more than the requirements of the general tourist whose primary interests are scenic and historic.

From 1876 until about 1920 several excellent annual tourist guidebooks were written by Walton Van Loan, Wallace Bruce and Ernest Ingersoll. Van Loan published and distributed his own guides, working from Catskill, N. Y. Bruce's books were sponsored by the Hudson River Day Line and were published by various firms through the years. Ingersoll's book was published by Rand McNally Co. The various railroads serving the region also sponsored annual guidebooks. With the changeover from water and rail travel to auto touring these guidebooks gradually went out of print. Various publications of the State of New York, the AAA and the oil companies devote a limited amount of space to the region, but the area has not been treated in depth for a considerable time.

It is to fill this need that this book has been written. The reader will find that the book falls into four major sections. The first three deal, respectively, with the geography, the history, and the literature and art of the region. The fourth section is a descriptive listing of all towns, locations and geographical features of the region, including some descriptive passages from the works of famous writers such as Washington Irving and James Fenimore Cooper. The reader will find that this book contains fewer statistics, and more material of general interest, than the *Guide to the Catskills*. We hope that the format will prove both attractive for browsing and handy for use on the road. I have taken the occasion of this new edition to update the original 1975 material.

Arthur G. Adams
September 15, 1989

Introduction

The Catskills—A Land of Illusion, Dreams and Memories.

. . . I was disturbed in my cogitations by a buzz among the guests near the door, and all I could hear was that the house was "going past on the outside." A waiter was quieting an old lady by telling her that all was quite firm at the foundations, for it was built on a rock.

We were all on the piazza in a few moments, and there, sure enough, was the perfect image of the vast building, plainly impressed upon a thicker cloud than the general envelope [of clouds and fog] that covered us. It was a great mass of vapor, moving from north to south, directly in front, and only about two hundred feet from us, which reflected the light of the sun, now beginning to appear in the east, from its bosom, like a mirror, in which the noble Corinthian pillars [of the mountain-top Catskill Mountain House], which form the front of the building, were expanded like some palace built for it by the Titans for the entertainment of their antediluvian guests. I had read of Catherine of Russia's famous palace of ice, all glittering with the gorgeousness that now beautifies the Kremlin; and how frequently that is produced, as emblematic of human glory; but here was something that more than recalled my early impressions of Aladdin's lamp, or the magician's wand.

The visionary illusion was moving with the cloud, and ere long we saw one pillar disappear, then another. We, ourselves, who were expanded to Brobdignags in size, saw the gulf into which we were to enter and be lost. I almost shivered when my turn came, but there was no eluding my fate; one side of my face was veiled, and in a few moments the whole had passed like a dream. An instant before, and we were the inhabitants of a "gorgeous palace" but it was the "baseless fabric of a vision" and now there was left "not a wreck behind."

from *The Dutch Dominie of the Catskills*
Rev. Dr. David Murdoch

See! Now ascends
the Lord of Day, waking with pearly fire
The dormant depths. See how his glowing breath
The rising surges kindles; lo! they heave
Like golden sands upon Sahara's gales.
Those airy forms disporting from the mass.
Like winged ships, sail o'er the wondrous plain.
Beautiful vision! Now the veil is rent,
And the coy earth her virgin bosom bares,
Slowly unfolding to the enraptured gaze
Her thousand charms.

from *The Wild*
Thomas Cole

Of all the scenery of the Hudson, the Kattskill Mountains had the most witching effect on my boyish imagination. Never shall I forget the effect upon me of my first view of them, predominating over a wide extent of country—part wild, woody and rugged: part softened away into all the graces of cultivation. As we slowly floated along, I lay on the deck and watched them through a long summer's day, undergoing a thousand mutations under the magical effects of atmosphere; sometimes seeming to approach; at other times to recede; now almost melting into hazy distance, now burnished by the setting sun, until in the evening they printed themselves against the glowing sky in the deep purple of an Italian landscape.

from *Autobiography*
of Washington Irving

Every change of season, every change of weather, indeed, every hour of the day, produces some change in the magical hues and shapes of these mountains, and they are regarded by all the good wives, far and near, as perfect barometers. When the weather is fair and settled, they are clothed in blue and purple, and print their bold outlines on the clear evening sky; but sometimes, when the rest of the landscape is cloudless, they will gather a hood of gray vapors about their summits, which in the last rays of the setting sun, will glow and light up like a crown of glory.

from *Rip Van Winkle*
Washington Irving

Fata-morgana, looming, changing colors—classic illusions, all on the same mountain escarpment, the famous "Great Wall of Manitou," which forms the eastern escarpment of the Catskills overlooking the Hudson Valley west of the village of Catskill. The English settlers called the Catskills the "Blue Hills," although they were manifestly green. The ever-changing atmospheric activity of this region awakens the imagination, and it is but one step further to tales of little men, Indian Witches, Ontiora the Evil Giant and similar fabulous beings.

And thus illusion leads to dreaming. And after a doze of twenty years, Rip, or Everyman, awakens to Memories, of which the reality has vanished. The Catskill Mountain House with its thirteen noble Corinthian Pillars has now in fact vanished as did Dr. Murdoch's fata-morgana. The visitor to Pine Orchard today will find but bare rock and wind-swept grasses. Yet, to the mind of the writer, when visiting the spot, the great building is still present—a noble ruin breasting the slings of fate and awaiting an inevitable doom. The Mountain House still lives as an idea and symbol of a noble view of life.

At the end of James Barre's play *Peter Pan*, the audience is asked, "Do you believe in fairies?" Walking up the old Mountain Road past sleepy hollow on the slopes of North Mountain, if the author should be asked by a solitary companion if he believed in dwarfs, trolls, imps, elves or similar "little men," he would fain have to assent to holding such belief. The landscape demands such belief. Other places demand similar belief: the Hartz Mountains of Germany, the shores of the Bay of Naples, Staffa, Loch Ness! The ancients believed that every tree, river, spring, flower, rock had its dryad, naid, nereid or nymph. More prosaically, these were called spiritus loci. The visitor to the Catskills who does not experience this feeling will lose much of the charm of the region. He will see merely low wooded mountains.

For many years High Peak and Hunter were thought the highest of the Catskills. Not until 1880 was Slide Mountain recognized as the monarch of the hills. Another illusion.

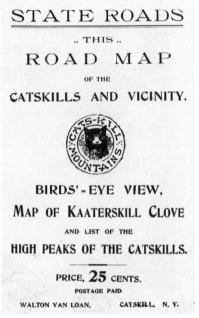

STATE ROADS
.. THIS ..
ROAD MAP
OF THE
CATSKILLS AND VICINITY,

BIRDS'-EYE VIEW,
MAP OF KAATERSKILL CLOVE
AND LIST OF THE
HIGH PEAKS OF THE CATSKILLS.

PRICE, 25 CENTS.
POSTAGE PAID.
WALTON VAN LOAN,   CATSKILL, N. Y.

Reprint of cover of a Van Loan Guide from 1914. Author's collection.

Holders of shares in the Hardenburgh Patent thought they would become rich—more illusion. People ransacked the mountains for gold, silver, and even coal—they saw silver mines "blowing off" on summer evenings. More illusion. But also a fatal attraction.

Marjorie Morningstar thinks she will meet her Prince Charming at a Catskill Resort. Dream always—illusion usually—sometimes fact.

The clerk buried in a concrete canyon dreams of the "Alpine Heights" of the Catskills. He is happy to spend the weekend in their cool woods. Always the Catskills seem something more than they actually are, but nonetheless the reality is satisfying and the memory magnified.

We all know that the Catskill Mountain House had small cramped bedrooms, poor ventilation, uncomfortable beds, was damp at times, was overpriced, had a limited menu and was a firetrap. Yet not only we, but the people who frequented it for many years, thought of it as a noble palace in the clouds—because it satisfied the soul and the imagination and the mind expanded in its environs. Its park had an Elfin Pass, Druid Rocks and a Fairy Spring—all on the path to the Grand Canyon of Kaaterskill Clove. On the other side were Sunrise and Sunset Rocks and Jacob's Ladder. Grand names all! Indeed this is a Romantic and enchanted land.

In memories of my own youthful visits to the Catskills I rode "great trains that sped over glistening rails." (They went at forty miles per hour over bumpy track.) Graceful ships glided up a smooth and noble river. The hotel rooms would not pass muster today compared with a Holiday Inn, but the views from the rooms were noble and the windows opened to the cooling breeze, or the noble spectacle of a thunderstorm in the mountains—Rip bowling! And never was the air keener or more delicious than in the morning after a stormy night.

Visitor! Raise your eyes to the hills. Forget the daily cares and give yourself to these hills, and they will give you enchantment and rest and memories for a lifetime.

PART I
GEOGRAPHY

Defining the Catskills

The precise definition of the Catskill Mountain Area is a subject that has been a center of controversy for many years. Originally the name applied only to those mountains west of the village of Catskill and lying entirely in Greene County and to the north of the Platterkill Clove behind Saugerties. They ranged northwest to Huntersfield Mountain north of Ashland and it was questionable if they included the Hunter Mountain massif or Plateau Mountain—Sugarloaf Mountain—Twin Mountain—Indian Head range. The center of these classic Catskills was at the Catskill Mountain House and the Kaaterskill Falls and Clove. North and South Mountains and the Kaaterskill High Peak were the best known portions of this area. The front escarpment was known as the Great Wall of Manitou, and it was atop this wall that sat the Mountain House.

With the development of tourism the name became popular and was appropriated by resort owners in the Overlook Mountain area in Ulster County and became firmly attached to the Hunter Mountain massif and Plateau-Indian Head Range, bringing the Platterkill Clove and Schoharie watersheds clearly into the Catskills.

In the early 19th century the part of the present Catskills incorporating Slide Mountain and the adjacent high peaks was known as the Shandaken Mountains. With the construction of the Ulster & Delaware Railroad and attendant development of adjacent resorts after 1875, the Shandaken Mountains also appropriated the name of Catskills. Decisive recognition of Slide Mountain as the highest peak in southern New York State by Arnold Henry Guyot in 1880 in his *Physical Geography and Hypsometry of the Catskill Mountain Region*, and John Burrough's book entitled *In the Heart of the Southern Catskills,* along with the promotional activity of the Grand Hotel at Highmount, ended all dispute and brought the Shandaken Mountains firmly into the definition of Catskills. Extension of the railroad to Bloomville on the West Branch of the Delaware River and construction of Churchill Hall (1883) and The Rexmere Hotel (1890) led to the appropriation of the Catskill name by Mount Utsayantha and the Moresville Range between the two branches of the Delaware River.

With development of the farm boarding house industry along the New York Ontario & Western Railroad around the turn of the century, the name Catskills was again appropriated—this time to the Sullivan County Hills. This was particularly resented by the people of Greene County who had seen their "trade name" constantly diluted. There was also an element of snobbism in that the Sullivan County boarding houses catered to what was then called "a mixed element," with whom the socialite visitors to the great Greene and Ulster hotels did not wish to be associated. The very name "Catskill" became déclassé and the richer socialites deserted the region en masse, bringing about the slow but inexorable economic decline of the great hotels in the classic Catskill Area. They soon were giving a hearty welcome to any guest who wished to sign in.

Development of auto travel on Route 17—The Quickway—firmly entrenched the idea that Wurtsboro, Monticello, Liberty and Roscoe were all in "The Catskills," which New York Cityites began to simply call "The Mountains," although this name also applied to places as diverse as West Orange, New Jersey and the Berkshires.

The name seemed to spread following the development of New York City oriented resorts. The Helderbergs, to the north, which had only very limited resort development around White Sulphur Springs near Berne, Cooperstown on the Susquehanna River and the Shawangunk Mountains of Orange and Ulster Counties seemed to escape the name. Possibly the reason for this with respect to the Shawangunks was the development of Lake Mohonk Mountain House and the Lake Minnewaska Mountain Houses in the towns of New Paltz and Gardiner by the Quaker brothers, Albert and Alfred Smiley. They catered to an entirely different clientele, drawn largely from Boston, Providence and Philadelphia—people of very conservative means and habits in the case of Minnewaska, and wealthy people of intellectual bent of mind at Mohonk. This distinction still holds in part today and the hotels in question emphasize the fact that they are located in the Shawangunk (pronounced Shongum) Mountains and not the Catskills. Geology is on their side as the Shawangunks, or "Gunks" as they are irreverently dubbed by rock climbers, are mountains of uplift and consist of limestone and quartz conglomerate rock not found in other parts of the Catskills.

However, the matter does not rest here. In 1973 the State of New York officially extended the definition of the Catskills when they established by an act of the legislature the Temporary State Commission to Study the Catskills and mandated them to study, as a unit, the ecology, sociology and economy of all of Greene, Delaware, Sullivan, Ulster and Schoharie Counties as well as of Otsego County and the towns of Berne, Coeymans, Knox, New Scotland, Rensselaerville and Westerlo in Albany County—an area of almost 4 million acres with a population of 373,000. This brought into the definition the Helderbergs, Shawangunks, Cooperstown area and Plattekill Hills of Southern Ulster County along the Hudson, which had always fought to retain their individual identity. Nonetheless, the grouping makes good social, economic and ecological sense. The entire region is subjected to the same outside pressures, is dependent upon tourism and agriculture and has suffered industrial decline—and to a large extent the ills of the region are amenable to the same treatment.

In his *Guide to the Catskills—With Trail Guide and Maps* the author more narrowly defined the Catskills for purposes of the hiker and outdoorsman. He there defined them as that area enclosed by an imaginary line running northwest from Carpenters Point, south of Port Jervis, along the Delaware River to Deposit, and thence following the watershed between the branches of the Delaware northeast to the neighborhood of Stamford, thence swinging east by northeast along an imaginary line to the neighborhood of Gilboa and thence east along the Manorkill to Huntersfield Mountain. From here the line follows the Great Wall of Manitou first southeast and then south to Overlook Mountain near Woodstock. From here he defines an imaginary line south to Hurley and High Falls on the Rondout Creek. The boundary is defined running south along Rondout Creek to Napanoch and thence south along Sandburg and Homowack Creeks and the Basha Kill and Neversink River to Carpenters Point. The present book will accept the definition of the Temporary Study Commission as it incorporates a convenient grouping for the tourist.

Many efforts have been made to arrive at the origin of the name Catskill. The word *Kill* in Dutch means creek, estuary or strait. However, the name is also so used in southeastern England and the word *Kyle* is common in Scotland, as in the "Kyles of Bute." The colonial Dutch applied the name more liberally. While the Arthur Kill and Kill Van Kull, separating Staten Island from New Jersey, are true Kills in the European sense, the early settlers were soon calling even small streams and brooks kills. As the English also used the word at home, it did not seem inappropriate for them to follow the Dutch useage—and corruption—of the word. Thus an allegedly hybrid word such as Catskill would not appear unusual to an early English settler. The most simple, and probably correct, explanation is that originally Catskill Creek was named because some wild cats were seen along its banks. The village that developed near its mouth also took the name and by extension the mountains immediately to the west became the Cat Creek Mountains. Both name and probable origin became abhorent to romantic-minded philological purists of the 19th century. Many attempts were made to discover, or in the lack of finding genuine ones, to coin "Indian names" for the Catskills. Thus we have Ontiora, which is supposed to mean "Land in the Sky," coined by Henry Rowe Schoolcraft and popularized by the Kingston lawyer-poet Henry Abbey in his poem "Onteora."

Other purists of linguistic bent coined such "all-Dutch" names as Katzbergs, used by Benson J. Lossing in his book *The Hudson*, and Kaaterskill Mountains or simply Katskill Mountains. The name Kaaterskill stuck to the creek, clove and waterfall of this name and was ultimately applied to a large luxury hotel, a narrow-gauge railway and an overnight steamship. Even an apartment house in New York City bore the name! William Cullen Bryant wrote a famous poem about the Kaaterskill Falls and he too tried to improve it into *Catterskill Falls*. The name Cauterskill was also used and still applies to a hamlet at the junction of Kaaterskill and Catskill Creeks near the village of Catskill.

In 1884 the Catskill Forest Preserve was created and in 1894 the enabling act was changed by an amendment to the Constitution of the State of New York ordaining that lands falling within the State Forest Preserve be kept "forever wild." The 705,500-acre Catskill Park is defined on official maps by a blue line. Not all the land in this area of almost 3,000 square miles is Forest Preserve land, however. There is also much private property within the blue line. At the present time the state is trying, through its administrative arm, the Department of Environmental Conservation (DEC) (formerly State Conservation Department), to consolidate parcels, obtain access corridors and generally neaten up the boundaries, as well as to acquire and either develop or preserve unique scenic or recreational areas falling outside the blue line.

State parks, marine and canal parks and many historic sites are administered by the Office of Parks and Recreation through the appropriate local arms. Zoning is a "hot issue" in the Catskills with many conflicting demands of conservationists, developers, summer home owners, farmers who want to quit and farmers who want to continue farming, people who want to build power facilities and those who don't want them. If you should ever be lonesome while visiting the Catskills, just visit any public gathering and make a positive statement—any kind of statement will do—about zoning or land use. You will soon find yourself in the center of a storm of controversy with teams of adversaries and supporters and may even have to escape from a general riot! The safe course is to keep such thoughts to yourself—and this is the voice of experience.

Now that we have defined the locus of the Catskills to nobody's entire satisfaction, but have nevertheless decided upon a serviceable definition for our tourist guide, let us return to our subject of physical geography.

Mountain Groupings

The Catskills proper are not even really mountains. They are a maturely dissected plateau. More illusion! During the Early Devonian Period, about four hundred million years ago, there were very high mountains in the New England area and a shallow inland sea covered most of what are now the states of New York, Pennsylvania, Ohio, Indiana and Illinois. Streams draining the mountains in New England carried soil, sand and gravel down and deposited them in this shallow sea's bottom. The sea was what geologists call the Appalachian Basin. During the Middle Devonian Period the eastern floor of the basin rose so that the water was deeper to the west and additional detritus was deposited in the shallow eastern portions. The material now forming the Hamilton Shales and Esopus and Schoharie Grits was deposited during this period. During the Late Devonian Period the basin continued to rise, forming alluvial deltas. During the following Carboniferous Period the floor of the basin rose dramatically. Rifts were forced in the Coastal Ranges which can still be seen in the Hudson Highlands, Delaware Water and Wind Gaps and at Nanticoke Gap on the Susquehanna. The waters drained off into the Atlantic Ocean. The former sea bottom rose to an elevation of five or six thousand feet above present sea level and formed a vast peneplain called by geologists the Allegheny Plateau. It consisted largely of shales and sandstones, and through the years has been constantly worn down so that the average heights of the present mountains fall between 4,180 ft. at Slide Mountain and 3,000. The modal average summit elevation is about 3,100 ft., and as the Catskills are an eroded plateau, there is a great uniformity of summit elevations, not often noted in real Alpine regions. The present-day cloves and ravines that are so picturesque were carved by fast running streams—and the work of erosion continues. Slide Mountain was named for the scars of a monumental landslide on its northwest slope in 1820, and landslides on the northern slope of High Peak in 1975 have caused very considerable siltation of Kaaterskill Creek in the Palenville area. In a few eons they won't be here anymore, so you had better enjoy them now.

About a million years ago (a more comprehensible time period) there was an Ice Age—the Pleistocene. There was glaciation, but apparently not very deep as there are few moraine deposits above 3,500 ft. During later glacial periods there was light scouring of exposed rock surfaces. The erratic boulders strewn about were left behind by the glaciers. Weathering has caused the breakdown of the conglomerate rocks and shales into soil and in some locations small quartz crystals can be found at higher elevations. Conglomerate is also locally known as Puddingstone, and a rock formation near the former Catskill Mountain House bore the name Puddingstone Hall. These conglomerates predominate at the higher elevations with red and blue shales at lower elevations. A very compact blue shale, when smoothly layed down, can be broken into slate or Bluestone slabs, and quarrying of this was once a major local industry, the slates being used extensively for paving and for sidewalks during the 19th century. The weathered rock provides a fair covering of soil which sustains a moderately rich vegetation. At the higher elevations fir and spruce are common along with southern escapes of plants more commonly found in Canada—as is the case all down the Appalachian chain into Georgia. At lower elevations birch, beech, maple and hemlock predominate. At higher elevations and with northern exposures there is some stunting of trees. This is particularly notable atop Kaaterskill High Peak where the stunted trees form what earlier writers called a "matting upon which you could rest." There is very little true Alpine vegetation. The area is well watered, however, and is well suited to the growth of forest cover. Many 19th-century mountainside and top farms are now well covred with second growth, with only the old stone pasture walls remaining in mute testimony.

The adjacent Pocono Mountains and Endless Hills in Pennsylvania were formed by the same forces as were the Randolph Hills between the Delaware and Susquehanna Rivers. The Helderbergs to the north were also formed in the same manner. The northern and eastern escarpments of the Helderbergs and Northern Catskills are precipitous with many cliffs and crags. The Indian Ladder region of the Helderberg Cliffs and the Great Wall of Manitou in the Catskills are notable examples and offer magnificent views of the Mohawk and Hudson Valley. The western slopes are generally more gentle and average elevation tapers off to the west. The Moresville Range between the two branches of the Delaware and the Randolph Hills are the westernmost major elevations.

Major groupings within the Catskills, aside from those described above, are the Slide Mountain Massif, the Dry Brook Range, parallel to and west of the Dry Brook between Balsam Lake and Arkville, and the Giant Ledge, Panther Mountain, and Garfield Mountain group north of Slide Mountain. The Beaverkill Range separates the Willowemoc to the south from the Beaverkill to the north and includes Mongaup Mountain. The Mill Brook Ridge, with its western extensions, separates the Beaver Kill from the East Branch of the Delaware and runs west to Twadell Point at their junction, with an average elevation of 2,700 ft. The Blackhead Range in Greene County has three notable peaks over 3,900 ft.: Mt. Thomas Cole, Black Dome, and Black Head. The Hunter Mountain Range continues west from Hunter Mountain separating the Schoharie Creek to the

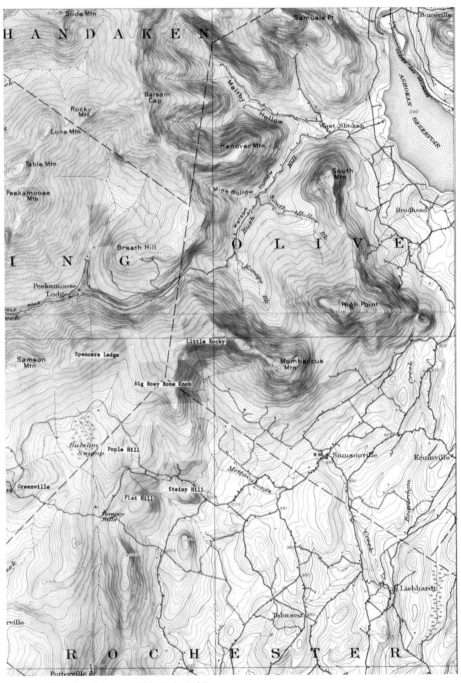

Slide Mountain area. U.S. Geological Survey.

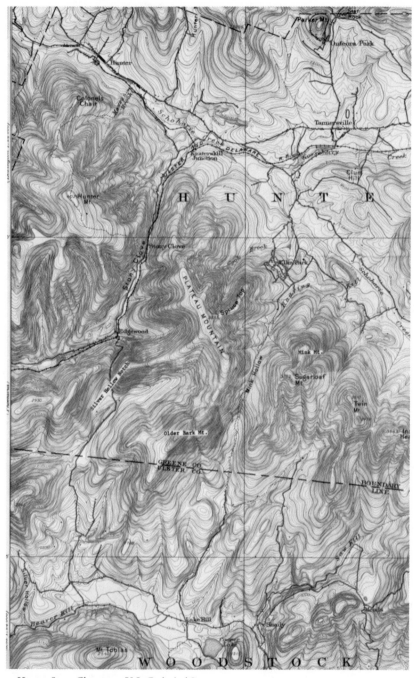

Hunter-Stony Clove area. U.S. Geological Survey.

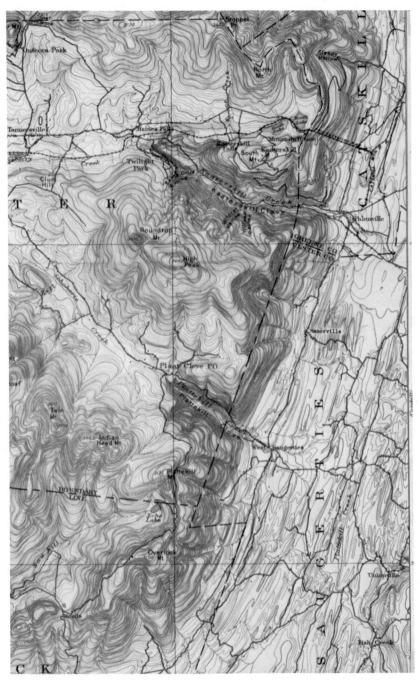

Kaaterskill area. U.S. Geological Survey.

Sherrill Mountain and Phoenicia. U.S. Geological Survey.

north from the West Kill to the south. Major peaks are Rusk, Evergreen, and Pine Island Mountains. The West Kill Range is parallel to and south of the West Kill in Greene County and includes Balsam Mountain (3,340 ft.), Mount Sherrill (3,540 ft.), North Dome (3,610 ft.), and West Kill Mountain (3,880 ft.) The Northern Front Range runs west from the Great Wall of Manitou at Acra Point and includes Windham High Peak (3,524 ft.), Richmond Mountain, Ashland Pinnacle, and Huntersfield Mountain. There are many minor ridges and extensive areas of indeterminate hills and high plateaus. There is a considerable escarpment along the northeastern shore of the Delaware River between Port Jervis and Hancock, with considerable cliffs at Hawks Nest south of Barryville. Among the more impressive ridges seen by most tourists is that composed of Cornell, Wittenberg and Slide as seen across Ashokan Reservoir, behind South Hanover, and Friday Mountains and Samuels Point. The Helderbergs are a series of indeterminate high hills with a dramatic northern and eastern escarpment, tapering off into the Schoharie Valley to the west.

The Shawangunks are a much older mountain range formed by upheaval. They are composed largely of limestone and quartz conglomerate and run from Pink Hill near Kingston at their northern end, southwest to the New Jersey border at High Point. The southeastern face is precipitous with many cliffs and crags, and an area known as the Trapps is popular with rock climbers. They divide the valleys of the Neversink, Basha Kill, Homowack and Sandburg Kills and Rondout Creek to the west from that of the Wallkill Valley to the east. Breached by Rondout Creek between High Falls and Rosendale, they continue south into New Jersey where they are called the Kittatinny Mountains, and in fact are the northern end of the famous Blue Ridge, which continues down through Pennsylvania, Maryland and Virginia into the Carolinas.

The rock is white and shines in the sun, providing vivid contrast with the foliage. The Shawangunks are blessed with some lakes of exceptional purity, some of them glacial in formation. At the northern end are the five Binnewater Lakes. Heading south we next have Mohonk Lake, with its exceptional beautiful green color and supporting vegetable and animal life. Next comes Lake Minnewaska with its mineral deposits and heavenly blue water surrounded by gleaming white cliffs. Further south are the large lake Awosting and shallow Haseco Lake or Mud Pond. Finally, atop Sam's Point (2,255 ft.), the highest point in the ridge, is Lake Maratanza. Notable points are Skytop near New Paltz, Bonticou Crag, The Traps, Millbrook Mountain, Gertrudes Nose, Castle Point and Sam's Point, now sometimes called Ice Cave Mountain, from a commercialized feature of the area.

The Shawangunks formed a great obstacle to early railroad builders and the Erie was the first to breach it near Otisville. At a later period the

Oswego Midland tunneled it near Wurtsboro. It is crossed by Route 17 and the Minnewaska Trail.

The last range of hills to be considered are the Plattekill Hills separating the Hudson River from the Wallkill Valley. They are of generally low elevation and run from north to south between Newburgh and the Rondout Creek south of Kingston. Major elevations are Schupeneak Mountain and Hussey's Mountain. There are numerous pools of tannin-dyed black water and here John Burroughs had his rustic retreat "Slab-sides."

Next to be considered are the waterways which supply drainage to this large area.

Waterways

Drainage of the Catskill region is through three major river systems: The Hudson-Mohawk, the Delaware and the Susquehanna.

THE HUDSON-MOHAWK SYSTEM

The Hudson River rises in numerous springs in the Adirondack region, but the generally recognized principal source is Lake Tear of the Clouds, at an elevation of 4,322 ft. on the south-western slope of Mt. Marcy, highest of the Adirondacks with an elevation of 5,344 ft. The outlet of Lake Tear of the Clouds is Feldspar Brook, which in turn flows into what is today called the Opalescent River. Formerly this stream was called the North or Main Branch of the Hudson River. What today is simply called the Hudson River was formerly called the West Branch. Its source is Hendrick Spring, northeast of Long Lake, whose waters flow to the St. Lawrence. The waters of Hendrick Spring are first collected in Fountain Lake. The North Fork has its head in Henderson Lake and joins the Opalescent River at the outlet of Sanford Lake. The West Branch flows from Fountain Lake south through Round Pond and Catlin Lake, then turns east and flows through Rich and Harris Lakes to the vicinity of Newcomb, where it is joined by the waters of the Opalescent—North Fork combined stream from the east. This is about 15 miles from Lake Tear of the Clouds.

From Newcomb the Hudson flows generally southeast to the community of North River, after receiving the waters of the Boreas River. It then continues south to Riparius, below which it receives the waters of the Mill Creek from the southwest. It continues south past The Glen to Thurman Station where it receives the waters of the Schroon River from the northeast. From here the river continues south, bowing slightly to the west where it receives the waters of Stony Creek. At Luzerne it receives the waters of the Sacandaga from the west. From here south to Corinth, at the head of Jesup's Great Falls, the river is broad and smooth flowing. Below the falls the river starts to curve first east and then northeast, forming crescent-shaped Moreau Lake. From here it flows generally northeast, making several loops, to the dam and falls at Glens Falls, where it is crossed by the Route 9–32 bridge just below the dam. A great deal of the water is diverted along power canals of the Finch Pruyn Company and the flow of water over the falls is disappointing. Before a recent reconstruction of the highway bridge it was possible to descend a stairway from midpoint on the bridge to one of numerous rocky islands in the falls, on which was located the cave described by James Fenimore Cooper in *The Last of the Mohicans*. All access to this famous cave is now closed off. It is 115 miles from Lake Tear of the Clouds to this point, and the river has been primarily a wilderness one to this point.

The next five miles to the confluence with the Champlain Canal at Fort Edward are full of rapids and Bakers Falls at the town of Hudson Falls. The banks are crowded with industry, including pulp and paper mills and chemical plants. The river first flows east and then turns decidedly south at Hudson Falls. The next 42 miles the river flows due south through a broad pastoral valley given largely to dairy farming in its upper reaches and industry in its nether reaches. It is in fact a canalized river, forming a part of the Champlain Canal, and with several locks along the way. It flows past Fort Miller, Thomson and Northumberland. Here it receives the waters of the Batten Kill from the east. Next south of here is Schuylerville, where it receives the waters of Fish Creek from the west. Here, running south to Bemis Heights, along the west bank is the Saratoga Historic Battlefield Park, where a deciding battle of the American Revolution was fought and the British under General Burgoyne were forced to surrender to General Gates in October of 1777. Near Stillwater the Hudson receives the waters of the Hoosic River from the east. The next major point southward is Mechanicsville and then Waterford where the New York Barge Canal enters from the west. Between here and the city of Cohoes, the Mohawk River, called the Maquaas Kill in early times, flows into the channel west of Van Schaick and Simmons Islands. On the east shore is the Lansingburg section of Troy. South of Van Schaick Island is Green Island and the Federal Lock is located between this island and Troy, on the east bank. The remaining 153 miles to New York Bay is tide water. The Hudson flows pretty much directly south with only a few bends in the Highlands. Principal long wide areas are, from north to south, Newburgh Bay, Haverstraw Bay and the Tappan Zee. The larger cities it passes are: Albany, Hudson, Catskill, Kingston, Poughkeepsie, Newburgh, Peekskill, Haverstraw, Nyack, Yonkers, New York City, Hoboken and Jersey City. The river is navigable by large river steamers to Troy and ocean-going vessels to the Port of Albany.

Principal tributaries from the Catskill region are the Schoharie-Mohawk, Vloman Kill, Normanskill, Hannacroix Creek, Catskill Creek, Sawyers Kill, Esopus Creek, Rondout Creek and Black Creek.

The first recorded discovery of the Hudson was by Giovanni da Verrazano, a Florentine in the service of Francis I of France in 1524. In 1609 Henry Hudson, an Englishman in the service of the Dutch East India Company, explored the river to the vicinity of Albany and made a full report of his findings. Adriaen Block, Cornelius May and Hendrick

NEW YORK – ALBANY (HUDSON RIVER DAY LINE)				
OUTWARD (Northbound)			HOMEWARD (Southbound)	
POINT	TIME	Dist. from N. Y.	POINT	TIME
New York			Albany..........Lv.	9 oo am
Desbrosses St....Lv.	9 oo am	—	Hudson.............	11 15
West 42nd St.......	9 20	—	Catskill.............	11 40
West 129th St......	9 40	—	Kingston Point.......	1 oo pm
Yonkers.............	10 15	17 m	Poughkeepsie........	2 oo
Newburgh..........	12 40 pm	6o m	Newburgh..........	2 50
Poughkeepsie........	1 30	75 m	Yonkers.............	5 oo
Kingston Point.......	2 25	90 m	New York	
Catskill.............	3 35	115 m	West 129th St......	5 40
Hudson.............	3 55	120 m	West 42nd St.......	6 oo
Albany..........Arr.	6 45	150 m	Desbrosses St .Arr.	6 30

1927 Timetable of Hudson River Day Line showing landings and all timings.

Christiansen of the United New Netherland Company were trading in the area in 1613 and built forts at Castle Island near Albany and on Manhattan. Actually they were armed trading posts. One had been built as early as 1540 at Albany by Frenchmen trading down from Canada at Castle Island. The Dutch called this Fort Nassau, but it was soon washed away by a flood. In 1623 Fort Orange was built on the mainland on the present site of the D & H Building in Albany. The Indians had no single name for the river but they did have for certain sections. Mahicannittuck was the section where the Mahicans dwelt and Cohohatatia was a section where salmon were caught. The Dutch called the river the Nassau River after the reigning house of Nassau and also the Mauritius River after Prince Maurice of Orange of the House of Nassau. More simply they called it The River of the Mountains or Great River. The English later called it the North River to distinguish it from the South River—the Delaware.

In 1807 commercial steam navigation was born with the successful trip of Robert Fulton's *Clermont* between New York and Albany.

The Hudson became important as a commercial corridor to the west with the opening of the Erie Canal in 1825. Later great railroads and highways followed its valley and it became the center of our first native school of painting and of 19th-century literati. The wealthy built magnificent villas on its shores and the arts and refinements of life were cultivated in its valley as commerce boomed at its ports, causing New York City to become the commercial capital of the United States.

The Mohawk River was originally called the Maaquas River after the Indians dwelling in its valley. It rises near Rome in central New York State and flows 140 miles east into the Hudson at Cohoes. For most of this distance it is canalized as part of the New York State Barge Canal. Earlier the Erie Canal had paralleled it as did the later railroads and highways. From Rome it flows east past Utica, Herkimer, Little Falls, Canajoharie, Fonda, Fultonville, Auriesville, Tribes Hill, Fort Hunter, Amsterdam, Schenectady and Crescent to the power dam above Cohoes Falls. In the early 19th century this was the site of a pleasure resort with terraces and gardens. With the building of the Harmony Mill in 1837 the water was diverted and large mill buildings and row houses erected for the workers. The area remains industrialized today and only a trickle flows over the falls. After going over some more rapids its flows into the Hudson's West Channel near Simmons and Van Schaick Islands. It is important for our purposes in that it receives the waters of Schoharie Creek at Fort Hunter near Tribes Hill.

The Schoharie River, sometimes called Schoharie Creek, rises on the slopes of Indian Head and Kaaterskill High Peak near Plaat Clove P. O. and flows west, being joined by the waters of Roaring Brook and Cook Brook. Further west it is joined by Gooseberry Creek at Kaaterskill Junction. Flowing over Red Falls at Hunter it continues west past South Jewett to a junction with the East Kill two miles east of Lexington and the West Kill a little west of the same town. A few miles east of Prattsville it receives the waters of the Batavia Kill from the north. At Prattsville it turns north and enters Schoharie Reservoir, where it is joined by the Manor Kill from the east. The former Devasego Falls was here.

North of Gilboa Dam it flows north past North Blenheim, Breakabeen, Fultonham, Watsonville and Middleburg to Schoharie, through fine and very fertile bottom lands especially well adapted to growing vegetables. It is some of the most fertile black soil in the world. The area was early settled by the Dutch and German Palatinates. Leaving the mountains it continues north past Central Bridge, Esperance, Burtonsville, and Mill Point to a confluence with the Mohawk at Fort Hunter near Tribes Hill, near which it is crossed by an old trestle of the Erie Canal.

Catskill Creek rises near Franklinton in Schoharie County and can be said to be the dividing line between the Helderbergs to the northeast and the Catskills to the southwest. It flows southeast past Livingstonville, Preston Hollow, Cooksburg, Oak Hill, East Durham, Freehold, South Cairo and Leeds to a confluence with the Kaaterskill Creek at Cauterskill, just west of Catskill village. It is paralleled for its entire distance by Routes 23 and 145 and was the projected route of the early Canajoharie &

Catskill Ry., which never got beyond Cooksburg. Its valley was used by the early Susquehanna and Schoharie Turnpikes. Principal tributaries from the north are Basic Creek at Freehold and Potic Creek near Leeds, where it is crossed by a famous old stone bridge. The Platte Kill and Shingle Kill are tributaries from the south. Above Cauterskill it flows through the picturesque Austins Glen, which is crossed by a bridge of the New York Thruway just south of Exit 21. Formerly the Catskill Mountain Railroad followed it through the Glen. Flowing under a high trestle of the West Shore Railroad (1883) and a lower footbridge, formerly used by the Catskill Mountain Railroad, it flows through the village of Catskill, where it is crossed by the Uncle Sam road bridge. Below this is the old port where the Catskill Evening Line boats used to tie up. From here it flows past the promontory of Hopp's Nose and into the Hudson at Catskill Point.

Potic Creek, a principal northern tributary of Catskill Creek, receives the waters of Cob, Grapeville and West Medway Creeks. It enters Catskill Creek above Leeds.

Basic Creek, a northern tributary of Catskill Creek, rises near Dormansville and flows south through the man-made Basic Reservoir (City of Albany), to Catskill Creek near Freehold. The reservoir is closed to the public.

Kaaterskill Creek is probably the most famous waterway in the Catskills. It rises in a marsh west of the village of Haines Falls and flows over the famous Haines Falls of 160 ft. at the head of Kaaterskill Clove, and east down numerous rapids and falls. In mid-clove it is joined from the north by the waters of Lake Creek. The waters of Santa Cruz, Wildcat, and Viola Falls join it from off Kaaterskill High Peak on the south. It flows over La Belle Falls just above Palenville at the foot of the clove, where it is crossed by Route 23A. Here it flows over Niobe and Fern Cliff Falls, to name but a few. East of Palenville it flows over the Kaaterskill High Falls, which are on private property and difficult and dangerous to see. East of here it dips down into Ulster County, then turns decisively north through pretty deep valleys, one of which is crossed by the New York Thruway. It empties into Catskill Creek at the hamlet of Cauterskill just west of Catskill.

Lake Creek is often mistaken for Kaaterskill Creek, as the famous Kaaterskill Falls are on it, rather than on Kaaterskill Creek as would be expected. It flows from South Lake, atop the Wall of Manitou, which is now connected by a manmade strait with North Lake, whose principal source is Ashley Creek, flowing down the south side of North Mountain. It flows west past Scribners to a junction with Spruce Creek from the north, and here turns south and goes over Kaaterskill Falls in two drops of 175 ft. and 85 ft. From the foot of the falls it runs over rapids to

Bastion Falls near the Horseshoe Curve on Route 23A. Just south of there it joins Kaaterskill Creek in Kaaterskill Clove just beneath Santa Cruz Park.

Plattekill Creek is the stream that created Plattekill Clove. It rises on the northern slopes of Indian Head Mountain and flows east, down the clove, over Plattekill Falls, where there were once rustic ladders, but which is now difficult and dangerous of access. Black Chasm is above the Plattekill Falls. Below them are Old Mill Falls, near the bridge on the Overlook Mountain Escarpment Road; Pomeroy, Rainbow, Lower Rainbow, Green (called "The Ghost" from fancied resemblance to a shrouded death's head figure, formed by the spray and mist) and Evergreen Falls. Next are Rocky Rapids and Gray Rock Falls, near the village of West Saugerties at the foot of the clove. The bed of this stream is dangerous, owing to overhanging precipices, a swift current and slippery footing. Several people have been killed in this area in recent years and their bodies removed with great difficulty. The rustic ladders and walkways that formerly made this a tourist mecca have been removed and the "purist" policy of the DEC has created a death trap, inasmuch as many people attempt to see these wonders even today. Until such time as a more enlightened policy prevails, we counsel the reader to let these sights rest in oblivion. From West Saugerties the stream meanders southeast to a junction with Esopus Creek near Glenerie, above the falls. It is crossed near its mouth by the Thruway.

Esopus Creek rises on the slopes of Panther and Slide Mountains in three branches; the combined stream begins near the settlement of Slide Mountain P.O. The source most easily seen by the auto tourist is Winnisook Lake on the northwestern slope of Slide Mountain, just east of where the road passes between Slide and Winnisook Lake Mountains, at an elevation of 2664 ft. This is an artificial lake owned by the Winnisook Club. Visitors are not encouraged, but the lake is easily seen from the road. Blossom Falls, on the middle branch, can be reached by an easy scramble from the auto road near the hairpin turn to the north of Winnisook Lake Pass. The North Branch rises on the south slope of Panther Mountain and flows down between Little Slide Mountain and Giant Ledge. The combined stream flows in a big curve first west and then north through the Big Indian Valley, with its numerous German resorts reminiscent of those in the Taunus Mountains of Swabia. At Big Indian the stream runs beside Route 28 and the U & D Railroad. Here it turns southeast by east past Allaben, where it is joined by waters from Schoharie Reservoir, conveyed hence through the Shandaken Tunnel. The outlet may be seen adjacent to the highway. It continues past Phoenicia where it receives the waters of Woodland Valley Creek and Stony Clove Creek. This section is a famous canoeing and kayaking area and the entire stream is famous as a trout stream. Continuing east from Phoenicia it flows past Mt. Pleasant and

Boiceville and enters the thirteen-mile-long Ashokan Reservoir, where it is damned at Olive Bridge, at the site of the former Bishops Falls. From here it continues east and southeast to near Lomontville, where it makes a bend to the northeast and flows through broad fertile flats between the Catskill foothills and the northern tip of the Shawangunks. It passes the early Dutch settlements of Marbletown, Hurley and Kingston, where it is crossed by the Thruway and Route 28 near Exit 19. Kingston is on the east bank. From here it flows north through marshes past the village of Lake Katrine to a junction with Plattekill Creek above Glenerie Falls. This portion of the creek is visible to the east of the Thruway which here parallels it. It turns sharply east under the West Shore Railroad bridge and goes over Glenerie Falls, which are quite spectacular during high water. The shores adjacent to the falls are private property and entry is not permitted. However, the creek turns sharply north at the foot of the falls and flows through a gorge which is paralleled by Route 9W. The falls can be seen at a distance from this highway. From the foot of the Glenerie Falls the creek flows through a rugged and narrow, but quite straight, gorge north to the vicinity of Saugerties. Here it is damned just below the Route 9W bridge and forms a fair-sized lake. In the 19th century the falls here were used for water power and the remains of several mills can be seen. The last major industry at the falls was the Martin Cantine Coated Paper Company on the north bank. The falls over the dam can be seen by turning off Route 9W on Dock St. just north of the Cantine mill. Below the falls the creek runs through a deep gorge and makes a sharp turn to the east where it becomes still tide water. The two shores are lined with marinas for the final short stretch to the Hudson, which it enters between tidal flats and jetties on either side. Here there is a Coast Guard station and a lighthouse on the north jetty.

Rondout Creek, along with the Esopus and the Neversink, is the third major stream to take its rise in the Slide Mountain massif. It rises in two branches, the west one of which rises between Rocky and Balsam Cap Mountains, whence it flows south between Lone, Table and Peekamoose Mountains on the west and Breath Hill on the east. It joins a stream flowing out of Peekamoose Lake and flows southwest to Sundown. Here it is joined by the East Branch which rises near Greenville, south of Bangle Hill and Samson Mountain, but to the north of East Mountain. This branch flows southwest to Sundown. From here the combined stream flows southwest to Lowes Corners where it enters the six-mile-long Rondout Reservoir, which runs from west to east. At the east end is the Merriman Dam, at Lackawack, near the junction of Routes 55 and 55A. It continues southeast through Honk Lake and over Honk Falls at Napanoch, where there was a hydroelectric plant above the highway bridge. At Napanoch the stream makes a sharp bend to the northeast

Peekamoose Lake on headwaters of West Branch of Rondout Creek. Photo by Alfred H. Marks.

along the northwestern foot of the Shawangunks, after receiving the waters of Sandburg Creek from the southwest. From here to tidewater it was followed by the old D & H Canal. It flows past Kerhonkson, Port Jackson, St. Josen, Accord, Alligerville, Kyserike and High Falls before starting through a breach in the Shawangunks. At High Falls is a hydro-electric plant and the falls which give the locality its name. Below the falls are the remains of an old canal aqueduct across the creek. Next come Bruceville, Lawrenceville and Rosendale. At Rosendale it is crossed by the 150 ft. high trestle of the Wallkill Valley Railroad, built in 1872. Here the stream is flowing due east and enters dikes of the Army Corps of Engineers. East of Rosendale it is crossed by the truss bridge on Route 32 and the high bridge of the New York Thruway. This bridge is near Lefever Falls. A short distance further east it is joined from the south by the waters of the Wallkill River, and here it makes a sharp bend to the north past Creeklocks and Bloomington to Eddyville where it falls to tidewater, and which was the end of the D & H Canal. Here it is crossed by Route 213 and broadens out into tide water with marshes at the border and with Gumaer Island in the middle. Barges come up this far to be loaded with aggregate. There were lime kilns along the shore here and bluestone yards at Wilbur, the next town downstream, where the creek is crossed by the 1,200 ft. long, 150 ft. high truss bridge of the West Shore Railroad, built

Rondout Creek and Route 32 bridge at Rosendale. Note flood dikes. Photo by Alfred H. Marks.

in 1883. Here the stream is flowing northeast with Hussey Hill to the east and Fly Mountain and the city of Kingston to the north. Continuing northeast are the canal villages of Connelly and Sleightsburg on the south bank and Rondout on the north. These formerly were connected by a cable ferry, since replaced by the Route 9W suspension bridge, from which fine views may be obtained. Just west of the bridge is the famous Island Dock where in past years immense piles of coal unloaded from canal boats awaited loading to river and coastal barges and schooners. On the north bank is the Strand section of Rondout, which was the former commercial center. The ferry house for the Rhinecliff Ferry was here. This ferry used to sail down Rondout Creek before crossing the Hudson. Also further east on the north bank are former limestone quarries, later used as mushroom growing caves, and the old community of Ponckhockie.

Rondout was the home port of the famous steamer *Mary Powell*, and there were many boatyards in the vicinity. Jetties extend out into the Hudson River on either side with mud flats to north and south. There is a navigation light at the tip of the south jetty and a two-story brick light house tower built in 1915 at the tip of the north jetty. Just north, on the Hudson River, across some mud flats, is Kingston Point.

The Wallkill River rises in Lake Mohawk in Sussex County, New Jersey, near Sparta, and flows northeast between the Kittatinny Mountains to the west and the Pimple Hills to the east to the vicinity of Pine Island in New York. Here it has several tributaries, including Papakating Creek and waters from Wickham and Wawayanda Lakes. It flows through large and immensely fertile bottom lands of "black dirt" where onions and other vegetables are grown extensively. This is in Orange County. It continues northeast, flowing beneath Route 17 and the Erie Railroad midway between Goshen to the east and Middletown on the west; past Montgomery, Walden, Wallkill and Gardiner, where it receives the waters of the Shawangunk Kill. It enters Ulster County just south of the village of Wallkill. It continues north along the eastern foot of the Shawangunks past New Paltz and, turning in loops to the east, passes under Route 32 and the Thruway south of Rosendale. Here it is spanned by Perrine's restored covered bridge, accessible from Route 213, and can be glimpsed to the east side of the Thruway. There is a power sub-station at Dashville, where it turns north and receives the waters of the Swarte Kill from the south before entering the artificial Sturgeon Pool near Rifton. The River is followed in parts by Routes 208, 32 and 213, and by the Wallkill Valley Railroad, between Montgomery and the vicinity of Rosendale. It flows into the Rondout Creek just below the dam at the north end of Sturgeon Pool.

Shawangunk Kill flows northeast from New Vernon, past Pinebush to Canahgote along the eastern base of Shawangunk Mountains. It empties into Wallkill River.

Black Creek rises on the western slopes of Illinois Mountain in the township of Lloyds in southern Ulster County. It flows north into Chodikee Lake and, going over several waterfalls and through some narrow gorges, turns to flow northeast by north to the Hudson at the town of Esopus. Its waters are dark with tannin from cedar trees—thus the name.

Normanskill Creek rises near East Berne in the Helderbergs and flows east through Normanskill Ravine or The Vale of Tawasentha (one supposed setting of Longfellow's *Song of Hiawatha*), to the Hudson River near Glenmont. The D & H Railroad follows the creek through the ravine.

Hannacrois Creek rises in the southern Helderbergs and flows through Ravine and over Dickinson Falls first southeast to Alcove Reservoir, then east and northeast to the Hudson River south of Barren Island at Coeymans, near Matthew Point.

THE DELAWARE RIVER SYSTEM

The Delaware River was called the South River by the early English settlers, although a name bestowed by an English adventurer, Samuel Argall, has stuck to the river. He named it after Lord De La Warr, the first colonial governor of Virginia. Henry Hudson entered the river in 1609, the same year he sailed up the Hudson River. Dutch and Swedes settled along its lower reaches as well as the English, and, of course, the Quaker followers of William Penn. The river is 315 miles long, from its sources near Stamford, New York to Liston Point, Delaware, where it flows into Delaware Bay, and in another 51 miles, the Atlantic Ocean at Cape May. The Delaware Indians who lived along its shores had migrated from the far northwest prior to white settlement. They were known as the Minsi or Lenni Lenape Indians and were generally friendly to the white settlers—especially with William Penn's followers. They were antagonistic to the Iroquois Confederation. After the Revolution they migrated to Ohio and, after Pontiac's Rebellion, they moved across the Mississippi and ultimately were dispersed. Remnants have intermarried with the Cherokees and a few live along the Trent River in Ontario, Canada today.

The river rises in two branches around the Stamford area. The West Branch is the more northerly and rises northeast of Stamford near Route 10. It flows southwest past Stamford, Hobart, South Kortright and Bloomville. In this section it is followed by the Ulster & Delaware Railroad and Route 10, which follows it all the way to Deposit. Continuing further southwest it passes Delhi, where it receives the waters of the Little Delaware River, De Lancey, Hamden and Walton, where it was formerly crossed by the NYO & W Railroad, which also had a branch along its west bank to Delhi. At Apex, below Walton, it enters the Cannonsville Reservoir, which extends 8 miles to Stilesville, where the dam is located. At Deposit it curves around and begins flowing southeast, paralleled by Route 17, and the Erie Railroad which follows its course all the way to Port Jervis. Starting at Hale Eddy it becomes the New York–Pennsylvania boundary.

The next major point is Hancock, where the river is joined by the East Branch flowing in from the north. Here it is left by Route 17, which follows up the East Branch. Route 97 follows its northeastern bank from here to Port Jervis and provides a most beautiful drive, although the river is best seen from either a canoe or an occasional Erie excursion train, as the highway is frequently inland and separated by dense forest. This is wild and beautiful country with much white water and rapids. In the early times there was extensive lumber rafting, as will be described in greater detail in our article on the Susquehanna.

Let us now retrace our steps to follow the East Branch, which rises to the southeast of Stamford, south of Grand Gorge village, in a narrow defile between Irish Mountain on the East and the Moresville Range on the West. In this shadowy glen there is barely sufficient room for the Ulster & Delaware Railroad, which follows the river to near Margaretville, and Route 30 which follows it to its junction with the Beaver Kill and Route 17 at East Branch, just east of Hancock. Here the river is a shallow, reed-filled stream and in places passes under driveways in corrugated pipe and meanders through meadows and pastures. It flows in a generally southwesterly direction past the towns of Roxbury, Halcottsville, Kelly Corners and Margaretville, where it is joined by the Bush Kill from the east. Here it is also crossed by Route 28. Between here and East Branch it was followed by the now abandoned Delaware Northern Railroad. At Dunraven it widens into the waters of Pepacton Reservoir, 18.5 miles long, to a dam at Downsville. There are roads all along both sides, but Route 30 crosses it at Shavertown Bridge, named after a drowned village, at about midpoint. Below Downsville it flows past Corbett and Shinhopple, where there are numerous campgrounds, to Harvard and East Branch, where it is joined by the waters of the Beaver Kill and Route 17 from the east. Here it turns decisively west past Fishs Eddy and Cadosia to its junction with the West Branch at Hancock. Formerly the NYO & W main line followed it between East Branch and Cadosia, where the old betowered depot can still be seen on the hillside. This branch was poetically named Pepacton by John Burroughs. His book *Pepacton* describes a rafting expedition down its length. The natives, however, call it simply the East Branch, reserving the name Pepacton to designate the reservoir.

Hancock is about sixty miles from both sources. The combined stream now flows 55 miles southeast to Port Jervis. Steep hills rise on either side and the tang of frontier life lingers on. There are rustic fishing camps, a recreation of old Fort Delaware at Narrowsburg, Roebling's pioneer suspension bridge for the D & H Canal at Lackawaxen and the Hawks Nest Cliffs below Barryville. A fitting but contrasting note is struck by St. Joseph's Franciscan Seminary above Callicoon, with its buildings reminiscent of a European Abbey. The towns passed in this section are Lordville, named for Eleazor Lord, promoter and first president of the Erie Railroad, Long Eddy, Callicoon, Cochecton and Damascus, Pa., across from it; Milanville, Pa., Narrowsburg, N.Y., Masthope, Westcolang and Lackawaxen, Pa. and Minisink Ford in New York.

Next downstream is Barryville, N.Y. with Shohola, Pa. across from it. Then comes Pond Eddy and Mongaup in New York and Millrift, Pa. followed by Sparrowsbush and Port Jervis, New York and Matamoras, Pa. across from it. Between Lackawaxen and Port Jervis the northern bank was followed by the now defunct D & H Canal. Much of this is a rugged gorge. The canal had to be blasted out of the foot of a cliff. The present Hawksnest Drive on Route 97 is high up on the cliffs and affords magnificent views. The Erie Railroad follows the Pennsylvania side in this section, which is also popular for canoeing.

At Port Jervis the Delaware is joined by the waters of the Neversink River from the north at Carpenters Point. Catskill tributaries to the Delaware between Hancock and Port Jervis are: Hoolihan Brook, Basket,

Hankins and Callicoon Creeks, Mitchell Pond and Clarks Pond Brooks, Ten Mile River, Grassy Swamp, Narrow Falls, Schumacher Pond, York Lake, Beaver, Halfway and Mill Brooks, Fish Cabin Creek and the Mongaup River.

Below Port Jervis the Delaware flows first southwest and then generally south, serving as the boundary between New Jersey on the east and Pennsylvania and Delaware on the west. It breaches the Blue Ridge at Delaware Water Gap where Mount Tammany is in New Jersey's Kittatinny Mountains (a southern extension of the Shawangunks) and Mt. Minsi is in the Pocono Mountains of Pennsylvania. They rise 1,200 ft. above the water. Two highways and the Lackawanna Railroad follow the river through the gap. Below the Gap the Delaware flows past Easton, Pa. and Phillipsburg, N.J. and then flows southeast to Trenton where there are rapids and it is crossed by U.S. Route 1 and the Pennsylvania R.R. Here again the river turns southwest and becomes navigable, and its banks are highly industrialized with steel mills and shipbuilding firms. Between Trenton and Delaware Bay at Liston Point it flows past Camden, N.J. and the Port of Philadelphia and Wilmington and New Castle in Delaware. There are many spectacular highway bridges across its lower reaches, including that of the New Jersey Turnpike at Deepwater. At the outlet of Delaware Bay into the Atlantic there is a ferry service between Cape May and Lewes, Del. and at this point it is so wide that one feels he is at sea.

MAJOR DELAWARE TRIBUTARIES:

Bush Kill Creek flows west from the Fleischmanns area to above Margaretville where it empties into the East Branch.

Dry Brook rises in Ulster County and flows north by northwest past Seager and Mapledale to junction with the Bush Kill Creek at Arkville. There are three covered bridges across it and its name possibly is derived from the German *Drei Brucke*.

Beaver Kill rises to the west of Doubletop Mountain. It is fed by Tunis Pond, Gulf of Mexico Brook, Black Creek, Balsam Lake, Beecher Lake, Scudder Brook and Alder Creek. It continues west past Hardenburg and Turnwood to Lew Beach where it is fed by Huggins Lake, then past Jersey Brook and Berry and Spring Brooks, where it turns south and flows into Junction Pool at Roscoe and is joined from the east by the waters of Willowemoc Creek. At Roscoe it turns to flow northwest past Cooks Falls, Horton and Peakville before flowing into the East Branch of the Delaware at East Branch. Major tributaries in this stretch are Russell, Horton, Trout and Spooner Brooks. This stretch was formerly followed by the O & W

Railroad, of which Route 17 now uses part of the alignment. It is a famous trout stream.

Willowemoc Creek rises in the vicinity of the village of Willowemoc, at the junction of Butternut and Fir Brooks. It flows west by southwest past Anderson and DeBruce to Livingston Manor, where it turns more westerly and flows past Deckertown and Hazel to its junction with the Beaver Kill at Roscoe. It is a notable trout stream. From Livingston Manor to Roscoe it was formerly followed by the O & W Railroad and is now followed by Route 17.

The Mongaup River rises northeast of Liberty and flows south past Liberty and Ferndale, where it was formerly crossed by a high trestle of the O & W Railroad, to Bushville, where it receives the waters of the East Branch, which have flowed south from Dixie Lake past Harris. From here it continues south to Mongaup Valley, where it is joined from the northwest by the waters of the West Branch which rises in Swan Lake, southeast of White Sulphur Springs. Here it enters the long and narrow Swinging Bridge Reservoir for six miles and receives the waters of Kinne Brook, Lake Brook and Burnt Meadow Brook. South of Swinging Bridge Reservoir it flows three miles through Mongaup Falls Reservoir into three-mile-long Rio Reservoir. From here it continues another three miles south to join the Delaware at Mongaup.

The Neversink River (formerly Mahackamack) is also called the Minisink River. Two branches rise on the west and east slopes of Slide Mountain and flow generally southwest to a junction at Claryville. From here they flow south into the Neversink Reservoir near Aden. The reservoir is five miles long approximately, and from here it flows south past Hasbrouck and Woodbourne to South Fallsburgh, where it was formerly crossed by a high trestle of the O & W Railroad. From here it continues south to Bridgeville on Route 17, site of a famous early covered bridge. It continues ten miles south through wild country to a junction with the Bush Kill at Oakland. Here it turns southeast for five miles past Paradise and Roses Point to Valley Junction at the foot of the Shawangunks, where it again turns southwest for seven miles, flowing past Godeffroy and Huguenot in Orange County, to a junction with the Delaware at Tri-State Rock on Carpenters Point south of Port Jervis. This last stretch between Oakland and Port Jervis was paralleled by lines of the O & W Railroad and by the D & H Canal between Roses Point and Port Jervis and by the present Route 209 for this stretch. Owing to action of the New York City Department of Water Supply in controlling outflows from its reservoirs the level of this river is subject to extreme fluctuation and there is also considerable pollution—both of which reasons have led to the deterioration of a once notable trout stream.

THE SUSQUEHANNA RIVER

Source of the Susquehanna River, Otsego Lake, Cooperstown. Photo by Alfred H. Marks.

Where Susquehanna pours his untamed stream . . .

Samuel Taylor Coleridge

And when I asked the name of the river from the brakeman, and heard that it was called the Susquehanna, the beauty of the name seemed to be part and parcel of the beauty of the land . . . that was the name, as no other could be, for that shining river and desireable valley.

from *Across The Plains*
Robert Lewis Stevenson

When you come here, I shall drive you to the Narrows of the Susquehanna. That is a word, nota bene, which, in this degree of latitude, refers not at all to the breadth of the stream. It is a place where the mountains, like many a frowning coward, threatens to crowd its gentler neighbor, but gives room at its calm approach, and annoys nobody but the passer-by. The road between them, as you come on, looks etched with a thumb-nail along the base of the cliff, and you would think it a pokerish drive, making no allowance for perspective. The friable rock, however, makes rather a smooth single track; and if you have the inside when you meet farmer Giles or the stage-coach, you have only to set your hub against the rock, and "let them go by as likes." The majestic and tranquil river sweeps into the peaked shadow, and on again, with the disdain of a beauty used to conquer. It reminded me of Lady Blessington's "do if you dare!" when the mob at the House of Lords threatened to break her chariot windows. There was a calm courage in Miladi's French glove that carried her through, and so, amid this mob of mountains, glides the Susquehanna to the sea.

from Letter VI
Letters from Under a Bridge
Nathaniel Parker Willis

The very name of Susquehanna has captured the imagination of poets and idealists ever since its first discovery. Talleyrand, the great French advocate of constitutional monarchy, took refuge here at "Asylum" in 1795 during the Reign of Terror and did not return to France until the establishment of the Directory; and European idealists and liberals imagined the valley of the Susquehanna as the native home of liberty.

Indeed a magical influence seems attached to the Susquehanna. The legends of very early Spanish settlement and treasures found at Carantouan or Spanish Hill near Tioga Point, the apparition of Peter, James and John to Joseph Smith on its banks near Oakland, Pennsylvania, and his subsequent finding of the golden plates containing the Book of Mormon near Afton, New York, all lend an aura of mystery to this river, as do the exciting military exploits enacted along its course.

The Susquehanna is one of America's great rivers. It flows for five hundred and twenty miles from its source in Lake Otsego in the far western foothills of the Catskills to its outlet into mighty Chesapeake Bay at Havre de Grace, north of Baltimore, in Maryland. It also has a great western branch, rising in the rugged Alleghenies near Altoona, Pennsylvania and, after circumscribing a great arc to the north, joining the main stream at Northumberland, Pennsylvania. The total fall is 1,200 ft. The river is generally shallow and turbulent and navigable only for a short distance near its mouth, although there were pioneer attempts at steam navigation on its upper reaches and around Harrisburg. Also, a canal was built along its lower stretches in Pennsylvania. However, its main navigational utility was for lumber and rafting, and it carried immense amounts of timber in the 19th century. Here is a brief description of this traffic by Nathaniel Parker Willis, who was living near Owego, New York, at his estate "Glenmary" at the time of writing in 1848:

One half the population of the neighborhood is engaged in what is called lumbering, and until the pine timber of the forest can be counted like the cedars of Lebanon, this vocation will serve the uses of the mobs of England, the revolutions of France, and the plots of Italy. I may add, the music and theatres of Austria and Prussia, the sensual indulgence of the Turk, and the intrigue of the Spaniard; for there is, in every people under the sun, a superflue of spirits unconsumed by common occupation, which, if not turned adroitly or accidentally to some useful or harmless end, will expend its reckless energy in trouble and mischief.

The preparations for the adventures of which I speak, though laborious, are often conducted like a frolic. The felling of the trees in mid-winter, the cutting of shingles, and the drawing out on the snow, are employments preferred by the young men to the tamer but less arduous work of the farm-yard; and, in the temporary and uncomfortable shanties, deep in the woods, subsisting often on nothing but pork and whiskey, they find metal more attractive than village or fireside. The small streams emptying into the Susquehanna are innumerable, and, eight or ten miles back from the river, the arks are built, and the materials of the rafts collected, ready to launch with the first thaw. I live, myself, as you know, on one of these tributaries, a quarter of a mile from its junction. The Owaga trips along at the foot of my lawn as private and untroubled, for the greater part of the year, as Virginia Water at Windsor; but, as it swells in March, the noise of voices and hammering, coming out from the woods above, warns us of the approach of an ark; and at the rate of eight or ten miles an hour, the rude structure shoots by, floating high on the water, without its lading [which it takes in at the village below,] and manned with a singing and saucy crew, who dodge the branches of the trees, and work their steering paddles with an adroitness and nonchalance which sufficiently shows the character of the class. The sudden bends which the river takes in describing my woody Omega put their steersmanship to the test; and, when the leaves are off the trees, it is a curious sight to see the bulky monsters, shining with new boards, whirling around in the swift eddies, and, when caught by the current again, gliding off among the trees, like a singing and swearing phantom of an unfinished barn.

At the village they take wheat and pork into the arks, load their rafts with plank and shingles, and wait for the return of the freshet. It is a fact you may not know, that, when a river is rising, the middle is the highest, and vice versa, when falling—sufficiently proved by the experience of the rafts-men, who, if they start before the flow is at its top, can not keep their crafts from the shore. A penthouse, barely sufficient for a man to stretch himself below, is raised on the deck, with a fire-place of earth and loose stone, and, with what provision they can aford, and plenty of whiskey, they shove out into the stream. Thenceforward it is vogue la galere! They have nothing to do, all day, but abandon themselves to the current, sing and dance and take their turn at the steering oars; and, when the sun sets, they look out for an eddy, and pull in to the shore. The stopping-places are not very numerous, and are well-known to all who follow the trade; and, as the river swarms with rafts, the getting to land, and making sure of a fastening, is a scene always of great competition, and often of desperate fighting. When all is settled for the night, however, and the fires are lit on the long range of the flotilla, the raftsmen get together over their whiskey and provender, and tell the thousand stories of their escapes and accidents; and, with the repetition of this, night after night, the whole rafting population, along the five hundred miles of the Susquehanna, becomes partially acquainted, and forms a sympathetic corps, whose excitement and esprit might be roused to very dangerous uses.

By daylight they are cast off and once more on the current, and in five or seven days they arrive at tide-water, where the crew is immediately discharged, and start, usually on foot, to follow the river home again. There are several places in the navigation which are dangerous, such as rapids and dam-sluices; and, what with these, and the scenes at the eddies, and their pilgrimage through a thinly settled and wild country home again, they see enough of adventure to make them fireside heroes, and incapacitate them, [while their vigor lasts, at least,] for all the more quiet habits of the farmer. The consequence is easy to be seen. Agriculture is but partially followed throughout the country, and while these cheap facilities for transporting product to the sea-board exists, those who are contented to stay at home, and cultivate the rich river-lands of the country, are sure of high prices and a ready reward for their labor.

Moral: Come to the Susquehanna, and settle on a farm. You did not know what I was driving at, all this while!

The raftsmen who "follow the Delaware" [to use their own poetical expression] are said to be a much wilder class than those on the Susquehanna. In returning to Owego, by different routes, I have often fallen in with parties of both; and certainly nothing could be more entertaining than to listen to their tales. In a couple of years the canal route on the Susquehanna will lay open this rich vein of the picturesque and amusing, and, as the tranquil boat glides peacefully along the river bank, the traveller will be surprised with the strange effect of these immense flotillas, with their many fires and wild people, lying in the glassy bends of the solitary stream; the smoke stealing through the dark forest, and the confusion of a hundred excited voices breaking the silence. In my trip down the river in the spring, I saw enough that was novel in this way to fill a new portfolio for Bartlett, and I intend he shall raft it with me to salt water the next time he comes among us.

It will be remembered that Bartlett was Willis's collaborator in his "American Scenery" venture, and did many fine drawings of the Catskills.

Many boom towns sprung up—instant cities with opulent homes, opera houses and fine stores, Lock-Haven and Williamsport, Pennsylvania among the most notable. With the coming of the Erie Railroad in 1848 impetus moved from water to rails. A few years later William Foster, older brother of Stephen Collins Foster, the composer, was working as a civil engineer for the Susquehanna Canal and living at Athens, near Tioga Point, where the Chemung joins the Susquehanna. Young Stephen came to live with him and while there wrote his first composition, "The Tioga Waltz," commissioned for the wedding party of one of the young civil engineers working for the Erie Railroad. It is interesting to note that Stephen died in Belleview Hospital in New York as a result of a fall in a

Bowery flophouse when dead drunk, while William became Vice President of the Pennsylvania Railroad. The years in the Susquehanna Valley were the last period when the Foster family were happy together.

The major port at the base of the Susquehanna was Port Deposit, Md., which even today retains its quaint early 19th-century charm. Here, in 1781, after the Battle of Yorktown which sealed the success of the American Revolution, General Lafayette paid a visit on his way back to New York.

The Susquehanna has two major branches:

The Main Branch starts at Cooperstown at the outlet of Lake Otsego, and flows south past Hartwick Seminary, Milford, where it is joined by Cherry Valley Creek, Colliersville, where the waters of Schenevus Creek join it and on to Oneonta. It continues south past Unadilla, after receiving the waters of Charlotte Creek. Unadilla was once known as Wattle's Ferry and was the western terminus of the Catskill & Suquehanna Turnpike. Sidney comes next, where it is joined by the Unadilla River from the northwest. Here the old New York, Ontario & Western Railroad crossed the river. It continues to flow south past Afton and Nineveh, New York and dips down into Pennsylvania for the first time to the great bend starting at Damascus. At the bottom of the bend it receives the waters of Starrucca Creek from the southeast. Between Sidney and the town of Susquehanna the river is paralleled on the east by the Randolph Hills, which form the divide between it and the West Branch of the Delaware. These hills served as a formidable barrier to the builders of the Erie Railroad, who finally found a low spot and dug a great cut at Gulf Summit, which was one of the great engineering achievements of the time. The great viaduct across Starrucca Creek, modeled after ancient Roman viaducts, is at Lanesville, Pa., just to the northeast of Susquehanna station, where the Erie built a great hotel-depot of red brick in the Gothic manner in 1848 and established their major car shops. The Route 17 Quickway crosses just above the state line between Damascus on the East Bank and Windsor on the West. Across from Susquehanna, Pa., on the northern bank is Oakland, formerly called Harmony, where Joseph Smith lived for a time around 1825. He boarded with Isaac Hale while working for Josiah Stoal. Smith claimed that in 1829 he received the Order of the Priesthood of Melchizedek from the hands of Peter, James and John, who appeared to him on the bank of the river between Harmony, Pa. and Colesville, N.Y. In 1827 he had eloped with Emma Hale, his landlord's daughter, to Afton, N.Y. where he claims to have discovered the golden plates of the Book of Mormon.

Flowing past Oakland at the bottom of the Great Bend, the river swings past the villages of Great Bend and Hallstead, Pa. and re-enters New York southeast of Binghampton. From here, after being joined by the waters of the Chenango River, the river flows west past Owego, N.Y. and Sayre, Pa. to Athens, Pa., where it is joined by Cayuta Creek. Here it turns and flows southeast and, at Tioga Point, just south of Athens, is joined by the Chemung River coming in from the northwest. This last named river, in conjunction with the tributary Canisteo River and the Genesee and the Susquehanna rivers, provided a natural all-water route between the Catskills and the Niagara Frontier which was used by the Indians and military expeditions in the French and Indian War and the Revolution. The route had only a few short portages and is described in many captivity tales. The general route from Kingston would follow: the Esopus, East Branch Delaware to Hancock, up the West Branch to Deposit, portage to Damascus, down the Susquehanna to Tioga Point, up the Chemung and Canisteo, then portage to the Genesee and down it to the shores of Lake Ontario. As the Susquehanna south from Tioga Point also provided easy communication, Tioga Point became an important place for Indian gatherings and councils, and was also of prime strategic military importance.

The central location of this stretch of the Susquehanna is important in understanding the story of Hiawatha and the powerful Iroquois Confederation. See Chapter 6 for these events.

Etienne Brule, an aide to Samuel Champlain, penetrated as far south as Tioga Point on the Susquehanna by 1616, coming down by way of the Chenango Valley from the Mohawk. Here, at Carantouan Hill, he saw ruined fortifications which the Indians told him were built by a party of Spaniards. To this day no one has gotten to the bottom of the facts of this tale.

Past Tioga Point the river continues southeast past Towanda, Pa. and the high Indian lookout of Wayalusing Rocks and the junction of Tunkhannock Creek at Tunkhannock, and past Pittston where it is joined by the Lackawanna River, also from the east. Further south at Wilkes-Barre it makes a bend to the southwest and is joined from the northeast by the Wyoming River. Here in 1773 the terrible Wyoming Massacre was perpetrated upon settlers from Connecticut by a band of Indians and Tories under John Butler. It was to avenge this and the Cherry Valley Massacre that General James Clinton mounted his famous expedition of 1779 down the Susquehanna that finally succeeded, in conjunction with that of General Sullivan at Elmira, in breaking the power of the Iroquois.

Continuing southwest through Nanticoke Gap in the Blue Ridge the river flows past Bloomsburg, where Interstate 80 crosses it, to the junction with the West Branch at Northumberland. The united stream now flows south past Sunbury, Selinsgrove, Harrisburg and Middletown to Columbia, Pa. Here it becomes very wild and flows through deep gorges, the crags of which are a nesting place for the bald eagle, till after a final fall it reaches tidewater at Port Deposit, Md. and flows into Chesapeake Bay.

Here it is crossed by high bridges of Routes U.S. 40 and Interstate 95 and the Baltimore & Ohio Railroad, and the long low-level bridge of the Pennsylvania Railroad at the very mouth of the river, at Perryville.

The West Branch rises in the Allegheny Mountains at Bakerton, Pa., twenty five miles northwest of Altoona, on the mainline of the Pennsylvania Railroad, near the famous Horseshoe Curve. It flows first northeast, then southeast, past Barnesboro, Curwensville, Clearfield, Renovo, Lock-Haven, Williamsport, Milton and Lewisburg to a junction with the main stream at Northumberland. This West Branch flows through some very rugged and still primitive country where it is rumored that even today the wolf is making a comeback. This branch saw the greatest lumber rafting activity, although it did not transport the great amount of farm produce that the North Branch was described as having. Clearfield and Williamsport were important railroad junction points for lines coming up from the coal fields and running north to Erie, Buffalo and the Rochester area. Today much of this area can be seen from Interstate 80.

It is not our purpose to describe the Susquehanna in detail in Pennsylvania and Maryland, but only to give the grand outlines of this great river that rises in Otsego Lake. Principal tributaries are: Oaks Creek, which is the outlet of Lake Canadarago, Cherry Valley, Schenevus, Charlotte, Otego, Ouleout Creeks and the Unadilla River. Starrucca Creek, Chenango River, Owego River, Cayuta Creek and the Chemung River at Tioga Point. Wysox, Wyalusing, Tunkhannock Creeks and the Lackawanna River. Wyoming River, and Fishing and Catawissa Creeks and the West Branch at Northumberland. Mahonoy, Mahantango, Wiconisco Creeks and Juniata River north of Rockville. Powell, Clark, Strong, Little Juniata, Sherman, Conewago, Conestoga, Pequea, Muddy and Octoraro Creeks.

Goodyear Lake, north of Colliersville in Otsego County, N.Y., is an artificial lake created for hydro-electric generation purposes. In times of low water the flood gates are opened wide only in the early morning—which should be of interest to canoeists. Also of interest to boaters are the coal dredges or "Susquehanna Fleet" on the river near Harrisburg, Pa.

The Susquehanna Valley is paralleled by many railroads, operating often along the very banks. They are: Cooperstown to Emmons: Cooperstown & Charlotte Valley. Emmons to Lanesville, Pa.: Delaware & Hudson, Albany & Susquehanna Division. Lanesville, Pa. to Binghamton and Athens, Pa.: former Erie Railroad portion of Erie-Lackawanna. Binghamton to Sayre: former Delaware, Lackawanna & Western portion of Erie-Lackawanna, now abandoned and used in part by Southern Tier Expressway, Route 17, on the south bank of the river. Sayre, Pa. to Wilkes-Barre: Lehigh Valley Railroad on the east bank. Wilkes-Barre to Northumberland on the west bank: Lackawanna Railroad portion of EL. Wilkes-Barre to Harrisburg and Port Deposit: various lines of the Pennsylvania on either side. Also D & H now operates some former Pennsylvania lines on the east bank south of Wilkes-Barre. Erie-Lackawanna and Lehigh Valley are now Conrail.

The Susquehanna River was discovered by Captain John Smith, of Pocahontas fame, in 1608 while exploring the western shores of Chesapeake Bay, which means Great Water in the Indian language. He did not get above the location of Port Deposit and the first falls, but he heard of a nation of "giant" redmen named the Susquehannocks, who lived upstream, and named the river after them. It is interesting to note that this was one year before Henry Hudson explored the Hudson River and only three years before Brule reached Tioga Point from the north. If there is any truth to the legend of Spanish Hill, it is possible that Spanish explorers, possibly a detachment of De Soto's men, had reached the Tioga area.

We will now let Cooper describe the beginning of the river in the outlet at Cooperstown, as told in his *The Deerslayer*:

It may strike the reader as a little singular, that the place where a stream of any size passed through banks that had an elevation of some twenty feet, should be a matter of doubt with men who could not now have been more than two hundred yards distant from the precise spot. It will be recollected, however, that the trees and bushes here, as elsewhere, fairly overhung the water, making such a fringe to the lake, as to conceal any little variations from its general outline.

"I've not been down at this end of the lake these two summers," said Hurry, standing up in the canoe, the better to look about him. "Ay, there's the rock, showing its chin above the water, and I know that the river begins in its neighborhood."

"And here is the river, Deerslayer," he continued, "though so shut in by trees and bushes as to look more like an and-bush than the outlet of such a sheet as the Glimmerglass."

Hurry had not badly described the place, which did truly seem to be a stream lying in ambush. The high banks might have been a hundred feet asunder; but, on the western side, a small bit of low land extended so far forward as to diminish the breadth of the stream to half that width.

As the bushes hung in the water beneath, and pines that had the stature of church-steeples, rose in tall columns above, all inclining towards the light, until their branches intermingled, the eye, at a little distance, could not easily detect any opening in the shore, to mark the egress of the water. In the forest above, no traces of this outlet were to be seen from the lake, the whole presenting the same connected and seemingly interminable carpet of leaves. As the canoe slowly advanced, sucked in by the current, it entered beneath an arch of trees, through which the light from the heavens struggled by casual openings, faintly relieving the gloom beneath.

"This is a nat'ral and-bush," half whispered Hurry, as if he felt that the place was devoted to secresy and watchfullness; "depend on it, old Tom has burrowed with the ark somewhere in this quarter. We will drop down with the current a short distance, and ferret him out."

"This seems no place for a vessel of any size," returned the other; "it appears to me that we shall have hardly room enough for the canoe."

Hurry laughed at the suggestion, and, as it soon appeared with reason; for the fringe of bushes immediately on the shore of the lake was no sooner passed, than the adventurers found themselves in a narrow stream, of a sufficient depth of limpid water, with a strong current, and a canopy of leaves upheld by arches composed of the limbs of hoary trees. Bushes lined the shores, as usual, but they left sufficient space between them to admit the passage of anything that did not exceed twenty feet in width, and to allow of a perspective ahead of eight or ten times that distance.

Neither of our two adventurers used his paddle, except to keep the light bark in the centre of the current, but both watched each turning of the stream, of which there were two or three within the first hundred yards, with jealous vigilance. . . .

In the Introduction to his novel *The Pioneers*, Cooper well describes the most interesting aspect of the punitive expedition against the Iroquois after the Wyoming and Cherry Valley Massacres:

In 1779, an expedition was sent against the hostile Indians who dwelt about a hundred miles west of Otsego, on the banks of the Cayuga. The whole country was then a wilderness, and it was necessary to transport the baggage of the troops by means of the rivers, a devious but practicable route. One brigade ascended the Mohawk, until it reached the point nearest to the sources of the Susquehanna, whence it cut a lane through the forest to the head of the Otsego. The boats and baggage were carried over this "portage," and the troops proceeded to the other extremity of the lake, where they disembarked, and encamped. The Susquehanna, a narrow though rapid stream at its source, was much filled with "flood wood," or fallen trees; and the troops adopted a novel expedient to facilitate their passage. The Otsego is about nine miles in length, varying in breadth from half a mile to a mile and a half. The water is of greath depth, limpid, and supplied from a thousand springs. At its foot, the banks are rather less than thirty feet high; the remainder of its margin being in mountains, intervals, and points. The outlet, or the Susquehanna, flows through a gorge in the low banks just mentioned, which may have a width of two hundred feet. This gorge was dammed, and the waters of the lake collected: the Susquehanna was converted into a rill. When all was ready, the troops embarked, the dam was knocked away, the Otsego poured out its torrent, and the boats went merrily down with the current.

General James Clinton, the brother of George Clinton, then Governor of New York, and the father of DeWitt Clinton, who died governor of the same state in 1827, commanded the brigade employed on this duty.

Thus we can see that the Catskill Massif is drained by three great river systems; the Mohawk-Schoharie-Hudson, the Delaware, and the Susquehanna and enters the Atlantic through the three great bays of our eastern seaboard; or to look at it in another way, all three great river systems find a principal source in the Catskill Region.

The Unadilla River, forming the boundary between Otsego County on the east and Chenango County on the west, rises in the neighborhood of West Winfield, in Herkimer County, and flows south past Unadilla Forks, Leonardsville, West Edmeston, New Berlin, South New Berlin, and Mount Upton to junction with the Susquehanna River at Sidney. The principal tributary in Otsego County is Butternut Creek, which flows into it below Mount Upton. In the past its valley was followed by the New York, Ontario & Western and Unadilla Valley railroads, both now abandoned. It is followed on its west bank, in Chenango County, by Route 8.

Cooper, in his *Wyandotte*, describes the early settlement of the Unadilla Valley area:

> Our adventurers made most of their journey by water. After finding their way to the head of the Canaderaga, mistaking it for the Otsego, they felled trees, hollowed them into canoes, embarked, and aided by a yoke of oxen that were driven along the shore, they wormed their way through the oaks into the Susquehanna, descending that stream until they reached the Unadilla, which stream they ascended until they came to the small river, known in the parlance of the country by the erroneous name of a creek, that ran through the captain's new estate. The labor of this ascent was exceedingly severe; but the whole journey was completed by the end of April, and while the streams were high. Snow still lay in the woods; but the sap had started, and the season was beginning to show its promise.
>
> The first measure adopted by our adventurers was to "hut." In the very centre of the pond, which, it will be remembered covered four hundred acres, was an island of some five or six acres in extent. It was a rocky knoll, that rose forty feet above the surface of the water, and was still crowned with noble pines, a species of tree that had escaped the ravages of the beaver. In the pond itself a few "stubs" alone remained, the water having killed the trees, which had fallen and decayed. This circumstance showed that the stream had long before been dammed; successions of families of beavers having probably occupied the place, and renewed the works, for centuries, at intervals of generations. The dam in existence, however, was not very old; the animals having fled from their great enemy, man, rather than from any other foe.
>
> To the island Captain Willoughby transferred all his stores, and here he built his hut. This was opposed to the notions of his axe-men, who, rightly enough, fancied the mainland would be more convenient; but the captain and the sergeant, after a council of war, decided that the position on the knoll would be the most military, and might be defended the longest against man or beast. Another station was taken up, however, on the nearest shore, where such of the men were permitted to "hut" as preferred the location.
>
> These preliminaries observed, the captain meditated a bold stroke against the wilderness, by draining the pond, and coming at once into the possession of a noble farm, cleared of trees, and stumps, as it might be by a coup de main. This would be compressing the results of ordinary years of toil

into those of a single season, and everybody was agreed as to the expediency of the course, provided it were feasible.

This novel gives a most complete and picturesque picture of early colonial life.

Cherry Valley Creek rises near Cherry Valley and flows southwest to the Susquehanna River at Milford.

Schenevus Creek rises southwest of West Richmondsville and flows generally southwest past East Worcester, Worcester, Schenevus, and Maryland to junction with the Susquehanna River near Colliersville.

Charlotte Creek rises south of Richmondsville in Schoharie County and flows southwest past Lutheranville, Charlottesville, South Worcester, Davenport, Davenport Center and West Davenport to the Susquehanna River at Emmons.

Otsego Lake rises twenty miles southeast of utica and twenty one miles northeast of Oneonta. Cooperstown is at its southern end. Springfield Center is ½ mile above the northern end. Route 80 runs along its west shore and offers the best views. Route 31 runs along the east shore, but views are screened by woods. Glimmerglass State Park is at the northeast tip of the lake.

Otsego Lake is the principal source of the Susquehanna River, which flows out of the lake at Cooperstown. The lake is nine miles long and at an elevation of 1,200 ft.

The lake is best described by Cooper in his novel *The Deerslayer* of 1841. The scene of the action is 1740, but the descriptions largely hold good today:

> In about ten minutes they both broke suddenly into the brilliant light of the sun, on a low gravelly point, that was washed by water on quite half its outline.
> An exclamation of surprise broke from the lips of Deerslayer, an exclamation that was low and guardedly made, however, for his habits were much more thoughtful and regulated than those of the reckless Hurry, when, on reaching the margin of the lake, he beheld the view that unexpectedly met his gaze. It was, in truth, sufficiently striking to merit a brief description. On a level with the point lay a broad sheet of water, so placid and limpid that it resembled a bed of the pure mountain atmosphere compressed into a setting of hills and woods. Its length was about three leagues, while its breadth was irregular, expanding to half a league, or even more, opposite to the point, and contracting to less than half that distance, more to the southward. Of course, its margin was irregular, being indented by bays, and broken by many projecting, low points. At its northern, or nearest end, it was bounded by an isolated mountain, lower land falling off east and west, gracefully relieving the sweep of the outline. Still the character of the country was mountainous; high hills, or low mountains, rising abruptly from the water, on quite nine tenths of its circuit. The exceptions, indeed,

Indian Ladder Cliffs in John Boyd Thacher State Park in the Helderbergs. Photo by author.

only served a little to vary the scene; and even beyond the parts of the shore that were comparatively low, the background was high, though more distant.

But the most striking peculiarities of this scene were its solemn solitude and sweet repose. On all sides, wherever the eye turned, nothing met it but the mirror-like surface of the lake, the placid view of heaven, and the dense setting of the woods. So rich and fleecy were the outlines of the forest, that scarce an opening could be seen, the whole visible earth, from the rounded mountain-top to the water's edge, presenting one unvaried hue of unbroken verdure. As if vegetation were not satisfied with a triumph so complete, the trees overhung the lake itself, shooting out towards the light; and there were miles along its eastern shore, where a boat might have pulled the branches of dark Rembrandt-looking hemlocks, "Quivering aspens," and melancholy pines. In a word, the hand of man had never yet defaced or deformed any part of this native scene, which lay bathed in the sunlight, a glorious picture of affluent forest grandeur, softened by the balminess of June, and relieved by the beautiful variety afforded by the presence of so broad an expanse of water.

"This is grand!—'t is solemn!— 't is an edication of itself, to look upon!" exclaimed Deerslayer, as he stood leaning on his rifle, and gazing to the right and left, north and south, above and beneath, in whichever direction his eye could wander; "not a tree disturbed even by redskin hand, as I can discover, but everything left in the ordering of the Lord, to live and die according to his own designs and laws!"

Several times the men ceased paddling, and looking about them at the scene, as new glimpses opened from behind points, enabling them to see farther down the lake, or to get broader views of the wooded mountains. The only changes, however, where in the new forms of the hills, the varying curvature of the bays, and the wider reaches of the valley south; the whole earth apparently being clothed in a galadress of leaves.

"This is a sight to warm the heart!" exclaimed Deerslayer, when they had thus stopped for the fourth or fifth time; "the lake seems made to let us get an insight into the noble forests; and land and water alike stand in the beauty of God's providence." . . .

"Does game abound?" suddenly demanded the other, who paid but little attention to March's raillery.

"It has the country to itself. Scarce a trigger is pulled on it; and as for the trappers, this is not a region they greatly frequent."

. . . "Do the redmen often visit this lake, Hurry?" continued Deerslayer, pursuing his own train of thought.

"Why, they come and go; sometimes in parties, and sometimes singly. The country seems to belong to no native tribe in particular; and so it has fallen into the hands of the Hutter [a trapper in the story] tribe. The old man tells me that some sharp ones have been wheedling the Mohawks for an Indian deed, in order to get a title out of the colony; but nothing has come of it, seeing that no one heavy enough for such a trade has yet meddled with the matter. [Eventually George Groghan, Sir John Johnson's associate, obtained the title.] The hunters have a good life-lease still of this wilderness."

And in Chapter IX we have another purple passage that is still an accurate description:

> Yet art thou prodigal of smiles—
> Smiles sweeter than thy frowns are stern;
> Earth sends from all her thousand isles
> A shout at thy return.
> The glory that comes down from thee
> Bathes, in deep joy, the land and sea.

It may assist the reader in understanding the events we are about to record, if he has a rapidly sketched picture of the scene placed before his eyes at a single view. It will be remembered that the lake was an irregularly shaped basin, of an outline that, in the main, was oval, but with bays and points to relieve its formality and ornament its shores. The surface of this beautiful sheet of water was now glittering like a gem, in the last rays of the evening sun, and the setting of the whole—hills clothed in the richest forest verdure—was lighted up with a sort of radiant smile, that is best described in the beautiful lines we have placed at the head of this chapter. As the banks, with few exceptions, rose abruptly from the water, even where the mountain did not immediately bound the view, there was a nearly unbroken fringe of leaves overhanging the placid lake—the trees starting out of the acclivities, inclining to the light, until in many instances they extended their long limbs and straight trunks some forty or fifty feet beyond the line of the perpendicular. In these cases we allude only to the giants of the forest— pines of a hundred or a hundred and fifty feet in height—for, of the smaller growth, very many inclined so far as to steep their lower branches in the water.

In the position in which the ark had now got, the Castle was concealed from view by the projection of a point, as indeed was the northern extremity of the lake itself. A respectable mountain, forest-clad, and rounded like all the rest, limited the view in that direction, stretching immediately across the whole of the fair scene, with the exception of a deep bay that passed its western end, lengthening the basin for more than a mile. The manner in which the water flowed out of the lake, beneath the leafy arches of the trees that lined the sides of the stream, has already been mentioned, and it has also been said that the rock, which was a favorite place of rendezvous throughout all that region, and where Deerslayer now expected to meet his friend, stood near this outlet, and at no great distance from the shore. It was a large isolated stone that rested on the bottom of the lake, apparently left there when the waters tore away the earth from around it, in forcing for themselves a passage down the river, and which had obtained its shape from the action of the elements, during the slow progress of centuries. The height of this rock could scarcely equal six feet, and, as has been said, its shape was not unlike that which is usually given to beehives or to a haycock. The latter, indeed, gives the best idea not only of its form but of its dimensions. It stood, and still stands, for we are writing of real scenes, within fifty feet of the bank, and in water that was only two feet in depth, though there were seasons in which its rounded apex, if such a term can properly be used, was covered by the lake. Many of the trees stretched so far forward as almost to blend the rock with the shore, when seen from a little distance; and one tall pine in particular overhung it in a way to form a noble and appropriate canopy to a seat that had held many a forest chieftain during the long succession of unknown ages, in which America and all it contained existed apart, in mysterious solitude, a world by itself; equally without a familiar history, and without an origin that the annals of man can reach.

Cooper also gives us a picture of the lake at night:

It would be difficult to convey to the minds of those who have never witnessed it, the sublimity that characterizes the silence of a solitude as deep as that which now reigned over the Glimmerglass. In the present instance, this sublimity was increased by the gloom of night, which threw its shadowy and fantastic forms around the lake, the forest, and the hills. It is not easy, indeed, to conceive of any place more favorable to heighten these natural impressions, than that Deerslayer now occupied. The size of the lake brought all within the reach of human senses, while it displayed so much of the imposing scene at a single view, giving up, as it might be, at a glance, a sufficiency to produce the deepest impressions.

The reader is referred to further descriptive material under the headings *Cooperstown*, *Council Rock* and *Susquehanna River*, as well as to the biography of James Fenimore Cooper.

Features:
Mohican Point
Three Mile Point
Six Mile Point
Sunken Island—Tom Hutter's *Muskrat Castle* location—a shallow area along Route 80 on the west shore
Kingfisher Tower with beacon light—lower east shore; see Cooperstown
Glimmerglass State Park—northeast end; see article
Boat rides launching site and marinas—foot of Fair St., Cooperstown; see Cooperstown

Note to boatmen: Otsego Lake, like many other mountain lakes, can get very rough very fast. Watch the sky to the southwest and, at the first signs of a storm, pull immediately to shore.

Fish: whitefish, lake trout, walleyed pike, large- and small-mouthed bass, salmon, pickerel, perch, ling.

THE DELAWARE & HUDSON CANAL

In addition to the natural waterways thus far described, the Catskill Region is notable for its artificial waterways consisting of reservoirs, aqueducts and canals. The earliest in time, having been completed in 1828, was the Delaware & Hudson Canal.

This early engineering marvel was worked upon by such famous engineers as John Bloomfield Jervis, after whom was named Port Jervis, Horatio Allen, America's first locomotive engineer, Benjamin Wright, a famous surveyor and John Roebling, the developer of suspension bridges.

The canal was the brainchild of two brothers, Maurice and William Wurts, after whom is named Wurtsboro. These brothers owned extensive anthracite fields in northeastern Pennsylvania. At the time anthracite was not generally recognized as an acceptable fuel. The Wurts brothers demonstrated its clean burning qualities to a group of investors in New York City in 1823 and immediately gained backing for construction of a canal from the coal fields to tidewater on Rondout Creek near Kingston— a total distance of 108 miles, with 109 locks, 15 aqueducts, and 14 boat

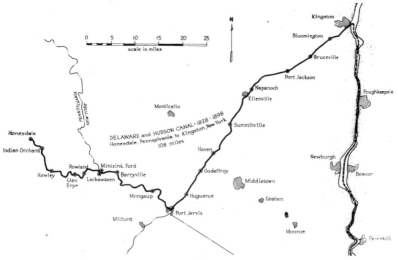

Map of Delaware & Hudson Canal. From The Technology Review.

basins. The projected canal was to be 4 ft. deep and 36 ft. wide at the water level and 20 ft. wide at the bottom. The bed was to be lined with clay to prevent seepage. Constant care was to be taken that it was not undermined by such aquatic animals as otters, beavers, muskrats and moles. The entire line was to be paralleled by the new telegraph, and this method of dispatching was to be used. Boats were to be hauled by mules; the only power vessel allowed was the paymaster's steam launch, *Minnie*. This was because a large bow wave or wake would undermine the banks. Speeding was strictly prohibited.

Philip Hone, soon to become Mayor of New York City, was elected the first president of the canal company in 1825. He was a personal friend of Washington Irving and a close observer of contemporary life. His famous diary is a valuable source of information on the period. The new town at the coalfield end of the canal in Pennsylvania was named in his honor: Honesdale. It was connected with the mine area by a gravity railroad whereon the loaded cars rolled down to the canal by gravity. The empty cars were hauled up by a combination of cables and winches in the steep sections and by one of the first steam locomotives used in the United States, the *Stourbridge Lion*, which had been built in England. Horatio Allen was the first locomotive engineer. He was no mere engine driver, but a true practical engineer and mechanic who made many practical improvements in the machinery. On August 8, 1829 he drove the first steam-powered train to move in America. The author's grandfather was associated with the Delaware & Hudson and the Hudson Coal Company for many years and on April 28 and 29, 1973 the author and his family participated in the D & H Sesquicentennial Celebration, part of which consisted of a steam-powered train excursion from Albany to Montreal.

From Honesdale the canal flowed along Lackawaxen Creek to Hawley and Lackawaxen on the Delaware River. Here it crossed the river and followed the north bank southeast to Port Jervis, along the foot of the Hawks Nest Cliffs, from which a right of way had to be blasted. The hard-drinking Irish construction workers had numerous bloody fights with the raftsmen on the Delaware who resented the canal, especially inasmuch as a dam had been built across the Delaware just below Lackawaxen so that canal boats could float across on slack water.

From Port Jervis the canal followed the Neversink River, Basher Kill, Homowack, Sandburg and Rondout Creeks to Eddyville near Kingston. At Rondout was built the famous Island Dock where the coal unloaded from the canal boats was stored prior to transshipment via coastal schooners and river barges. The canal followed the northwestern foot of the Shawangunk Mountains for many miles. Total distance in the Catskill Region was 84 miles and many remains can be seen in the form of old locks, earthworks and bridge abutments. However, there are very few

The Island Dock coal transfer station in Rondout Creek near end of Delaware & Hudson Canal, c1895. Photo by Lionel De Lisser.

water-filled sections left. It is largely paralleled today by Routes 97, 209 and 213, although it will be necessary to often use parallel secondary roads to follow the route closely. Eventually the dam at Lackawaxen was replaced by a suspension bridge that carried a water-filled trough. This was completed in 1848 and consisted of four spans varying from 132 ft. to 142 ft. in length. It is still in use as a vehicular bridge with the water trough removed, and has been designated a National Historic Landmark. Other Roebling suspension bridges were at Lackawaxen Creek (1848; 228 ft. in two spans), Cuddebackville across the Neversink River (1850; 170 ft. in one span), and across the Rondout Creek at High Falls, where is located the Delaware & Hudson Canal Historical Society Museum. Here remains of the stone foundations of the viaduct may be seen, as well as some locks. From Lackawaxen the route was as follows: Barryville, Pond Eddy, Mongaup, Port Jervis, Huguenot, Godeffroy, Roses Point, Cuddebackville, Westbrookville, Haven, Wurtsboro, Summitville (formerly Beatysburg), Phillipsport, Ellenville, Napanoch, Wawarsing, Kerhonkson (formerly Middleport), Alligerville, High Falls, Bruceville, Lawrenceville, Rosendale, Creek Locks and Eddyville. The highest point between the Hudson and the Delaware was at Summitville. The first through shipment of coal was received in Kingston on December 5, 1828. Revenue operation had commenced on April 22nd of that year. In 1842 the canal depth was increased to five feet, enabling the boats to carry an additional ten tons. In 1847 depth was again increased to six feet.

Rondout Creek near Island Dock in 1976. Photo by Alfred H. Marks.

John Novi's "DePuy Canal House Tavern," built 1797. High Falls. Photo by Alfred H. Marks.

Old D & H Canal lock at High Falls. Constructed 1828. Photo by Alfred H. Marks.

The captain and his family lived on board the canalboat in a cabin measuring 12 ft. square. The trip from end to end took a week and the canal was closed on Sundays. Whole families grew up, lived and died on the canal. Always essentially a single commodity canal, traffic began to dwindle with improvements in the parallel railroads, which could operate year round. In November 1898 the D & H Canal Company sent the last load of coal through and in 1899 reincorporated as the Delaware & Hudson Railroad. They sold the canal to S. D. Coykendall of Kingston, who operated towboats on the Hudson and was a factor in the Wallkill Valley and Ulster & Delaware Railroads. He operated the canal between Rondout and Ellenville until 1904 for the transport of Rosendale Cement and general merchandise. The canal was totally abandoned in 1904. A ghost story of the canal is told in C. G. Hine's *The Old Mine Road*. Excellent books on the subject are:

Canal Boats to Tidewater by Manville Wakefield
Delaware & Hudson by Jim Shaughnessy
Old Mine Road by Charles Gilbert Hine
Delaware & Hudson Canalway by Dorothy H. Sanderson

In his short story "Great Day in the Morning" (*Saturday Evening Post*, June 25, 1960), George Sumner Albee gives a vivid description of life on the canal. The "canalers" were a rough and tumble lot and hard drinking was the norm, with many taverns along the line. They were also a musical lot, singing at their work. Popular songs included, "As I Went Down to Port Jervis," "Haul on the Bowline" and the comic "Mule Song," with its concluding verse, "Never take the hind-shoe from a mule."

THE CATSKILL RESERVOIR AND AQUEDUCT SYSTEM

In 1904 a drought left New York City with only five days supply of water. At this time the City depended principally upon the Croton System on the east side of the Hudson. This situation had been developing for some time and shrewd speculators had acquired water rights to most of the watersheds near the city in the Highlands and Ramapos. Consequently the City decided to go further afield to the Catskills, one hundred miles away. There were a number of legal battles before the City's rights of condemnation were recognized, but by 1909 construction began on the Ashokan Reservoir on Esopus Creek.

Ashokan Reservoir is the largest component of the Catskill reservoir system. It impounds the waters of Esopus Creek.

Length, 12 miles; area, 10,000 acres; average depth, 40 ft.; capacity, 132 billion gallons. Completed 1919.

There are two major sections separated by a spillway. The western section is at an elevation of 590 ft. and the eastern of 587 ft. The system of dams and dikes is four miles long. The main dam is at Olive Bridge and is 1,000 ft. long, 240 ft. high and 190 ft. thick at the base, built of boulders embedded in concrete and faced with bluestone. It supports a two-lane auto road. A forty-mile scenic highway encircles the reservoir (Routes 28 and 28A). There is a 5,000-acre wooded watershed zone. At Olivebridge aeration fountains form a curiously antiseptic Tivoli beneath the dam. Water is inducted here into the 92-mile-long first segment of the Catskill Aqueduct to a distribution reservoir at Kensico in Westchester County. Construction necessitated the removal of eight communities, 2,600 graves, 64 miles of road and 11 miles of railroad. It took ten years to build and was completed in 1917. It is extremely attractive; peaks surrounding the western end rise to 3,000 ft.

Schoharie Reservoir was completed 1924. Impounds waters of Schoharie Creek. Dam at Gilboa. Length, 6 miles. The Shandaken Tunnel conveys waters from here to Allaben on Esopus Creek, above Ashokan. It is 18 miles long. The outlet of this tunnel may be seen adjacent to Route 28.

Catskill Aqueduct is a surface-level gravity-flow aqueduct. It passes under the Hudson River at 1,400 ft. beneath high water at Cornwall-on-Hudson through a pressure siphon. Waters are collected in Kensico Reservoir in Westchester County. Here waters are chlorinated and sent 17 miles further

POINTS of INTEREST

1. **West Hurley Dike.**
   Road over top of the dike.

2. **East Dike. Waste Weir. Spillway and Bridge over Spillway Channel**

3. **Beaver Kill Dike**—from East Dike to Olive Bridge Dam—road over top of dike.

4. **Beaver Kill Bridge over the Waste Channel.**

5. **Upper Gate Chamber on Dividing Weir Dike.** Controls water in East and West basin and from either basin into the pressure aqueducts.

   A. **Lower Gate Chamber controls the water** from upper Gate Chamber.
   Aerating Basin.
   Screen Chamber.
   Aqueduct to New York City.

6. **Ashokan Bridge of 15 Spans over Dividing Weir.**

7. **McClellan Triangulation Monument.**

8. **Olive Bridge Dam across the Esopus.** Roadway over top of Dam.

9. **Watson Hollow Inn.** On the South Shore Drive overlooking the Reservoir. Trails to High Point and South Mountain begin here.

10. **Bush Kill twin bridges of reinforced concrete.**

11. **Traver Hollow Bridge**—a beautiful reinforced concrete structure over the hollow from which it takes its name.

12. **Reinforced Concrete Bridges.** The Boiceville Bridge spans the Ulster & Del. R. R. and the Esopus Bridge of 5 spans crosses the Esopus Creek.

13. **Cross Road leading from North to South Shore Drive over the Ashokan Bridge and main Ashokan Dam.**

Distances to Watson Hollow Inn

	Miles
From New York City via Newburgh	100
Albany	77.6
Newburgh	53
Catskill	41.7
Poughkeepsie	40
Ellenville via cross roads from Stone Ridge	30
Saugerties via Woodstock	29
Centerville via Phoenicia	26.7
Grand Hotel	24
Pine Hill	23
Kingston via North Shore Drive	21
Kingston via South Shore Drive	18
Woodstock via North Shore	17.7
Chichester via Phoenicia	13
Phoenicia	12
Stone Ridge via cross roads through Atwood	12

MAP of ASHOKAN RESERVOIR TOUR AND THE VICINITY
ULSTER COUNTY, N.Y.
FROM OFFICIAL SURVEYS
SCALE 2 MILES TO 1 INCH

MAIN ROADS
COUNTRY ROADS
TOWNS & VILLAGES

J. Waldo Smith Monument and Grove, Ashokan Reservoir. Smith was chief engineer of the New York City water supply system. Photo by Alfred H. Marks.

to Hillview Reservoir in Yonkers and from there it is distributed to Manhattan and Brooklyn through a deep-level 18-mile-long tunnel blasted through solid rock. From Brooklyn a bell and spigot pipeline continues under the Narrows to Silver Lake on Staten Island, the southern end of the Catskill Aqueduct. The total length is 120 miles.

Bishop Falls, now under site of main dam on Ashokan Reservoir. Photo 1896 by Lionel De Lisser. Author's collection.

THE DELAWARE RESERVOIR AND AQUEDUCT SYSTEM

By the 1930s New York had to again look for additional water supplies. It was determined to tap the waters of Rondout Creek and the Neversink River as well as the two branches of the Delaware.

Rondout Reservoir impounds the waters of Rondout Creek with the Merriman Dam at Lackawack. Length, 6 miles. Encircled by Routes 55 and 55A. Average depth, 75 ft. Serves as collection reservoir for waters from Neversink, Pepacton and Cannonsville Reservoirs. Completed 1955.

Neversink Reservoir impounds waters of the Neversink River. Length, 4.5 miles. Dam at east end. Seen from Route 55. Waters conveyed from here to Rondout Reservoir by Neversink Tunnel. Completed 1955.

Pepacton Reservoir impounds waters of the East Branch of the Delaware River. Dam is at Downsville at the west end. Length, 18.5 miles. Completed 1955. Encircled by highways, including Route 30, which crosses it at midpoint at the Shavertown Bridge. Its waters are conveyed to Rondout Reservoir by the 26.5-mile deep-driven East Delaware Tunnel.

Cannonsville Reservoir impounds waters of the West Branch of the Delaware with a dam at the west end near Stilesville. Length, 7.75 miles. Area, 5,000 acres. It is followed for its entire length by Route 10. Waters are conveyed to Rondout Reservoir by the 42-mile West Delaware Tunnel, completed in 1965. The reservoir itself was completed in 1967.

Delaware Aqueduct, a deep-driven pressure tunnel through solid rock from Merriman Dam at Lackawack to Hillview Reservoir in Yonkers. Total distance 85 miles.

At the present time recreational use of the New York City reservoirs is limited to tightly controlled fishing from non-power boats. There is presently much local agitation to open them up to other recreational use.

For further details on the Catskill and Delaware reservoirs and aqueducts see *Guide to the Catskills with Trail Guides and Maps*, by Adams, Coco and Greenman (Walking News, Inc. New York, 1975) and *Water for a City* by Charles H. Weidner, a detailed history of New York City water supply system.

Present-day Rail Lines

There are eight operating rail lines in the Catskill Region today, only one of which provides regularly scheduled passenger service. There are various studies under way for restoration of service on several others, and special excursion trains are run from time to time on most routes. The Cooperstown & Charlotte Valley ran daily excursion steam train service through 1974. Amtrak and Delaware & Hudson trains from New York to Albany, Montreal, Buffalo, Toronto, Detroit and Chicago operate on the Hudson River Division of Conrail along the eastern bank of the Hudson, providing panoramic views of the Catskills and local access via Poughkeepsie, Rhinecliff, Hudson, and Albany stations. Since 1976 Amtrak offers direct coach and Pullman service from Boston and Chicago to the Catskill region and is now operating new high-speed trains between Buffalo and New York City. Amtrak trains continue west from Albany over the Penn-Central Mainline with stops at Schenectady, Amsterdam and Utica, providing access to Schoharie and Otsego County points.

Reprinted herein are copies of old timetables of certain of the rail lines which, besides being of historical interest, will be of use to present-day riders and excursionists, as modern timetables do not provide names of stations where stops are no longer made nor such detailed mileage information.

NEW YORK CENTRAL MAINLINE (NOW CONRAIL), HUDSON AND MOHAWK DIVISIONS

This was the great route of the *Twentieth Century Limited* and *Empire State Express*. It follows closely the east bank of the Hudson River from Grand Central Terminal in New York to Albany-Rensselaer, where it crosses the river, providing a continuous view of the Hudson surpassed only from a boat and panoramic distant views of the Catskills from Overlook Mountain near Kingston to Windham High Peak, including Plattekill, Indian Head, Kaaterskill High Peak, Round Top, South, North and Thomas Cole Mountains. These can be seen from just south of Rhinecliff station to Castleton and are most impressive at twilight with the sun setting behind the mountains. The mouths of Rondout, Esopus and Catskill creeks, with their respective lighthouses, may be seen, as well as Esopus Meadows and Hudson Lights on small islands in the river. It is virtually impossible to see anything on the east shore as the train runs right along the edge of the water with a steep slope immediately to the

2 6

NEW YORK, ALBANY, UTICA, SYRACUSE and ROCHESTER to BUFFALO and NIAGARA FALLS

Miles	Table No. 12	◆699 Ex. Sat.& Sun. Note	◆ 9 Daily	175 Ex. Sun.	55 Daily	51 Daily	95 Daily	143 Daily Note	667 Ex. Sun.	39 Daily	165 Sat. Only	49 Daily	41 Daily	161 Ex. Sat.& Sun.	159 ◆ Sat. & Sun. Only	1 Daily	65 Daily	27 Daily	167 Daily	157 Ex. Sat.& Sun. Note	15 Daily
0	Lv New York (Grand Central Terminal) (E.T.)	AM	AM 2 05	AM 6 01	AM 7 10	AM 8 00	AM 8 15	AM 9 00	PM	AM 11 00	AM 11 28	PM 1 00	PM 2 30	PM 2 47	PM 2 47	PM 3 00	PM 3 00	PM	PM 3 45	PM 3 56	PM 4 00
4 2	Lv New York (125th St.)		h 2 15	h6 14	h7 20	h 8 10	h 8 25	h9 10		h11 10	h11 38	h 1 10		h2 57	h 2 57					h 4 06	
5 0	Lv The Bronx (138th St.)																				
14 5	Lv Yonkers		2 40		h7 37		h 8 41	d9 26		h11 26		h 1 26		3 13	3 13	W325				4 22	
24 3	Lv Tarrytown		3 08								12 05			3 27	3 27						
30 2	Lv Ossining		3 28								12 14			3 37	3 37						
32 7	Lv Harmon		3 35	6 55	h8 00	h 8 48	9 03	h9 48		11 48	12 18	1 48	h3 17	3 42	3 42	h3 48	h3 48		h4 32	4 44	h4 46
40 8	Lv Peekskill		4 17	7 32			9 27			12 13	12 46	2 10		4 19	4 19				5 05	
45 4	Lv Manitou			7 40			b 9 35				12 54			i4 26	4 26					
49 1	Lv Garrison		4 31	7 47			9 40				1 01			4 33	4 33				5 18	
51 8	Lv Cold Spring		4 38	7 55							1 06	2 24		4 39	4 39				5 23	
56 5	Lv Dutchess																			
58 3	Lv Beacon(Newburgh–Note W)		4 53	8 08	8 38		9 54	d1026		12 35	1 16	2 33		4 45	4 49				5 07	5 33
61 5	Lv Chelsea			8 14							1 22			4 55	4 55					5 42
64 4	Lv New Hamburg		5 05	8 22							1 28			5 00	5 00					
67 5	Lv Camelot													5 05	5 05					
72 8	Lv Poughkeepsie		5 20	8 35	8 55		10 15	10 46		12 54	1 40	2 50		5 12	5 12				5 24	5 54
72 8	Lv Poughkeepsie	5 40	5 50		8 55		10 15	10 46		12 54		2 50	t 4 02	5 35		T4 38	T4 38			5 24	
78 5	Lv Hyde Park		6 00											5 52						
82 9	Lv Staatsburg		6 09											6 02						
88 4	Lv Rhinecliff	5 57	6 19				10 35				1 13	3 08		6 14					5 45	
93 0	Lv Barrytown	6 05	6 30				10 44					3 16		6 30						
98 2	Lv Tivoli	6 11	6 39									P 3 24		6 37						
103 6	Lv Germantown	6 19	6 45											6 44				H609		
105 3	Lv North Germantown		6 54																	
113 7	Lv Hudson(Catskill–Note W)	6 30	7 04		9 34		11 07			1 41		3 41		7 15				6 22		
117 9	Lv Stockport																			
121 1	Lv Newton Hook	6 40	7 19											7 25						
125 5	Lv Stuyvesant	6 45	7 26											7 35						
129 6	Lv Schodack Landing	6 53	7 40																	
133 5	x Castleton-on-Hudson	6 59	7 56									Z 4 04		7 40						
141 6	x Rensselaer																			
142 2	Ar Albany	7 15	8 15		10 10	10 43	11 45			2 22		4 20	5 10	8 00			5 45	6 51		6 37
148 4	Ar Troy	△	△		11 20	△	△	12 16		3 05		△	△	△			△			△
142 2	Lv Albany		9 30		10 20	10 48	12 01			2 37		4 40	5 20	D550	5 50		7 01		6 45	
150 0	Lv Schenectady		10 05		10 47	c11 15	12 30			3 04		5 07	5 50	D617	6 17	J 7 07	7 28		7 11	
174 9	Lv Amsterdam		10 29				12 50			3 25							7 48			
189 5	Lv Tribes Hill																			
185 5	Lv Fonda (Fultonville)		10 47				1 07			3 39							8 10			
196 0	Lv Palatine Bridge (Canaj.)		b11 00				1 24										8 23			
200 0	Lv Fort Plain						1 34										8 29			
205 9	Lv St. Johnsville						1 44										8 38			
215 6	Lv Little Falls						1 56										8 48			
222 9	Lv Herkimer (Mohawk-Ilion)						2 07			4 25							8 58			
225 0	Lv North Ilion (Ilion)																			
236 6	Ar Utica		11 45		12 03	12 26	2 30			4 43		6 18	7 03	D729	7 29		9 20		8 28	
	Lv Utica		12 35		12 06	12 31	2 38			4 50		6 23	7 08	D734	7 34				8 27	
243 3	Lv Oriskany																			
250 4	Lv Rome		12 53		12 22		2 55			5 07		6 40		D751	7 51					
259 0	Lv Verona		1 11		12 36		3 18			5 26										
263 5	Lv Oneida																			
266 3	Lv Wampsville		1 20		12 42		3 27													
268 6	Lv Canastota																			
278 8	Lv Kirkville																			
284 1	Lv Minoa																			
284 7	Lv East Syracuse																			
289 5	Ar Syracuse		1 50		1 12	1 24	4 00			6 00		7 25	8 02	D835	8 35	J 9 07	9 19			
	Lv Syracuse				1 17	1 29			3 00	6 10		7 30	8 07	D840	8 40	J 9 12	9 24			
327 0	Lv Clyde								3 37	6 47										
334 0	Lv Lyons								3 46	6 59										
341 5	Lv Newark								3 55	7 11		8 22								
347 0	Lv Palmyra								4 04	7 23										
362 0	Lv East Rochester																			
369 4	Ar Rochester				2 31	2 43			4 29	7 50		8 52	9 22	D954	9 54				10 38	
	Lv Rochester				2 35	2 47			4 30	7 55		8 57	9 27	D959	9 59				10 41	
401 0	Lv Batavia				3 14				5 04	8 34										
435 4	Ar Buffalo (Cent. Term.)				3 50	4 00			5 40	9 15		10 15	10 40		11 32				11 53	
461 0	Ar Niagara Falls				5 06	5 05														
		AM	PM	AM	PM	PM	PM	PM	PM	AM	PM	PM	PM	PM	PM	PM	PM	PM	PM	PM

For explanation of Reference Marks, see Page 5   For Pullman, Coach and Dining Car Service, see

Reprint of 1952 New York Central System Mainline Timetable showing only half of scheduled westbound passenger trains. There were about 100 daily passenger trains at this time. Notice such famous names as Empire State Express, Ohio State Limited *and* Commodore Vanderbilt. *Author's collection.*

east of the track, cutting off the view. The wise traveller will do well to select a seat on the river side, although if he is bound for Montreal, this will put him on the wrong side along Lake Champlain.

Also, a fine panoramic view of Albany is obtained when crossing the Hudson. The scenery along the Mohawk Division is unimpressive from Albany to just west of Schenectady when the train begins to follow the canalized Mohawk River. The timetable reproduced is from 1952 when service was at an all-time high and lists all stations and mileages north and west of Peekskill. The many local stations between New York and Peekskill were shown on a separate timetable.

WEST SHORE RAILROAD (FORMERLY NEW YORK, WEST SHORE & BUFFALO, NOW CONRAIL)

This line formerly connected with 42nd St. and Cortlandt Street in New York City by ferry boats. The southern terminus was at Weehawken, New Jersey, opposite 42nd Street in Manhattan. Here the trains immediately entered a two-mile-long tunnel under the Palisades to North Bergen and turned north through the Hackensack River meadows and through suburban Bergen County, New Jersey to the New York state line at Tappan, to the west of the Palisades and out of view of the Hudson. From Tappan it continues north through Orangeburg and past Lake DeForest and Congers Lake to south of Haverstraw where it again passes through a one-mile-long tunnel under the mountain and comes out on a ledge high above Haverstraw Bay with a sweeping view of the Hudson River Valley and Highlands of the Hudson. The tracks gradually work their way down to waterlevel north of Haverstraw and continue north past Stony Point, Iona Island and Bear Mountain to West Point depot. North of the depot the line plunges into a mile-long tunnel beneath the Parade Grounds, coming out at waterlevel at the foot of Crows Nest Mountain opposite Cold Spring. It contines along the foot of the cliffs of Crows Nest and Storm King, with great views of Mts. Taurus and Breakneck across the river and of the Fishkill Range and Mount Beacon. Cornwall-on-Hudson and Newburgh are next passed with fine views of Newburgh Bay and some of the great estates on the East Bank. The tracks follow the river to Highland, just opposite Poughkeepsie, and turn inland through West Park and Esopus to just south of Wilber, where they cross Rondout Creek on the high Wilber Trestle (built 1883, 1,200 ft. long, 150 ft. above the water), from which fine views are obtained of the old river port and canal terminal. After passing through a short tunnel beneath Montrepose Cemetery the train comes to the site of the former Union Depot where the West Shore is joined from the south by the line of the Wallkill Valley Railroad and crossed at right angles by the Ulster & Delaware.

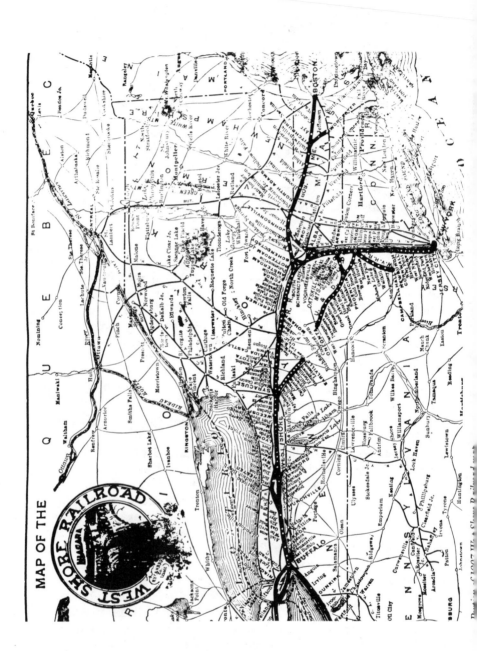

WEST SHORE RAILROAD
(NEW YORK CENTRAL & HUDSON RIVER R.R. CO., Lessee.)

ALL TRAINS RUN FROM WEEHAWKEN, N. J., AND CONNECT WITH FERRIES TO AND FROM WEST 42d STREET STATION AND THE DOWN-TOWN STATION AT FOOT OF DESBROSSES STREET, NEW YORK.

TIME TABLE IN EFFECT FEBRUARY 7, 1909.

REVISED APRIL 7, 1909

Trains run on Eastern Standard Time.   Light face figures denote A. M. time.   Dark-face figures denote P. M. time.

GOING WEST.

From Lake Katrine to West Athens the Catskills may be seen to the west, but the Hudson River remains out of sight until Glenmont is reached just south of Albany on the West Shore Albany Branch. Mount Marion, Route 32 (Kings Highway) and the Thruway may be seen from the train. Esopus Creek is crossed above Glenerie Falls between Lake Katrine and Mount Marion stations. The Saugerties and Malden stations are to the west of town. At Cementon the line hugs the eastern base of the Kalkberg and extensive cement plants can be seen near Alsen, cutting off the view of the river to the east. The line passes through the west side of Catskill and crosses Catskill Creek, just north of the station, on another high viaduct, from which a fine view of the Catskills may be obtained. From here north to Ravena the line runs through farm country out of sight of the river. At Ravena the West Shore's Albany Branch (shown on the River Division timetable reproduced below) continues north along

the river past Selkirk, Wemple and Glenmont to a junction with the
Delaware & Hudson at Kenmore Junction, just south of the former Albany
Union Station. From Ravena the West Shore Mainline swings gradually
west around the foothills of the Helderbergs past Feura Bush, New Salem
and Guilderland Center to Rotterdam, south of Schenectady. Here it
comes out high above the Mohawk River and runs northwest to Rotterdam Junction, where it connects with the Boston & Maine Railroad
Mainline from the east. Just west of Rotterdam Junction the trains cross
the high bridge to Hoffmans. The original West Shore line continued west
to Buffalo along the south bank of the Mohawk River. However, much of
this has now been ripped up and there is no longer any through line. Parts
are still used for industrial switching with connections from the New York
Central Mainline. Other segments have been utilized by the New York
Thruway. There is a major freight line of the Boston & Albany Railroad
that crosses the Hudson at Castleton and the Albany Branch of the West
Shore at Selkirk. Just west of the Albany Branch it has a junction with the
West Shore Mainline, and here is located the gigantic Alfred E. Perlman
Freight Classification Yard, a major interchange point of the Conrail
System. The West Shore also has another short branch from Bethlehem to
South Bethlehem. The timetable here reproduced shows all stations and
mileages from Weehawken to Albany.

ULSTER & DELAWARE (FORMER PENN-CENTRAL CATSKILL MOUNTAIN BRANCH)

This line formerly ran from a steamer connection at Kingston Point all
the way to the Delaware & Hudson at Oneonta, with several branches
into the high Catskills. Today the line remains from Rondout to Roxbury,
57 miles from Kingston Union Depot. This line enters the Central
Catskills via the valley of the Esopus. It formerly ran where are now the
waters of Ashokan Reservoir, but has been relocated along its northern
shore. Just west of Pine Hill there is a Horseshoe Curve and a steep climb
to Highmount or Grand Hotel Station. From here the waters of Bush Kill
Creek are followed to Arkville and the track here cuts west to the East
Branch of the Delaware near Kelly's Corners. The line contines north past
Roxbury to Grand Gorge at the Delaware headwaters and turns west
along the north side of Mt. Utsayantha to Stamford. Beyond Stamford
the line runs southwest along the West Branch of the Delaware to
Bloomville, the present terminus. Formerly it continued across Delaware
County to Oneonta and connection with the Delaware & Hudson. The
timetable reproduced here shows the entire route from Kingston to
Oneonta. Excursions are operated over several segments.

WALLKILL VALLEY RAILROAD (CONRAIL)

This line ran along the Wallkill River along the southeastern foot of the Shawangunk Mountains from a junction with an Erie branch at Montgomery to Kingston. It was a route of great pastoral beauty. The line passed Walden, Wallkill, Gardiner and New Paltz on its way to Rosendale. Here considerable elevation had been gained and just north of the depot it crossed Rondout Creek on a 150 ft. high trestle built in 1872. North of the trestle some abandoned cement mines were passed before reaching Binnewater Station at the foot of Williams Lake. From here the line headed northeast through picturesque hilly country to Greenkill Avenue in Kingston, where it joined the West Shore line south of the former Union Depot. This line was contemplated as a major freight route in the Conrail system. It was formerly a popular route to Lakes Minnewaska and Mohonk. With SUNY at New Paltz and Shawangunk recreational areas it was a not unlikely candidate for restored service to New York/Hoboken via the Erie-Lackawanna from Montgomery. But the line was abandoned in 1982.

CENTRAL NEW ENGLAND RAILWAY (CONRAIL)

In past years this line has been controlled by the Philadelphia & Reading and the New York, New Haven & Hartford. It is still known to local residents simply as the New Haven. This route runs from a connection with the Erie-Lackawanna and Lehigh & Hudson railroads at Maybrook in Orange County to Devon, Connecticut on the former New Haven (now Conrail) Shoreline Route near Bridgeport. It crosses the Hudson River on the great Poughkeepsie Bridge, built in 1889. This bridge is two and a half miles long, of which 3,094 ft. are over the water. It is 212 ft. above the water and allows a clearance of 165 ft. above high tide over the main channel. It was part of a major bypass route around New York City and much traffic from southern New England industry passed over it bound for the south or the west via the Erie-Lackawanna and Chessie Systems. There was no passenger service over it for a great many years since the *Federal Express* between Boston and Washington near the turn of the century. It was too far from major population centers. However, occasional railfan excursions operated over it and sometimes excursion trains were parked on the bridge for the viewing of crew races on the river below. The bridge vibrated tremendously and this provided a thrilling sensation. The views up and down the river from the Catskills to the Highlands were unsurpassed. In 1973 the track timbers of the bridge

CATSKILL MOUNTAINS VIA KINGSTON

527 Daily except Sunday	Miles	EASTERN TIME	528 Daily except Sunday	
AM			**PM**	
......	....	Lv N.Y. Cortlandt St...... Ar	......	....
1 35	....	Lv N.Y., foot W. 42d St..... Ar	6 40	....
1 49	0	Lv Weehawken............. Ar	6 25	....
4 50	89	Ar Kingston(Union Sta.).... Lv	4 05	....
5 30	0	Lv Kingston (Union Sta.).... Ar	3 45	....
f 6 42	6	Ar Stony Hollow........... Lv	f 3 30	....
6 55	8	Ar West Hurley........... Lv	3 25	....
7 05	14	Ar Ashokan............... Lv	3 15	....
f 7 14	20	Ar Cold Brook.......... Lv	f 3 05	....
f 7 20	22	Ar Mount Pleasant........ Lv	f 3 00	....
7 30	25	Ar Phoenicia............ Lv	2 55	....
8 20	39	Ar Grand Hotel Station...... Lv	2 20	....
8 30	42	Ar Fleischmann's.......... Lv	2 10	....
8 50	46	Ar Arkville............. Lv	2 00	....
f 8 56	49	Ar Kelly's Corners........ Lv	f 1 50	....
f 9 02	51	Ar Halcottville........... Lv	1 45	....
9 15	57	Ar Roxbury.............. Lv	1 33	....
9 28	63	Ar Grand Gorge.......... Lv	1 20	....
9 37	68	Ar South Gilboa.......... Lv	f 1 08	....
9 50	71	Ar Stamford............ Lv	1 00	....
10 00	75	Ar Hobart............. Lv	12 50	....
10 10	79	Ar South Kortright........ Lv	12 40	....
10 25	84	Ar Bloomville........... Lv	12 30	....
10 50	95	Ar East Meredith.......... Lv	12 05	....
11 01	97	Ar Davenport Center....... Lv	11 59	....
f11 06	100	Ar West Davenport........ Lv	f11 53	....
11 15	104	Ar Oneonta.............. Lv	11 45	....
AM			**AM**	

Reprint of 1951 Catskill Mountain Branch [Ulster & Delaware] timetable. Author's collection. Note inconvenient connection at Kingston that led to decreased use of the service.

caught on fire and it was projected to abandon the bridge. Other connecting railroads protested vigorously because of diversion of freight from their lines to those of the Penn-Central, and some even suggested sabotage on the part of Penn-Central. In our Catskill Region the line ran northeast from Maybrook past St. Andrews, Modena, and Clintondale where it cut through the Plattekill Hills to Highland at the western end of the bridge. In past years streetcars used to be pulled across from Poughkeepsie by steam engines to Highland. From Highland an electric railway extended to New Paltz. A long freight train crossing the mighty bridge at a snailpace was a fascinating sight. The line is now abandoned.

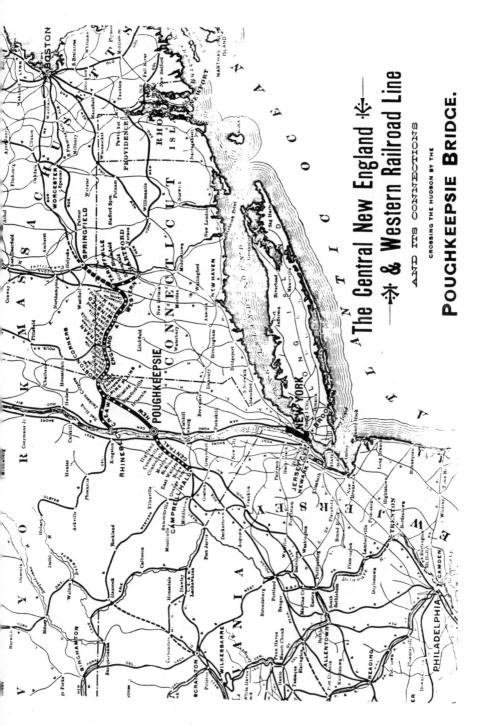

The Central New England & Western Railroad Line

AND ITS CONNECTIONS

CROSSING THE HUDSON BY THE

POUCHKEEPSIE BRIDGE.

DELAWARE & HUDSON MAINLINE (ALBANY & SUSQUEHANNA RAILROAD)

The Catskill Mountains are contained within a triangle consisting of the lines of the D & H, West Shore and Erie Railroads, with the angles at New York (Weehawken-Jersey City), Albany and Binghamton. It is 142 miles from Weehawken to Albany and also exactly 142 miles from Albany to Binghamton. It is 215 miles from Binghamton to Weehawken via the Erie Railroad.

The D & H Line, however, is the only leg that cuts through the Catskill region for almost its entire length. From Albany to Binghamton the major points of interest are as follows. South of Albany's Union Station the line turns west through the Vale of Tawasentha, or more simply called the Normanskill Ravine, where it is crossed by high bridges of Route 9W and the New York Thruway. From here the line runs northwest along the foot of the Helderberg Mountains to Delanson. This is picturesque hill country. From Delanson the line trends southwest and crosses the Schoharie River at Central Bridge. Next passed is Cobleskill. At Warnerville Richmondville Summit is crossed. This is the divide between Mohawk River waters and those of Schenevus Creek, which is Susquehanna River water. From here the waters of Schenevus Creek are followed to their junction with the Susquehanna River at Colliers, also known as Colliersville. Here is a junction with the Cooperstown & Charlotte Valley Railroad. From here to Nineveh the railroad follows the Susquehanna River, passing Oneonta, Unadilla, Sidney and Bainbridge. At Nineveh the line formerly split. The old Albany & Susquehanna line turns westward over the hills to Binghamton. Another line continued south along the Susquehanna into the Great Bend country as far as Lanesboro, where it turned south up the valley of Starrucca Creek and under the great Erie Railroad viaduct. This line continued over the Pennsylvania hills into the coal fields, with major stations at Carbondale, Scranton and Wilkes-Barre where there is a major interchange with the Lehigh Valley Railroad. The timetable reprinted dates from 1953 and shows the passenger service between Albany and Binghamton. The line is now freight only.

ERIE RAILROAD (ERIE-LACKAWANNA, NOW CONRAIL)

The former Erie Railroad mainline ran from Jersey City to Chicago. Even after merger with the Delaware Lackawanna & Western, the former Erie Mainline remained the principal line. It was the route of the former *Erie Limited, Pacific Express, Atlantic Express* and *Lake Cities Ltd*, as well as innumerable accommodation trains. This is a highly scenic line, 121 miles of which are in our Catskill Region—from Howells, west of Middletown

| TABLE 7 | | | MAIN LINE ALBANY AND BINGHAMTON | | | | |

READ DOWN						READ UP	
208 Daily			Mls.	205 Except Sun.	209 Sunday Only		
PM				Lv. ALBANY Ar.	AM	PM	
3 45	....	....	0	......ALBANY......	10 45	6 20	....
k3 57	....	....	5.5	.......Delmar......	f10 33	f6 07	....
4 04	....	....	10.8	.....Voorheesville.....	10 26	f6 00	....
4 15	....	....	17.2	.....Altamont......	10 16	f5 52	....
4 32	....	....	26.8	......Delanson......	10 01	5 38	....
4 49	....	....	36.2	....Central Bridge.....	9 46	5 23	....
4 56	....	....	39.2	...Howe's Cave.....	9 39	f5 17	....
5 09	....	....	44.7	......Cobleskill......	9 30	5 08	....
5 19	....	....	49.9	....Richmondville.....	9 19	f4 57	....
5 33	....	....	56.9	.....East Worcester...	9 07	f4 46	....
5 40	....	....	61.5	......Worcester......	8 59	4 40	....
5 48	....	....	66.5	.....Schenevus.....	8 51	4 31	....
v6 00	....	....	76.3	......Colliers. ✛	f8 37	f4 16	....
6 07	....	....	81.7	Ar.....Oneonta...Lv.	8 30	4 10	....
6 18	....	....	81 7	Lv...Oneonta....Ar.	8 17	3 55	....
6 31	....	....	89.6	......Otego......	8 04	3 42	....
v6 37	....	....	94.0	.....Wells Bridge....	7 58	f3 36	....
6 44	....	:....	98.8	.......Unadilla......	7 51	3 30	....
6 58	....	....	103.3	.......Sidney.......	7 43	3 23	....
7 09	....	....	108.4	.....Bainbridge......	7 29	3 09	....
7 17	....	....	114.3	.......Afton......	7 19	f3 01	....
7 25	....	....	118.8	......Nineveh.✛	7 12	f2 55	....
h7 28	....	....	120.3	....Harpursville.....	7 09		....
h7 42	....	....	127.0	......Tunnel......	6 58		....
h7 51	....	....	132.5	...Sanitaria Springs....	6 47		....
8 10	....	....	142.5	..BINGHAMTON....	6 30	2 15	....
PM				Ar. Lv.	AM	PM	

Trains 208, 205 and 209 will stop at former site of Esperance Station (located between Delanson and Central Bridge), to pick up and discharge passengers.

Delaware & Hudson, Albany and Binghamton Mainline timetable from 1953. Author's collection.

in Orange County to Susquehanna, Pa. There is still suburban passenger service between Port Jervis and Hoboken and talk of possible restoration of Hoboken to Binghamton service under a State of New York subsidy or possibly use of the route by Amtrak for a Southern Tier New York to Buffalo train. It is a popular route for steam train excursions. This route provides the finest continuous viewing of the Delaware River between Port Jervis and Deposit. For much of the way of line follows the Pennsylvania side of the river between Mill Rift and Tusten. The scenery around Narrowsburg as seen from the train is magnificent. From Hoboken the train uses tracks of the former D L & W through a tunnel under the

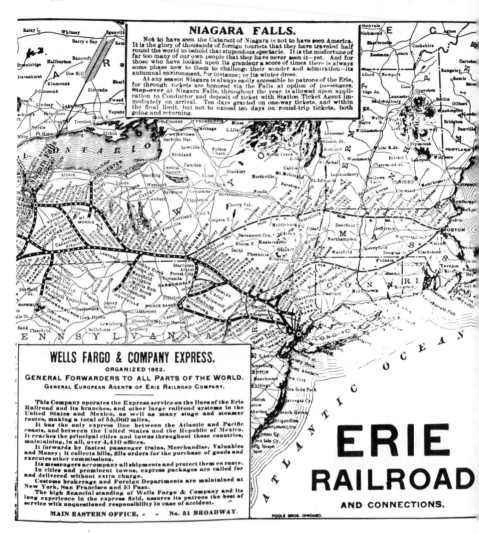

Palisades and turns onto former Erie Railroad track a mile west of the western portal. Here the line splits. One lines goes via Passaic and Paterson to Ridgewood, N.J. The other line, known as the Bergen County Railroad, cuts across the Hackensack Meadows to Rutherford and Fairlawn, N.J. and rejoins the other line at Ridgewood in the suburbs. From Ridgewood the line begins to climb the northernmost slopes of the Watchung Ridge to Hohokus and there are extensive views to the east. Here it begins to cross a plateau past Waldwick, Allendale and Ramsey to the Ramapo Valley at Mahwah. The line crosses into New York State at Suffern and begins to follow the Ramapo Clove through the mountains

NEW YORK—BINGHAMTON

TABLE 2
WESTBOUND

For additional train service from Hoboken and Jersey City, not shown in this table, please refer to local time tables.

Hudson and Manhattan Tube Trains operate between New York and Erie-Lackawanna Station in Hoboken.
To Erie-Lackawanna Station, Hoboken—Train marked "Hoboken"— Fare 20 cents.
From Uptown New York —Train marked "Hoboken"— Fare 20 cents.

Eastern Standard Time Read Down	51 Daily Ex. Sun.	53 D'ly Ex. Sun.	71 Sun. only	1 Daily	73 Sat.& Sun. only	55 Daily	57 Daily Ex. Sun. and Hol.	75 Daily Ex. Hol. only	85 Runs Nov. 6, 12, Feb. 12 only	59 Daily Ex. Sat., Sun. and Hol.	61 Daily Ex. Sun. and Hol.	77 Sun. and Hol only	5 Daily	79 Sun. only	7 Daily Ex. Sat.	9 Sat. only
NEW YORK Rockefeller Center Terminal, 11 Rockefeller Plaza.....Lv	AM	AM	AM	AM 8.40	PM	PM	PM	PM	PM	PM	PM	PM	PM	PM	PM	PM
W.34th St.at 9th Ave. (Hotel New Yorker) (Ferry)				8.47									7.25		11.20	11 20
													7.33		11.27	11 27
Barclay St..... Lv	12.45	④4.30	8.45	⑨ 9.10	12.15	2.15	4.00	5.15	★ 5.15	★529	6.15	6.15	⑨ 8.00	8.15	12.15	12.15
Hoboken, N. J.	1.15	4.45	9.00	9.30	12.32	2.30	4.14	5.30	★ 5.30	★542	6.38	6.47	8.15	8.55	12.45	12.45
Rutherford, N. J.	1.29	5.00	9.14		12.46	BG		5.44	5.44		7.00		9.09			
E. Rutherford..	1.43	5.09	9.21	BR 9.49	12.56	2.47		5.54	5.54		7.09	BJ 8.34	9.19			
Passaic......	1.56	5.27	9.29	BP 9.56	1.04	2.54		6.03	6.03		7.19	BH 8.42	9.29			
Paterson......	2.08	5.40	9.38	BP 1005	1.16	3.03	4.40	6.14	6.14		7.29	BH 8.51	9.39			
Ridgewood....	2.11	5.47			1.19	BG		6.17	6.17	6.11		7.32	9.43			
Hohokus......	2.14	5.51			1.22	BG		6.20	6.20		7.35	9.46				
Waldwick.....	2.17	5.56	♦		1.25			6.23	6.23		7.38	9.49				
Allendale.....	2.20	6.01			1.28		BL449	6.26	6.26		7.41					
Ramsey......	2.24	6.07			1.32			6.30	6.30	6.24	7.46					
Mahwah.....	2.27	6.14	9.50	BR 1018	1.36	3.17	4.53	6.33	6.33	6.28	7.49		9.54			
Suffern....N.Y		6.30	9.56		f 1.41		4.59	6.35	6.35	6.31	7.38	7.58	9.59			
Hillburn.....		6.37	10.00		f 1.45	f 3.23	5.04	6.40	6.40	6.37	7.43	7.59				
Sloatsburg...		6.43			f 1.51	BK 3 31	5.11	6.45	6.45	6.42						
Tuxedo......		6.47			f 1.55		5.16	6.52	6.52							
Southfields..		6.54	10.13		1.59		5.20	7.01	7.01	6.57	7.55	8.11	10.14	Ex. Sun.		
Arden......		7.00	10.17		2.03	3.41	6.25	7.05	7.05	7.01	8.04	8.15	10.18			
Harriman....		7.11			2.11	BD 3.50	5.34	7.14	7.14	7.11	8.09	8.26	10.26			
Monroe......	3.08	7.28		f10.49	2.13	3.57	5.42	7.23	7.23	7.19	8.17	8.35	f 9.38	10.33		
Chester.....		7.40					5.47									
Goshen.....	3.50	8.00		f11.00	2.27	4.08	5.56	7.33	7.33	7.30	8.27	8.49	f 9.49	10.44	2.08	2.04
New Hampton..		8.10					6.04	7.40	7.40	7.30						
Middletown. N.Y		8.25				BW240	BF 4.18		7.40	7.38				10.56		
Howells.....		8.50		11.30		BW300	BM 4 35	6.30	8.05	8.05	8.05	10.18	11.15	2.45	2.35	
Otisville....				11.40								10.26		2.55	2.45	
Port Jervis...Ar																
Port Jervis...Lv																
Sparrowbush..N.Y																
Mill Rift....Pa.					12.05							BC10 51				
Pond Eddy...					12.11							BC10 57				
Parker's Glen..																
Shohola.....																
Lackawaxen..					12.27							f 11.11	3.41	3.31		
Westcolang Pk..					1.06											
Tusten....N.Y.																
Narrowsburg...																
Hoadalb, Pa.BU.Ar					BN12.40							f 11 30	4.07	3.57		
Skinners...N.Y.Lv					12.49											
Cochecton..N.Y.																
Callicoon...N.Y.																
Hankins....					1.27							f 12.05	4.46	4.36		
Long Eddy..																
Lordville...																
Hancock....					1.46							f 12.21	5.08	4.58		
Hale's Eddy...					2.12							12.46	5.36	5.26		
Deposit.....					2.14							12.48	5.38	5.28		
Gulf Summit..																
Susqrh'n'a, Pa..Lv																
Great Bend..					2.50							1.20	6.16	6.06		
Binghamton, N.Y.Ar	AM	AM	AM	AM	AM	PM	PM	PM	PM	PM	PM	AM	PM	AM	AM	

ALL ABOVE PASSENGER TRAINS ARE DIESEL POWERED

All Conditional Stops are for Revenue Passengers Only.

Trains 59 and 85, operate from Jersey City Station only with Ferry connection from

BM On Holidays arrives Port Jervis (4.50 P. M.).
BN Stops to discharge passengers from Ridgewood and east and receive

Reprint of January 1960 Erie Railroad Mainline timetable. Author's collection.

to Harriman. It is paralleled by the New York Thruway and Route 17. At Harriman the line again split. The old mainline turned west across the Orange County Hills and dairylands past Monroe and Goshen into the Wallkill Valley at Middletown and then on to Howells. This line is now abandoned. The other line is known as the Graham Line after the surveyor who layed it out. It was built as a low-grade line for heavy freight trains. It is somewhat longer, but offers magnificent views. It continues straight north from Harriman past Central Valley and Highland Mills along Woodbury Creek. Here it begins to climb along the east side of Schunemunk Mountain to the long, high viaduct across Moodna Creek. Here there is a fine view of the Northern Highlands and Fishkill Range to the east and the Shawangunks to the west. The line then runs west, bypassing Middletown to the north and rejoins the mainline at Howells. This is the line used by passenger trains today. Here the line climbs the Shawangunks to a tunnel near Otisville. At the west end of the tunnel the tracks come out on a high ledge, offering fine views of the Southern Catskills and the Neversink Valley. The line then runs southwest down the mountainside into Port Jervis. From Port Jervis the route runs up the east side of the Delaware to just beyond Sparrowbush, where it crosses over to the Pennsylvania side at Mill Rift. From Mill Rift to Lackawaxen there are good views of the Hawks Nest Cliffs across the river. Just below Tusten the line crosses back into New York State and follows the beautiful river valley to Deposit, where it crosses the West Branch and begins to follow the the bed of McClure Brook up towards the defile at Gulf Summit. From here the line drops down into the valley of the Susquehanna River, crossing 1,200 ft. long, 110 ft. high Starrucca Viaduct, built in 1847 and offering beautiful views of the Susquehanna Valley. The D & H Wilkes-Barre Line ran beneath this bridge, a description of which can be found in the Gazetteer section under the heading Lanesboro. The unique Victorian depot at Susquehanna is also described under the heading Susquehanna. From here the line followed the river northwest to Binghamton and thence to Chicago. Reproduced are timetables showing all stations and mileages on the New York and Delaware Divisions.

COOPERSTOWN & CHARLOTTE VALLEY (DELAWARE–OTSEGO SYSTEM)

This line was leased for many years by the D & H and known as the Cooperstown Branch. It is again under independent operation by the Delaware-Otsego System between Colliersville and Cooperstown along the uppermost stretches of the Susquehanna River. This is idyllic farming country with meadows and pastures. The line also passes Goodyear Lake. Until 1975 this line offered steam excursions out of Cooperstown on a

FROM NEW YORK			WESTBOUND				
EASTERN DAYLIGHT SAVING TIME	**81** Sat. only	**1** Daily	**55** Daily	**57** Fri. only	**5** Daily	**7** Daily ex. Sun.	**9** Sun. only
Lv. NEW YORK Rockefeller Center Terminal	AM	AM	PM	PM	PM	PM	PM
Motor Coach (11 Rockefeller Plaza)......	8.00	8.40				7.25	10.45	10.45
West 34th St. & 8th Ave.........	8.07	8.47				7.33	10.52	10.52
(Hotel New Yorker)								
Barclay St. Ferry...............	8.15	④9.10	2.15	4.00	⑥8.00	12.15	12.15
Hoboken Station................	8.45	9.30	2.30	4.14	8.15	12.45	12.45
Lv. Sparrowbush.................	f 10.55			6 45				
Mill Rift.....................	10 59		4.55	f 6.48				
Pond Eddy....................	f 11.11		5.06	f 7.00				
Parker's Glen.................	f 11.16		⑥5.11					
Shohola (Yulan, Eldred, Highland Lake)④........	11.24	12.05	5.18	7.13	n 10.51		
Lv. Lackawaxen.................	11.32	12.11	5.26	7.21	n 10.57		
Westcolang Park...............	f 11.37		⑥5.31					
Tusten.....................								
Narrowsburg.................	11.52	④12.27	5.45	7.42	④11.11	3.41	3.31
Lv. Honesdale...................	1.05	1.05	⑥6.20	8.30			
Lv. Cochecton (Lake Huntington)④....	12.06	⑥12.40	5.58	7.59			
Callicoon..................	12.15	⑥12.49	6.10	8.09	④11.30	4.07	3.57
Lv. Kenoza Lake.................	1.00	1.30	6.50	7.20			
Jeffersonville..............	1.30	2.00	7.20				
Lv. Hankins	12.26		6.21	8.18			
Long Eddy..................	d 12.34		6.29	8.26			
Lordville..................	12.44	② 1.12	6.38	8.35			
Hancock...................	1.00	① 1.27	6.53	8.50	④12.05	4.46	4.36
Deposit...................	1.20	f 1.46	7.13	9.10	⑥12.21	5.08	4.58

Reprint of Summer 1958 Erie Railroad Delaware Division Timetable showing all local stops. Author's collection.

regular basis and even operated "Dinner Trips" with a traditional dining car. New federal track standards caused this service to be suspended. This line has also purchased and is operating the former Central New York Railroad, alias Utica, Chenango & Susquehanna Valley and Delaware Lackawanna & Western Richfield Springs Branch, between Richfield Springs and Clayville on the Erie-Lackawanna Utica Branch. The former Lackawanna lines between Binghamton and Utica and Syracuse, and the Erie line between Lakawaxen and Honesdale, Pa., are also operated by the D-O's new subsidiary, the New York, Susquehanna & Western. The Southern New York Railroad is only a freight switching line in the environs of Oneonta.

Major Highway Routes

Most tourists will be visiting the Catskill Region by automobile, and they will find a great many attractive drives, ranging from super highways to quiet back lanes. The scenery as viewed from the Quickway or Thruway is analogous to that seen from a train in that you can gain only a fleeting general impression of the grand panorama. Neither road gives any feeling of intimacy with the area. They were designed for fast transit through the region or speedy access to resort areas. It will be noted that many of the routes described below either have descriptive names or bear those of old turnpikes which they roughly parallel. In those cases descriptions will be found in the Gazetteer section.

THE NEW YORK THRUWAY

The Thruway runs from the Bronx to the Pennsylvania state line at Ripley on Lake Erie. It generally follows the route of the New York Central Railroad up the Hudson and across the Mohawk Valley and then on to Buffalo and Cleveland. It crosses the Hudson River at its widest point at Tappan Zee near Tarrytown and Nyack. Here it cuts west along the Ramapo Mountains to the Ramapo Clove at Suffern and turns north, following the Erie Railroad and Route 17 along the Ramapo River to Harriman, where the Quickway bears off to the West via the Delaware Valley and Southern Tier route. From Harriman it passes between Schunemunk Mountain on the west and the Hudson Highlands on the east, with distant views east to the Fishkill Range and Mount Beacon. However, after crossing at Tappan Zee, you do not again see the Hudson River as the route is inland through rolling farm country. There are distant views of the Shawangunks and Catskills all along the route to just south of Albany, and from Albany to Rotterdam there are similar distant views of the Helderbergs. West from Rotterdam it utilizes sections of the former New York West Shore & Buffalo Railroad to Syracuse. It is a toll road. There are a limited number of service stations, restaurants and rest areas along the way. It is generally pleasant driving and good for making time, but not really a good route for sightseeing.

THE QUICKWAY—SOUTHERN TIER EXPRESSWAY—ROUTE 17

The same comments can be made in reference to sightseeing that were made relative to the Thruway. It provides panoramic views of the Shawangunks and Southern Catskills and portions of both branches of the

Delaware, before crossing the hills to Binghamton and the west. It is roughly analogous to the Erie Railroad. The old Route 17 now bears various suffixes in different stretches and gives a more intimate view of the country.

Note: In the following descriptions only major features will be noted. The reader should refer to a map and separate articles for each town in the Gazetteer section.

ROUTE 20—THE CHERRY VALLEY TURNPIKE

This is a major U.S. Highway running from New England to the West. The section that concerns us is from Albany to Bridgewater, south of Utica on New York Route 8.

Chartered in 1799 from Albany to Cherry Valley, the Turnpike was extended to Manlius in 1803 and work was completed by 1811. It was built to unusually high standards for the time and followed high ridge lines, providing good drainage as well as the bonus of excellent views. It was an important route for western migration and later on for shipping farm products to the Hudson. Later it was a principal route to the spas at Sharon and Richfield Springs and also for traffic to Cooperstown. It is followed generally by Route 20 today, which, however, bypasses Cherry Valley to the north. It is now a modern divided highway on which good time can be made, and offers good panoramic views of both the Catskills and Mohawk Valley as well as of the Helderbergs.

ROUTE 32—THE KINGS HIGHWAY

This is a meandering secondary route from Harriman to Hudson Falls. The segments that concern us are from Newburgh to Albany. This route is rich in old villages and houses, as it follows the pre-revolutionary Royal Mail route in many stretches. It is a well paved road without much traffic and an average speed of 45 mph can easily be maintained. The Shawangunks and Catskills are in view for much of the way, and this route gives the best idea of the Plattekill region of Ulster County, and routes you through historic Kingston. It gives you a taste of the Wallkill Valley as well as of the Hudson between Kingston and Saugerties. A very satisfying route.

ROUTE 9W—THE RIVER ROAD

Before the Thruway this was the main road to Albany from New York City. It runs from the New Jersey side of the George Washington Bridge to downtown Albany and is a four-lane road most of the way and in many stretches very lightly used today. It offers the best continuous views of the Hudson River available from any main highway. Major features along the route are: The Palisades, Tappan Zee, Haverstraw Bay, The Highlands, Bear Mountain, West Point, Crows Nest, Storm King, Newburgh, Highland, Kingston, where it crosses Rondout Creek, old Saugerties, the cement area and Kalkberg, Catskill and the rich farmlands several miles in from the river between there and Albany. Above Catskill it is necessary to deviate to Routes 385 and 144 if you wish to follow the "River Road." There are many historic sites, villages and homes along the route and probably the best choice of dining and sleeping places. The trucks that once plagued this beautiful route are now mostly on the Thruway and you can slow down and enjoy the scenery with no fear of getting killed in the mad rush as in past years. However, do not count on averaging better than 45 mph overall.

ROUTE 7

This route is analogous to the Albany & Susquehanna Division of the Delaware & Hudson. For much of the way it is a two-lane road with rather heavy and rushing truck traffic. Its main virtue is that of providing easy access to major tourist attractions. While the scenery is generally pleasing, it is not outstanding. At the northern end the Helderbergs are seen and further south Schenevus Creek and the Susquehanna River are followed. The route takes you through the center of Oneonta, which can be slow going, but there is a bypass. It is a busy road and there is not too much charm along the way, although accommodations and eating places are plentiful and there are some superior ones.

ROUTE 23—THE SUSQUEHANNA TURNPIKE

The name of this route is only a rough analogy. The section that concerns us is from the Rip Van Winkle Bridge at Catskill to Norwich on the Chenango River. The old Turnpike only extended to Wattle's Ferry near Unadilla on the Susquehanna River. This is a real tourist's delight, passing through grand countryside and quaint villages and towns of the Northern Catskills. It varies from a two to four lane road and bypasses a few towns such as Cairo, while also serving as the Main Street of Stamford and Oneonta. However, it is a road with character. The views between South Durham and East Windham are spectacular—especially that from Five State Lookout on Kate Hill, also known as Point Lookout. Pratts Rocks are passed east of Prattsville and a sidetrip to Mt. Utsayantha near Stamford is feasible. The section west of Oneonta traverses a pleasing countryside. Accommodations are ample but it is best to plan to eat at regular mealtimes as there are few "always-open" restaurants along route.

ROUTE 23A—THE RIP VAN WINKLE TRAIL

This is possibly the most scenic route in the region and runs from Catskill to Prattsville via the tremendous Kaaterskill Clove and Hunter Mountain. It penetrates the heart of the classic Catskills and is the best access to North Lake, Kaaterskill Falls and Hunter Ski Bowl. It is a two-lane road with a number of bottlenecks in towns. Count on taking your time and savoring the scenery. Ample accommodations but limited dining facilities outside of hotels.

ROUTE 28—THE ONTEORA TRAIL

This is the main route through the central Catskills, running from Kingston to Oneonta. It roughly parallels the Ulster & Delaware Railroad route as far west as Arkville, but here it cuts across country rather than following the branches of the Delaware via Stamford as does the railroad. The original Route 28 ran through the center of many villages. Now many of them are bypassed and you can make good time on this highly scenic route. The present route is the direct descendent of the old Dutchess, Ulster & Delaware Turnpike. Those not in a hurry will probably enjoy using the closely parallel Old Route 28 which goes through all the villages. You cannot see the Ashokan Reservoir from the main highway. it is suggested that you take the slightly longer Route 28A which runs along the south side if you wish good views, or you can take a short sidetrip south from Shokan on the main road to the separation wier and dam, where there are unsurpassed views of the surrounding mountains and the reservoir and aeration fountains. Principal scenic attractions are Esopus Creek, and Phoenicia area, Pine Hill, Andes and Delhi with their interesting architecture. Many rugged higher peaks are in view, but not intimately approached as on Route 23A. The route probably has the widest variety and greatest number of good sleeping accommodations and restaurants. It provides prime access to the Hunter Ski Bowl, Woodland Valley, Big Indian Valley, Slide Mountain and Belle Ayre Ski areas.

ROUTE 209—THE OLD MINE ROAD

The original Old Mine Road is allegedly the oldest highway in America and ran from the copper mines near Pahaquarry in New Jersey to Kingston along the east bank of the Delaware and the northwestern foot of the Shawangunks. It was built sometime in the early 1600s. Today's Route 209 closely parallels the old road between Kingston and Port Jervis. Many portions of the original Old Mine Road are still so named and in use for local traffic. It is recommended that the tourist interested in old houses and forts utilize the older route, although the old and new do run concurrently in many places. This was also the general route of the D & H Canal between Accord and Port Jervis and branches of the former O & W Railway for the entire distance. There are many markers commemorative of Indian raids and many well preserved stone houses along the way. Hurley and Stone Ridge are real gems of well preserved colonial villages and the entire route is an antiquarian's delight. The Catskills are seen in the distance to the northwest and there are excellent views of the more rugged portions of the Shawangunks' western slopes between Naponoch and Port Jervis. Ellenville and Wurtsboro preserve some of the flavor of the early 1800s and the Greek Revival architecture of that era. There is fairly heavy traffic on a route which varies greatly in quality as far as alignment and surfacing is concerned. There are numerous places to eat and sleep but without the sophistication of establishments found on the other routes. Best plan to eat at Kingston or Port Jervis, if you want more than a snack.

ROUTE 97—THE HAWKS NEST TRAIL

This is a true pioneer wilderness trail, although close to major cities. The Delaware between Port Jervis and Hancock is an unspoiled and extremely beautiful stream and the area preserves the flavor of the colonial frontier. While Port Jervis and Sparrowbush still retain the aura of a milltown and railroad junction, this is soon left behind as the road enters and climbs the rugged Hawks Nest Cliffs between Mongaup and Barryville. Here there are extensive views up and down the river and across to the distant Poconos of Pennsylvania. The old D & H Canal followed the base of these cliffs and there are a few remains of the old embankments. The trains on the Erie Railroad across the river look like toys, but they are all that is to be seen of civilization in this apparent wilderness.

At Barryville is Reber's Hotel and Restaurant—possibly the finest in the Catskills—featuring both traditional German menu and high cuisine items in an opulent setting that includes a large oil copy of Leutze's famous painting, *Washington Crossing the Delaware*, and numerous other fine paintings. The service is impeccable. We mention this as you may wish to schedule your trip through this extensive area with limited restaurant facilities to hit Barryville at mealtime. They do not accept credit cards or large personal checks.

From Barryville to Minisink Ford the road follows the river, where there are many small fishing camps along the wayside. Here it cuts more inland and runs through beautiful wild forest lands. At Narrowsburg there is a re-creation of the pioneer Fort Delaware. From there to Callicoon the road is up on the hillside and there are fleeting views of the river. Callicoon

Creek is crossed on a high viaduct and north of town are the beautiful buildings and grounds of St. Joseph's Franciscan Friary and Seminary. From Callicoon to Hankins the road cuts inland through beautiful wild forestland. While not providing as fine views of the Delaware as obtained from the Erie Railroad, this road still provides a supreme woodland experience.

ROUTE 52—THE SHAWANGUNK TRAIL

This is somewhat of a misnomer—or rather an inadequate name, as the route shows the traveller much more than just the Shawangunks. It provides a good look at the fertile Wallkill Valley and the valley of the Callicoon as well as the older Borsht Belt resort area of Sullivan County. It runs west from Newburgh through Walden in the Wallkill Valley and past Pine Bush on the Shawangunk Kill. Here it climbs the Shawangunk Ridge at Walker Valley and provides access to Cragsmoor and Sams Point (Ice Cave Mountain). The really spectacular portion, however, is the descent of the west side of the Shawangunks, atop and along high cliffs and with magnificent views of the Catskills. Just outside Ellenville a high waterfall is visible from the road. From Ellenville to Liberty the road runs through the older resort area and beyond Liberty enters the wilder western portion of Sullivan County, terminating at Callicoon on the Delaware. Limited accommodation and food for casual tourists.

ROUTE 44—THE MINNEWASKA TRAIL

This is the western extension of a highway that traverses New England and only the New York State portion west of the Hudson bears the name Minnewaska Trail. It starts at Highland on the Hudson and provides good views of the Plattekill Hills and orchard country around Modena and the Wallkill Valley at Gardiner. Here it climbs the spectacular Traps portion of the Shawangunks with hairpin turns and great views to the distant Taconics, Berkshires and highlands to the east. The sheer face of Millbrook Mountain is seen when approaching the Shawangunks and it is not unlikely that the observant tourist will see rock climbers scaling the cliffs or dangling like spiders from an overhanging precipice. At the top of the Traps the road goes under what looks like a railroad bridge. It actually carries the carriage road that connects the Lake Mohonk and Lake Minnewaska resorts. In this area the highway runs through lands of the Mohonk Trust, Lake Minnewaska Mountain Houses and Minewaska State Park—all regions of surpassing beauty with picturesque rock formations and delicate woodlands with many ferns and huckleberry bushes. In June the mountain laurel is at its height. This is the prime access to the

Minnewaska resorts and State Park. Awosting Falls are near the road and may be visited for a small fee. The descent of the western side of the ridge offers unusually fine panoramic views of the central and northern Catskills. The road terminates at Kerhonkson in the Rondout Valley.

ROUTES 17K, 17, 17B AND 114—THE COCHECTON TURNPIKE

The old Cochecton Turnpike was an important early avenue of western commerce and migration running from Newburgh on the Hudson to Cochecton on the Delaware. It was a great stagecoach route and some of the old stagecoach hotels are still standing and in operation. It first traverses the rich farming areas cultivated by colonial governor Cadwallader Colden and the present-day dairy and stud-farm areas of Orange County, crossing the wide and fertile Wallkill Valley amidst scenes of pastoral beauty. This section, known as 17K, ends at Bloomingburg on the Shawangunk Kill at the eastern foot of the mountains. Here it followed the route of the present Old Route 17 across a low point in the mountains to the old canal port of Wurtsboro on the Basher Kill. From here to Monticello, the old Shiretown of Sullivan, it follows Old Route 17. Many older buildings are reminiscent of staging days. The route west of Monticello is known as 17B and passes through the old Moravian settlement of Bethel, site of the famous "Woodstock Festival" from August 14 through 17, 1969. It was held on the farm of Max Yasgur between Bethel and White Lake. From Fosterdale to Cochecton the turnpike is now called Sullivan County Route 114. Cochecton was a big lumber rafting center and is now a center for white-water canoeists.

ROUTE 145—THE SCHOHARIE TURNPIKE

This was another important route of western migration to the Schoharie and Susquehanna valleys. It follows Catskill Creek from the Hudson to its headwaters. The original Schoharie Turnpike started at Athens and followed what are now back roads to Cooksburg, where it picked up the present alignment of Route 145 to Middleburgh and that of Route 30 to Schoharie. Our present-day route utilizes Route 23 west to Cairo and Route 145 to Cooksburg, Livingstonville and Middleburgh and 30 to Schoharie. This route was also utilized by the early Canajoharie & Catskill Railroad between Catskill and Cooksburg. It forms the dividing line between the Catskills to the south and the Helderbergs to the north, with fine views of the northern Catskill escarpment. Much of the area retains the flavor of "patroon days." It makes an interesting alternate to Route 23, but is short of sleeping and dining accommodations. Many old buildings.

ROUTE 30

While not boasting a name, this route provides pleasing continuous views of the Schoharie Valley and that of the East, or Pepacton, Branch of the Delaware. It is an important present-day commercial road, but not as busy as Route 7, and provides comfortable touring. There is a modicum of sleeping and dining accommodations around Schoharie, Grand Gorge and Margaretville, but many "long dry stretches" in between. Chief scenic features are the Grand Gorge at the headwaters of the Delaware, where it is paralleled by the Ulster & Delaware Railroad and the river is merely a trickle, and Pepacton Reservoir. The southern end at East Branch is at the confluence of the Beaver Kill amid rugged hills. Here it joins Route 17. Schoharie has many interesting historic buildings and Middleburgh and Roxbury are very attractive. This is a good way to achieve Prattsville and portions of Route 30 find their way into many interesting circular tours. We do not recommend its entire length as an axis of any scenic tour as other routes have more to offer.

ROUTE 10

This may be called the dairyland highway. For our purposes it may be considered as running from Canajoharie on the Mohawk to Deposit on the Delaware. It enters our region at the old spa town of Sharon Springs and continues southeast to Cobleskill and then southwest by south to Stamford. Here it runs southwest, following the West Branch of the Delaware. Interesting old towns are Stamford, Hobart, Bloomville, Delhi and Walton. Scenic attractions include Mt. Utsayantha and the Cannonsville Reservoir, which is followed for its entire length. It parallels the Ulster & Delaware Railroad from Stamford to Bloomville and former lines of the O & W from Delhi to Apex. There are ample dining and sleeping accommodations at Sharon Springs, Cobleskill, Stamford and Delhi, but they are quite sparse in between.

PART II
HISTORY

The Indian Period

It is difficult to pinpoint the date when aboriginal man first visited the Catskill area. The New York State Archeological Association owns a site near Athens in Greene County where it is believed that prehistoric Indians mined flint stones 12,000 years ago. Other archeologists date the first aboriginal occupation at 8,000 years ago. There is a distinct possibility that this area served as hunting grounds during late inter-glacial periods. However, it is extremely difficult to assign any specific dates and the amount of remains suitable for dating by radio-carbon tests is extremely limited.

Jumping ahead to the period of recorded, or legendary, history, it is pretty well agreed that the people who later comprised the Iroquois nations occupied upper New York State about 1300 A.D. It is quite possible that actual, but unrecorded, occupation was at an earlier date.

Columbus first landed in the New World in 1492 and by 1498 John Cabot was exploring the North Atlantic Coast for England. Giovanni da Verrazano and Estevan Gomez visited the mouth of the Hudson in 1524 and 1525 respectively. Some historians believe it likely that there was sporadic visitation by French traders to the Hudson River valley from 1525 until 1609. In 1534 Jacques Cartier explored the St. Lawrence for France and it is believed that Franch traders, penetrating down from Canada, built a stockade on Castle Island near Albany around 1540.

During this period there had been internecine warfare between the tribes that later comprised the Iroquois Confederation. During the 1560s they were threatened by foes from the Middle West. These powerful western tribes had been beating the New York tribes singly in battle when a visionary leader appeared. This leader, a follower of the prophet Degan-awidah, was named Haya-watha or Hiawatha. According to legend, he was meditating on an island in the Susquehanna River near Owego when he had a vision. He was shown a single arrow—and how easily it could be snapped in two. Then he was shown a vision of five arrows banded together—they could not be broken.

Hiawatha then summoned a great council of the five New York tribes to meet at the island. The original five tribes were the Mohawks, Oneidas, Onandagas, Cayugas and Senecas. Hiawatha, a Mohawk, was respected for his visions and mystical powers and gained a sympathetic audience from the represetatives of the beleaguered tribes. This meeting at which was formed the Iroquois Confederation was around 1570.

These tribes called themselves the "Ogwanonhsioni" or "long-house builders," after the type of homes they constructed. They conceived of their Confederation as a great "long house" extending across the State of New York. The Mohawks were fond of calling themselves the "guardians of the eastern door of the long house." The name Iroquois is actually a Delaware one, and a derogatory one at that. It means "real snakes" or "adders." The Mohawks called themselves the Kanyengehaga or "people of the place of flint," referring to the area around Cohoes. Mohawk is a corruption of the Delaware word Maquaas, which means "those who eat people." This is a deprecatory term and arose from their cannibalistic practice of eating some of the flesh of their victims in order to attain some of their prowess in battle. Possibly it also could have arisen simply from their warlike behavior. In any event the Confederation served its major purpose of resisting western encroachment and the Iroquois became an important power right down to after the American Revolution. About 1722 the Tuscaroras, who had originally come from the South, were "adopted" by the Oneidas, at which time the Iroquois became the Sixth Nations. The newfound "strength in unity" of the Iroquois Confederation inspired Benjamin Franklin in his conception of a Confederation of the English Colonies. A rather less beneficial result was that the Iroquois became bullies to their neighbors. The powerful Huron and Algonquin tribes of Canada feared them and their raids on the annual western fur caravans to Montreal. They had good reason for such fear as they were friends of the French and the French were the mortal enemies of the Iroquois. This situation had come about in the following manner.

On July 29, 1609, Samuel Champlain, on an exploring expedition accompanied by Hurons, opened fire on some Iroquois near the south end of Lake Champlain. As the Iroquois were unfamiliar with firearms, and the Hurons were operating out of their own territory, this action was considered to be "dirty pool" and was much resented. They became implacable enemies of the French and attached themselves to the English—even to their detriment after the American Revolution. Only the Oneidas adhered to the colonial side during the Revolution. The Iroquois did much to help the English win Canada from the French in 1763.

Although this behavior of the Iroquois was understandable, the treatment they accorded to their neighbors to the east and south was arrogant and unworthy. They encroached upon their territory, demanded tribute, attempted to exercise hegemony and derided them as "women." Let us now consider these other neighbors.

The Delaware or Lenni Lenape Indians dwelt along the Delaware River and in eastern Pennsylvania and New Jersey. They, like the Iroquois, were Algonkian-speaking Indians. Their culture was higher than that of the Iroquois and of the Indians of New England. They had stone implements and good pottery; they raised corn, squash, pumpkins and beans and used fish as fertilizer. Unlike the Iroquois, they dwelt in round houses. A sub-tribe named the Minsi dwelt in northern New Jersey and in the Port Jervis area. This name was also corrupted to Munsi, Munsee, Monsey, Muncie and Minnisink. A further subtribe known as the Wooranecks or Warana-wankongs, composed of a mixture of Minnisinks, Minsi and Nanticokes from Pennsylvania, lived in the Esopus or Kingston area. The Indian word for river or large creek is Seepus, and as these Indians dwelt along Esopus Creek and the Hudson River, the Dutch settlers came to call them Seepus or Esopus Indians. They occasionally came into conflict with some small settlements of Mohawks near Shandakan and Beechford. The entire area southeast of Otsego Lake was a disputed domain between the Delawares and Iroquois. Basically they were peaceful Indians, somewhat dependent upon agriculture and fishing in the Hudson, and found life somewhat easier than tribes that had to depend more upon hunting and that had to contend with the harsher inland winter climate. In the eyes of the Iroquois this made them "soft." Even down until late colonial times the Iroquois exacted tribute from them and held them up to ignominy. The Delawares were relatively friendly to the white settlers and generally on the English side during the French and Indian Wars. During the American Revolution they frequently banded together with Tories in raiding parties but by the end of the Revolution had pretty much moved north and west to Ontario, Wisconsin, Oklahoma and Kansas.

Perhaps the most romantic tribe of all was the Mohicans or Mahicans, who dwelt mainly on the east side of the Hudson but who did occupy the west shore from around Catskill north to the beginning of Mohawk territory near Albany. It is not clear whether they ever had a much stronger hold on the western bank of the river. Gradually the Mohawks drove them back to the east. In 1664 the Mohawks forced them to move their council fire from Schodack Island near Coeymans to the neighbor-hood of Stockbridge, Massachusetts. The name Schodack derives from Scoti-ack or "place of ever-burning council fire." In 1680 "King" Aepgin of the Mahicans sold to the Van Rensselaers "all that tract of country on the west side of the Hudson, extending from Beeren Island up to Smacks Island and in breadth two days' journey." By around 1750 a decisive final battle had been fought between the Mohawks and Mahicans at Rodgers Island near Catskill; the Mahicans were badly beaten and their power broken. Several years earlier a similar disastrous battle had been fought at Wanton Island, the details of which are given by Lionel De Lisser in his *Picturesque Ulster* under the heading "The Legend of Blossom Falls."

Finally the Mahicans drifted back eastward to join their relations the Mohegans of Connecticut. Even today there are Mohegans who claim Mahican descent. They live mainly around New London. James Fenimore Cooper's *The Last of the Mohicans*, set in 1757 during the French and Indian War, describes the exploits of one of the Mahican chiefs after the dispersal of his tribe. Cooper's *The Deerslayer*, the action of which takes place in 1740, tells of how this same chief, Chingachgook, goes to the Lake Otsego area to rescue his beloved, Wah-Ta!-Wah, a Delaware maiden, who had been kidnapped by the Iroquois.

It seems that the Mohicans and Delawares fared rather badly between the upper and nether millstones of White and Iroquois encroachment. By the end of the first quarter of the 19th century only a few Indians lingered anywhere in the Catskill area. They are remembered primarily by the names they have left. Inasmuch as smaller game favors "edge" areas round cleared lands and rivers the Indians did not have much impetus to enter the higher mountains except when hunting large game. In their travels, both for trade and on the warpath, they favored canoe travel on navigable streams and lakes, with which the Catskills were not plentifully provided except around the perimeter. There were several trails along the Esopus and the Schoharie, but for the most part Indian settlement concentrated along the major rivers rather than in the higher mountains.

Exploration and Settlement

After the early explorations of Columbus (1492), Cabot (1498), Verra-zano (1524) and Gomez (1525), the most important event as affects the Catskill area was Jacques Cartier's penetration of the St. Lawrence in 1534. Shortly after this, French traders began filtering down into the Adirondacks and even to the Albany area, where it is suspected that they erected a trading post on Castle Island around 1540. In 1544 Captain Jan Alfonce Saintongeoise penetrated the area. In 1581 a Walloon named Adrian Van Loon arrived in Canada and by 1598 he was trding actively throughout the Adirondacks. Years later his descendants were to migrate to the area of Athens in Greene County and change the spelling of their name to Van Loan, after having purchased the Loonenburg Patent. In 1598 several Dutch captains visited the mouth of the Hudson River, although formal exploration of the tidal river awaited that of Henry Hudson in 1609. He was an Englishman in the employ of the Dutch East India Company. He and his ship did not get above the Overslough Bar near Castleton, but some of his men in a small boat explored as far as the mouth of the Mohawk River. It was obvious that the Hudson River was not the Northwest Passage for which he was searching. His first mate, Robert Juet, kept a journal which describes the land and the many Indians they encountered. He made one particular stop near the present site of Catskill; this is the first recorded visit of a white man to the Catskills— September 15, 1609. There he found "very loving people, and very old men: where we were well used. Our Boat went to fish, and caught great store of very good fish." On September 25th they went ashore somewhere near present-day Athens and reported as follows: "We rode still, and went on Land to walke on the West side of the River, and found good ground for Corne, and other Garden herbs, with great store of goodly Oakes, and Wal-nut trees, and Chest-nut trees, Ewe trees, and trees of sweet wood in great abundance, and great store of Slate for houses, and other good stones."

Although Hudson was working for the Dutch, in 1606 James I of England had laid claim to the entire Atlantic seaboard under the Charter of Virginia. However, this did not stop the Dutch from establishing a trading post at Pavonia, in present-day Jersey City, in 1610, nor the Dutch captains Block, May and Christaensen from trading here between 1611 and 1613, nor the Dutch from chartering the "Merchants of North Holland" who traded along the Hudson River in 1614. They had a redoubt or trading post at Rondout. The main attraction was furs—

especially beaver fur. The Iroquois welcomed an opportunity to purchase firearms with which to fight the French, and a brisk trade was soon flourishing. Also in 1614 the Dutch established Fort Nassau on Castle Island under the command of Hendrick Christiaensen. In 1615 Champlain again invaded New York territory and this time was defeated by the Iroquois near Oneida Lake.

A year later, in 1616, a Frenchman, Etienne Brulé, penetrated as far as Tioga Point on the Susquehanna River. He travelled south down the Chenango Valley. This seems to represent the furthest point of French penetration in the Catskill area. No doubt individual traders continued to do business here for many years afterwards, but the French were never a real factor in the region.

Bergen, near downtown Jersey City, was settled in 1616 and in 1617 and 1618 Sir Samuel Argal raided the primitive settlements at New Netherlands in an attempt to assert English sovereignty. A minor disaster occurred in 1617 when Fort Nassau was destroyed by a flood, but apparently trading continued because in 1619 the governor of the Plymouth Colony, who also claimed the area, agreed to "protect Dutch trading on the River." This did not prevent the Dutchmen from refusing the Puritans a right to settle along the river in 1620, however. In 1621 the Dutch West India Company was chartered and prepared for development of trade along the Hudson. This led James I to complain to The Hague, which did not prevent the Dutch West India Company from sending out thirty families of Walloons to settle in the Albany area in 1623. In 1624 they arrived and built Fort Aurania on Castle Island. This same year some Frenchmen attempted to settle on Staten Island, but were soon chased out by the Dutch. From this time forward Dutch settlement continued on a regular basis.

An interesting event bordering on the Catskill region was the capture of the French Jesuit priest Isaac Jogues by the Iroquois in 1643. He was taken to their settlements and tortured. In 1644 he escaped through Albany in a Dutch ship. In 1646 he returned to Canada and went to Auriesville, New York to negotiate peace with the Iroquois. After a third visit to the Iroquois he was seized, tortured and beheaded, and thus became the first American martyr. There is a shrine at Auriesville today.

DUTCH SETTLEMENT

To foster settlement as well as trade the Dutch West India Company established a form of the manorial system known as the patroon system. Under this semi-feudal system large grants of land were given to entrepreneurs who undertook to build a manor house, bring over settlers and commence agricultural development. The settlers became tenant farmers, owing rent to the landlord, or patroon. The patroon usually refused to sell land in fee simple and the preferred method of tenure was by three-life leases. Prior to establishment of the patroon system individual settlers could obtain title to lands they settled upon after "extinguishing" the Indian title by paying the Indians. At a later date many settlers who had paid the Indians for their land and had been confirmed in possession of their homesteads found that the government was including their homesteads in large grants of land under the patroon or manorial system and that they automatically became tenants of the Lord of the Manor, even though they had paid the Indians for the land and had what they thought were valid titles in fee simple. Naturally this created a great deal of ill feeling.

The first large grant was made in 1629 to Kilaen Van Rensselaer, a pearl and diamond merchant. This tract centered on Fort Orange and was on both sides of the Hudson River and covered an area of 24 by 48 miles. It was the only one of six major Dutch patroonships to survive under later English domination. Kilaen Van Rensselaer was the uncle of wouter Van Twiller, a director of the Dutch West India Company and later the third governor of New Netherlands. Van Rensselaer himself did not venture to the new world but sent his relative Roelf Janssen as overseer. The tenants had to buy all supplies from the commissary and have their grain ground at the patroon's mill. By 1637 the Patent covered 700 square miles. On April 8, 1680, Van Rensselaer had purchased from King Aepgin of the Mahicans "all that tract of country on the west side of the Hudson, extending from Beeren Island up to Smack's Island, and in breadth two days' journey." In 1642 the Van Rensselaers built Fort Crailo at Greenbush, and by the time of the governorship of Peter Stuyvesant (1647–1664) Kilaen Van Rensselaer thought himself so powerful that he instructed his henchman Nicholas Koorn to build a fort on Barren Island and demand tribute tolls from passing vessels by "wapen recht!" (For an entertaining description of the entire episode as told by Washington Irving in his *Knickerbocker History of New York* see the article in the Gazetteer section under the heading "Bear Island.") The power of the Van Rensselaers was becoming intolerable to the Company and Director General (Governor) Peter Stuyvesant ordered the laying out of the town of Beverwyck adjacent to Fort Orange. This was to be considered "company property" and was placed under the jurisdiction of three magistrates and was completely independent of the Manor of Rensselaerwyck, which surrounded it for miles on all sides. This was the nucleus of the present city of Albany. Later on in 1685 Kilaen's grandson was confirmed in his rights to the Manor of Rensselaerwyck by the English.

Aside from this major grant on the upper river, other settlements had been made. In 1625 a fort was staked out on Manhattan Island and this was the start of New York City. In 1626 Peter Minuit purchased the island from the Indians for 60 guilders, or roughly $24.00.

Other grants were made on the lower river. Pavonia was created in 1630 and Adriaen Van der Donck was given a tract in the neighborhood of present-day Yonkers in 1646. Closer to the Catskill region Brandt Van Schlechtenhorst purchased a tract on the Catskill Creek in 1649 and in 1661 Pieter Bronck settled in the neighborhood of Coxsackie. In 1665 an Indian chief named Caniskeek sold a large tract near Athens which later was resold to Jan Van Loan and was known as the Loonenburgh Patent. In 1652 Thomas Chambers settled at Esopus and in 1658 the area of Kingston was settled.

We will not concern ourselves with political developments at New Amsterdam nor with developments on the east shore of the Hudson or below the present Ulster County. Suffice it to say that during this period there was some conflict between the patroons and the agents of the Dutch West India Company. The English kept asserting their claims to the area and there were various troubles with the Indians, assertions of mismanagement on the part of the governors and changes in command. The "big action" was still in the fur trade and pelts were being brought in to Albany from as far west as Saskatchewan. This acerbated the French in Canada and was one of the prime causes of the various French and Indian Wars, along with the long-standing feud between the Hurons in Canada and the Iroquois in New York. In effect Albany and Montreal became competing centers of an important trade extending west to the Rocky Mountains. When the English ousted the Dutch from New Netherlands, they then came into conflict with the French for this important trade.

One other important point should be kept in mind with respect to the Indians. Maize or corn agriculture was important to certain tribes, especially to those along the Esopus Creek near Kingston and the Wallkill River. When settlers began to encroach upon their corn lands serious resistance began. As early as 1655 there was a general Indian uprising on both sides of the Hudson, which was quickly surpressed. However, in 1659, shortly after the settlement of Kingston, or Wiltwyck as it was then called, the First Esopus War broke out. Up until this time the settlers had spread out in individual homesteads. During the war they took refuge in the village, leaving their farms subject to the depredations of the savages. In fact, Wiltwyck had been built at the order of Peter Stuyvesant after the 1655 general Indian uprising. Stuyvesant advocated the grouping of settlers in fortified towns. However, the settlers preferred to remain on their own homesteads and between hostilities there was considerable fraternization with the Indians. Construction of fortifications gave the Indians the idea of constructing their own "forts" or "castles," which they did near Bruynswick and Kerhonkson. The First Esopus War was quickly ended in 1660 when the settlers successfully attacked these Indian castles and freed prisoners. This quelled the uprising, but they made one very bad mistake in selling an Indian chief into slavery on the Dutch plantations at Curacao in the Caribbean. later, after he had escaped and made his way home, this was greatly resented by the proud Indians and led to the Second Esopus War in 1663. On June 7th two hundred Indians attacked Wiltwyck and Hurley, massacring many of the inhabitants. Troops were levied and a full-scale summer campaign was undertaken wherein the strength of the Indians was effectively broken once and for all. Except for working in concert with the French, or later the Tories and British, they were never again an independent threat in the Catskill area.

ENGLISH COLONIZATION

In 1664 a small British fleet under the command of Sir Robert Carr and Richard Nicolls sailed into New York harbor and captured New Amsterdam after an abortive resistence under Peter Stuyvesant. King Charles II of England gave the former Dutch colony to his brother, the Duke of Albany and York, later King James II. The colony was renamed New York, as well as the town on Manhattan Island. Fort Orange, the former Fort Aurania, as well as the village of Beverwyck, was given the new name of Albany, after his other title. Wiltwyck became Kingston. Few changes were made in the way of life and the Dutch language still remained in common usage. The settlers were treated well by their new masters and the powers to control taxes, make laws, regulate trade and grant land were transferred from the Dutch West India Company to the Duke. Richard Nicolls was appointed governor from 1664 to 1668 and Francis Lovelace from 1668 to 1673. Governor Nicolls established the first counties in New York.

Shortly after English occupation some troops were sent to Esopus under the command of a Captain Brodhead. The troops were uncouth and quarrelsome and picked fights with the equally pugnacious Dutch-men. The Huguenots soon joined in with the Dutchmen and the entire situation seems to have degenerated into a general brawl and there is great difficulty in attempting to ascertain which side was the more at fault. Finally Governor Nicolls sent up two privy counsellors and the entire matter degenerated into a court contest, with many charges and counter charges. The general public soon lost interest and finally, after taking much evidence, four of the Dutch burgomasters were taken to New York City for sentencing. It is not recorded what, if any, sentence was inflicted. This episode later came to be called the Esopus Mutiny.

In 1673, on August 9th, the Dutch, who were again at war with the English, recaptured New York. The name was changed back to Nieuw

Amsterdam and the colony was put under the command of Cornelis Evertsen and a Council of War. Shortly thereafter Anthony Colve was appointed Governor General.

Prior to this, about 1670, several Christian Iroquois villages had been formed and the initial English-Dutch War had been settled by the Treaty of Breda in 1667, at which New York had been ceded to the English. In 1668, under English rule, a tract of 160,000 acres had been given to Robert L. Livingston (1654–1728) and Livingston Manor was formally given full manor status in 1686. All this land was on the east side of the Hudson, but subsequent generations of Livingstons acquired extensive holdings in the Catskills as well.

Dutch rule did not last for long, however, as the Treaty of Westminster in 1674 confirmed the earlier Treaty of Breda and returned the English to control of New York. In 1674 Edmund Andros was appointed governor.

The year 1683 is notable in that Governor Thomas Dongan called the first elected Representative Assembly in the colony and on July 22nd granted a "Charter of Liberties." Ten counties were then created. Under the new Charter the elected representatives had the power to approve or reject all taxes. This put the colonists almost on a par with the people in England under Parliament. In 1686 New York and New England were consolidated into the Dominion of New England, and in the same year the City of Albany was incorporated with Peter Schuyler as first mayor. Also, the last wolves and bears were driven from Manhattan Island.

In 1685 the Duke of York had become King James II of England and the colony became the property of the Crown. However, James was a Catholic and was unpopular at home because of his attempts to abrogate the powers of Parliament. In 1688 James was overthrown in the "Glorious Revolution" and the Protestant William of Orange and Queen Mary were set upon the English throne.

In 1688 King William's War with the French broke out and the Canadian border became an area of skirmishing. In 1689 the union of New York and New England was dissolved and the democratic "rebel" Jacob Leisler seized control of the government in New York until he was deposed by Richard Ingoldesby and Governor Henry Sloughter in 1691. Leisler was hung. In 1690 the settlement of Schenectady was massacred by French and Indians. The First Continental Congress was called at New York City in 1690 to discuss ways to prosecute the war with the French and in 1691 a popular assembly was also called and liberal laws promulgated. Peter Schuyler and Dutchmen from Albany conducted an expedition and defeated the French at La Prairie in Canada in 1691. Finally in 1697 peace was concluded.

1702 saw the outbreak of Queen Anne's War, the American manifestation of the War of the Spanish Succession. Few incidents of this war impinged upon the colony of New York; at its settlement in 1713 the Treaty of Utrecht recognized that the Iroquois were subject to British sovereignty. An expedition against Canada in 1711 from New York had been unsuccessful.

Meanwhile, in 1708 Governor Lord Cornbury had granted a patent of almost two million acres in the Catskills to Johannis Hardenbergh and six other grantees, who were merely "front men." This tract covered most of the present-day Greene, Sullivan and Ulster Counties and large portions of Delaware County. There was some vagueness about the western boundary and it was not fully surveyed until 1749, after which there was much litigation. This patent hung like a cloud over the Catskills for almost a hundred years and did much to hamper settlement. Eventually the Livingstons bought into the Hardenbergh Patent.

In 1731 the French built a fort at Crown Point near the southern end of Lake Champlain and in 1744 hostilities broke out again in King George's War, which was the American equivalent of the War of the Austrian Succession. In 1745 Saratoga was destroyed by French and Indians and in 1746 William Johnson was made Head of the Indian Department. He called a great Indian Council at Albany in 1748 and generally gained their trust and respect. He took the sister of the Mohawk chief Joseph Brant as mistress and closely allied himself with the Iroquois.

War and Revolution

THE FRENCH AND INDIAN WAR

The French and Indian War, and its predecessors, King William's, Queen Anne's and King George's Wars, were direct precursors of the American Revolution in that the cost of these wars was one of the principal bones of contention between the colonies and the mother country. The colonists claimed that these wars were merely extensions of European conflicts and that they had contributed more than their fair share in men and arms in protecting British interests on the North American Continent. The English took the view that they had made large expenditures to protect the colonies from the French and Indians. A large war debt had been incurred and someone would have to pay more taxes to cover the debt. England imposed such taxes on the colonies despite their protest, and this "taxation without representation" became one of the principal causes for the Revolution. Perhaps New York did not contribute as spectacularly as New England in the prosecution of the war, but its northern borders were an arena of much bloody fighting, although hardly any formal action took place in the Catskill region.

Before reviewing the principal events of this war let us note an event which took place between the years 1710 and 1713. Queen Anne had been largely dependent upon Scandinavian sources for such naval stores as tar, pitch and turpentine. An influx of refugees from the German Palatinate was posing problems in England and the thought arose that possibly these people could be settled on the banks of the Hudson and put to work making turpentine. Little thought was given to the fact that these people were completely untrained for such work nor that the type and quantity of pine trees in the neighborhood were poorly suited for the production of such materials. Nevertheless these people were transported to the Hudson north of present-day Saugerties and settled on either side of the river in what are still known as East Camp and West Camp. Robert Livingston contracted to supply them with food and supplies—on a meagre basis. Governor Robert Hunter at New York was given the thankless charge of the entire project. The project did not work out and the people were left to their own means. They felt deeply cheated as they had been promised land and a start in the new world, and now they were left to shift for themeselves at the start of what turned out to be a long and hard winter. Fortunately many of them were skilled at hand crafts and these gradually drifted to the towns while others who knew something of farming moved to the Schoharie Valley and to the neighborhood of

Newburgh. Ultimately many of the original Newburgh settlers moved on to Pennsylvania to join their compatriots. A relative few remained along the Hudson, as the terms of tenancy on manor lands was not particularly attractive.

Hostilities commenced in 1754 and a meeting was held at Albany to form a Plan of Union. Benjamin Franklin was a delegate at this conference and here he gained some of the expertise he was to utilize in conjunction with the Revolution. Military action during 1754 and 1755 consisted primarily of attacks against French forts in the West and Canada. The attempt to capture Fort Duquense under Braddock's leadership was a costly failure, as were attempts on forts Frontenac, Niagara, Ticonderoga and Crown Point. It was during this period that George Washington gained his first active military experience. The tide turned in 1758 when Lord Jeffrey Amherst took Louisburg on Cape Breton Island. However, in that same year Montcalm repulsed Abercromby at Ticonderoga in a particularly bloody engagement. This expedition is well described in James Kirke Paulding's novel *The Dutchman's Fireside*. In 1759 Amherst succeeded in capturing Ticonderoga. Sir William Johnson and his Iroquois allies secured northern New York and the war became a contest for control of the St. Lawrence and consequently of the entire North American Continent. In 1759 the English under General Wolfe defeated the French under Montcalm on the Plains of Abraham at Quebec. Both brave commanders fell in the battle. A subsequent battle at Montreal gave the British full control and France had lost out entirely in North America. The fortunes of battle were formally recognized by the Treaty of Paris in 1763.

During the course of the war there was an important meeting of colonial governors at New York in 1755, and Fort Edward was erected that same year. There was also a victory known as the Battle of Lake George. In 1756 the French took the forts at Ontario and Oswego and in 1757 the British surrendered Fort William Henry, at the south end of Lake George, to the French and Indians. The surrender was followed by an Indian massacre. This is the opening event in Cooper's novel *The Last of the Mohicans*. However, starting with Amherst's success at Ticonderoga in 1759, all French posts in New York were back in British hands by the end of the year. It was during this war that the British started the practice of paying Indians for enemy scalps. During the French wars this did little harm in the Catskill region, but during the Revolution, with the British on the other side, it led to many bloody incidents in the Catskills. This conflict served as military training for residents of the area, and this experience was put to good use during the Revolution.

Frontier life was hard and often lonely. The original forest cover of the region was dense, with large hemlocks and other evergreens predominating over large expanses. The forests were dark and gloomy and harbored such animals as wolves, mountain lions and panthers. It was a far cry from today when the principal forest cover is composed of such hardwoods as birch, beech, maple, oak and chestnut and the most dangerous animals to be encountered are bobcats, Canadian Lynx and an occasional irritated mother bear. The new settler had first to find a spring or other source of good drinking water and then start to clear the land for planting. He would erect a crude lean-to type of shelter and gradually replace this with a log cabin as he felled trees. He made no attempt to clear the stumps but planted between them, and it was often many years before they rotted or he would get around to pulling them. Initial crops were usually for the farmer's own consumption as there were no facilities at first to take grain for milling except along the principal streams. The pioneer farms had an unkept appearance. Often the pioneer depended largely upon hunting and fishing and some minor trading with the Indians. Often the Indians were friendly and helpful, but they could be treacherous and it was most difficult to tell when you had aroused their superstitious fears or broken a taboo—or when the thought of a fee for your scalp overcame neighborly feelings.

However, during this period many a white child made friends with young Indians and became adopted into neighboring Indian tribes. The early settlers thus became expert woodsmen and learned many of the Indian skills. Buckskin clothing was common. Owing to poor transportation to the interior, few manufactured articles of any size found their way to the frontier. Social activity generally consisted of getting drunk on "home brew," with the local Indians frequently participating. Hunting was enjoyed both as a sport and source of food. It was not until the development of turnpikes after the Revolution that this basic pattern would change—and at that time many of the frontiersmen had developed such a taste for the rugged life that they moved on west, leaving the farms to newcomers from the seaboard to further develop and cultivate.

Prior to the Revolution there was considerable exploration of upstate New York. In 1757 Indians led British troops to the Great Sulphur Spring at present-day Richfield Springs. The valley of the Schoharie had been settled as early as 1724 and Cherry Valley in 1740. Saratoga was settled in 1773. Closer to home in the Catskill region the Kingston Academy opened in 1774.

THE AMERICAN REVOLUTION

On April 19, 1775, was fired "the shot heard round the world." At Lexington, Massachusetts a small, determined group of patriots resisted British troops and war had begun.

The Catskill region did not see many major battles, but nonetheless there was plenty of action and the bordering Hudson and Mohawk valleys were of strategic importance. It was the grand strategy of the English to gain control of the Hudson Valley between Canada and New York City and thus split New England from the other colonies. To resist this Washington determined to hold the Highlands of the Hudson and the upper valley at all costs. In the great British campaign of 1777 the chief strategy was for General John Burgoyne to march down from Canada via Lake Champlain and hook up with Sir William Howe and Sir Henry Clinton, who were to move up from New York, and with Barry St. Leger, who was to march from the west via Oswego and the Mohawk Valley. Burgoyne was halted at the Battle of Saratoga and St. Leger at the Battle of Oriskany. For reasons that are not yet determined, Howe and Clinton failed to move north from New York according to schedule. Thus the campaign was abortive and the American victories were a turning point in the long war. The British never did succeed in splitting the colonies, although they made a foray as far north as Clermont on the Hudson in 1777 and burned Kingston.

However, things were far from peaceful on the frontier. The Iroquois, except for the Oneidas, were aligned with the British and Tories under command of Joseph Brant (also called Thayendanegea), the Mohawk chieftain and brother of the mistress of the Tory leader Sir William Johnson. Johnson, his son Sir John Johnson, Colonel John Butler and his infamous Tory Rangers, and Butler's son, Captain Walter Butler were all with Brant. They made the frontier along the Susquehanna and Mohawk Rivers a place of constant nightmare and made forays as far south and east as Port Jervis, Kingston and Cairo. They also made a practice of abduction and brought the prisoners to Fort Niagara for stipulated rewards. Remains of a Tory blockhouse or fort have been found atop Round Top near Kaaterskill Clove, and this was a jumping off point for many raids down to the Hudson Valley.

Conditions in the Mohawk Valley have been well described by Benson Lossing in his *Pictorial Field-Book of the Revolution*:

> From the commencement of hostilities the Mohawk Valley was a theater of great activity, and all through the eventful years of the contest it suffered dreadfully from the effects of partisan warfare. Every rod of ground was trodden by hostile parties, and for seven years the fierce Indian, and the ofttimes more ferocious Tory, kept the people in continual alarm, spreading death and desolation over that fair portion of our land. So frequent and sanguinary were the stealthy midnight attacks or open daylight struggles, that Tryon* county obtained the appropriate appellation of the "dark and

*Note: Tryon County, erected in 1772 from parts of Albany County, was renamed Montgomery County in 1784.

bloody ground," and long after peace blessed the land, its forests were traversed with fear and distrust.

Brant and his warriors, with a large number of Tories . . . organized scalping parties and sent them out upon the borderers. The settlers were cut off in detail. Marauding parties fell upon isolated families like bolts from the clouds, and the blaze of dwellings upon the hills and in the valleys nightly warned the yet secure inhabitant to be on the alert. Their dwellings were transformed into block-houses. The women were taught the use of weapons, and stood sentinels when the men were at work. Half-grown children were educated for scouts, and taught to discern the Indian trail, and every man worked armed in his field. Such was the condition of the dwellers of Tryon county during almost the whole time of the war.

On May 10th the Second Continental Congress met in Philadelphia and on June 5th George Washington was appointed Commander in Chief. On June 7th Israel Putnam successfully defended Breeds Hill in the Battle of Bunker Hill. This raised the colonists' spirits and on July 6th Congress issued a *Manifesto*. Shortly thereafter Ethan allen and Benedict Arnold captured Fort Ticonderoga and Crown Point and General Richard Montgomery led an ill-fated expedition against the Province of Quebec and was killed during the attack on Quebec City, after successfully capturing Montreal. The expedition was a failure.

In February of 1776 the British engaged Hessian mercenaries, but on March 17th found it expedient to evacuate Boston. On April 1st the British fleet appeared off Sandy Hook and General Charles Lee and Washington were sent to prepare the defense of New York City. In June British troops landed in Charleston, South Carolina and General William Howe and his elder brother Admiral Richard Howe arrived with Governor William Tryon off Sandy Hook and made an initial landing on Staten Island.

On July 4, 1776 Congress, assembled in Philadelphia, issued the Declaration of Independence, and it was soon promulgated throughout the colonies. On August 27th the British under Generals Grant, Cornwallis, Percy and Henry Clinton, accompanied by Hessians under General De Hiester, landed at Brooklyn. The Americans under Generals Putnam, Sullivan and Lord Sterling put up a noble defense, among which that of the Maryland Brigade was notable. However, the fortunes of battle went against the Americans and on August 29th 9,000 men, under the command of General Knox, made a strategic retreat to Manhattan under cover of early morning dark and fog.

Manhattan proved untenable and Washington ordered retreat. By September 15th Manhattan was in the hands of the British, who held it until after completion of the peace treaty in November 1783. Notable engagements occurred at Kipps Bay and Fort Washington. The main body of troops was withdrawn to White Plains, where another major battle was fought on October 28th. The entire situation around New York City proved so untenable that on November 18th Washington ordered abandonment of Fort Lee in New Jersey and retreat to the Delaware on December 12th. The next day the British occupied Newport, R.I. They also gained control of New Jersey.

On Christmas Day, December 25, Washington conducted a surprise attack on the British and Hessians at Trenton and Princeton. This ended action for the year.

1777 saw the British in control of Philadelphia after the American Defeat at Brandywine Creek on September 11th, but this was shortly offset by the defeat of Burgoyne at Saratoga on October 17th. We have already discussed the great Saratoga Campaign. American victory here was a turning point and gained for us the active assistance of France.

On April 20, 1777, the government of the State of New York was established at Kingston and the 1st Constitution was issued. George Clinton was elected governor on July 30th. This temerity, and vindictiveness on the part of the British over the defeat of the Saratoga Campaign, led Sir John Vaughan and Sir Henry Clinton to lead a marauding expedition up the Hudson after the defeats of Forts Clinton and Montgomery in the Hudson Highlands. They sailed up the river in 30 ships, shooting at Staatsburg and landing at and firing Clermont. On October 13th Kingston was set to the torch with great damage. This expedition had little military value for the British except to relieve frustration. In Cooper's *The Pioneers* Natty Bumpo describes this atrocity as witnessed from Pine Orchard.

During this period there was a great split of the population of the Catskills between Loyalists and Revolutionists. Many of the Patriots joined the New York Rangers who operated in guerilla fashion in the Highlands under Washington's general direction. The Loyalists rallyed together under the Johnsons and Butlers with the Iroquois as allies. Their depredations were concentrated to the north and west. Most of the freehold farmers in the Hudson Valley and the large landlords were on the American side. However, as they felt they would not have much to gain by an American victory, many of the tenant farmers were loyal to the Crown.

1778 saw General Clinton withdraw his British troops from Philadelphia back toward the Jerseys. Washington inflicted some punishment on him at the Battle of Monmouth in New Jersey. On August 9th the French fleet under D'Estaing failed to recapture Newport. There was much manoeuvring across the Jerseys during the summer. On November 11th the Indians and British made a bloody raid on Cherry Valley, which is described under that heading in the Gazetteer section. Another massacre occurred at the Wyoming Valley settlements in Pennsylvania.

In 1779 General Anthony Wayne led a brilliant attack upon Stony Point on the Hudson and recaptured it for the Americans. However, as it had little real strategic value and was difficult to hold he again abandoned it. The capture had great value for morale, however. In August Generals John Sullivan and James Clinton (brother of Governor George Clinton) led an expedition down the Susquehanna to avenge the Wyoming and Cherry Valley Massacres. On August 29th they defeated the British and Iroquois at Newtown, near Elmira. Some interesting incidents of this expedition are described in the article on the Susquehanna River.

On July 20th Joseph Brant and three hundred Iroquois warriors attacked Minnisink (Port Jervis), wreaking much havoc and killing many settlers. They started to retreat back up along the Delaware. On July 22nd they were overtaken by Colonel Tusten and the Goshen Militia near Barryville, where a pitched battle was fought. The Indians massacred the whites and escaped. There were only thirty white survivors. On October 22nd the property of Tories was declared forfeit.

The year 1780 saw much manoeuvring of the armies and Indian and Tory raids in the Mohawk and Schoharie Valleys. Benedict Arnold's treason plot was uncovered and Major André captured, tried and executed as a spy. Although belonging to the enemy camp, he was a very aimiable young man and well liked by all who knew him, but the stern letter of the laws of war were executed nonetheless.

1781 saw the decisive victory of the war. Action had moved to the South during 1780 and 1781 and on October 25th the French and Americans beat the British near Yorktown, Virginia in the last major battle of the war. Washington withdrew his army to Newburgh to defend the Highlands during the winter of 1781–1782, where he remained for the rest of the year while negotiations were conducted at Paris.

In 1783 Washington received the infamous Nicola letters and refused the crown with noble simplicity and expressed sorrow that anyone would have believed him capable of subverting the revolution he had just led. The author would like to make the personal observation that he considers this one the most noble individual acts in secular history and can never visit the Newburgh–New Windsor area without a strong consciousness that, in these hills, the spirit of liberty came to its finest flower. The Treaty of Paris was signed on January 20th and cessation of arms was announced on April 11th. Details of the Treaty were cleared up by September 3rd and on November 25th the British, under Sir Guy Carleton, evacuated New York.

Washington bid farewell to his officers in New York on December 4th and went to Philadelphia to resign his commission on December 23rd. On December 13th Congress ratified the Treaty of Paris.

Peace and a New Nation

During 1784 the Continental Congress moved to New York and the State Legislature also met there. For the next three years the various states were busy setting up their governments and there was a great deal of discussion about the possible form a federal government might take. In 1787 the Constitutional Convention met in Philadelphia and drew up the Federal Constitution. Shortly thereafter John Jay and Alexander Hamilton of New York and James Madison of Virginia issued the *Federalist Papers*, explaining the benefits of the new constitution. It now became necessary for the various states to ratify it. Also in 1787 the Act Disenfranchising Tories was repealed. The wounds of the war were slowly beginning to heal; but many confiscated properties had changed hands and the great Phillipse Patent had been broken up.

In 1788 the New York Legislature, meeting at Poughkeepsie, ratified the Federal Constitution and elected representatives to Congress. On April 30, 1789 (also the year of the French Revolution), George Washington was inaugurated on the steps of Federal Hall in Manhattan and Congress met in New York, which was declared the capital, although not then the largest city in the United States. However, in 1790 the capital was moved to Philadelphia pending building of a new federal capital.

POSTWAR DEVELOPMENTS

Of interests to the Catskills was the Whiskey Excise Act of 1791. Many frontier farmers had no way to economically get their grain crops to market. Distilling added value while decreasing bulk and the finished liquor could more easily be transported to market. The frontier farmers greatly resented the new excise tax and the Whiskey Rebellion was under way. While the Rebellion was not as virulent in the Catskills as elsewhere, there was shared sympathy nonetheless. This was the first real test of the powers of the new federal government. Eventually federal power was recognized and the question of coinage became paramount. As it is not our purpose to write a history of the United States, from here on we shall confine ourselves to area developments and those in the state and greater world which can serve as points of reference.

The tenant farmers still chafed under the odious three-life lease system. New settlers shunned the Catskills and Hudson Valley region and went further west. Many new freeholders went to what are now the Otsego and Montgomery County areas where they could own their own land. It was during this period that Cooperstown saw its first significant growth, and it is suggested that the reader will here take the time to read the Cooperstown article in the Gazetteer section.

In 1795 John Jay was elected governor and John Fitch's steamboat was demonstrated in New York. In 1797 Albany was made the permanent state capital. The Cherry Valley Turnpike was incorporated in 1799. The year 1802 saw the United States Military Academy established at West Point and in 1804 the tragic duel between Alexander Hamilton and Aaron Burr at Weehawken, New Jersey ended two brilliant political careers and Hamilton's life.

Perhaps 1807 is the most significant year for our area, as in that year Robert Fulton's "North River Steamboat of Clermont" made its first successful commercial trips between Albany and New York. The enterprise was backed by Fulton's father-in-law, Chancellor Robert Livingston, and Fulton and Livingston obtained a chartered monopoly on steamboats in New York State. The advantages of the new mode of transport were soon apparent and soon others were seeking to break the monopoly.

In 1811 the Erie Canal to connect Lake Erie with the Hudson River was authorized. This was to make New York the great seaport for the interior of the new nation. It was finally opened in 1825.

THE WAR OF 1812

Most present-day Americans are rather unclear about the causes of the War of 1812. They consider is as a sort of "second round" of the American Revolution inflicted upon us by the British. Actually the United States declared the War. American merchants felt that the British were hampering American trade. British "Orders in Council" forbade neutral trade with France. American seamen were being impressed at sea by British warships and the British generally were making it difficult for those who sought to break their Continental Blockade and deal with Napoleon.

On the other hand the frontiersmen were seeking new lands in the West and Northwest. They claimed that the British in Canada were stirring up the Indians and arming them. In this there was probably some truth. Soon a movement developed to "take Canada." The War Hawks persuaded James Madison to declare war on Britain in 1812.

It soon became apparent that America was not ready for such a major undertaking. We could not "take Canada at a blow." An attack upon Detroit by General William Hull was unsuccessful and he surrendered to a smaller force under General Isaac Brock.

The U.S. did better at sea that year. The *Constitution* under Isaac Hull captured the British man-of-war *Guerriere*, and the *United States* under

Stephen Decatur captured the *Macedonian*. Our privateers carried the action to the very shores of Britain and one such action is well described in Cooper's *The Pilot*. However, a land attack on Queenstown Heights, on the Niagara, was beaten back.

In 1813 the tide turned against us. The *Shannon* defeated the U.S. ship *Chesapeake* under Captain James ("Don't give up the ship!") Lawrence. American forces were beaten at the Battle of the Raisin River near Detroit. The Americans under James Wilkinson were unsuccessful along the St. Lawrence and the British captured Ogdensburg and also burned Buffalo and Black Rock on the Niagara frontier. They were, however, beaten at the battle at Plattsburg.

Our luck was better on Lake Erie. In September of 1813 Captain Oliver Hazard Perry won a decisive battle near Presque Isle, at which he uttered the memorable aphorism "We have not yet begun to fight." Under his protection American forces under General William Henry Harrison succeeded in capturing Detroit, the British forces burning it upon retreat to Canada.

In 1814 things looked bad for the U.S. The British invaded Chesapeake Bay and captured Bladensburg and Washington, where they burned the Capitol and the White House. Their advance was checked at Fort McHenry on the Patapsco River near Baltimore. It was during this battle that Francis Scott Key wrote *The Star Spangled Banner*. This action took place in August. Earlier in the year American forces had crossed the Niagara River and won engagements at Chippewa and Lundy's Lane (Ontario), under the command of General Jacob Brown.

On the other hand, the British captured Fort Ontario at Oswego and invaded northern New York. The war was becoming unpopular in New England, whose extensive shipping interests were idled and a Convention was called at Hartford where possible seccession was considered. The culminating action of the year was in September when Sir George Prevost led a force down the west side of Lake Champlain toward the Hudson Valley. This campaign was checked on the water by Captain Thomas MacDonough, who defeated the British fleet at the Battle of Plattsburg, sometimes called the Battle of Lake Champlain, near Valcour Island.

By this time things were at a stalemate. John Quincy Adams, Henry Clay and Albert Gallatin were dispatched to Ghent were negotiations took place, culminating in the Treaty of Ghent on December 24, 1814.

One major action, the Battle of New Orleans, took place after the signing of the Peace Treaty when Andrew Jackson won a decisive victory on January 8, 1815. This was the end of hostilities. The War of 1812 served to strengthen the Union and a feeling of nationalism and to open up the West. A strong feeling of isolationism developed after the war.

COMMERCIAL DEVELOPMENT

The War of 1812 cleared the way for full scale expansion of the new nation and of the State of New York. In 1817 New York State abolished slavery, which had become an established institution along the Hudson. Final emancipation took effect in 1827. Many of the slaves did not favor emancipation, according to Cooper's novel *Satanstoe*, and remained with their old masters. Others drifted to the towns, especially to Albany, or All-Bonny as they called it.

Prior to the war, turnpike construction began in the Catskill region. Early roads included the Susquehanna Turnpike from Catskill to Wattle's Ferry near Unadilla; the Schoharie Turnpike from Athens to Schoharie; the Cherry Valley Turnpike; the Newburgh & Cochecton Turnpike, connecting the Hudson and the Delaware; the Dutchess, Ulster and Delaware from Connecticut to Margaretville via Kingston and Phoenicia; the Jeffersonville & Monticello Turnpike; etc. Later, under the impetus of tanning industry requirements, many more, such as the Mt. Hope & Lumberland, Callicoon Depot & Rockland, and Ulster & Orange Branch Turnpike, were built. Most of them are now state or county highways. These were all originally privately built and tolls were collected. Many of them were financially unsuccessful, despite their great importance in opening up the area. The Dutchess, Ulster & Delaware gave birth to the word "DUD."

This was also the great age of canal building and steamboat development. In 1823 the Champlain Canal, connecting the Hudson with Lake Champlain, was completed. This same year saw incorporation of the Delaware & Hudson Canal to run between Honesdale in the Pennsylvania coal fields and Rondout on the Hudson River. In 1824 a Supreme Court decision written by John Marshall in the case *Gibbons vs Ogden* broke the Livingston-Fulton monopoly on steam navigation and led to a great burst of steamboat building on the Hudson and other U.S. waters. Finally, in 1825, the Erie Canal was completed and an immense celebration held, as this assured the primacy of New York as a seaport.

Agriculture was the backbone of the Catskill area economy. Products included maple syrup, hops, vegetables, grain, tobacco, milk, butter, eggs, honey, wool and livestock.

Abundant water power along the many streams also led to development of industry at an early date. Grist mills, sawmills, fulling mills, paper mills, iron works, carding works and woolen factories sprang up. The Catskill Creek was particularly heavily industrialized. In 1830 the Port of Catskill shipped "substantial quantities" of butter, tallow, wool, hay, potash and shingles—also 3,000,000 board feet of lumber and 250,000 sides of sole leather.

This last item indicates the rising importance of the tanning industry in the Catskills. Before the automobile, leather had great importance for saddles and harnesses in addition to its traditional role as footwear. Tannin, obtained from the bark of the hemlock tree (Tsuga Canadensis), was the major source of tanin. As a great deal of this bark was required to obtain a small quantity of tannin, it became cheaper to carry the hides to the forests where the hemlock grew. Thus many large tanneries grew up in the Catskill region, with their stinking vats and fumes. Great wagons loaded with hides would be pulled up into the mountains by straining horses over the primitive roads and turnpikes. These hides often came from as far as the Argentine, and the finished leather was exported all over the world. Vast tanneries were established near Palenville, Tannersville, Hunter, Prattsville, Phoenicia, Samsonville, Claryville and in many other now forgotten spots. Millions of large Hemlock trees were cut down only for their bark, and the bleached timbers left to dry and eventually rot or serve as fuel for great forest fires. The tanneries moved to follow the hemlock supply. Later, when the hemlocks were virtually depleted, the tanners turned to oak, and the industry moved generally south from Greene to Sullivan and Ulster counties. There was a great boom in tanning in Sullivan County during the Civil War. However, the industry was pretty well dead by the end of the 19th century. Many towns took their names

Hoop Makers, c1895. Photo by Lionel De Lisser

from local tanners, and the industry is thus remembered. Today the
hemlock is making a modest comeback on the Catskill mountainsides.
Only those in inaccesible ravines and on high peaks had been spared by
the tanners.

Other early industries included barrel making, hoop shaving, dyeing,
brick making, brewing and shipbuilding along the Hudson. Gradually the
old sloops on the Hudson gave way to steamboats and tows of barges.
However, these too passed from the scene. On September 6, 1971, the
S.S. Alexander Hamilton of the Hudson River Day Line made the last trip
by a scheduled steamboat on the Hudson. She was a sidewheeler, as was
Fulton's *Clermont*, the first Hudson steamboat. Next season saw the
Hamilton in a museum and a new diesel vessel on the Day Line route. Her
freight-carrying sisters had disappeared by the 1950s and remaining water
traffic on the Hudson consists of large ocean-going tankers and cement,
traprock oil and paper barges, pulled by diesel tugs, and pleasure boats of
all descriptions.

After the decline of tanning, bluestone, or flagstone, cutting became
the principal Catskill industry. This stone, also called slate, was "lifted"
from deposits of sedimentary rock. It was an attractive blue-gray in color
and had the additional advantage of not becoming slippery when wet.
This made it an excellent sidewalk paving stone. During the second half
of the 19th century immense amounts of bluestone were quarried for
America's growing cities. The largest slab ever cut was in Sullivan County.

*Bluestone cutters near Wilbur, c1895. Rondout Creek and West Shore RR Viaduct in
background. Photo by Lionel De Lisser.*

It was floated down the Delaware River and sent by ship from Philadelphia to New York City, where it was layed in front of City Hall porch.

Principal centers of quarrying were at Woodstock, Platte Clove, Phoenicia, Palenville, Ashokan and in Delaware and Sullivan Counties. A very limited amount is still cut for decorative stonework and garden walks. Many miles of bluestone walls may be seen around Woodstock and Ashokan Reservoir.

The Catskills were always difficult to farm and many early hillside farms were abandoned; their stone pasture walls still run up the side of many a mountain. With later development of the railroads dairy farming took precedence over field crops. This still remains the case today, especially in Delaware, Ulster and Sullivan Counties. The Schoharie Valley once was a center of hops growing until the industry was ruined by a blight. Today, it is famous as a vegetable growing region, with some of the most fertile soil in the world. Dairying dominates in Otsego County.

Lumbering, once a major industry, has been limited by state acquisition of park lands. Most present-day lumbering is selective cutting of hardwoods, although some pulpwood is still cut for processing in a pressed board plant near Deposit. With proper management Delaware County can sustain a small pulpwood industry indefinitely. Principal industries in the region include International Business Machines at Kingston, Rotron Company in Woodstock, Channel Master in Ellenville, and Kolmar Laboratories in Port Jervis. The Dairylea Cooperative in Delaware and Otsego Counties is an important marketing organization for the dairy farmers.

In 1885 large parts of the Catskills were included in the Forest Preserve Act and in 1894 the act was made an amendment to the constitution. During the early 20th century the manufacture of wood alcohol and acid was a major industry in western Sullivan and Delaware Counties. The primary products were wood alcohol, acetate and charcoal. Much of this product was used for explosives, ammunition and embalming fluid. However, when cheaper synthetic substitutes were discovered during the First World War, this industry faded away. Certain areas had considerable charcoal burning, wood turning and furniture manufacturing industries. Most of these have come and gone. We have intentionally deferred any mention of the area's principal industry, tourism, and the growth of the railroad system which made this growth initially possible, and of the great artistic, literary and cultural movement that gave it impetus. However, before going into the detailed histories of the railroad and resort industries, let us take a quick look at the general history of the region as it relates to that of the nation.

THE ANTI-RENT WAR ("DOWN-RENT WAR")

On July 4, 1845, the long-festering anti-rent discontents broke out again when a group of farmers met in the old red brick Lutheran Church in Berne to draft a new Declaration of Independence. They vowed to stop paying rents to the Van Rensselaers and other large landowners for lands which they and their ancestors had cleared and improved themselves. The movement soon spread into Rensselaer, Columbia, Greene, Delaware, Schoharie, Ulster and Sullivan Counties. The farmers dressed as Indians with masks, calico costumes and other paraphernalia. They resisted rent collectors and law officers and gave warning of their approach by blowing on loud tin horns. Much hard feeling ensued. Resistence was made at Lake Hill and Cooper Lake. Sheriff Schoonmaker of Ulster County had to send a force of one hundred men to Bearsville. The ringleaders in that incident were indicted by a grand jury in Kingston in 1845.

Also in 1845 Dr. Smith Boughton, alias "Big Thunder," was brought to trial and convicted at Hudson, in Columbia County, of inciting a riot. In September he was given a life sentence. This was during the governorship of Silas Wright, who was friendly to the landowner class.

In 1846 there was a bloody incident at Lake Delaware, near Delhi, and popular sentiment began to show itself in the political arena. In 1846 John Young, a Whig, was elected governor for the term 1847–1849. His first move was to pardon Dr. Boughton. Soon legislative action abolished the old system by a constitutional act. Henry Christman's book *Tin Horns and Calico* tells of this exciting period and its importance in the formation of the Republican Party.

LATER EVENTS

The years 1860 through 1865 saw the Civil War with its great draft riots of 1863 in Troy and New York City. Many local men saw action in the war. The war was followed by a great boom, which gave rise to the new resorts of the Catskills, followed by a great financial panic in 1873. Later developments were mainly tangential to the Catskills and might better be tabulated as follows:

1869 New York & Oswego Midland Railroad (NYO & W) completed.
1875 Ulster & Delaware Railroad line completed from Kingston to Stamford.
1881 President Chester A. Arthur visits Catskills.
1884 West Shore Railroad completed.
1901 Theodore Roosevelt becomes president—another Catskill visitor.
1917 Ashokan Reservoir completed.
1918 New York State Barge Canal (successor to Erie Canal) opened.
1924 Bear Mountain Bridge opened.
1924 *Alexander Hamilton*, last Hudson sidewheeler, built.
1928 Franklin D. Roosevelt elected governor of New York.
1932 Franklin D. Roosevelt elected president of U.S.
1932 Enlarged Port of Albany opened to ocean-going ships.
1957 NYO & W Rwy. abandoned.

Railroad Fever

The 19th century has often been called the Railroad Age, and indeed it was so in the Catskill area. Major trunk lines to the West ran up the Hudson and Mohawk Valleys on the east and the north, while the New York & Lake Erie ran along the Delaware River to the south. Today these routes remain as the main lines of the Penn-Central and Erie-Lackawanna systems. Other routes were soon built to serve the Catskill heartland. First they were built to serve the farms and small local industries. Later they catered to the developing resort industry which they fostered. The New York & Oswego Midland was originally built as a trunk line competing with the Erie and New York Central; later on, under the name New York Ontario & Western it concentrated upon carrying passengers, anthracite coal and milk. Other small lines grew, thrived and died, primarily to serve the resort industry. Let us take a look at the individual lines from their inception to the present day.

The first railroad to influence the Catskill region was built in Pennsylvania as an adjunct of the Delaware & Hudson Canal. It was a 16-mile-long "gravity" railroad from mines near Carbondale to the canal at Honesdale. Completed in 1829, cars were originally pulled upgrade by horses and allowed to coast back down grade. On August 8, 1829 the first steam engine, the English-built *Stourbridge Lion*, pulled a load on this line. In 1866 the line was extended to Olyphant, Pa. and stationary steam engines were being used to pull loads uphill. This line ran until 1898 when the D & H Canal was closed, and the railroad was eventually converted into a regular steam railroad, known as the Honesdale Branch of the Delaware & Hudson Railroad. The D & H hauled coal from the Carbondale region via Lanesville and Oneonta to Albany, and the old "gravity line" has been completely abandoned.

CANAJOHARIE & CATSKILL

Within the Catskill region proper the first railroad was the Canajoharie & Catskill, chartered in 1828 as the Catskill & Ithaca; it was completed from Catskill to Cooksburg in 1840. It was not a financial success, and after a disastrous accident in 1842, it was abandoned. A famous painting by Thomas Cole, dated 1841, shows a C & C train crossing Jefferson Flats, with the Catskills in the distance. Various culverts and abutments can still be found along Route 23.

PENN-CENTRAL SYSTEM PREDECESSORS

In 1831 the Albany & Schenectady, later reincorporated as the Mohawk & Hudson Railroad, was completed. The first through train was powered by the steam locomotive *De Witt Clinton*. The passenger cars were built like Concord coaches. This was the first segment of the later New York Central System.

By 1840 there were a series of connecting railroads all the way from Albany to Buffalo, and by 1851 the Hudson River Railroad had been built from Manhattan to Greenbush, across the river from Albany, under the promotion of William C. Redfield. In 1853 the various lines between Albany and Buffalo were consolidated into the New York Central Railroad. The trip between New York City and Buffalo was broken only by a ferry crossing at Albany.

Commodore Cornelius Vanderbilt, a successful coastal and river steamboat operator, completed construction of the New York & Harlem Railroad from New York City to Hudson and Greenbush in 1868. This line ran along the western foot of the Taconic Mountains near the Connecticut and Massachusetts borders and proved longer than that of the Hudson River Railroad. Shortly thereafter Vanderbilt acquired control of both the Hudson River Railroad and the New York Central and built a bridge to connect them at Albany. Both lines were then amalgamated with the New York & Harlem to form the New York Central & Hudson River Railroad, forerunner of the giant New York Central System, which eventually stretched from Boston and New York City to Chicago, St. Louis and Cincinnati.

This line provided important access to the Catskills on both the east and north. After many years as one of the greatest railroads in the United States the New York Central began to experience serious financial difficulty in the 1950s. The Vanderbilt family lost control to Robert R. Young and Allen Kirby in a famous proxy fight. The new owners installed Alfred E. Perlman as president. In what the author considers ill-considered attempts to maintain dividends to suit the stockholders, Mr. Perlman cut maintenance to the point of causing frequent costly breakdowns and limitations on ability to provide proper service. The road was in such bad shape by the mid 1960s that it sought merger with its principal competitor, the Pennsylvania Railroad Company, which was also suffering difficulties. On February 1, 1968, the two roads were merged to form the Penn-Central Railroad (later Penn-Central Transportation Company). The new entity was beset by many external economic difficulties and possibly gross mismanagement. Bankruptcy was declared in June of 1970. The line was kept operational only by Federal financial aid pending incorporation into the projected Consolidated Railroad Corporation—Conrail, which commenced operations on April 1, 1976. Since May 1st, 1971, all passenger service over this line has been operated by the National Railroad Passenger Corporation, popularly known as Amtrak. Service has been greatly improved and new trains added. Access to the Catskill region is provided at Utica, Amsterdam, Schenectady, Albany-Rensselaer, Hudson, Rhinecliff and Poughkeepsie stations from Grand Central Terminal in New York and from Buffalo, Toronto, Detroit and Chicago and all points west. Pullman service from the west has been restored.

THE ERIE-LACKAWANNA SYSTEM

In 1841 the New York & Lake Erie Railroad was completed from Piermont-on-Hudson in Rockland County to Goshen, in Orange County. By 1848 this line had been pushed across the Shawangunks to Port Jervis and up the Delaware and over the Randolph Hills to Binghamton on the Susquehanna River. By 1851 the line was completed across the southern tier of New York State to the port of Dunkirk on Lake Erie. Subsequently the name of the line was changed to Erie Railroad and extensions built to Buffalo, Chicago and Cincinnati. In 1960 it was merged with the former Delaware Lackawanna & Western Railroad to form the Erie-Lackawanna Railway. The E-L was controlled by the Dereco Company, a creature of the wealthy and profitable Norfolk & Western Railway. However, because of flood damage, slowdown of steel shipments and economic depression,

Historic Erie Railroad locomotives. Top: articulated pusher, largest in the world in 1914, capable of hauling a train 4½ miles long. Bottom: "Berkshire-type" locomotive. Erie Railroad Co. photos.

the Erie-Lackawanna became bankrupt despite the fact that it was a basically strong railroad. N & W did not seem to be willing to offer the necessary financial assistance and the Erie-Lackawanna petitioned for inclusion in Conrail. Much excellent modern passenger service is operated in New Jersey and Orange County in New York State as far west as Port Jervis from a terminal in Hoboken, N.J., which is reached from Manhattan by the PATH system (former Hudson Tubes or H & M subway). It does not belong to Amtrak and there has been no passenger service between Port Jervis and Binghamton since 1969, although restoration under a State of New York subsidy is being considered.

The former D L & W once controlled the Utica, Chenango & Susquehanna Valley Railroad which operated a branch from Richfield Junction to Bridgewater and Richfield Springs, known as the Richfield Springs Branch. Subsequently they sold it to the Central New York Railroad Corporation, and in November of 1974 it was acquired by the independent Cooperstown & Charlotte Valley Railroad for operation as a freight shortline, connecting with Erie-Lackawanna at Richfield Junction on the E-L's Utica Branch.

THE DELAWARE & HUDSON SYSTEM

The D & H was one of the few strong and profitable railroads in the northeastern United States until its recent bankruptcy. It was the corporate descendant of the old Delaware & Hudson Canal. Its main lines ran from the coal fields near Scranton and Wilkes-Barre, Pennsylvania and from Binghamton to Nineveh, Oneonta, Albany, Saratoga and Montreal. It handled much interchange traffic with the Boston & Maine and Lehigh Valley railroads as well as with the Canadian lines.

A railroad from Binghamton to Albany (142.5 miles) was first proposed by A. Keyes of Bainbridge in 1844. On April 2, 1851 over 2000 citizens met at Oneonta to organize and Railroad Conventions were held along the proposed route in 1852. The line was incorporated and Joseph H. Ramsey was appointed its first president. The Albany & Susquehanna Railroad was completed from Albany to Central Bridge by 1863 and to Binghamton by December 31, 1868. The first passenger train was operated over the entire line on January 12, 1869. Regular passenger service was continued until the mid 1960s. Originally the Albany & Susquehanna was built to the original six-foot wide gauge of the Erie Railroad to provide for the interchange of cars. In 1869 Jay Gould and Jim Fisk of the Erie decided that they would move in and take over the Albany & Susquehanna. It was a complicated financial and legal battle which soon degenerated into pitched physical warfare known as the "Erie War." It has been colorfully described by W. A. Swanberg in his *Jim Fisk: The Career of an Improbable Rascal*, and by Jim Shaughnessy in his monumental and completely fascinating *Delaware & Hudson*. The upshot of the Erie War was that a compromise was reached and the Albany & Susquehanna was leased by the Delaware & Hudson in February of 1870. Finally in 1945 the Delaware & Hudson purchased the line outright, and operates it as their Susquehanna Division.

Closely associated with the Delaware & Hudson are several branches and connecting shortlines. In 1868 the Albany & Susquehanna backed construction of the Cherry Valley & Mohawk Railroad Co., running 23 miles between Cherry Valley and Cobleskill via Hyndsville, Seward, and Sharon Springs. It was completed by the Delaware & Hudson in 1870 and ran as the Cherry Valley Branch until abandoned in 1954. When Route 20 was upgraded in the 1950s a substantial overpass bridge was built for this line, but tracks have never been put down over it. This may be seen west of Sharon Springs.

Closely associated with the D & H were the Schoharie Valley Railroad, the Middleburg & Schoharie Railroad, and the Southern New York Railway, an electric interurban line.

The Schoharie Valley Railroad was 4.3 miles long, running from Schoharie Junction, near Central Bridge, to Schoharie. It was built in 1865 and acquired by the Delaware & Hudson in 1906. It was finally abandoned in 1942.

The Middleburg & Schoharie Railroad was built in 1867 to run 5.7 miles from a connection with the Schoharie Valley Railroad at Schoharie to Middleburg. It hauled considerable amounts of hops, timothy and lumber and was abandoned in 1937. An old car may be seen on display at the restored station in Schoharie.

The Southern New York Railway was built near the turn of the century as the Oneonta & Mohawk Valley Railway, an electric interurban line between Oneonta and Richfield Springs, with a branch to Cooperstown. The longer routes have long been abandoned but some industrial trackage survives near Oneonta and is operated by the independent Cooperstown & Charlotte Valley for interchange with the D & H.

COOPERSTOWN & CHARLOTTE VALLEY

The Cooperstown & Susquehanna Valley RR was incorporated in 1869 to connect Cooperstown with the Albany & Susquehanna at Colliersville. In 1887 it was leased by the Cooperstown & Charlotte Valley Railway, which was building east from Colliersville to Davenport, with plans to push on eastward to Harpersfield, Cooksburg and Catskill. Construction never got beyond Davenport Center. In 1903 the Delaware & Hudson leased the Cooperstown & Charlotte Valley and discontinued passenger service between Davenport and Cooperstown Junction (Colliersville). The entire line between Cooperstown Junction and Davenport was pulled up in 1930. In 1970 the D & H applied to abandon what was then known as the Cooperstown Branch. In 1971 the independent short line (16 miles) Cooperstown & Charlotte Valley Railroad was organized under the direction of Malcolm Hughes. This line continues to provide freight service in interchange with the D & H and, until promulgation of new Federal Railroad Administration track standards, operated steam passenger excursions from Cooperstown with even a dining car service! The D-O system, the parent company, also operates the Central New York Railroad and Southern New York Railroad for freight only.

NEW YORK ONTARIO & WESTERN

The sobriquets "Old Woman" and "Old & Weary" were affectionate as the O & W held a warm place in many hearts in the Catskill region. It was the first Class I railroad in the United States to be completely abandoned, and had made valiant efforts against long odds to remain in operation.

All three of its economic mainstays had given way: coal, milk and passengers. The decline in use of anthracite for home heating, coupled with competition from new and more direct highways for milk and tourist traffic, spelled her doom. The O & W did not connect enough large manufacturing centers and managed to go all the way from Weehawken, N.J. to Oswego without hitting any towns larger than Middletown or Norwich, although it did have a branch to Utica. What is more, the route was indirect and ran over high mountains with many tunnels, trestles and other operational difficulties, although this made the line very scenic and a passengers' delight. The O & W was the first Class I railroad to completely dieselize in an attempt to save money and they made a valiant attempt to please both passengers and shippers until the bitter end. At one time it was a busy and profitable hauler of anthracite coal from the Scranton area to tidewater at Cornwall-on-Hudson and Weehawken and to southern New England via the Poughkeepsie Bridge route. Today portions of its former right of way are used by Route 17, the Quickway or Southern Tier Expressway between Roscoe and Cadosia.

Originally incorporated as the New York & Oswego Midland Railroad, large portions were completed by 1869. In 1872 a branch had been completed from Summitville down the Mamakating Valley to Port Jervis via Wurtsboro, and a branch from Summitville to Ellenville had been completed in 1871. The main line was completed near Roscoe and the first through train from Jersey City to Oswego ran on July 10, 1873. Eventually through Pullmans were to operate as far west as Chicago over connecting lines. Also in our Catskill region the New Berlin Branch had

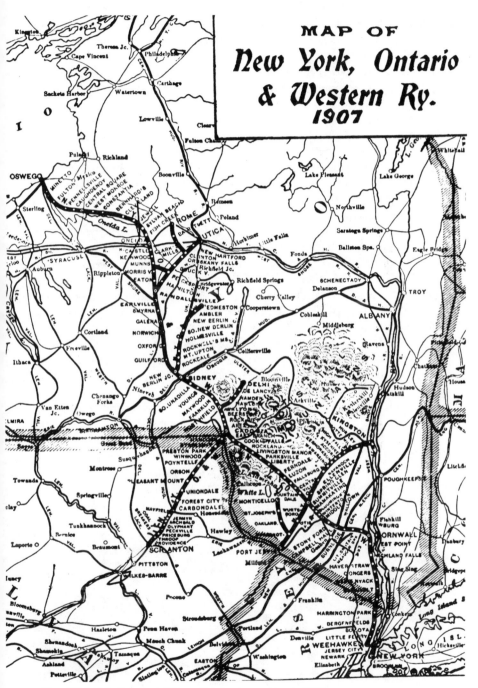

Map of New York, Ontario & Western Rwy. and connections in 1907.

been completed along the Unadilla River from New Berlin Junction, north of Sidney, to New Berlin (20 miles) in 1869. The independent Wharton Valley Railroad was built from New Berlin to Edmeston, a distance of 7 miles, in 1888. It was originally planned to build east to Richfield Springs, but this was never done. In 1889 it was leased by the Oswego Midland and incorporated into the New Berlin Branch.

Originally Midland trains reached Jersey City from Middletown over the tracks of the New Jersey Midland Railroad (now Middletown & New Jersey and New York, Susquehanna & Western). This was a very round-about and unsatisfactory route. Later, equally unsuccessful attempts were made to connect via the Erie south from Middletown. Eventually, in 1873, during the great panic, the Midland went bankrupt and was reorganized as the New York Ontario & Western in 1880.

A progressive management began to develop milk traffic from Chenango, Otsego, Delaware, Sullivan and Orange Counties. They also built a line to Scranton to tap the coal fields and built their own line from Middletown to Cornwall-on-Hudson where they built a coal pier and made a connection with the new West Shore Railroad so that trains could operate down to Weehawken, N.J. over that line, whence ferries connected to Manhattan.

In 1878 the railroad started publication of a booklet entitled *Summer Homes*, which listed resorts, boarding houses, hotels, etc. and which for many years was a dominant factor in the development of the resort industry in the Southern Catskills.

Monticello had been left off the mainline and in 1871 they formed the Port Jervis & Monticello Railroad to connect with the Erie. In 1872 the

The Mountaineer *at West Englewood.*

name was changed to Port Jervis, Monticello & New York and in 1903 the
entire operation was taken over by the O & W as the Monticello Branch
with connection with the mainline at Summitville. Passenger service was
discontinued in 1941.

As early as 1898 hearings were held on the proposed Rondout Valley
Railway between Ellenville and Kingston. This line was completed under
the name Ellenville & Kingston Railroad in 1902, providing through
O & W service to such resorts as Lake Minnewaska and Lake Mohonk via
Kerhonkson and Alligerville.

*Open observation platform of NYO & W Train #2, The Mountaineer, at Roscoe, N.Y. in
1952. This coach was originally a luxurious parlor car. Photo by author.*

	Main Line — New York to Roscoe				
			WEEK DAY TRAINS		**SUNDAY TRAINS**
Miles from New York	**Eastern Standard Time** STATIONS		Daily Except Sunday	Friday Only	Sunday Only
			1	8	1
	New York—		AM	PM	AM
...	Cortlandt St. Ferry	Lv	(1) 8 00		
...	West 42nd St. Ferry	"	8 15	6 40	8 15
...	**Weehawken**	Lv	8 30	6 55	8 30
...	**Cornwall**	Lv	9 50	....	9 50
57	Firthcliffe	"	N 9 59	....	N 9 59
59	Meadow Brook	"	N10 02	....	N10 02
66	Rock Tavern	"	....	....	....
67	Burnside	"	....	....	....
70	Campbell Hall	"	N10 13	....	N10 13
74	Crystal Run	"	....	....	....
80	**Middletown**	Ar	10 33	8 58	10 33
	Station for Pine Bush, Circleville, etc.	Lv	10 38	9 08	10 38
87	Winterton	Lv	N10 51	....	N10 51
90	High View	"	N10 57	N 9 27	N10 57
	Station for Bloomingburg, Burlingham, Walker Valley				
91	Mamakating	"	N11 02	....	N11 02
	Station for Mamakating Park, Rock Hill, Wurtsboro, Wurtsboro Hills				
95	**Summitville**	Ar	11 06	N 9 37	11 06
	Station for Ellenville Branch points	Lv	11 06	N 9 37	11 06
103	Mountaindale	Lv	11 24	9 53	11 24
	Station for Dairyland, Greenfield Park				
106	Woodridge	"	11 30	9 59	11 30
	Station for Glen Wild, Dairyland				
109	Fallsburgh	"	11 39	10 06	11 39
	Station for Kiamesha Lake, Monticello, Sackett Lake, So. Fallsburgh, Woodbourne				
113	Luxon	"	11 47	10 13	11 47
	Station for Hurleyville, Loch Sheldrake, Divine Cor's.				
116	Ferndale	"	11 56	10 23	11 56
	Station for Swan Lake				
120	Liberty	"	12 03	10 30	12 03
	Station for Bethel, Bradley, Curry, Jeffersonville, Kamronga Lake, Neversink, Swan Lake, White Lake, White Sulphur Springs, Youngsville				
125	Parksville	"	12 12	10 40	12 12
131	Livingston Manor	"	12 21	10 50	12 21
	Station for Beaverkill, De Bruce, Lew Beach, Sand Lake, Shandelee Lake, Union Grove				
137	Roscoe	"	12 31	11 00	12 31
	Station for Cooks Falls, Horton, Rockland, Tennanah Lake				
			PM	PM	PM

Reprint of 1953 New York, Ontario & Western Rwy. timetable.

The great years of the O & W were from 1880 until 1918; there was a continuous flow of long coal trains and many passenger trains ran in several sections of up to sixteen cars each. Parlor car service was provided as well as overnight Pullmans with connections to the North and West.

With development of better highways and the general decline of Borscht-circuit hotels the O & W began to suffer loss of passengers. This was abetted by the development of bus service and hacks that would take passengers directly from the mountains to Brooklyn and Bronx without recourse to ferry and local transit transfers at the New York end. By 1953 passenger traffic had dwindled to a handful when the last train ran on September 10th. Such name trains as *The Mountaineer* were only a memory.

Decreasing freight loadings led to complete abandonment on March 29, 1957, after a long drawn out bankruptcy. For many years there had been a close alliance with the New York, New Haven & Hartford with a through route via the Poughkeepsie Bridge. However, by this time the

New Haven was itself in serious trouble and there was nobody left to help out the Old Woman.

A short line named the Unadilla Valley Railroad had run for many years between New Berlin and Bridgewater through South Edmeston, Sweets, West Edmeston, Leonardsville and River Forks in Chenango and Madison Counties, just outside our area. It connected with the D L & W Richfield Springs branch at Bridgewater and the N Y O & W New Berlin Branch at New Berlin. This original route was 19 miles long. In 1940 the Unadilla Valley acquired both the Edmeston and New Berlin Branches of the O & W, along with trackage rights over the O & W Mainline to Sidney and Norwich, where connections were made with the D & H and the D L & W Utica Branch. This entire operation was freight only and was totally abandoned in 1960.

THE ULSTER & DELAWARE SYSTEM

In 1866 citizens of Kingston began to look for a rail line to the West. That year a group of them obtained a charter for the Rondout & Oswego Railroad, and construction was started in 1869. By 1870 passenger service had been inaugurated as far as Mount Pleasant. The name of the line was changed to New York Kingston & Syracuse in 1872, and, after further financial reorganization, to Ulster & Delaware in 1875. That same year the line reached Stamford. The line finally attained its goal of a connection with the D & H in Oneonta in 1900.

In 1872 the Wallkill Valley Railroad had been completed from a connection with the Erie Railroad at Montgomery to Kingston via Walton and New Paltz. This line soon came under Ulster & Delaware dominance, and is notable for its high viaduct across Rondout Creek at Rosendale. The line was abandoned in 1982.

Ulster & Delaware trains made connections with Hudson River Day Line steamers at Kingston Point, and for many years there was a close alliance between the Day Line and the U & D. Passengers were always to be an important factor on the U & D and the track was maintained to high standards for fast running. There was a steep grade and spectacular double horseshoe curve near Pine Hill which could be seen from the railroad-built and owned Grand Hotel at Highmount. The road soon began issuing a Summer Guide and developing passenger traffic.

In order to reach the popular mountaintop resorts at Hunter the narrow-gauge (3 ft. wide) Stony Clove & Catskill Mountain Railroad was built in 1882 from Phoenicia to Hunter. In 1883 a connecting narrow-gauge line, the Kaaterskill Railroad, was built from a junction near Hunter to Tannersville, Laurel House and Kaaterskill Station at the west end of South Lake, convenient to the Hotel Kaaterskill and Catskill Mountain

THIS MAP SHOWS THE ONLY STANDARD GUAGE RAILROAD TO THE CATSKILL MOUNTAIN!
IT ALSO SHOWS THE ROUTE OF THE THROUGH CAR LINE BETWEEN PHILADELPHIA, JERSE
CITY, NEW YORK AND ALL POINTS IN THE CATSKILLS VIA PENNSYLVANIA, WEST SHOR
AND ULSTER & DELAWARE RAILROADS.

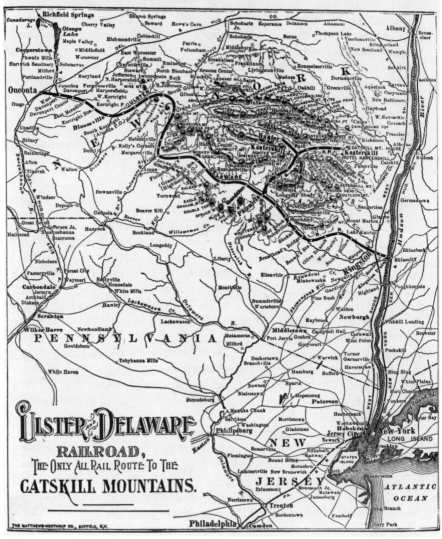

House. In 1893 the Ulster & Delaware acquired both roads and in 1899 converted them to standard gauge for operation of through trains from Weehawken, N.J. via the West Shore Railroad. Through parlor and sleeping cars operated to points as far away as Washington, D.C., Philadelphia, Montreal, Saratoga and Niagara Falls, and the crack *Rip Van Winkle Flyer* was a through parlor car train from Weehawken to Kaaterskill

Station. Connections continued to be made with the Day Line at Kingston Point.

In 1932 the entire Ulster & Delaware system and the Wallkill Valley were acquired by the New York Central. The same adverse factors were working against the U & D as on the O & W. In 1940 the Hunter and Kaaterskill Branches were completely abandoned. A semblance of passenger service, with an inconvenient West Shore connection at Kingston, lingered on until 1954. In 1965 twenty-one miles of track between Oneonta and Bloomville were abandoned, thus assuring the New York Central a longer haul on grain and feed consigned to Roxbury, Stamford and Bloomville. Shortly after Penn-Central bankruptcy in 1970 application was made to abandon the U & D. To provide for possible take-over as a short line the Catskill Mountain Transportation Company was formed by local citizens in 1973. The 1975 Preliminary System Plan of the United States Railway Association has labelled the U & D (Catskill Mountain Branch of Penn-Central) as potentially surplus. The Delaware & Ulster (formerly Ulster & Delaware) has renovated track between Highmount and Halcottville and operates passenger excursions from Arkville to both terminii. The entire Wallkill Valley line has been abandoned.

THE WEST SHORE RAILROAD SYSTEM

The West Shore was built as a nuisance road by interests that may have been backed by the competing Pennsylvania Railroad. The idea was to directly parallel the highly profitable New York Central from Albany to Buffalo while serving some new markets on the west side of the Hudson River between New York and Albany. These cities had been completely dependent upon steamboats and ferry connections to the Hudson River Railroad on the east bank.

The Saratoga & Hudson River Railroad had been built from Athens to Schenectady in 1863, connecting at Athens with steamers operated by Daniel Drew. The line never paid off and was known as the White Elephant Line.

In the 1870s the New York, West Shore & Chicago was surveying a route but the enterprise was abandoned in 1877 during a financial panic. This included part of the former Ridgefield Park Railroad of 1866 from Jersey City to Ridgefield Park, N.J. In 1873 the Jersey City & Albany Railroad was commenced along the west side of the Palisades and had progressed as far as South Haverstraw (Congers) by 1880 when funds ran out before a tunnel could be bored to Haverstraw.

In 1880 the Wallkill Valley began building a "Northern Extension" from Kingston to Athens. In 1881 this was purchased and incorporated into the newly formed New York, West Shore & Buffalo. The New York,

Ulster & Delaware RR Depot at Phoenicia in 1896. Photo by Lionel De Lisser.

West Shore & Buffalo reached Buffalo on January 1, 1884, operating from a terminal at Weehawken, N.J., where there were ferry connections to West 42nd Street and Franklin St. (later transferred to Cortlandt St.).

The new railroad was under-capitalized and was soon engaged in a vicious rate war with the New York Central. By 1885 they were bankrupt and sold out to the New York Central, who set up the subsidiary West Shore Railroad Company.

Passenger service continued on a deluxe through train basis up until the First World War. The top train was the *Continental Limited*, which continued from Buffalo to Chicago over the Grand Trunk System. Through trains were operated from Washington and Philadelphia to Saratoga and Lake Champlain in conjunction with the Pennsylvania Railroad and the Delaware & Hudson. Similar through lines were run in conjunction with the Ulster & Delaware. New York Ontario & Western trains utilized West Shore tracks from Weehawken to Cornwall-on-Hudson, where their own line began. Passenger service was provided to Kingston and Albany until 1958 and local commuter service in New Jersey until December 10, 1959, on which run the author was the last passenger ever to board a scheduled West Shore train.

Today the line has been single-tracked. It is the main Conrail freight route into New York and extremely busy. As this is a key segment of Conrail, it is to be hoped that some multiple track sections will be restored. The State of New Jersey and Rockland County also have plans to restore limited passenger service. Hopefully this will enable trains to again be run to a U. & D. connection at Kingston. In 1976 Conrail did substantial track upgrading.

 only standard gauge line to the
CATSKILL MOUNTAINS

THIS TIMETABLE SUBJECT TO CHANGE WITHOUT NOTICE.

Rip Van Winkle used as advertising motif on Ulster & Delaware timetable, c1900. Author's collection.

DELAWARE & NORTHERN RAILROAD

This line was conceived in 1904 as part of a new through route from the coal fields near Wilkes-Barre to Schenectady. The Delaware & Eastern Railroad was organized in 1904 and construction began in 1905. The line ran from the NY O & W at East Branch to the U & D at Arkville, along the East Branch of the Delaware, a distance of 37.5 miles, with a 9.5-mile-long branch to Andes from near Union Grove. The line opened October 28, 1905, but was soon bankrupt; the proposed northern and southern connections were never built and there was no through traffic. It was reorganized as the Delaware & Northern Railroad in 1911. The line was again bankrupt in 1921. In 1925 the Andes Branch was abandoned and in 1928 directors petitioned for abandonment. It was purchased by Samuel Rosoff and reorganized as the Delaware & Northern Railway. The line was run on a shoestring with passenger service being provided by a gasoline railcar called the "Red Heifer." Dairy products, bluestone and lumber products were the main commodities hauled. In 1939 the City of New York bought the line for the site of the Pepacton Reservoir. It was used to haul in materials for this project and then finally abandoned in 1943. Much of its former right of way is now beneath the reservoir, along with the villages it served.

DELAWARE-OTSEGO RAILROAD

This line ran as a tourist line from 1966 till 1971, utilizing 2.5 miles of the former Ulster & Delaware east from Oneonta. It was operated by Malcolm Hughes, who now controls the Cooperstown & Charlotte Valley.

New York, West Shore & Buffalo Rwy. freight house at Saugerties. Photo by Alfred H. Marks.

The state acquired most of the line for the route of the Susquehanna Expressway.

CATSKILL MOUNTAIN RAILROAD

This was a narrow-gauge shortline built by Charles L. Beach in 1882 from Catskill Landing to Palenville to serve his Catskill Mountain House at Pine Orchard. It followed the former alignment of the Canajoharie & Catskill along Catskill Creek through Austin's Glen and then turned south along the Kiskatom Flats to Palenville. Passengers for the Catskill Mountain House changed for stage coaches where the line crossed the Old Mountain Turnpike near Saxe's Farm. The line had a branch built to Cairo, along the old C & C alignment in 1884, which was incorporated as the Cairo Railroad. Both lines operated until 1918, when they were sold for scrap. Charles Beach also controlled the Catskill Evening Line of steamers to New York, the flagship of which was the *Kaaterskill*. The Catskill Mountain Railroad was also supported by the Hudson River Day Line, with whose ships it made through connection at Catskill.

OTIS ELEVATING RAILWAY

With completion of the Ulster & Delaware Railroad's Kaaterskill Railroad to South Lake in 1883 the stagecoach connection began to prove unpopular and the Catskill Mountain Railroad lost patronage. To combat

Union Station or West Shore Depot, Kingston, N.Y. in 1896. View looking southwest. Tracks parallel to long side of the station are the mainline of the West Shore RR. Other two tracks are those of Ulster & Delaware, also later used by NYO & W. Photo by Lionel De Lisser.

this, Charles L. Beach built the Otis Elevating Railroad from Otis Junction, just north of Palenville on the Catskill Mountain Railroad, to Pine Orchard near the Catskill Mountain House. Construction was started on a cable funicular railroad straight up the Wall of Manitou in 1892. The line was incorporated in 1885 with the help of the Otis Elevator Company, who designed and equipped the line. Actual design was by their chief engineer, Thomas E. Brown, Jr. who had designed the still-functioning elevators for the Eiffel Tower in Paris in 1879. The Otis Elevating Railway was opened for business on August 7, 1892. It was 7,000 ft. long with a rise of 1,630 ft. and a maximum grade of 34% and average grade of 12%. The line was of three rails or two tracks, the middle rail serving in common with a passing section at midpoint. Two cars were counterbalanced and the cables ran around a drum turned by powerful stationary steam engines at the summit. Much of the line was on a high wooden trestle and provided magnificent views of the Hudson Valley and distant Taconic and Berkshire Mountains. The gauge was the same as on the Catskill Mountain Railroad and cars could be pulled up on it. This was done with baggage and coal for the engines, but never with passengers, who had to change at both bottom and top. The line ran until 1918 when it was abandoned with the other Beach-owned railroads.

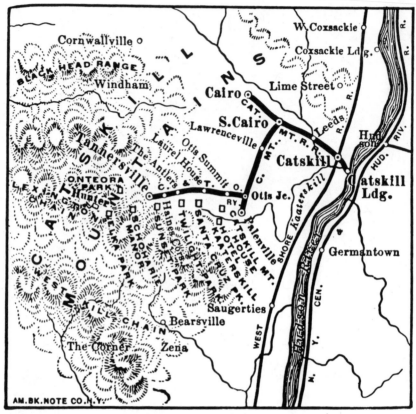

Map of Beach-owned Catskill Mountain, Otis Elevating, and Catskill & Tannersville Railroads.

CATSKILL & TANNERSVILLE RAILROAD

This line was built by Charles L. Beach in 1892 to connect the top of the Otis Elevating Railway with the then narrow-gauge Kaaterskill Railroad at Kaaterskill Station at the west end of South Lake. It ran from the Otis Summit Station along the south shore of North Lake, between the two lakes and along the north side of South Lake. Here cars ran over the Kaaterskill Railroad to Tannersville. The entire line was operated by Kaaterskill Railroad crews until 1896, when there was a dispute between the owners. The Catskill & Tannersville then began construction of their own line and this was completed to Tannersville by 1899. Thus for three years there were two separate competing narrow-gauge lines on top of the mountain. The Kaaterskill Railroad was acquired by the Ulster & Delaware and changed to standard gauge in 1899.

The Catskill & Tannersville ran to the north of the Kaaterskill Railroad. It was a lightly built line catering primarily to passengers and got its nickname, "the Huckleberry Route," because crews would make unscheduled stops to accommodate berry pickers. The line ran, along with the Otis and Catskill Mountain Railroads, until 1918.

The Catskill & Tannersville, Otis Elevating Railway and Catskill Mountain Railroad sold through tickets to New York via the Catskill Evening Line, Hudson River Day Line, West Shore Railroad and New York Central (reached via ferry from Catskill to Greendale—also Beach-owned). It competed with the Ulster & Delaware/Day Line/West Shore combination for the mountaintop traffic to and from the Catskill Mountain House, Laurel House and Hotel Kaaterskill, as well as from the various parks and boarding house towns. Changing fads in resorts, the automobile and the First World War all helped to kill this miniature transport empire, and only in Switzerland can anything like this be observed today, where a combination of lake steamers, narrow-gauge railways, funiculars and standard-gauge trunk lines serve a major resort region.

The Consolidated Railroad Corp. (Conrail) acquired all former Penn-Central and Erie-Lackawanna properties and commenced operations in 1976. Delaware & Hudson remains independent.

This concludes our survey of the railroads serving the Catskill region. It has covered lines ranging from heavy-duty transcontinental trunk lines to lightweight lines such as only seen in amusement parks today. This intriguing subject has been well covered in recent years by some very excellent books, among which we recommend:

Delaware & Hudson by Jim Shaughnessy (Berkeley, California: Howell North Books, 1967)

O. & W.: The Long Life and Slow Death of the New York, Ontario & Western Railway by William F. Helmer (Berkeley, California: Howell North Books, 1959)

The Ulster & Delaware: Railroad through the Catskills by Gerald M. Best (San Marino, California: Golden West Books, 1972. Mr. Best grew up in Port Jervis)

Rip Van Winkle Railroads by William F. Helmer (Berkeley, California: Howell North Books, 1970)

To the Mountains by Rail by Manville B. Wakefield (Grahamsville, New York: Wakefair Press, 1970)

Famous Hotels

All the literature and artistic interest in the Catskill area served to create a desire on the part of many to visit the region. The nineteenth century was also a time when many wealthy people spent summer-long vacations. This was particularly the case with Southerners who wished to escape their sultry, and often unhealthy, climate in the cool North. Philadelphia and New York City because unbearably hot and malaria and other epidemics became common. It must be remembered that there was no air conditioning and that water supplies in the cities were limited and sewerage systems inadequate. The Catskills were the nearest mountains of any extent and size that could easily be reached by boat or train. The Adirondacks were still largely unknown and difficult to reach, and the White Mountains too distant except for residents of New England. All the ingredients were present to stimulate the grwoth of a major tourism and vacation hotel industry.

At first the older stagecoach inns began taking in tourists and summer vacationers. Among the early ones, still remaining in operation today, were Perez Steel's Windham House at Windham. It is a gracious old building with Ionic columns and a Garrison Colonial-style second-floor gallery. Built in 1800, it has been recently restored. Other old inns still

Windham House, Windham. Photo by Alfred H. Marks, 1963.

Catskill Mountain House, showing final evolution after 1845. From old advertisement.

operating are the Tunnicliff Inn of 1802 in Cooperstown, a good example of a town type inn; the Unadilla House of 1804, on Main Street in Unadilla; and the Delaware House of 1813 in Stamford, now operating as the Delaware Motor Inn. Theodore Roosevelt stayed here.

While the old taverns and inns helped somewhat, they were usually located in villages and along busy highways, and were not always comfortable nor within easy reach of the great scenic attractions. To meet the need for more attractively located hotels and the requirements of wealthy and demanding clients, the Mountain House type of hotel was developed. These were the forerunners of today's large resort hotels. Some of the old

Catskill Mountain House, c1900.

Catskill Mountain House, c1957. Photo by author.

mountain houses remain in operation today. We shall take a look at some of the more important and famous ones in the balance of this chapter. However, it is important to take note that there soon developed other hotels and boarding houses too numerous to discuss here. Many are now out of business, having been succeeded in popularity by cottage colonies, private summer homes, and outdoor camping. Also, with development of first the western railroads, and later air travel, distant spots are now competing for the attention of vacationers and there is less requirement today for elaborate hotels in the Catskills than in the past. Let us review some of the more interesting ones:

West front of Catskill Mountain House, c1957. Photo by author.

CATSKILL MOUNTAIN HOUSE

In 1823, partially at the instigation of stagecoach operator Erastus Beach, a group of Catskill Village businessmen formed the Catskill Mountain Association to build accommodations at Pine Orchard on the top of the Wall of Manitou.

On July 4, 1824, a primitive hotel opened its doors. It consisted of ten rooms, including a ballroom and male and female dormitories with bunk beds. A good time was had by all and the view over the Hudson Valley was highly acclaimed. Pine Orchard was then reached by an old wood road from Palenville.

The fame of the view soon spread and demands for accommodation grew rapidly. Soon control of the enterprise came under Charles L. Beach. He improved the old Turnpike Road of 1805 from Catskill to Pine Orchard via Saxe's Farm and made additions and betterments to the hotel. The Mountain House was easily reached from the Hudson River steamboats and was approximately half way between New York City and the popular spa at Saratoga Springs, as well as on the route to Niagara Falls and the West. It soon became a "must" for tourists. Also, Southerners visiting at Newport for the summer developed the habit of taking a tour to Lebanon Springs, Saratoga and the Mountain House. It was during this period that literary personages began writing glowing descriptions of the locale.

By 1845 it had been expanded to fifty rooms, and ultimately, with the addition of two large wings, grew to three hundred. Architecturally it was a patchwork. Initially it was a simple Federalist style structure, but with the addition of a long colonnade with thirteen Corinthian columns

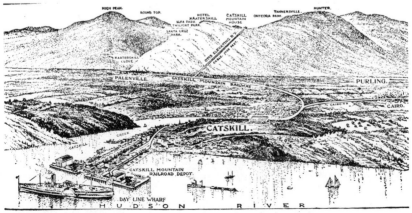

BIRD'S-EYE VIEW OF THE CATSKILLS FROM CATSKILL LANDING

fronting the Hudson Valley, it became an impressive example of Greek Revival architecture. The guest rooms were simple and small, but the quality of the food and drink and service were exemplary for the period. Eventually it was eclipsed by newer and grander hotels, but the Mountain House always retained a faithful clientele and a tone of social superiority. It was always expensive compared to other hotels.

The Mountain House eventually acquired a large estate of three thousand acres including North and South Lake and much of South and North Mountains. Paths and trails were layed out to points of interest and lookout places, with such quaint names as Elfin Pass, Fat Man's Delight, Druid Rocks, Puddingstone Hall, Palenville Overlook, Artists Rock, Bears Den, Glen Mary, Newmans Ledge and Inspiration Point. Until a rather late date the "lawn" was kept rustic and the feeling of the forest came right to the doors of the hotel.

Entertainment included dances, impromptu concerts and amateur theatricals. Sunday was a day of quiet with religious observances. The meals were of the old-time "ordinary" type with "family style" service and no choice of menu—you ate what the host provided. However, the wine cellar was extensive and of notable quality. A popular activity was to rise to see the sunrise. Run by members of the Beach family for most of its history, in the 1930s, with changing clientele, it was leased to an operator named Andron who ran it as a Kosher resort. The last open season was 1942, after which it gradually fell into ruin and the property was acquired by the state for development into the North Lake Camping area. In 1963 the hulking ruin was burned down by the state as the crumbling building was becoming a menace to life and limb. Thus ended "The noblest wonder of the Hudson Valley" in a fiery Götterdämerung.

During the great years there were many famous guests: writers such as the Reverend Charles Rockwell, Lucy C. Lilly, Harriet Martineau, Mark Twain, Henry James and Oscar Wilde; the poet William Cullen Bryant; clergymen Timothy Dwight and Newman Hall; performers Jenny Lind and Maude Adams; composer Charles K. Harris, who wrote the popular ballad *After the Ball Was Over*; inventor Alexander Graham Bell, who exhibited his telephone when a line was established between the Mountain House and Catskill; artists Thomas Cole, Asher B. Durand, Sanford Gifford, Jasper F. Cropsey, William H. Bartlett, Harry Fenn and Winslow Homer; social commentators such as Nathaniel Parker Willis and journalist Thomas Nast. Indeed the great and famous were drawn here. General William Tecumseh Sherman and President Chester A. Arthur visited, as did ex-president Ulysses S. Grant.

To make the hotel easy of access the Beach family operated the famous Otis Elevating Funicular Railroad, the narrow-gauge Catskill Mountain and Catskill & Tannersville Railroads and the Catskill Evening Line of steamers to New York City—not to mention a steam ferry from Catskill to the New York Central at Greendale. Later the Ulster & Delaware had a direct line in conjunction with the West Shore Railroad and private cars and through Pullmans and parlor cars came from as far as Washington, Chicago and Montreal. This was all in addition to the lines of stages they operated and extensive livery stables. Proximity to the famous Kaaterskill Falls also led to development of an extensive one-day excursion trade, many of the excursionists taking a meal at the Mountain House.

Today all vestiges are gone, except for a memorial marker on the site, written by Roland Van Zandt, whose book *The Catskill Mountain House* so well chronicles the history of this institution. There is a remarkable wooden model of the hotel on exhibit at the Bronck House Museum of the Greene County Historical Society on Route 9W near Coxsackie. Extensive reminiscences have been recorded by Greene County historian Mabel Parker Smith and railroad historians Gerald Best and William Helmer.

The Catskill Mountain House summed up the spirit of the Romantic Age in the Catskills and served as prototype for all following large resorts.

Laurel House. Library of Congress.

LAUREL HOUSE

Need soon arose for auxiliary, and less expensive, accommodation. In 1852 Peter Schutt built the Laurel House at the top of Kaaterskill Falls. It was a simple colonial-style building and accommodated fifty guests. It was enlarged in 1881 and 1884 when it gained a large Victorian wing, a cupola and impressive portico, almost doubling its size. It was served by its own railroad stations on two different lines! Remaining in operation until 1963, it had become a ruin by the time it was burnt by the state in 1967. The property has been added to the Catskill Preserve.

MEAD'S MOUNTAIN HOUSE

To the south George Mead erected a modest inn in 1863 in a col at 1700 ft. between Mt. Guardian, then called Sawkill Head, and Overlook Mountain above Woodstock. It was a rather small Greek Revival structure, but it commanded fine views of the Hudson Valley to the southeast and north to the Indian Head Range. It soon came to be simply called "Mead's." For many years it served as a refreshment stop on the road to Overlook Mountain. Today it is a retreat center.

OVERLOOK MOUNTAIN HOUSE

Overlook Mountain, above Woodstock, commands one of the finest views in the entire Catskills. In 1870, a hotel was erected at the 2,978 ft. level by a corporation headed by Artemus Sahler. In 1873 it was enlarged to accommodate 300 guests. A famous guest was President Grant, who made it the "Summer White House" during a short visit. The first hotel

Mead's Mountain House. Photo by Alfred H. Marks.

was destroyed by fire in 1875. One replacement was shortly thereafter built by the Kiersted Brothers (1878). It was anchored to the rock of the mountain by strong cables to keep it from being blown away. Its three stories, 200 feet long with room for 150 guests, presented considerable broadside to the wind.

Soon the Overlook began catering to tubercular guests and assumed the atmosphere of a sanitorium. In 1915 it was purchased by G. Newgold. It again burned down in 1926. Newgold Brothers formed a new corporation to rebuild, this time in fireproof poured concrete. Construction began in 1928, but ceased when the Stock Market crashed in 1929. Materials and fixtures on the jobsite soon disappeared and the unfinished walls still stand, a melancholy landmark. There are rumors that the state may acquire the property.

MOUNT TREMPER HOUSE

Thus far all the hotels have been on mountain tops. In 1878 Captain Jacob H. Tremper, Jr. built the Mount Tremper House on a terrace above the railroad station in Phoenicia, along the Esopus Creek, beneath the slopes of Mount Tremper. It had 130 rooms and was popular with South Americans and high society, the jet set of the times. Its grounds were laid out with fountains and formal gardens, lawns and walks and it generally was a more "finished" specimen than the mountain houses.

LAKE MOHONK MOUNTAIN HOUSE

The year 1870 saw the erection of the Mohonk Mountain House by Albert K. Smiley in the Shawangunks. This hotel is still in vigorous operation.

Mohonk Lake is in Ulster County, west of New Paltz, east of Alligerville, north of Minnewaska and south of Rosendale, atop the Shawangunk Ridge. The name, from the Indian word Moggoneck, later corrupted to Maggoneck, Mohunk and ultimately to Mohonk, means "lake in the sky." The high point immediately east of the lake, now called Skytop, was formerly called Moggoneck Point, Mohunk Point and Paltz Point. Its elevation is 1542 ft. Lake Mohonk is at an elevation of 1246 ft. and covers 17 acres. It is a glacial lake and of a light green color. The lake supports vegetation and fish life. It is spring fed. There is a foot trail around the lake and sand bathing beaches (open to hotel guests only) on the west shore. The Lake Mohonk Mountain House is at the northwest end, where is also located the boat dock. The outlet of the lake is beneath the hotel! It drains into Mossy Brook.

Three hundred acres immediately around the lake were purchased by

*Albert K. Smiley, of Lake Mohonk. Author's
collection.*

*Daniel Smiley, of Lake Mohonk. Author's
collection.*

Albert K. Smiley, a Quaker, in 1869 as a summer home. It soon became
obvious that he could not support such a large tract on his own, and in
1870 he opened the house to paying guests. Previously the tavern standing
on the present site of the Mountain House belonged to a farmer in the
valley named John F. Stokes. The tavern was a popular spot for picnics,
parties and dances. When drunks got out of order, Mr. Stokes would
chain them to trees! Under Mr. Smiley the hotel became a temperance
house and only in recent times have drinks been sold in the dining room,
and till this day there is no bar or cocktail lounge. Strict Quaker principles
prevailed and proper decorum is still a house tradition.

The present large picturesque "Chalet" of over 300 rooms grew from
several small frame structures erected in the 1870s. However, there have
been many replacements, additions and rebuildings and the house has
been kept thoroughly comfortable with modern facilities while retaining
the attractive traditional decor. Much of the present building is of massive
stone and steel construction. Many rooms have their own fireplaces and
balconies, many having extensive, spectacular views. Air conditioning is
not needed, owing to the prevalence of cool breezes, large windows and
high ceilings, and the modifying effect of stone construction. The large
parlor boasts a fine pipe organ, used at daily prayers and for concerts.
Lectures and musicals of unusually high quality and interest are a Mohonk

Lake Mohonk and Lake Mohonk Mountain House looking northwest from Skytop. Catskill Mountains in distance.

tradition. The dining room is also unique. It occupies its own wing and is oval in shape, with a large central fireplace. Picture windows offer a spectacular view of the Catskill Mountains.

The Mountain House has always attracted people of means and of distinguished position in the church, education and government. Presidents Rutherford B. Hayes, William Howard Taft and Woodrow Wilson were among the prominent guests, which also included such noted personages as Andrew Carnegie, Charles G. Dawes and John Burroughs. Albert K. Smiley was interested in the welfare of the American Indian and the cause of world peace; he held various Indian conferences at Mohonk as well as several conferences on international arbitration around the turn of the century. These were important in the formation of the League of Nations. The Smiley family retains their interest in world peace and is host to many members of the United Nations and still holds conferences at Mohonk. The Mohonk Trust is now responsible for work in this field.

The Smileys were pioneer naturalists and eventually expanded the estate from the original 300 to almost 8,000 acres (abutting the 10,000-acre Minnewaska tract to the south). This property embraced crags, cliffs, crevices, lakes, valley, woodland, pastures, farms and rhododendron swamps and the famous Traps. The highest point is Skytop, crowned by the Albert K. Smiley Memorial Tower which was completed in 1923. It

Arial View of Lake Mohonk and Lake Mohonk Mountain House looking southeast, with Wallkill Valley in background. Skytop and Albert K. Smiley Memorial Tower on left with Eagle Cliff on right.

Memorial Gateway, Lake Mohonk Mountain House Estate.

has a beacon light and forest ranger observation station and is open to the public. Views are extensive in all directions. Several quarries atop Skytop have been allowed to fill with water and serve as reservoirs for the Mountain Houses' sprinkler system, providing a fine head of water while remaining inconspicuous. They are over 300 ft. above the hotel. A monumental Testimonial Gateway was erected near New Paltz in 1908, which is now used as the Mid-Hudson-Catskills Museum. The old carriage drive from the valley has been replaced by shorter motor roads and it is no longer possible to enter the grounds through the gateway. Entrance is now effected at Mountain Rest Gatehouse atop the ridge on the public highway. The Mohonk Golf Course and Bonticou Ski Area

Albert K. Smiley Memorial Tower atop Skytop. Photo by author.

and Lodge are also near Mountain Rest. Auto access is strictly controlled at this point.

From the very beginning, formal gardens were laid down and today the floral displays are a famous attraction. There is also an extensive arboretum and experimental garden. The greenhouses are open to the public. There are 60 miles of shale roads, 30 miles of bridle trails, 25 miles of paths and many additional hiking trails and 140 summerhouses on the grounds. Horse-drawn transportation (carriages and sleighs) is still extensively used at Mohonk, and only in recent years have automobiles been allowed to approach the hotel. There is a small "village" near the hotel to house employees, and the residences of the Smiley family are located here. While the hotel is now owned by a corporation, control of this corporation is vested in the family and they still keep a close interest in the daily, as well as overall, operation of the hotel and estate.

In 1963 the Smiley family set up the Mohonk Trust to work on environmental and social concerns. About 6,000 acres of Mohonk land are being transferred to the trust. This land will remain open to both hotel guests and the general public on a nominal fee basis. This has proven necessary to assure preservation of this unique scenic area which could no longer be supported by hotel operations. The land immediately adjacent to the hotel and lake will remain owned by the hotel corporation.

The hotel is open year-round and meals are available to day guests, but reservations are mandatory, especially on holidays and weekends. It is usually impossible to get beyond the Mountain Rest Gatehouse unless you are on the "expected arrivals" list. Telephone 914-255-1000 for reservations, ski and other information. Whatever your planned activity it is a good idea to call to avoid possible disappointment. Rock climbing is popular at the Traps and it is usual to find experienced members of the various mountain clubs. This activity is closely supervised and a fee is charged. Inexperienced persons should not attempt this activity and all climbers must sign in with the patrol. Mohonk and Minnewaska are connected by a carriage road but at the present time through vehicle travel is impractical because of obstructions. The road offers attractive hiking and is still usable by carriages as far south as Traps Bridge over Route 44. There are also various day-use and overnight camps on the grounds. Check with the ranger for locations. Nominal day-use fees are charged on both Trust and Hotel grounds, although day guests are not allowed to use hotel facilities unless taking a meal; limits are clearly posted. Maps are available showing all the various paths and roads and principal points of interest.

There are separate entries in the Gazetteer for the following: The Traps, Eagle Cliff, Skytop, Cope's Lookout, Arching Rocks, Newlin's Cave, the Labyrinth, Gate of the Winds, Cave of Aeolus, Zaidee's Bower. There are simply too many points of interest to list and the Mohonk grounds will bear many rewarding years of exploration. Dogwood and laurel blossom times are particularly attractive.

LAKE MINNEWASKA MOUNTAIN HOUSES

Minnewaska Lake is in Ulster County, south of Lake Mohonk and north of Lake Awosting atop the Shawangunk Ridge, west of Gardiner and east of Kerhonkson. The name means "frozen waters." Lake Minnewaska is a glacial lake, oval in shape, with an area of 38 acres and an elevation of 1,650 ft. The water is crystal clear; the acidity of the water prevents the growth of algae or vegetation. Conglomerate cliffs, covered with pitch pines, laurel, hemlock and white birch, rise to 145 ft. above the lake. A scenic footpath encircles the lake. There is bathing and canoeing and good scuba diving. The lake empties into Coxing Kill at the east end.

Cliff House and Wildmere, the Lake Minnewaska Mountain Houses, overlooked the lake from the north and west, respectively. These mountain houses were founded by Alfred H. Smiley, cousin of the Lake Mohonk

Smileys, in 1879. Mr. Smiley was a Quaker and maintained a conservative and simple atmosphere in a more rustic manner than that of Lake Mohonk. The estate gradually grew to 10,000 acres, incorporating Lake Awosting to the south. Mr. Smiley's original land purchase was in 1876. In 1970 the owners, the Phillips family, disposed of 7,000 acres to the Palisades Interstate Park Commission for formation of the Minnewaska State Park. This incorporates Lake Awosting, but not Lake Minnewaska proper. The Park is a wilderness type operation and offers water sports, camping, snow-mobiling, picnicking,

Alfred Homans Smiley, founder of Lake Minnewaska.

rock climbing and crosscountry skiing. Mud Pond, or Haseco Lake, is a significant site for the study of ecology.

The Mountain Houses continued in operation on the remaining 3,000 acres, which include Lake Minnewaska. There are many miles of carriage roads, riding and hiking trails. The Wildmere was in year-round operation and had a dining room open to day visitors and was fully licensed, the old Quaker restrictions no longer being in effect. Many of the rooms in this charming Victorian building offered private fireplaces and balconies. Old traditions such as hymn sings, carriage rides and theatricals were maintained in conjunction with the emphasis on such new activities as ski touring and golf. The hosts were Ken Phillips, Senior and Junior, and their charming wives—thus maintaining the old Mountain House tradition of family owned and managed resorts. Cliff House burned down on January 1, 1978. The Wildmere closed on January 1, 1980, and burned down in 1986. After much dispute about the future of the property it was acquired by the Palisades-Interstate Park Commission.

Scenic features in the Minnewaska area (see individual entries) are: Haseco Lake (Mud Pond), Murray Hill, Margarets Stone Parlor, Jacobs Ladder, Margarets Cliff, Wolf's Jaw, Awosting Lake, Hamilton Point, Castle Point, Battlement Terrace, Litchfield Ledge, Huntington Ravine, Overlook Point, Fly Brook, Stony Kill and Falls, Rainbow Falls, Kempton Ledge, Echo Rock, Palmaghatt Ravine, Gertrude's Nose, Millbrook Mtn., Pattersons Pellet, Dallas Pool, Peters Kill, Awosting Falls, the Amphitheatre, Beacon Hill, Pine Cliff, Coxing Kill, Sheldon Falls, Dickie Barre, the Traps and Ski Minnie.

Cliff House, Lake Minnewaska. Photo by Alfred H. Marks.

PROSPECT PARK HOTEL

During the 1860s a fine hotel was erected overlooking the Hudson River within the village limits of Catskill. It is described as follows by Wallace Bruce in his *The Hudson by Daylight* of 1901.

> Just out of the village proper, on a beautiful outlook, stands the charming Prospect Park Hotel, unrivaled in its beauty of location. It has a most delightful piazza, four hundred feet long, sixteen feet wide, supported by Corinthian pillars twenty-five feet high, with many private balconies, and

The Wildmere at Lake Minnewaska, from Cliff House. Catskill Mountains in distance. 1960. Photo by author.

Lake Minnewaska and Cliff House. Photo by Alfred H. Marks.

Wildmere Hotel, Lake Minnewaska. Photo by Alfred H. Marks.

Prospect Park Hotel from the southeast, c1875. Note entrance to Catskill Creek.

charming views from every room. The main building is two hundred and fifty feet front, with wing one hundred and fifty feet by forty, situated in a large and beautiful park. This handsome park adjoins the best residence portion of the village, thus affording miles of elegant shady walks and drives near at hand. The views and scenery from the "Prospect" are unsurpassed . . . etc.

The site is now occupied by St. Anthony's Friary.

HOTEL KAATERSKILL

The year 1881 saw the opening of several large and pretentious hotels. A Philadelphia millionaire lawyer, George Harding, had been the "star boarder" at the Catskill Mountain House for a number of years. His daughter required a special diet, and when Charles Beach refused to meet his request for some "fried chicken," but adhered to the rigid ordinary policy, Mr. Harding realized that a more modern and accommodating hotel was required. He soon acquired property atop the western slope of South Mountain, between the Catskill Mountain House and the Laurel House, and erected what was then the world's largest summer hotel. It was four stories high with two towers of six stories, long colonnades and piazzas in the Mansard style. It had rooms for one thousand guests, deluxe cuisine, its own symphony orchestra, and extensive grounds with a private road down Kaaterskill Clove to Palenville. Soon the nearby Kaaterskill Station offered railroad service to all other eastern resorts and to cities as far away as Washington. It was popular with high society and politicos such as President Chester A. Arthur until after the First World War II. It then went into a rapid decline and burned to the ground in 1924. It was never rebuilt. Some ruined foundations can still be seen. The state now owns the property and maintains the private carriage roads for hiking and horseback riding.

Hotel Kaaterskill. Library of Congress.

Grand Hotel, Highmount. Library of Congress.

GRAND HOTEL

1881 saw the height of the "Gilded Age" in the Catskills, with the opening not only of the Kaaterskill Hotel but also the gigantic Grand Hotel and Mount Meenahga House in the Shawangunks. The Grand was built by the Ulster & Delaware Railroad along its line on Monka Hill near Highmount, later called Grand Hotel Station. This is near the present Bellayre Mountain ski resort. The Grand commanded spectacular views of the Central Catskills and of Slide Mountain, recently recognized as the highest mountain in the Catskills by geographer Arnold Henry Guyot of Princeton University.

The hotel was copied after the then famous Oriental Hotel at Coney Island and was of Victorian Mansard construction, with four towers and a long portico adorned with latticework decorations. It was one eighth mile long, straddling the Ulster and Delaware County line. The bar could be moved from end to end of the building as the townships and counties within which the building stood alternately went "wet" or "dry" in those days of temperance agitation. The hotel featured the Diamond Spring for drinking water; a fountain stood in the central lobby wherein the sparkling waters were collected in a marble basin.

Originally the Grand Hotel appealed to the clergy, but later became popular with such socialities as Jay Gould. Because of its railroad backing it retained a high class of service for longer than any other hotel of its type and period. It operated as a first-quality hotel until its closing in 1966. Today a private club occupies the site.

MOUNT MEENAHGA HOUSE

This hotel was erected by U. E. Terwilliger in 1881, 1,200 ft. above Ellenville in the Shawangunk Mountains. It was a five-story wooden chalet with peaked dormers and turrets in the Queen Anne style. It sported one of the first golf courses in the area and catered to the carriage trade. An advertisement of 1901 states, "Laurel, Sweet Brier, and Wild Flowers in Profusion—Miles of Walks and Drives." The view out over the Rondout valley was spectacular. Meenahga means huckleberry in Indian, and picking them was a popular activity, as were walks and picnics to Sam's Point and Verkeerdekill Falls and Lake Maratanza. In 1921 the Terwilliger family sold the hotel and the place suffered a decline. It burned down in 1963. The area is now known as Mt. Cathalia and is a ski resort.

CHURCHILL HALL

Far to the west at Stamford a physician, Dr. Stephen E. Churchill, built a magnificent rambling hotel and casino inside the village, which is on the headwaters of the Delaware and beneath Mt. Utsayantha. It was a very elegant establishment. Opened in 1872 and enlarged in 1883 and 1890, it was the largest hotel west of the Grand and boasted tennis courts, artifical lakes and a music hall. In its later years it operated as an apartment hotel and was known as the Maslynn. It was acquired by the village in lieu of taxes and torn down in 1944.

REXMERE

The Churchill Hall proved such a success that the good doctor soon had to build another hotel. It adjoined the Churchill Hall property and had a golf course, stables, bridle paths and a swimming pool. It had one of the first elevators in the Catskills and appealed to wealthy Cubans and South Americans and the "sporty" set in society. It was acquired by the Redemptorist Order in 1954 and renamed Villa Alphonsus and used as a seminary. It now houses the Rural Supplementary Education Center and offices of the Board of Cooperative Educational Services.

HOTEL WAWONDA

Toward the end of the 19th century the towns along the O & W Railway in Sullivan County began to develop as resorts. In 1892 the Wawonda was built near Liberty by Young, Messiter and Scott. It was the largest structure in Sullivan County. Special trains were run from New York for the gala opening, and the hotel enjoyed great success for a short time. However, as Liberty acquired a reputation as a tuberculosis resort, it fell upon hard times and burned to the ground in a spectacular fire in 1914.

YE LANCASHIRE INN

A peculiarly graceful large Queen Anne structure, with a great arched porte-cochere and bracket verandahs, this hotel was built in 1894 for Frederick William Lancashire, who operated it until 1908. It attracted the super rich, such as Pierre Lorillard and Rosita Sardinia of Cuba, who married into the Spanish royal family. In 1920 it burned to the ground.

SHA-WAN-GA LODGE

Situated atop the Shawangunk Ridge just north of where Route 17 crosses the mountain at Highmount, and easily accessible by O & W Railway, the Sha-wan-ga Lodge was opened in 1895. The view included both the Catskills to the northwest and the Hudson Highlands and Ramapos. It was built for D. G. Carpenter. It was a massive house with over 3,000 sq. ft. of piazzas along with many fireplaces, parlors, dining rooms, etc. The original hotel burned in a spectacular blaze in 1926. Successor hotels operated on the site until the 1960s. It was the southernmost of the large hotels.

OTESAGA

Far to the west at Cooperstown a magnificent hotel opened its doors in 1909. The O-te-sa-ga was built by Stephen C. Clark and Edward S. Clark, who were associated with the Singer Sewing Machine Company and residents along Lake Otsego. The new hotel was of Georgian red brick design with a graceful lantern and Ionic portico. It was the most up-to-date construction possible at the time. Located in the village limits right on the lake front, it commands a superb view up Lake Otsego and is near the Fenimore House and various museums. It soon gained, and has retained, a strong following of well-to-do guests. Today it is possibly the only large hotel operating in the old "grand manner," with functioning ballroom, concerts, a sting orchestra playing at dinner, all sports facilities and elegant public and private rooms. It is superbly maintained and the service is elegant. In past years it was occupied during the winter by a female finishing school. Today it is closely allied with the neighboring Cooper Inn. The Templeton Lounge perpetuates a name familiar to readers of Cooper's novels.

NEVELE

Founded as the Nevele Falls Farm House (named for "eleven" sisters, spelled backwards), this hotel in Ellenville, at the foot of the towering Shawangunk Cliffs, is known today for its tall, round tower and top-grade golf course. It has always remained modern for its time and is among the more luxurious of today's hotels.

GROSSINGERS

Possibly the best known modern hotel in the Catskills, Grossingers was actually located in Ferndale, just outside of Liberty. A sprawling "Tudor Manor" type complex, it overlooks the Southern Tier Expressway. Grossingers prided themselves on having every possible facility, including golf courses and large indoor swimming pools. They featured gourmet Kosher cuisine and big name entertainment. It was founded by Selig and Malke Grossinger in 1914 in a ramshackle seven-room farm house. The food was good and the hosts accommodating and it grew steadily through the years. Later it lost its strong ethnic overtones and assumed a place among the great international resort hotels. It closed in 1986 and is being converted to condominiums.

YOUNGS GAP HOTEL

Located at the highest point on the former O & W Railway and Route 17 between Liberty and Parksville, the massive brick and steel Youngs Gap Hotel was built in 1928 on the site of the former farmstead of William Young. It was among the first Sullivan County resorts to operate year round and featured a large swimming pool, sun parlors, gymnasium and many stores. It accommodated 400 guests, and was also known for its entertainment. It operated until 1967 and now stands abandoned.

THE CONCORD

The newest of the large resorts is the Concord at Kiamesha Lake near Monticello. Arthur Winarick, who made a fortune selling Jeris Hair Tonic, purchased the old Kiamesha Ideal Hotel and remodeled it as the Concord Plaza. By 1941 it was called simply The Concord and it has grown tremendously ever since. It offers all amenities, big name entertainment and deluxe cuisine. It is very posh and also has become a popular center for conventions.

Many other large hotels have operated over the years, not to mention the multitudes of small inns and boarding houses, but the above described ones give a representative sampling of styles in resorts.

Some Famous Catskillians

In the course of our narrative we have told of many famous people who have crossed the stage of Catskill area history, and in Part III we will meet a number of important writers and artists. In this chapter we would like to tell about a few additional colorful people.

SAM GONSALUS

Sometimes spelled Gonzales or Consawley, Sam was born and brought up in the vicinity of Mamakating in the Shawangunks. He was a farmer and lived during the period of the French and Indian Wars. His knowledge of the terrain and the habits of the Indians was such that his counsel was held in high esteem in planning military operations. Also, his bravery and self sacrifice in the cause of his people was widely recognized and appreciated. Possibly of Spanish descent, his family remained in the area for many years. He is best remembered for a spectacular feat of daring.

According to Philip H. Smith, in his *Legends of the Shawangunks*, one day in September of 1758 Sam was hunting atop the ridge, near the Traps, when he was surprised by an Indian scalping party returning from a foray in the Wallkill Valley. The Indians hated Sam and took after him in pursuit, they themselves being chased by a party of irate settlers from the valley below. Sam was a swift runner and knew the topography well. He directed his flight southward towards what was then known as the Big Nose of Aioskawasting, which terminated in a precipitous cliff, and which is the highest point in the Shawangunks. As the Indians were gaining upon him he ran to the brink, and with a whoop of defiance, he jumped off the cliff rather than let himself be caught.

Sam, however, had no intention whatever of committing suicide. He knew that there was a thick clump of hemlocks about forty feet below and he directed his fall so as to land among them. He received only a few scratches and bruises and made his way home. The Indians were unpleasantly surprised a short time later to find him still alive and active.

The point was shortly thereafter renamed in his honor—Sam's Point, which name it still bears.

TOM QUICK

Tom Quick was a famous Indian killer. He was born and raised in the neighborhood of Milford, Pennsylvania, where his father had settled deep in the forest. As a youth he lived among the Indians and learned all their ways. His father was a true friend of the natives and for many years they too treated him well. You can imagine Tom's surprise when one day they treacherously murdered his father. At that time Tom made a vow of vengeance against the redmen. Exact data on Tom's life are scarce, but he is generally believed to have lived between 1710 and 1795 and to have worked at times as a farmer, lumberman and hunter. Later in life he settled permanently near Flatbrookville, New Jersey.

While still young, he and his wife and children settled near Neweiden in Sullivan County. One day, while he was away on a hunting trip, the Indians massacred his wife and children. This did it! Tom became a monomaniac about killing Indians. He hated them all and would hunt them down like animals. He considered them subhuman and had no compunction about luring them into deadly traps and ambushing them. He would even go out of his way to murder even young and totally innocent ones. The Indians became terrified of him. This is hardly surprising inasmuch as it is documented that he killed at least twenty of them and more likely over one hundred! He himself lived a charmed life, which led the Indians to believe that he was under the special care of the Great Spirit. This unusual and tormented man survived to die in his own bed at an advanced age. However, his memory lives on in many a "haunted glen" in the Sullivan County hills.

GROSS HARDENBERGH

Gross Hardenbergh was gross. He was tall and weighed over 250 lbs. He would visit taverns nightly and ask that the table be covered with candles and bottles of wine and viands and enter into orgies of debauchery.

Who was this man? He was the son of Johannis Hardenbergh, to whom was granted the famous Hardenbergh Patent. Gross lived from 1733 till 1808, when he was ambushed and shot by irate tenants in Sullivan County, near Fallsburgh, in the Neversink Valley where his holdings were concentrated.

While an avid patriot in his youth and somewhat a hero in the frontier operations of the American Revolution, in later age his debauched habits gained the ascendency. His father disinherited him and bequeathed his wealth to his wife and children. However, his wife and children died before Gross, and he became their heir.

The Hardenbergh Patent was the subject of much dispute about titles. It was Gross's intention to reclaim lands that had been settled on and improved. To this end he made the lives of his tenants miserable in an attempt to "buy them out cheap." He kicked women and cheated the men.

Finally the poor populace would take no more and he was shot while riding his horse.

SULLIVAN COUNTY HUNTERS

In the wild and woolly days of early settlement, each man and boy had to provide his own meat by hunting and protect himself and those under his care from the depredations of wild beasts such as wolves, panthers, bears, rattlesnakes and wildcats. These animals also attacked the domesticated livestock and not unfrequently attacked and mauled and ate little children. Weapons were more primitive than today and hunting was often quite a dangerous occupation.

Several early natives are remembered for unusual exploits. Cyrus Dodge fought seven panthers at one time. Nelson Crocker cleaned out an entire swamp full of panthers. However, the greatest bravery was that of a spirited little fellow named William Lane who, armed with only a hunting axe and dirk, crept into the den of a wounded panther to dispatch him.

The neighborhood of Forestburgh produced many famous bear hunters, including the Brown brothers, the Burnham and Horton boys and Zephaniah and Nathan Drake. The author is informed by a friend, Mark Sherwood, himself an avid Nimrod, that the bears in the Mongaup Valley still offer a formidable challenge even with modern weapons.

ZADOCK PRATT

Zadock Pratt was an eccentric back-country genius. He was very ingenious and perspicacious and indeed very far-sighted. In addition, he was somewhat of an altruist and philanthropist and, to say the least, an egotist.

Pratt was born in Stephentown, New York, in the western foothills of the Taconics, in 1790. Around 1802 his family moved to the Catskills, finally settling in Jewett Center, in Greene County, after sojourns in Windham and Lexington. While yet a boy he worked at various jobs such as fur trading and store clerking. He went into business on his own in 1812 as a harness maker and saddler.

Tanning was the big business of the time and in 1824 he went to the Palatinate community of Schoharieville to build a tannery. Soon he owned the largest and most modern tannery in the mountains, utilizing much new machinery of his own invention. He began to bring about improvements in the community as well as on his own properties and soon became greatly beloved of the townspeople, who changed the name of the town to Prattsville in his honor. He had many forward-looking ideas about such subjects as town planning, ecology and regional economics. He became an honorary colonel and served for two separate terms in Congress. There he was instrumental in bringing about completion of the Washington Monument and in creating the National Bureau of Statistics.

He was fond of practical jokes such as bundling up in a fur coat on a hot July day and having his team take him for a sleigh ride. He also enjoyed militia re-enactments of famous battles. Once when an itinerant sculptor visited Prattsville he commissioned him to cut bas reliefs in a cliff outside of town to commemorate his achievements. The reliefs include portraits of himself, his children and a favorite horse; they were painted white and are still maintained to this day. There is now a picnic grove at the foot of Pratts Rocks, and a tumulus

Zadock Pratt. Author's collection.

over the grave of some favorite horses. Zadock outlived seven wives and died in 1871. He is buried in the village cemetery at Prattsville and his home on Main Street is now a museum.

JAY GOULD

This famous Catskill native has been much maligned. While not above the sharp financial practices common in his day, he nonetheless maintained a comprehensive vision of a great transcontinental railroad system which, if accomplished as he planned, would have prevented a great deal of the problems besetting that industry today.

Jay could was born in Roxbury in 1836, near the birthplace of John Burroughs. In his youth he worked as a store clerk and, in his spare time, wrote an excellent *History of Delaware County*, and *The Border Wars of New York*. He then worked as a surveyor's assistant and when he had accumulated some money he began investing in railroad stocks. He made the acquaintance of two scoundrels, Jim Fisk and Daniel Drew, who used him as a front man in gaining control of the Erie Railroad. This group ran the Erie into the ground by lack of maintenance, watering the stock and living high on the hog at company expense. There is evidence that Gould did not always go along with this policy of depreciating the property, but that he was outvoted by his associates.

However, it is likely that he was much less innocent in his attempt to

Jay Gould. Author's collection.

corner the gold market. This scheme involved attempts to manipulate President Grant and culminated in a stock market collapse in 1869 known as Black Friday.

After this debacle the stock and bondholders of the Erie finally forced him out of control. He then turned his attention to an attempt to build a transcontinental railroad system. He ultimately gained control of the Union Pacific and Missouri Pacific and approximately half the railroad mileage in the Southwest. His other holdings included control of the New York Elevated Railroad and Western Union Telegraph Company.

Personal idiosyncrasies included belief in crystal ball gazing and taking his "personal cow" with him on his travels. He was tubucular and suffered from a weak stomach. His home at Lyndhurst, south of Tarrytown on the Hudson, where he was a neighbor of Washington Irving, was one of the most famous estates of the time. His daughter Helen continued to live part-time in Roxbury, and after his death in 1892 the family built a Memorial Church there in his memory. His great-grandson Kingdon Gould, ambassador to the Netherlands, still lives at Furlough Lake.

THURLOW WEED

This famous American journalist and political leader was born at Acra in Cairo township, New York, in 1797. He learned printing and worked for several newspapers in western New York State. He published the Anti-Masonic Inquirer and was a leader of the Anti-Masonic Party. He later became a great power in the Whig Party and backed William Henry Harrison, Henry Clay and Zachary Taylor. In 1854 he joined the new Republican Party and eventually became one of Lincoln's staunchest supporters. As a consummate machine politician he helped further the political career of William H. Seward.

Lincoln sent Weed on an important diplomatic mission to England during the Civil War. Weed was very handsome and personally likeable— but thoroughly unscrupulous. He became one of the most famous men of his time and is best remembered as one of the pioneers of "machine" politics. He died in 1882.

OWEN D. YOUNG

A more modern leader of industry is Owen D. Young. Born in Van Hornesville, in Herkimer County, in 1874, Young attended St. Lawrence University and Boston University Law School, where he graduated in 1896. After lecturing there for several years, he moved to New York City and eventually became general counsel for the General Electric Company. From 1922 till 1939 he was chairman of the board. He was also largely responsible for the formation of the Radio Corporation of America (RCA). He served with Charles G. Dawes on the reparations conference after the First World War, and in 1929 he presented the Young Plan.

For much of his life he maintained a home at Van Hornesville and he restored several old houses and a gristmill dating from 1791. He also donated a park, a school and a municipal swimming pool. Mr. Young died in 1962.

PART III
LEGENDS, LITERATURE
AND ART

Legends

THE ROMANTIC ERA

While all the developments documented in the foregoing chapters were going forward the Catskills were also accumulating a Romantic aura. The late 18th and early 19th centuries saw the birth of the artistic and literary movement commonly called the Romantic Movement.

The Romantics saw history through a golden haze and there was a great interest in the antique, the adventurous and the legendary. Associated with this point of view was an almost mystical veneration of nature—and especially of mountains.

While only averaging around 3,500 ft. in its higher peaks, the Catskills were the most easily accessible mountains to the eastern seaboard and especially to New York City. The Hudson River Valley soon became the cynosure the American Romantics found most compelling. It was not long before the adjacent Catskills came in for their share of attention.

Washington Irving, in his *Autobiography*, makes the following statement which well describes the prevailing sentiments of the period:

> Of all the scenery of the Hudson, the Kaatskill Mountains had the most witching effect on my boyish imagination. Never shall I forget the effect upon me of my first view of them, predominating over a wide extent of country—part wild, woodly and rugged; part softened away into all the graces of cultivation. As we slowly floated along, I lay on the deck and watched them through a summer's day, undergoing a thousand mutations under the magical effects of atmosphere; sometimes seeming to approach; at other times to recede; now almost melting into hazy distance, now burnished by the setting sun, until in the evening they printed themselves against the glowing sky in the deep purples of an Indian landscape.

Most necessary to the Romantic turn of mind were legends. However, the country had not been long enough occupied to have accumulated any great store of them. In 1835 a young physician and poet, Joseph Rodman Drake, had performed a tour de force in his *Culprit Fay*, set amidst the Hudson Highlands. This lyric epic in the manner of Wieland's *Oberon* (translated in 1798 into English by John Quincy Adams), deals with elves, ouphes and similar creations of European fancy set amidst American scenery, while offering some of our finest examples of native lyric art:

> The stars are on the moving stream,
>   And fling, as its ripples gently flow,
> A burnished length of wavy beam
>   In an eel-like, spiral line below;
> The winds are whist, and the owl is still,
>   The bat in the shelvy rock is hid,
> And naught is heard on the lonely hill
> But the cricket's chirp and the answer shrill
>   Of the gauze-winged katy-did;
> And the plaint of the wailing whip-poor-will
>   Who mourns unseen, and ceaseless sings,
> Ever a note of wail and woe,
>   Till morning spreads her rosy wings,
> And earth and sky in her glances glow.

Elves and ouphes do not really take well to our American forests. Sources closer to home are required to create a convincing mythology, and what better sources than the aboriginal redskins? The stock of genuine Indian legends was somewhat limited, but soon white American writers were hard at work "improving" or "inventing" "Indian legends." Let us sample a few of their efforts.

THE MAN IN THE MOUNTAINS

Among the early writers in this idiom are Henry Rowe Schoolcraft (1793–1864) and Henry Abbey (1842–1911). Schoolcraft was born in Albany and spent much of his life in the West studying the area and the Indians, and their legends. Abbey was born in Rondout and, for some years, was a journalist in New York City. Later he returned to Rondout, where he was a merchant until his death. He wrote a considerable quantity of verse, some of it with local backgrounds.

What these two gentlemen had in common was a dissatisfaction with the name "Catskill." Schoolcraft claimed that the proper Indian name for the Catskill Mountains was "On-ti-ora" or "Land in the sky." He claimed that according to Indian legend, the mountains were originally a giant who was turned into mountains by the Great Spirit. North and South Lakes were his eyes and the flowing waters of Lake Creek his tears. Indeed the front range does look like a reclining giant from the neighborhood of Hudson and can be well described as such from the Parade in Hudson or from the decks of a steamer in that vicinity or from a southbound Amtrak train. This fact was apostrophized by the late Wallace Bruce:

    Where Manitou once lived and reigned,
      Great Spirit of a race gone by,
    And Ontiora lies enchained
      With face uplifted to the sky.

However, it remained for Henry Abbey to immortalize the legend:

ONTEORA

Moons on moons ago
In the sleep, or night, of the moon,
When evil spirits have power,
The monster, Onteora,
Came down in the dreadful gloom.
The monster came stalking abroad,
On his way to the sea, for a bath,
For a bath in the salt, gray sea.

In Onteora's breast
Was the eyrie of the winds,
Eagles of measureless wing,
Whose screeching, furious swoop
Startled the sleeping dens.
His hair was darkness unbound,
Thick, and not mooned nor starred.
His head was plumed with rays
Plucked from the sunken sun.

To him the forest of oak,
Of maple, hemlock and pine,
Were as grass that a bear treads down.
He trod them down as he came,
As he came from his white-peak'd tent,
At whose door, ere he started abroad,
He drew a flintless arrow
Across the sky's striped bow,
And shot at the evening star.

He came like a frowning cloud,
That fills and blackens the west.
He was wroth at the bright-plumed sun,
And his pale-faced wife, the moon,
With their twinkling children, the stars.

But he hated the red men all,
The Iroquois, fearless and proud,
The Mohegans, stately and brave,
And trod them down in despite,
As a storm treads down the maize,
He trod the red men down,
And drove them out of the land,
As winter drives the birds.

When near the King of Rivers,
The river of any moods,
To Onteora thundered
Manitou out of a cloud.
Between the fountain's crystal
And the waters that reach to the sky
Manitou, spirit of God,
To the man-shaped monster spoke:

"You shall not go to the sea,
But be into mountains changed,
And wail to the last, and weep
For the red men you have slain.
You shall lie on your giant back
While the river rises and falls,
And the tide of years on years
Flows in from a depthless sea."

Then Onteora replied:
"I yield to the heavy doom;
Yet what am I but a type
Of a people who are to come?
Who as with a bow will shoot
And bring the stars to their feet
And drive the red man forth
To the land of the setting sun."

So Onteora wild,
By eternal silence touched,
Fell backward in a swoon,
And was changed into lofty hills,
The mountains of the sky.

This is the present sense
Of Onteora's name,
"The mountains of the sky."
His bones are rocks and crags,
His flesh is rising ground,
His blood is the sap of trees.

On his back, with one knee raised,
He lies, with his face to the sky,
A monstrous human shape
In the Catskills high and grand,
And from the valley below,
Where the slow tide ebbs and flows,
You can mark his knee and breast,
His forehead, beetling and vast,
His nose and retreating chin,
But his eyes, they say, are lakes,
Whose tears flow down in streams
That seam and wrinkle his cheeks,

For the fate he endures, and for shame
Of the evil he did, as he stalked
In the vanquished and hopeless moon,
Moons on moons ago.

THE WITCH OF THE CATSKILLS

We have already alluded to Washington Irving's *Autobiography*. It will
be worthwhile to peruse another excerpt:

My whole voyage up the Hudson was full of wonder and romance. I was
a lively boy, somewhat imaginative, of easy faith and prone to relish
everything that partook of the marvelous. Among the passengers on board
the sloop was a veteran Indian trader, on his way to the Lakes, to traffic
with the natives. He had discovered my propensity, and amused himself
throughout the voyage by telling me Indian legends and grotesque stories
about every noted place on the river, such as Spuyten Devil Creek, the
Tappan Sea, or the Devil's Dans Kammer, and other hobgoblin places. The
Catskill mountains, especially, called forth a host of fanciful traditions. We
were all day slowly tiding along in sight of them, so that he had full time to
weave his whimsical narratives. In these mountains, he told me, according
to Indian belief, was kept the great treasury of storm and sunshine for the
region of the Hudson. An old squaw spirit had charge of it, who dwelt on
the highest peak of the mountain. Here she kept day and night, shut up in
her wigwam, letting out only one of them at a time. She made new moons
every month, and hung them up in the sky, cutting up the old ones into
stars. The great Manitou, or master spirit, employed her to manufacture
clouds. Sometimes she wove them out of cobwebs, gossamers, and morning
dew, and sent them off, flake after flake, to float in the air and give light
summer showers. Sometimes she would blow up black thunder-storms and
send down drenching rains, to swell the streams and sweep everything away.
He had many stories, also about mischievous spirits who infested the
mountains, in the shape of animals, and played all kinds of pranks upon
Indian hunters, decoying them into quagmires and morasses, or to the
brinks of torrents and precipices. All these were doled out to me as I lay on
the deck, throughout a long summer's day, gazing upon these mountains,
the ever-changing shapes and hues of which appeared to realize the magical
influences in question. Sometimes they seemed to approach, at others to
recede; during the heat of the day they almost melted into a sultry haze; as
the day declined they deepened in tone; their summits were brightened by
the last rays of the sun, and later in the evening their whole outline was
printed in deep purple against an amber sky. As I beheld them, thus shifting
continually before my eye, and listened to the marvelous legends of the
trader, a host of fanciful notions concerning them was conjured into my
brain, which have haunted it ever since.

LOTOWANA

With the coming of the railroads and full-scale tourism, it became
desirable that the stock of "legends" be increased. Clarence E. Hawkes

obligingly provided a tale in the style of the popular novels of the day
entitled:

THE TRAGEDY OF THE GREAT TABLE ROCK: A LEGEND
OF THE CATSKILLS

Soon after the great Hudson first navigated the beautiful river that bears
his name, and woke its silent cliffs and dreamy highlands with the thunder-
ous vibrations of his guns, and took possession of the same in the name of
the Dutch sovereignty, there was formed at the confluence of the Hudson
River and Catskill Creek a small settlement and trading post—the site of the
present town of Catskill. What with the natural beauty and fertility of the
surrounding country, and the abundance of fur-bearing animals in the great
woods to the north and west, the community prospered but the sovereign
will of its landholders and the extensive territory granted them by the
authorities long made the settlement a straggling one.

The dreamy highways and shady lanes of the quaint Dutch community
were steeped in the cool delicious balm of a June evening; from far down
the roadway on the wings of the breeze came the dreamy roll of the river;
from a distant elm or maple came the whirring notes of the tree-toad, while
the cricket chirping in the long grass by the pathway, added his musical
mite to the deep symphony of nature.

Suddenly the door of the village inn, by the wayside, is thrown open, and
a tall, lithe figure, in foreign dress, strides hastily through the yard and into
the highway. It is Norsereddin, the strolling Egyptian, and magician and
astrologist, who says that the purest blood of the Pharaohs of Egypt throbs
in his own hot veins. But now his black eyes are shining in the gathering
gloom like the bright stars, his scornful lips are parted in a sneer. "And they
dared to say that I could not win the hand of Lotowana, and my host has
dared to wager me a hundred pieces of gold that I could not do it," he
hissed between his teeth, "and I the lineal descendant of the great Pharaohs,
while she is but the lowly daughter of a savage chieftain! What though they
call him the great Shandaken of the Wabingas, and her the peerless Lotowana, wisest and sweetest of the dusky daughters of the woods—I would
bring the proud old chief upon his knees at my feet, and win the love of his
daughter were he twenty times sachem of the Wabingas."

The following morning saw Norsereddin fully equipped, on his way
toward the mountains, to the great table rock, which was a favorite camping
ground with the old sachems. For the first few miles the trail led through
broad green valleys, watered by placid streams dotted by the sycamore and
maple trees and bordered by distant hills, but by degrees the opposite hills
came nearer and nearer together, their verdant sides became dark with the
spruce and pine, and the broad deep streams were changed to impatient
mountain torrents. And here the deep, cool woods were filled with a myriad
pleasant sights and sounds. The fair anemone and the shy forget-me-not
peeped out from among fragile ferns and silver mosses; the poison laurel
and fragrant swamp pink stood side by side, vying in floral beauty, while
the wild cherry lifted its spotless pennon high among the verdant branches.
The noisy woodpecker tapped on the distant trees; the wary partridge
sprang from the densest cover, while a host of the sweetest songsters flooded
the fragrant forest with their lilting songs. By the time the bright June sun

had reached his zenith, Norsereddin was deep in the mountains, near to the great flat rock and precincts of Shandaken. And now a sudden turn in the trail brings him out on the mountain side, in full view of the Indian village. Not far to the east lies the placid Hudson, winding through peaceful green meadows, while far beyond the eastern hill, [now Berkshire], picturesque and broken, fringed the distant horizon. When Norsereddin entered the village he found the old sachem, sitting by his wigwam, smoking with his beautiful daughter beside him. "Welcome my son," said the old chief to the young Egyptian, as Norsereddin approached. "Welcome to the lodge of Shandaken; though his wigwam is small, his heart is great."

It needed but one glance at the beautiful Lotowana, and the proud Egyptian, who had come to the wigwam of the dusky maiden a conqueror, was changed to a captive and a slave. But who will essay to paint the beauty of this child of the woods; to catch the radiant light that fell from her deep dark eyes, like the smile of heaven upon the soul of the young Egyptian; to praise the glossy sleekness of her raven hair, and trace the perfect lines and curves of her graceful form; or portray her movements, which were like the bending corn that sways in the gentle south wind? She was a pure child of Nature, unfettered and unsullied by the cankering chains of civilization—a spiritual incarnation of the beauty and grace and the freedom of the fields, the flowers and the woods. The old sachem was a grave and venerable man, who had learned his wisdom of the creatures of the earth, and the fowls of the air, and his heart was like the heart of a child. For the next four months the lot of Norsereddin was that of the woodsman and hunter. By night he slept on the boughs of the fragrant pine, and by day he roamed in the mountains, seeking the haunts of the deer and the beaver, watching the flight of the wild fowl and imitating the ways of the red men. But all this time he lost no opportunity for visiting the old sachem and doing homage to his beautiful daughter. The fair Lotowana received these advances as a natural tribute to her grace and beauty. Yet in her maiden heart she feared and disliked the haughty stranger. With her father, who had never ventured beyond the confines of the forest, Norsereddin fared better, and the old chief would listen for hours, with wonder and pleasure, to his stories of the land beyond the great sea, where the dark pale-faces dwelt, and builded monuments and temples so high that the topmost stones were e'en among the stars; and so it happened that the young Egyptian was much in the camp of the Wabingas. But by her father's wigwam, or far away among the distant mountains, the thoughts of Norsereddin were ever with the peerless Lotowana. In the dancing sunbeams upon the mountain torrent he beheld the sunshine of her eyes, in the spotless purity of the wild flower an emblem of her spirit; and so the months went by, until far up on the mountain sides the early frosts had enfolded the oak and the maple in garments of crimson and gold, and deep down in the swamps and valleys had kindled the watch-fires of autumn. The heart of Norsereddin grew so turbulent with passion that he could hold his peace no longer. So he sought the wigwam of the sachem, for permission to throw himself at the feet of the purest and fairest of his children and speak his love. The venerable chieftain was seated by his doorway, contemplating the distant mountains with a look of mingled pleasure and sorrow, when the hopeful young Egyptian approached him. "My father," said the humble suitor, standing with bowed head before the old warrior, "the heart of the dark pale-face is burning within him, and he can find no happiness in his life until the great chieftain gives him his beautiful daughter, and he leads her away to his lodge." A look of sorrow and surprise passed over the face of Shandaken, and he bent his eagle gaze long and earnestly upon the young Egyptian, then slowly and sadly made answer, "My son, it cannot be. The spirit of the Great Manitou has never yet lied to his children, and the rising sun flings the shadow of the old chieftain's daughter toward the land of the Mohawks, and Onondaga, the bravest of warriors and chief of the nation, is waiting to wed her."

All the haughty pride and vengeful anger of Norsereddin's nature mounted to his swarthy cheek, and flushed in his darkly-gleaming eyes. "But I am of the Pharaohs of Egypt," he cried, "and he an untutored savage."

"True, my son," replied the old sachem, mildly, "but he is a red man and a warrior, a child of the forest, filled with the spirit of the rushing torrents; Lotowana, too, is a child of the woods, with the bloom of the wind flowers upon her cheek, the song of the birds upon her lips, and the joy of the glad young deer in her heart; as she was born so she must remain. And it is well, for the fawn does not mate with the panther, or the sparrow with the eagle. Go back, my son, to the land of thy fathers, and choose thee a wife from thine own people, one who will fill thy days with joy and do honor to the son of the great Pharaoh."

Burning with shame and anger at his failure and deeming himself dishonored and insulted by the refusal, Norsereddin struck the old sachem full in the face and felled him to the earth. Instantly an infuriated throng of braves were on the spot, brandishing their clubs and tomahawks, and crowding around the young Egyptian, who stood at bay, with his back to the lodge; and in a moment he would have been hewn down, had it not been for the old sachem, who interceded for him. "Back, my braves," he cried, in a voice that brought each owner's weapon to his side, "Back to your lodges and leave Shandaken to settle with the dark pale-face." As quickly as they had come, the warriors disappeared, and the two were left standing by the lodge, Norsereddin still brandishing his long knife. "Put up thy knife," said Shandaken, "the old chief seeks not thy blood; thou are young and thy blood is hot. Go thy way in peace." Slowly the young Egyptian wended his way down the mountain and along the beautiful valleys that had now grown so familiar to him. But he saw not and heard not, for his heart was filled with passion. All his former love for Lotowana and respect for her father was turned to hatred and scorn, and insatiable thirst for a dark and dire revenge burned in his wicked heart. Once more in the village streets the tall form of the young Egyptian became a familiar figure and again he frequented the old lounging-places. Many were the taunts and queries that were showered upon him concerning his love-making, all of which he met with a scornful silence, only informing his host, secretly, that he had won the dusky maiden, and should some day claim his gold.

About three weeks after the return of Norsereddin to the village, a courier from the mountains brought tidings of the great preparations that were being made in the camp of the Wabingas for the marriage of the beautiful Lotowana to the brave young chief of the Mohawks. Then once more Norsereddin wended his way toward the distant mountains. Once upon the journey he drew from the folds of his long cloak an antique jewel case, exquisitely carved and set with precious stones; then breaking a twig from an overhanging tree, as he strode along, he cautiously touched the spring of the casket with one end. Instantly the case flew open and a poisonous spine of the narcona, brought from the swamps of Nyanza, firmly fixed upon a spiral, shot forth with a vicious thrust, and to make the device more sure, Norsereddin had dipped the spine in a deadly poison, known only to the dark art of the alchemist. Closing the box, while a sinister smile played around his lips, he replaced the casket in the folds of his cloak. All was bustle and confusion on the Indian village, but Norserreddin heeded not the busy squaws, or the lounging braves, but went straight to the lodge of Shandaken. "The heart of the dark pale-face is softened," he said; "he comes bringing tribute to the fair Lotowana and begging her father's forgiveness." So saying, he placed the glittering casket in the hands of the dusky maiden, bowed low to the old sachem, and passed out of the lodge. Then the beautiful Lotowana, with eager fingers, touched the fatal spring, the dainty casket flew open, and the poisonous thorne sank deep into her innocent hand; with a wild shriek, she fell to the earth. In an instant Shandaken was bending over his prostrate child, sucking the nauseous poison from the dark wound. But his efforts were futile, the swelling arm grew livid, great drops of sweat gathered upon her icy temples, while one fearful paroxysm of pain succeeded another, until by degrees, her piteous moaning grew fainter and fainter, the light faded from her closing eyes, and the flower of the Wabingas lay dead at her father's feet.

By this time Norsereddin was far down the mountain, flying from the revenge that he knew would follow on the wings of the wind. Soon he heard the cries of his pursuers, and turning, he saw they were close upon him. He was fleet of foot and the race would have been a long one, but just as they were nearing the valley, the flying wretch stepped upon a rolling stone that hurled him far down the hillside. Stunned and bleeding, Norsereddin staggered to his feet, but before he could gain the thick cover, his pursuers were upon him, and escape was impossible. There was a short but desperate struggle, in which more than one red man received a death thrust from the Egyptian's knife; but he was soon overpowered, bound hand and foot and taken back in triumph. Here a council of the warriors was called, and a bloodthirsty yell soon announced that the sentence was passed. Norsereddin was then placed upon the great table rock in front of the village, fagots of pine and knots from the hemlock were piled about him till only his dark, gleaming eyes and glossy hair were seen. Then a band of hideously painted braves joined hands around the pyre and the wild dance of death was begun. As the first yell broke upon the stillness of the evening air, a torch was applied to the pile and a bright flame shot upward. At first the shrieks and moans of the agonized victim blended with the yells of his tormentors, but soon his feeble moaning died away, as the flames leaped higher and higher. The fury of the fire was soon spent, and in the dying embers the ashes of the cruel Egyptian were common dust with the cinders of the spruce and pine. The same night the sorrowing Wabingas laid their old chieftain and his beautiful daughter [both victims of the deadly poison] side by side beneath the monarchs of the forest.

But who can foreshadow the changes of time? The red men have departed and the tourist and woodsman have taken their places; on the camp ground of Shandaken gleam the white pillars of a famous summer house, and the idle lounger, seated upon the table rock, dreams not of its story of love, hatred and anguish.

It is not unlikely that his legend was written at the behest of the owners of the Palace Hotel, the "famous summer house" mentioned.

WINNISOOK, "THE BIG INJIN"

Travellers on the Onteora Trail, as was the case with passengers on the Ulster & Delaware in former times, often express curiosity about a hamlet named Big Indian, which also gives its name to a valley west of Panther Mountain. This area is surrounded by some of the highest Catskill peaks, including Slide Mountain. Similar curiosity is sometimes also expressed about the name of the Winnisook Club and Winnisook Lake at the foot of Slide Mountain.

There are several accounts of Winnisook, who was the "big Indian." This is the way the legend is told by Lionel De Lisser in his *Picturesque Ulster*, written between 1896 and 1905.

> This little hamlet takes its name from the cognomen given a very large Indian who lived for some time in the locality. His proper name was "Win-ni-sook," and he was said to have been a little over seven feet in height, well formed and a Samson in strength. This muscular giant fell in love with Gertrude, a beautiful white girl, a daughter of one of the earlier settlers named Molyneaux. But the maiden although she loved the dusky warrior, married a young man of her own race, called Bundy, in deference to her parents' wishes. He proving of bad temper and habits, she lived an unhappy life with him for some time thereafter. Win-ni-sook seeing how matters stood, abated none of his love-making, but visited her in secret and finally gaining her consent to elope, he proved his gallantry and lack of morals by running off with her. In his wigwam and among his people they passed several years of happiness, undisturbed by the threats of revenge from the deserted husband that would reach the Indian village now and then. The Dutch settlers who had located in the fertile valleys and plains suffered much from the lawless raids and forays of their copper colored neighbors of the mountains who would steal their sheep and cattle and run them off up the different ravines that open into the Shandaken valley to their mountain fastnesses.
>
> Win-ni-sook and a band of his tribe were returning from one of these raids, which had been successful, a large number of fine cattle having been secured, when they were overtaken at the entrance to the Big Indian valley at a spot now occupied by the Ulster & Delaware Railroad's big curve. Win-ni-sook and a few of his men attempted to hold the angry farmers in check while the plunder was being driven to a place of safety, but Joe Bundy, who was among the pursuers, catching sight of the tall figure of his hated rival, planted a bullet near his heart, the dying giant taking refuge in a hollow tree that stood near, and in which he was afterwards found standing upright and dead by his grief stricken Gertrude. Win-ni-sook was buried at the foot of the pine tree in which he had been found, Gertrude and her dusky children living near the grave until the time of her death.

Wallace Bruce, in his *Hudson by Daylight* of 1901, gives a somewhat different version:

> It is said that about a century ago, a noble red man dwelt in these parts, who early in life, turned his attention to agriculture instead of scalping, and won thereby the respect of the community. Tradition has it that he was about seven feet in height, but was overpowered by wolves, and was buried by his brethern not far from the station, where a "big Indian" was carved out of a tree near by for his monument. An old and reliable inhabitant stated that he remembered the rude statue well, and often thought that it ought to be saved for a relic, as the stream was washing away the roots; but it was finally carried down by a freshet, and probably found its way to some fire-place in the Esopus valley. "So man passes away, as with a flood." There is another tale, one of love but less romantic, wherein he was killed by his rival and placed upright in a hollow tree.

THE LEGEND OF BLOSSOM FALLS

While our thoughts are in the Big Indian Valley let us consider a much longer tale as also told by Lionel De Lisser. This story is considerably closer to "Indian mentality" than that of Lotowana, and might well contain some germs of truth. It is well to remember the political situation between Mohawk, Iroquois and Mohegan as described in our chapter on Indian Period history.

> In the winter of 1890, late one afternoon, I found myself astray after a fruitless bear hunt over the Big Indian Mountain. I had followed the tracks since daybreak and with the coming of night was searching for the trail that leads from Dry Brook in Hardenburgh to the Big Indian valley in Shandaken. Unable to find it, I was prepared to pass the night in the woods, when I was more than delighted to see a light glimmering through the trees. Making my way to it through the deep snow, I found a rough bark shanty into which I was made welcome by the tenant, an old man. He was engaged through the day, he said, in cutting hoop poles. The straight black hair, high cheek bones and coppery complexion of my host attracted my attention and excited my curiosity. After supper I learned that the old man was nearly, if not, a full blooded Iroquois Indian, the last descendant of a tribe that had formerly occupied this region for a time. I found him an interesting companion around the fire that night, full of the weird stories and legends of his people. One of Blossom Falls told to me before the dying embers of the open wood fire, late into the night seemed worthy of record, so after looking up the historical parts, I present it to the reader.
>
> At the time of the discovery of the Hudson, that part of the present counties of Greene and Ulster which borders on this river was inhabited by the Mingua Indians, a mixed band composed of branches or clans of the Minnisinks, Nanticokes, Mincees and Delawares. They had emigrated from the upper valley of the Delaware, a region known to the early Dutch settlers as the "Land of Baca," and following the Neversink River and the Esopus Creek had reached the banks of the Hudson. Here they were classed and

known to the settlers as the "seepus" or River Indians. Their principal village and fort was located at Wiltwyck, a spot lying a little to the west between the sites of old Kingston and Rondout.

Along the east bank over the river, resided the Mohicans or Mohekander Indians. More inland and extending from Castle Island northward to the lakes on the east side, were the Maguaas or Mohawks and the Iroquois. The Mohawks and the River Indians were bitter enemies, numerous battles being fought between them for the supremacy, victory in wanton fickleness smiling first on one and then on the other.

Brown, in his history of Schoharie county, and Rev. Charles Rockwell ["The Dutch Dominie of the Catskills"] in his "Catskill Mountains and The Region Around," as well as other early historians, relate that the final battle was fought on an island near the mouth of the Catskill Creek for the honor of naming a head chief from their own tribe to preside over all. The battle raged for a whole day with changing fortune until evening, when the Mohegans obtaining the advantage, the Mohawks retired to another island and resorted to stratagem. They built numerous fires and hanging their blankets upon the bushes, draped them so as to represent men on guard, and dressing the fallen trees and logs in the same manner to represent a sleeping army, they awaited in ambush the expected attack. The Mohegans falling into the snare and believing the Mohawks to be off their guard and sleeping, dropped quietly into the river and silently swam to the island of their enemies, forming on the dark beach and with hideous yells and whoops, making a terrific onslaught upon the supposed sleeping camp. The trap laid for them by the Mohawks was successful, the bright fires disclosing them plainly to their foes, who shot from their ambush and then fell upon them with knife and tomahawk. The Mohegans were defeated with severe loss, and finding themselves unable to continue the struggle further, a treaty of peace was made by the terms of which the Mohawks were to elect the King, whom the Mohegans were to reverence and furthermore to call them, as a title of honor, "Uncle," for evermore. The war chief of the Mohegans, he who had led his tribe to victory in the earlier battle and headed them in their disastrous attack upon the sham camp, was called "Wanatuska," or Black Thunder. He was an old warrior long respected in his tribe for his wisdom and bravery, and loved for his misfortunes and sorrows, his wife and three sons having been killed in a night raid and surprise upon the village by their fierce neighbors, the Iroquois. Not only had they been killed, but their scalps had been torn from them and carried off by their exultant enemies. The old chief had refused to be comforted or select a new wife from either the many maidens offered from among his own tribe or neighboring ones, preferring to share his wigwam alone with his only remaining child, a boy who bid fair to inherit all those qualities of bravery in the field and wisdom in the council that had so endeared the father to his tribe. Wanatuska was the sole tutor of his boy, perfecting him in the use of such simple instruments of war-fare as was then employed, and ever instilling in his young mind a hatred for the destroyers of his home. In the morning when the old chief arose, he would say to the sleeping boy beside him, "Arise Lotowanka, the moon has gone to sleep deep in the great salt water. The sun is here. Many scalps are swinging from the scalp pole of our lodge, but I see none of the dogs of Iroquois among them." In the evening as they sat before their humble meal, he would say, "Our wigwam is empty. Old age comes upon me with each night. The leaves are dropping from the tree and soon the blasted trunk will fall and you will be alone. Then when the soft spring winds blow so still and warm and melt the snow upon the Onteoras, our mountains of the sky, thy heart will melt beneath the warm love light of some dark eyed maiden of our tribe, and yearning in thy solitude for love and home, you will forget as does the mountain brook its course when filled with winter's melting snow, the trail that leads towards the setting sun. The dower for thy wife should be four scalps torn from the Iroquois with thy own hand. My son, let no maiden raise the curtain of thy lodge till then, for I shall watch thee from the spirit land." It is not to be wondered at, that the young Lotowanka grew up full of hatred for the despoilers of his home and with a firm resolve of fulfilling his father's commands and his own desires. The old chief had taught his son to shoot the arrow and wield the tomahawk and knife, and with knee pressed hard upon the prostrate body of a fallen foe, the grim old chief had taught his boy to tear the reeking scalp from bleeding crown. Instructed by his father he had passed through the trying ordeal deemed necessary to prove a warrior and awaited with impatience the opportunity to win the eagle feather of a brave.

The dispute between the Mohegans and Mohawks over which tribe should elect a common King or Sachem had waxed warmer and warmer, until the hot bloods of each tribe resolved on war. The tomtom had been beaten and the weird scalp dance had been danced in the Mohegan village. The war party formed with Black Thunder as chief, included Lotowanka and nearly all of the best warriors of the tribe. One by one they had fallen into place and bedecked in feathers and painted with all the hideous art of savagery, had wended their way from out the little clearing that surrounded the village and silently treading in each others footprints, disappeared in the dark foliage of the surrounding forest. We will not follow them on their way as they moved like a huge serpent in and out among the trees along the trail that led to the river. Arriving there they found their enemies encamped and waiting for them on Wanton Island, near the present village of Catskill. Crossing the river in canoes some distance below and passing through the woods along the west bank until they reached a spot some distance above the island, they threw themselves into the river, and taking advantage of the current soon effected a landing, and a terrible battle unsued in which the Mohawks were beaten and fled at nightfall to a neighboring island. There they plotted and carried out the stratagem told in the opening notes. Young Lotowanka had fought with great bravery, earning from his old father a grunt of satisfaction, accompanied by the single word, "Good," and exhausted by the long march and struggle that had followed, had sought a place to rest amid the slain that lay upon the battle field. In the distance could be plainly seen the camp fires of the Mohawks, and by the light they shed could faintly be discerned the forms of the sleeping warriors as they lay shrouded in their blankets, while here and there the upright, motionless figure of a sentinel silhouetted against the light. Old Black Thunder sleepless and watching hidden had noted all this and more, for what rashness was this? The east side of the island was left unguarded, once gained, the slumbering camp was at their mercy. Quietly the Mohegans were aroused and one by one silently without a splash entered the water, and wading out as far as possible committed themselves to the rapid stream, which soon landed them upon the unguarded beach. Forming in a semicircle they crept through the underbush to arise at a signal from their chief and rush with yells and whoops upon the motionless forms before them. Too late they discovered the trap into which they had been decoyed. Answering yells and whoops resounded from all about them and from every side could be heard the twang of the bow as showers of arrows on their mission of death sped from out the surrounding gloom, to find their victims so plainly disclosed by the light of the camp. Trying to rally his braves, Wanatuska, pierced with a number of arrows, had fallen. Lotowanka, hearing his father's death cry, and in his grief, regardless of all else. rushed to his side and raised the head of the dying chief. "Lotowanka! It is good," said old Black Thunder faintly. "We are beaten. Save yourself for the Iroquois. Do not forget. Leave me for I have but a few minutes to live. Save my scalp if you can." There was but a moment ot think. The Mohawks had arisen from their ambush, and with tomahawk and knife uplifted were ready for the final rush upon their demoralized and fearfully diminished foes. Lifting the expiring chief with superhuman strength over his left shoulder and grasping his tomahawk firmly in his right hand, he sought and found in the melee that followed an opening to escape, but not without a struggle. Seen and pursued, he had nearly eluded his pursuers and gained the bank, when he found that he had been headed off. Dropping the dead chief upon the ground, without a moment's hesitation, he severed the head from the body, and clutching it by the warlock wormed his way through the dense undergrowth that lined the shore and lowering himself with one hand by a tree branch into the dark water of the river, floated with the stream past the disastrous scene of the fight, now made hideous by the cries of the wounded who were being tortured and the triumphant yells of the victors. Trailing his ghastly burden he soon drifted out of sight and hearing them striking out he swam with the current, reaching the west shore in a little cove just above the site now occupied by the village of Malden. Here he crept up under the shelter of the thick foliage which overhangs the river, and placing the still bleeding and hideously painted head upright upon its stump in front of and facing him, he bowed his head upon his clasped knees in silent grief and watched with patience through the long night until the grey light of morning came. During his lonesome vigil, unbroken save by the ripples which, breaking on the beach would wash to his very feet to carry back a crimson stain, he had thought of the future and formed his plans for it. His father and the best of his tribe were slain. No kin remained. Nothing was now left him but revenge. First his father's trust, "the old score with the Iroquois," then the new one. Kneeling before the fearsome, ashen head, he placed his hands reverently upon it and looking into the staring, sightless eyes he said softly, "Father, hear thy son, Lotowanka will not forget." Then arising to his feet as the first rays of the sun shot upward in the east he lifted his arms with clinched hands far above his unturned head and cried "Then the Mohawks." After washing the war paint from his face and body he carefully infolded his father's head in birch bark and proceeded on his way westward in search of the Iroquois. He knew that a branch of that large tribe was located to the west, somewhere among the "big mountains," in a country known to the Indians in their tongue as Shandaken, so he traveled in that direction, guided by the sun and the bark of the thickly growing hemlocks, until he reached the Esopus, near the present postoffice of Beechford, from there he followed the creek until he saw a small party of Indians a short distance ahead, whom he recognized by their paint as Iroquois.

Hiding the head in a small cave that was near at hand, he joined them and learned that he was in the land of rapid waters. In answer to their questions he told them that he was a Seepus or river Indian and that in a quarrel he had killed the son of a chief and had been forced to leave his tribe, and made a request to remain with them.

The Iroquois, seated in a circle about him, gravely listened to his story in silence, expressing neither doubt or belief. When he had finished their headman arose and said, "Our brother has spoken, and his words seem good. The Iroquois are at peace, they have washed the red paint from their faces and the tomahawk has been buried many moons, but the wild deer knows not when the hungry wolf will spring from the covert nor the grouse the moment of the hawk's swift swoop. Our ears have heard your words. Our tongues shall speak them to the wise men of our village and they shall answer them. Till then, unharmed, remain with us."

Lotowanka placing his tomahawk and knife at the feet of the spokesman, the party formed in Indian file, with Lotowanka near the centre, and started on the back trail for the Iroquois village. Their way lay through the beautiful Big Indian Valley, then an unbroken forest of giant hemlocks, and up the steep hill that commences at Dutchers' to the flat just above the site, now occupied by "Hawk's Roost," the Summer home of the Rev. Mr. Lewis. Here the Iroquois had planted their village, surrounded on all sides by a country teeming with game and numerous streams that contained an exhaustless supply of fish. On arriving, Lotowanka was placed in confinement until the following morning, when the head chiefs and the older men of the tribe assembled at the council lodge—a square log house thatched with bark that stood near the centre of the encampment.

Entering one by one they seated themselves gravely against the sides of the hut. When all entitled to share in the council had entered and were seated, a pipe was lighted and passed in silence around the circle, each in turn taking a few whiffs and handing it to his neighbor. Then the party that had brought Lotowanka to the village entered, and placing themselves at one side of the circle their head man arose and told of the meeting with Lotowanka, his story to them, and request. The pipe was again passed and Lotowanka was brought in and seated opposite an old warrior and chief, who, by right of his age and rank, presided over the council. After a short silence, the aged chief arose and addressing the young Mohegan said: "The ears of the Iroquois are open; let the young man speak; but let him think first so that his words may be straight, for words are like the waters of our mountain brooks, they come not back when passed."

Lotowanka then told his story as he had told it to the hunters and in answer to the questions put to him by different members of the council further stated that his name was Kohokee, and that he was a Mohegan, that in a fight between his tribe and the Mohawks, that had taken place a few days previous, on one of the islands of the river, his tribe had been beaten and their warriors nearly all killed, only himself and a small band escaping to the main land.

A dispute had arisen between the survivors as to who should succeed to the chieftainship made vacant by the death of Wanatuska, who had been killed on the island. Lotowanka, his son, a very young man with but little experience, made claim to the vacancy with so much warmth that the dispute ended in a quarrel and finally in a fight in which Lotowanka had been killed, and that fearing the anger of his people he had fled. This story was artfully contrived, for Lotowanka knew that the Iroquois would hear, if they had not already heard, of the fight on the island and death of Wanatuska, as well as of his own disappearance.

When he had finished he quietly seated himself and awaited the decision of the council. The pipe was again passed from hand to hand, each one as it was received drawing a whiff or two in silence and passing it to his neighbor or holding it in his hand, addressed the meeting.

When all had finished and the pipe had again reached Krapatoa [the old chief], he arose and holding it by the long reed stem, advanced toward the center and said, "My son has spoken with a straight tongue. His mouth is not crooked, neither is his tongue forked like the serpent, for our young men have brought us word of the river fight and the death of the Mohegan Wanatuska and his son.

It is good; the lodges of the Iroquois are open; let the Mohegan enter; let him prove himself a brave; then we will change his blood and he shall take a wife from among us and so forget forever Cohohatatia, the mighty river of the Onteoras."

Then knocking the ashes from the pipe into the smouldering council fire the meeting was dismissed and Lotowanka was free to come and go as he would and to work out the dark purpose that had brought him to the land of the Iroquois. Months passed, the heavy foliage on the mountain side had changed from green to golden yellow, purple, crimson, red and brown. The white blossoms of the mountain laurel long had fallen and the clearings now were all aglow with sumach and the golden rod. Lotowanka, skilled in woodcraft and the chase, had proved himself a hunter, and in consequence the recipient of many a warming glance and smile from the brown, dark-eyed maidens of the tribe, for the Aborigines not unlike their pale faced sisters of to-day saw much to admire in a good provider, but he heeded them not nor heard the low plaintive notes of the love song that come softly to him as he passed the berry patch or village spring. Silently he passed into the forest in the morning and as silently returned at night or when ready, to drop some game or venison before Kra-pa-toa's lodge and pass on to his own abode. Such gifts were welcome to the old man who could hunt but little himself and had several mouths to feed. Late in the fall trouble broke out with the Mohawks, who had become very annoying in their encroachments and extremely arrogant since their great victory over the Mohegans. In the several battles that followed, Lotowanka distinguished himself, a number of fresh scalps hanging from his lodge pole that had formerly belonged to his old enemies. At the close of hostilities, late in the winter, he was adopted into the tribe with all due formality, drinking a mouthful of blood from a vein opened in the arm of Kra-pa-toa so as to be of the same blood as his foster father and receiving the name of Skat-nek-ta [the silent one.] The soft south winds blew through the hemlocks and shook the white coverlets from their branches. Old winter that had robbed the forest of its leafy dress and had been asleep so long, awoke to slink away down the mountain side in tears, that swelled the Esopus to a roaring torrent. From out the dripping moisture of the hills the arbutus raised its tiny petals and perfumed all the land. The wild dove cooed and sought a mate. Lotowanka, since his adoption, had been thrown more into the society of old Kra-pa-toa and his family which consisted of an aged wife, a crippled son and an only daughter, a young girl of rare beauty named Ta-wa-sen-ta [Blossoms of Spring.] She had a willowy, graceful figure, large soft brown eyes, small mouth, but lips that were full and red and shaped like her sire's bow, and long straight black hair that fell from the birch band about her brow nearly to the fringe around the bottom of her deer skin skirt.

Lotowanka or Skat-nek-ta as he was known to her had told her that her voice was like the singing of a low-land brook, and he had told her to look down into the shady spring at dusk and she would see the fairest maiden of her tribe. She knew not what he meant, but she had looked and seeing only her own face reflected, she told Skat-nek-ta so, but he had laughed and said, "My little sister must look again." So every evening when she went to bring the water for the night, she would look down deep into the spring, until at last seeing but her own face, it came to her what he meant and the warm blood flushed the brown face, and she became very shy when he was near and would sit no more at his feet to hear the legends of the tribe, but steal away and looking into the spring would sit and think over what Skat-nek-ta had said to her. One day he came quietly upon her and standing over her, as she bent over the spring, his own face had been reflected in the pool beside her own. Startled, she had attempted to arise, but he caught her in his arms, and bending her head backward and kissed her on her eyes and on her mouth, saying, "Ta-wa-sen-ta has found the lady. Skat-nek-ta's heart and wigwam are empty. Will the early blossom enter both?" And he said many words that she could not remember, for it was like a dream to her. When he had let her go, she fled through the woods like a startled fawn back to the village without replying. Lotowanka, unable to make her speak and mistaking her silence for denial, sadly wended his way [when she had fled from him] back to his lonely lodge, for he knew but little of women and loved the girl with all the wild passion of his Indian nature. In the morning he bid Kra-pa-toa good bye and departed without a word to Ta-wa-sen-ta on an extended hunt. She watched him through the opening of her father's lodge until out of sight, then passing out she followed his trail a little way and stooping to the earth pressed her lips deep into a foot mark he had left imprinted in the sandy soil. Old Kra-pa-toa, who had seen all from his lodge, smiled, a rare thing for him to do, and turning to his aged wife said, "It is well. After the blossom comes the fruit. Kra-pa-toa's heart will be glad." Days passed. Ta-wa-sen-ta worked patiently upon a pair of dainty moccasins for Lotowanka, the measure for which she had taken from his foot prints. Her little store of beads, tiny pierced shells and colored quills, were nearly exhausted, but still she worked, adding and changing with the patience known only to a woman when working for a man she loves. A week or more had passed when one evening, she who had listened and watched through the day and night without ceasing, heard a footstep approach; then some game was dropped within the enclosure and the steps went on to Lotowanka's lodge. "Skat-nek-ta is here," said the maiden to her father. Ta-wa-sen-ta must go to him, and taking the finished moccasins with her she passed out and over to where Lotowanka sat before his tent and kneeling before him unloosened his soiled and worn moccasins from his feet and replaced them with the ones she had embroidered. Then folding her hands and still kneeling, she said softly, "Tawansenta has heard the wild buck calling from the forest on the mountain side and seen the timid doe go forth to meet him. She had heard a song bird singing on the branches of a tree until a little feathered mate would flutter to the twig beside him. 'Spring Blossoms' has heard the 'Silent One' a calling through the day and night and she has come to him." And Lotowanka, after the manner of an Indian, was glad and comforted her and in due time bargained for her with old Krapatoa and all arrangements were completed for the simple ceremony that would make her his wife. Lotowanka now moved his lodge away from the village to a wild spot called by the Indians "Da-yeh-ju-ga" [the place where the storm clouds meet in battle with the great serpent,] so as to be nearer to the best hunting grounds, which lay on the south mountains of the Big Indian Valley. Here near the bank of a mountain torrent, called by the natives "Tears of the Cloud," on account of its source being high up on the mountain top, he erected his wigwam and awaited the day that would bring Tawasenta to him, but not in idleness, for the bargain that old Kra-pa-toa had made with him for his daughter called for many furs and pelts and he must need to work hard to win her. At last, one morning when he had nearly completed his task, just as he was setting out from his lodge for the day's hunt, he caught sight of a large grey wolf gnawing at something in the brush a little way above him. Scenting danger the animal tried to escape when Lotowanka's arrow laid it low and the strange thing on which it was feeding, and which it had attempted to carry off, rolled down the hillside to the hunter's feet. It took but a few minutes for the horrified Mohegan to discover that the half eaten, dried up, shriveled thing at his feet was the head of Wanatuska, his father. Recoiling, he prostrated himself before it in superstitious horror for he saw in this peculiar visitation the wrath of his parent at his neglect and failure in fulfilling the trust that had been left with him. Murmuring, "Lotowanka will not forget," the conscience striken Indian lifted the ill-omened thing, talking to it as he would have done to a thing of life and promising to keep the trust, carried it to his lodge. There he painted it and himself in the war paint of the Mohegans. Then dressing as a warrior of his nation, he gathered up his pelts and departed for the Iroquois village, saying, "Wanatuska shall see Lotowanka has not forgotten."

Kra-pa-toa was sitting before his tent dozing in the sunshine. Near him reclined the crippled son engaged in extracting numberless small hedge-hog quills from the mouth of a favorite hound. A thin curl of blue smoke arose from the opening at the top of the wigwam from within which could be heard the voice of Ta-wa-sen-ta singing as she helped her mother about her household duties. Suddenly Lotowanka appeared, and striding up to the old man threw the bundle of pelts before him saying, "Shat-nek-ta has come for Tawasenta." Surprised to see the young man painted and dressed as a Mohegan, that costume having been discarded since his adoption, Kra-pa-toa sat motionless and without raising his eyes said, "Tawasenta awaits the coming of Skat-nek-ta. Hodenosawnee [of the people of the long house—the Iroquois] when he comes she is ready." Disregarding the insinuation, Lotowanka folded his arms and drawing himself up to his full height proudly answered. "The blood of a great war chief, a Mohegan sachem flows through my veins. The mouthful of Iroquois blood I have taken is not strong enough to make me forget. Skat-nek-ta would appear before his bride as becomes a warrior of his rank. It is the custom of his people. When a Mohegan goes forth to take a wife he paints as if for war to signify the strife and hardship of a single life. The bride on entering his lodge washes the paint from his body to signify her new duties and the peace that enters with her in the married life to come." "Hump," said old Kra-pa-toa, "The Mohegans are a strange people. I thought it went the other way." The explanation was satisfactory, however, so after counting the skins, the two entered the lodge and Ta-wa-sen-ta was given in marriage to Lotowanka. At the close of the simple ceremonies, while the bride was gathering her few belongings together preparatory to her departure for her home, Kra-pa-toa began singing in a low tone, swaying his body back and forth in unison with the rhythm of the monotonous chant. He was proud of his son by adoption and marriage and had listened to his boast of lineage and fighting blood with satisfaction and pleasure, but not wishing to be out-done and desiring to stand well in his son-in-law's esteem, was reciting the history of his past greatness, the battles he had fought, the enemies he had killed and the manner of their killing, as his people were wont to do at scalp dances. As the chant proceeded and he recounted his exploits of war and blood, the old warrior became more and more excited and pointing to the dried scalps hanging before him in succession, he would creep about the inclosure to spring upon an imaginary enemy, an act with tomahawk or knife in the manner in which they had been gathered in. Finally he came to a bunch of four, one of which had the long hair of a woman. The story he chanted of them caused the muscles in Lotowanka's impassive face to twitch for it was the story that Lotowanka had heard so often from the lips of Wanatuska and he realized that the withered things at which Kra-pa-toa was pointing with his bony finger were the scalps of his mother and of his three brothers. When the chant was finished he left the lodge in silence followed by Tawasenta and strode back toward his abode. When they came to the Esopus Creek he bade the girl remain and await his return. Creeping through the forest with murder in his heart, he stealthly approached the isolated habitation of old Kra-pa-toa, and finding the crippled son asleep in the sunshine dispatched him with a stroke of his tomahawk, and entering the lodge hurled the same weapon dripping with the blood of her son at the head of the old squaw, then turning to Kra-pa-toa, who half asleep had started from his couch, he cried, "I am Lotowanka, the son of Wanatuska the Mohegan," and tearing the scalps of his people from their fastenings and shaking them in the face of the old Iroquois he continued, "Wanatuska has sent me for them and for yours!" and uttering a wild whoop the crazed Indian hurled the deadly axe at the aged chief, who had half arisen and was in the act of drawing his knife to defend himself. Lotowanka's aim had been true, but the handle of the weapon revolving rapidly as it sped in its flight struck the center pole of the lodge, deflecting its course slightly so that the sharpened blade was buried in the old man's shoulder instead of his head, as he intended. In a second Kra-pa-toa was on his feet and the two stood with heads bent forward face to face, armed alike with a knife only. Watching for an opening, they cautiously crept around and towards each other and for a moment, standing with crouched bodies and drawn muscles, then with the shrill war cry of his tribe the old Iroquois warrior sprang at the Mohegan, clasping him about the waist and with a quick stroke thrust the knife into his side. Badly hurt, Lotowanka pressed the old chief's head backward from him exposing the throat and plunged his long knife downward deep into it. Pushing him away again the knife descended, the stricken man staggering blindly for a moment and falling at his feet a corpse. With a few quick strokes Lotowanka removed the scalps of his three victims, and leaving the bodies as they lay, staunched his wound as best he could and returned to the place he had left Ta-wa-sen-ta. Seeing the scalps, and her husband besmeared with blood and wounded, the girl was naturally amazed and frightened. In answer to her hurried question of alarm Lotowanka said nothing, but bid her follow him. Accustomed to blind obedience from childhood she took her place behind him and crossed the creek. They ascended the mountain to Da-yeh-je-ga, the spot selected by Lotowanka for his hatibation. Reaching the wigwam he drew the curtain aside and bade her enter, which she did, but only to recoil with horror at the sight of the grotesque head that confronted her. Pushing the trembling girl before him her husband entered and laid his trophies before the horrid object, then turning to the young wife who had fallen upon the ground and hid her face, he told the wretched story of his father's trust and the manner in which he had fulfilled it.

By the time he had finished, the loss of blood from his wound, which was a fatal one, had so weakened him that he was unable to stand steadily upon his feet. It had also served a better purpose, for his insane frenzy was passing from him and his clearing mind began to realize the enormity of the inhuman acts he had committed. The silence that followed his story was unbroken for some time except by the low wail that came from the prostrated girl. Then the rapidly sinking man continued in a voice much weakened, "Lotowanka would have killed and taken the scalp of Ta-wa-sen-ta, but the evil spirit that has possessed his soul has departed from him and his heart is filled with grief and sorrow at what has been done. Let the daughter of Kra-pa-toa avenge the death of her people." Reaching his stained tomahawk toward her he continued, "A Mohegan brave fears not death. It is but just."

Dazed by the rapidity of which one horror had succeeded another during the few hours that had followed her marriage, Ta-wa-sen-ta had remained motionless upon the spot on which she had fallen on first entering the lodge. As the trembling and much weakened voice of the man she loved reached her ears it penetrated and awakened her numbed brain and opened the flood gate of her bursting heart. With a cry of anguish she sprang to her feet and caught the tottering man in her arms and laid him upon what was to have been their nuptial couch, and raising his head upon her lap she pressed her lips upon his damp forehead and on both closed eyes, moaning, "Ta-wa-sen-ta has no people. Thy people are my people." But he heard not for exhausted and unconscious he had passed into that deep sleep that comes before death.

Just as the sun was sinking behind the distant hills and the shadows that had crept upward from the deep valley below lay long upon the mountain side, the dying man awoke, delirious, calling, "Yes my father, I come, but the way is long and rough. I will need the moccasins my sweet lover has made for me. My Ta-wa-sen-ta. My wife." Semiconscious for a moment he bid her place the shoes upon his feet and help him arise. Then supported by her arms and carrying the scalps and head they passed out of the lodge and up the side of the ravine a little way to the flat rock above the falls that now bears the name of the girl. The stream was full at this time, the spring rains having filled "The tears of the cloud" [as it was called] to overflowing. It rushed down its steep bed, carrying all before it, and leaping from the rocky ledge on which the two were standing to fall far down and break into foam and spray on the rocks below and rush madly on through the debris that clogged the way in its path, to the Esopus in the Valley. Drenched with the spray, as they stood at the very edge of the overhanging rock, Lotowanka threw the hideous head and the scalps afar down into the boiling water. Then taking his wife in his arms he pressed her to his heart and kissed her saying, "My wife must not weep. The journey is long, but Lotowanka will rest on the border of the spirit land and wait with arms wide open to greet his love when she comes." But she refused to untwine her arms from about him or lift her head from his breast, whispering, "My husband will have need of me for the way is long and dark. I must not leave him." And again and again she murmured the tender, trusting words of Ruth of old that has found and will find an echo in the hearts of all women of all nations and color for all time: "Whither thou goest, I will go." Suddenly Lotowanka paused in his efforts to free himself and with upturned face and eyes staring into the darkening blue ether above, stretched his arms wide open as if in greeting and attempted to utter the cry of his people, but the sound died away in a choking gurgle as his life blood welled from his open mouth down upon the dark hair that nestled on his breast, then swaying for a moment the lovers fell from the rock into the deep abyss beneath them, and crushed and mangled, their bodies still locked in that last embrace, were swept by the seething torrent far down the mountain and lost. Honest mountaineers returning from their toil in the wood at dusk in the spring time, have told repeatedly that when the stream is wild, as they express it just at sunset, they have seen two forms half hidden by the spray standing on the flat rock above Blossom Falls, and watching seen them totter and fall, but have never been able to find the bodies. They shake their head now when questioned, but avoid the spot after dark.

There can be no question that the foregoing story is very highly colored and romantic—but rather bloody and gory. To suit the tastes of a more delicate sentimentality Eugene A. Bouton, a native of Stamford in Delaware County, fashioned the poignant tale of *Utsayantha* while a student at Yale University. It first appeared in the pages of the *Yale Literary Magazine,* but subsequently gained far wider circulation and was seized upon by the Ulster & Delaware Railroad and the resort operators of Stamford.

According to Bouton's poem an Indian maiden falls in love with a white man and bears him a child. Her angry father drowns the baby in a lake and the grief-maddened Utsayantha throws herself from the mountain that now bears her name into the lake that also bears it.

The poem first appeared in 1872. By the 1880s "Princess" Utsayantha's grave had been "discovered" up on the mountain. And so legends acquire a life of their own.

The works of James Fenimore Cooper more properly belong to the realm of literature. He worked mainly from accurate historical materials, but some of his archetypical characters have become legendary, as is the case with Washington Irving's *Rip Van Winkle.*

Literature

THE COLONIAL PERIOD

Closely allied to, and partly arising from, the romantic aura of the Catskill region there developed a considerable body of formal literature. The region serves as setting for a number of novels and various features served as subject matter for poems, contemplative essays and descriptive sketches. While the neighboring Hudson River valley was one of the cradles of American literature, as embodied in the Knickerbocker School, the Catskill region itself did not give birth to any writers of distinction until John Burroughs. Most writers who used the Catskills as a setting came from neighboring regions: Irving from New York City, Cooper from New Jersey and Paulding from Dutchess County. However, the scenic allure served as a magnet and, along with the Hudson River, the Catskills soon became a popular theme in 19th-century literature.

Early New Amsterdam produced two local poets writing in Dutch: Jacob Steendam and Nicasius De Sille. Their writings had a limited circulation among the early settlers, although those of the Dutch poet Jacob Cats were more popular. Most reading in early times was confined to the Bible and the theological treatises of the Reformed Church.

At a somewhat later date Orange County was home to a distinguished scholar and statesman: Cadwallader Colden (1688–1776). Born in Scotland, he attended the University of Edinburgh and studied medicine in London. He came to America in 1710. In 1720 he was appointed surveyor general and in 1721 was appointed to the Governor's Council. After 1761 he became lieutenant governor of New York and remained a staunch loyalist. Having studied Newton's *Principia Mathematica*, he wrote a critique entitled *The Principals of Action in Matter* (1751) and other scientific treatises. In 1727 he published a *History of the Five Indian Nations*.

WASHINGTON IRVING

The first writer of note to use the Catskills as a setting was Washington Irving (1783–1859). His tale *Rip Van Winkle* was published, along with *The Legend of Sleepy Hollow*, in a volume entitled *The Sketch Book of Geoffrey Crayon, Gent.* (London, 1820). It soon gained international fame and remains the most famous literary treatment of the Catskills. The complete tale is included in *The Hudson River in Literature* (Arthur G. Adams, ed., Fordham University Press, 1989).

It is generally considered that the village of Catskill and the slopes of North Mountain above Saxe's Farm on the Old Mountain House Road were the setting. However, Irving had no specific locality in mind and was amused by the efforts of hotel owners and other local boosters to appropriate the tale to a specific local setting. A ravine on the slopes of North Mountain is still known as Sleepy Hollow and for many years Rip's Rock was pointed out to visitors. What is confusing is that another Sleepy Hollow in North Tarrytown in Westchester County is the setting for the completely un-related *Legend of Sleepy Hollow*, with its famous Headless Horseman. Lit-

Washington Irving; oil portrait by Henry F. Darby, c1858. Courtesy of Historic Hudson Valley.

erary critics have pointed out that Irving probably drew his inspiration from the old legend of the long sleep of the Emperor Frederick Barbarossa. No matter; the story fits equally well on the henpecked Dutchman. In later years the actor Joseph Jefferson wrote a popular play on the subject and the French composer Robert Planquette turned it into an operetta.

Robert Planquette (1850–1903) is best known for his other operetta *Les Cloches de Corneville* or *The Chimes of Normandy* (1877) and famous military march, "Sambre et Meuse," which was popular during the First World War. *Rip*, with a libretto by Meilhac, Gille and Farnie, was first given at the Theatre des Folies-Dramatiques in Paris in 1884. There is some very evocative storm music in the second act. The plot deviates considerably from Irving's story.

The American composer Reginald De Koven (1859–1920), born in Middletown, Connecticut and a graduate of Oxford, was a successful composer and music critic in New York and Chicago. He studied composition under the ballet and opera composer Leo Delibes in Paris. His best known work is the operetta *Robin Hood*, which contains the well-known Wedding Song "Oh, Promise Me." Other works are the operetta *Maid Marion* and opera *Canterbury Pilgrims*. De Koven's last and finest stage work, based upon a libretto by Percy MacKaye, the American folklorist, is entitled *Rip Van Winkle*. It was first performed in Chicago in 1920. MacKaye took considerable liberties with Irving's story in his three-act setting, introducing such characters as Dirck Spuytenduyvil, "mate of the

Rip Van Winkle used as an advertising motif by Ulster & Delaware RR on timetable cover, c1900. Author's collection.

Half Moon." Revival of this interesting work would be a suitable project for a local musical organization or college.

A third operatic setting of the Rip Van Winkle story is entitled simply *Rip Van Winkle* (London 1897), by the Italian-English composer Franco Leoni (1864–1937), who is best known for his verismo shocker *L'Oracolo*. A revival of interest in Leoni's music bodes well for a revival of Rip.

JAMES FENIMORE COOPER

The next writer to dwell upon Catskill subject matter was James Fenimore Cooper (1789–1851). In 1790 William Cooper, founder of Cooperstown, brought his family there from Burlington, N.J. Little James Fenimore was only one year old. William Cooper was the leading citizen of the new town and was later made a judge. In 1802, at the age of thirteen, James Fenimore matriculated at Yale but was expelled in 1805, possibly a result of immaturity. He returned to his father's home, Otsego Hall, at Cooperstown, for two months, and then went to sea as a merchant sailor. In a few years he entered the Navy in which he remained until 1811. Shortly thereafter he married Susan DeLancey, of a prominent old Tory family, and settled in Scarsdale in Westchester County, where he lived the life of a country gentleman.

About 1815 he moved to Cooperstown and built a smaller home for himself which he called "The Chalet," but in 1817 he moved back to Westchester and began a period of extensive European travel and residence. He also began a writing career, beginning first with some rather commonplace Gothic tales such as *The Heidenmauer*, Jane-Austin-like social comedy such as *Precaution* and Byronesque adventure tales such as *The Bravo*. However, his forte was not in being a follower of Walpole, Lewis and Radcliffe but in more original fields.

He soon turned to writing sea stories such as *Wing and Wing, The Pilot, Red Rover*, and *The Water-Witch*, for which his former career and knowledge of sailing and the sea well qualified him. His eye for topography and interest in the events of the Revolution led him to write *The Spy* in 1821 with its setting in Westchester, Putnam and Dutchess Counties. *Lionel Lincoln* is a similar tale. His knowledge of oldtime manor life in New York led to the Littlepage Papers—*Satanstoe, The Chainbearer* and *The Redskins*, which concerns itself with anti-rent sentiment.

However, Cooper found his greatest success with the *Leatherstocking Tales*. The character of Leatherstocking, alias Natty Bumppo, La Longue Carabine, Hawkeye and Pathfinder, is based upon that of an old Cooperstown huntsman named Shipman who wore leather footgear. The five novels were written in somewhat reverse order of the chronology of the action. The following tabulation will be of interest:

The famous actor Joseph Jefferson as Rip Van Winkle in the play he adapted from Washington Irving's story. Author's collection.

Title	Locale	Date of Action	Date Published
The Deerslayer	Otsego Lake	1740	1841
The Pathfinder	Upper NY & Lake Ontario	1756	1840
Last of the Mohicans	Lake George & Adirondacks & Glens Falls area	1757	1826
The Pioneers	Otsego Lake — allusions to the Catskills	1793	1823
The Prairie	The Western Plains	1804	1827

These, and *The Spy* and *The Pilot*, are the central canon that established Cooper's international reputation.

While residing in Paris he became famous for his buckwheat pancake breakfasts—this in the world's culinary capital! The conversation must indeed have been good. Cooper also imbibed aristocratic prejudices while abroad, and these caused him to become personally unpopular upon his

James Fenimore Cooper. Artist unknown.
Author's collection.

return home. Certain books, including *Homeward bound* and *Home as Found*, make unfavorable comparisons between American and European mores and society, much as did Mrs. Trollope's *The Domestic Manners of the Americans*. Many Americans thought that his marriage into a Tory family and his sympathetic treatment of Mr. Wharton and his family in *The Spy* were not quite becoming for an American writer.

Upon his return to Cooperstown in 1834, this time for good, he converted Otsego Hall into a fake-Gothic castle such as Sir Walter Scott's home, Abbotsford, and Horace Walpole's estate at Strawberry Hill, with crenelations and ogee windows. He also forbade the townsfolk to continue their practice of using Threemile Point, which he owned, as a pleasure and picnic ground. This last measure was too much for the natives. They contested their right of entry, but lost. Thereafter Cooper's popularity with the natives hit a new low. It may be recalled that Cooper's father, old Judge Cooper, had suffered a similar decline in popular esteem after his unpopular prosecution of Jedediah Peak under the Alien and Sedition Law. Cooper attempted to justify his attitude in *Home as Found*, of 1838, which is a veiled account of the episode.

In 1839 Cooper completed his monumental *History of the Navy of the United States*. He died in 1851 and is buried in the cemetery of Christ Episcopal Church in Cooperstown. He had written thrity-three novels. His statue by V. Salvatore is on the Cooper Grounds, and the present Fenimore House Museum stands on the site of Otsego Hall, which burned down in 1853.

For examples of Cooper's descriptive writings see the following headings in the Gazetteer section: Ostego Lake, Unadilla River, Cooperstown, Coeymans, Saugerties. The most famous descriptive extracts are in *The Pioneers* (1823), wherein Leather-stocking describes Kaaterskill Falls and the view from Pine Orchard.

"I have travelled the woods for fifty-three years, and have made them my home for more than forty; and I can say that I have met but one place that was more to my liking; and that was only to eye-sight, and not for hunting and fishing."

"And where was that?" asked Edwards.

"Where! Why up on the Cattskills. I used often to go up into the mountains after wolves' skins and bears; once they paid me to get them a stuffed panther, and so I often went. There's a place in them hills that I used to climb to when I wanted to see the carryings on of the world, that would well pay any man for a barked shin or a torn moccasin. You know the Cattskills, lad; for you must have seen them on your left, as you followed the river up from York, looking as blue as a piece of clear sky, and holding the clouds on their tops, as the smoke curls over the head of an Indian chief at the council fire.

Scenes from Cooper's Leatherstocking Tales. *Author's collection.*

Well, there's the High-peak, and the Round-top which lay back like a father and mother among their children, seeing they are far above all the other hills. But the place I mean is next to the river, where one of the ridges juts out a little from the rest, and where the rocks fall, for the best part of a thousand feet, so much up and down, that a man standing on their edges is fool enough to think he can jump from top to bottom."

"What see you when you get there?" asked Edwards.

"Creation," said Natty, dropping the end of his rod into the water, and sweeping one hand around him in a circle: "all creation, lad. I was on that hill when Vaughan burned 'Sopus' [Kingston] in the last war; and I saw the vessels come out of the Highlands as plain as I can see that line-scow rowing into the Susquehanna, though one was twenty times farther from me than the other. The river is in sight for seventy miles, looking like a curled shaving under my feet, though it was eight long miles to its banks. I saw the hills in the Hampshire [in Vermont, ed. note] grants, the Highlands of the river, and all that God had done, or man could do, far as eye could reach— you know that the Indians named me for my sight, lad; and from that flat on the top of that mountain, I have often found the place where Albany stands. And as for 'Sopus' the day the royal troops burnt the town, the smoke seemed so nigh that I thought I could hear the screeches of the women."

"It must have been worth the toil to meet with such a glorious view."

"If being the best part of a mile in the air, and having men's farms and houses at your feet, with rivers looking like ribbons, and mountains bigger than the 'Vision,' seeming to be haystacks of green grass under you, gives any satisfaction to a man, I can recommend the spot. When I first came into the woods to live, I used to have weak spells when I felt lonesome; and then

I would go into the Cattskills, and spend a few days on that hill to look at the ways of man; but it's now many a year since I felt any such longings, and I am getting too old for rugged rocks. But there's a place, a short two miles back of that very hill, that in late times I relished better than the mountain; for it was more covered with the trees, and natural."

"And where was that?" inquired Edwards, whose curiosity was strongly excited by the simple description of the hunter.

"Why, there's a fall in the hills where the water of the two little ponds, that lie near each other, breaks out of their bounds and runs over the rocks into the valley. The stream is, maybe, such a one as would turn a mill, if so useless a thing was wanted in the wilderness. But the hand that made that 'Leap' never made a mill. There the water comes crooking and winding among the rocks; first so slow that a trout could swim in it, and then starting and running like a creatur' that wanted to make a far spring, till it gets to where the mountain divides, like the cleft hoof of a deer, leaving a deep hollow for the brook to tumble into. The first pitch is nigh two hundred feet, and the water looks like flakes of driven snow afore it touches the bottom; and the stream gathers itself together again for a new start, and maybe flutters over fifty feet of flat rock before it falls another hundred, when it jumps about from shelf to shelf, first turning thisaway and then turning thataway, striving to get out of the hollow, till it finally comes to the plain."

"I have never heard of this spot before; is it mentioned in the books?"

"I never read a book in my life," said Leather-Stocking; "and how should a man who has lived in towns and schools know anything about the wonders of the woods? No, no, lad; there has that little stream of water been playing among the hills since He made the world, and not a dozen white men have ever laid eyes on it. The rock sweeps like masonwork, in a half-round, on both sides of the fall, and shelves over the bottom for fifty feet; so that when I've been sitting at the foot of the first pitch, and my hounds have run into the caverns behind the sheet of water, they've looked no bigger than many rabbits. To my judgement, lad, it's the best piece of work that I've met with on the woods; and none know how often the hand of God is seen in the wilderness, but them that rove it for a man's life."

"What becomes of the water? In which direction does it run? Is it a tributary of the Delaware?"

"Anan!" said Natty.

"Does the water run into the Delaware?"

"No, no; it's a drop for the old Hudson, and a merry time it has till it gets down off the mountain. I've sat on the shelving rock many a long hour, boy, and watched the bubbles as they shot by me, and thought how long it would be before that very water, which seemed made for the wilderness, would be under the bottom of a vessel, and tossing in the salt sea. It is a spot to make a man solemnize. You can see right down into the valley that lies to the east of the High Peak, where, in the fall of the year, thousands of acres of woods are before your eyes, in the deep hollow, and along the side of the mountain, painted like ten thousand rainbows, by no hand of man, though without the ordering of God's providence."

"You are eloquent, Leather-Stocking," exclaimed the youth.

PAULDING AND WILLIS

Less well known today is the once famous James Kirke Paulding (1779-1860). He was a popular novelist and was active in politics, serving as secretary of the navy under Van Buren. His estate, "Placentia," in Hyde Park commanded a panoramic view of the Catskills. His satirical guidebook to the Hudson entitled *New Mirror for Travellers & Guide to the Springs*, issued anonymously in 1828, extolled the scenery of the Kaatskills. The mountains also serve as background to his 1831 novel, *The Dutchman's Fireside*.

Nathaniel Parker Willis (1806-1867) was born at Portland, Maine. After graduating from Yale he became active in journalism. For a while he lived on a farm, "Glen Mary," on the Susquehanna River, where he wrote his essays *Letters from Under a Bridge* and *Glenmary Poems* (1849). An extract from the former was included in our article on the Susquehanna River. In 1836, in conjunction with the artist W. H. Bartlett, he wrote the text for a popular illustrated book entitled *American Scenery*, which gave prominence to Catskill views.

James Kirke Paulding. Artist unknown. Author's collection

WILLIAM CULLEN BRYANT

William Cullen Bryant (1794-1878) was born in the neighboring Berkshires but lived most of his life in and around New York City. One of America's finest nature poets, he rarely localized his poems. However, he frequently visited the Catskills with his friends Asher B. Durand and Thomas Cole, two of our greatest landscape painters. His poem "Catterskill Falls" soon became famous—and in turn brought attention and fame to the falls themselves.

William Cullen Bryant writing in his study in Roslyn, L.I. Attributed to Asher B. Durand.

CATTERSKILL FALLS

Midst greens and shades the Caterskill leaps,
    From cliffs where the wood-flower clings;
All summer he moistens his verdant steps,
    With the sweet light spray of the mountain-springs,
And he stakes the woods on the mountain-side,
When they drip with the rains of autumn-tide.

But when, in the forest bare and old,
    The blast of December calls,
He builds, in the starlight clear and cold,
    A palace of ice where his torrent falls,
With turret, and arch, and fretwork fair,
And pillars blue as the summer air.

For whom are those glorious chambers wrought,
    In the cold and cloudless night?
Is there neither spirit nor motion of thought
    In forms so lovely, and hues so bright?
Hear what the gray-haired woodmen tell
Of this wild stream and its rocky dell.

'Twas hither a youth of dreamy mood,
    A hundred winters ago,
Had wandered over the mighty wood,
    When the panther's track was fresh on the snow,
And keen where the winds that came to stir
The long dark boughs of the hemlock-fir.

Kaaterskill Falls, 1971. Photo by Robert R. Clark.

Too gentle of mien he seemed and fair,
   For a child of those rugged steeps;
His home lay low in the valley where
   The kingly Hudson rolls to the deeps;
But he wore the hunter's frock that day,
And a slender gun on his shoulder lay.

And here he paused, and against the trunk
   Of a tall gray linden leant,
When the broad clear orb of the sun had sunk,
   From his path in the frosty firmament,
And over the round dark edge of the hill
A cold green light was quivering still.

And the crescent moon, high over the green,
   From a sky of crimson shone,
On that icy palace, whose towers were seen
   To sparkle as if with stars of their own,
While the water fell with a hollow sound,
'Twixt the glistening pillars ranged around.

Is that a being of life, that moves
   Where the crystal battlements rise?
A maiden watching the moon she loves,
   At the twilight hour, with pensive eyes?
Was that a garment which seemed to gleam
Betwixt the eye and the falling stream?

'Tis only the torrent tumbling o'er,
   In the midst of those glassy walls,
Gushing, and plunging, and beating the floor
   Of the rocky basin in which it falls.
'Tis only the torrent—but why that start?
Why gazes the youth with a throbbing heart?

He thinks no more of his home afar,
   Where his sire and sister wait.
He heeds no longer how star after star
   Looks forth on the night as the hour grows late.
He heeds not the snow-wreaths, lifted and cast
From a thousand boughs, by the rising blast.

His thoughts are alone of those who dwell
   In the halls of frost and snow,
Who pass where the crystal domes upswell
   From the alabaster floors below,
Where the frost-trees shoot with leaf and spray,
And frost-gems scatter a silvery day.

"And oh that those glorious haunts were mine!"
   He speaks, and throughout the glen

Thin shadows swim in the faint moonshine,
    And take a ghastly likeness of men,
As if the slain by the wintry storms
Came forth to the air in their earthly forms.

There pass the chasers of seal and whale,
    With their weapons quaint and grim,
And bands of warriors in glittering mail,
    And herdsmen and hunters huge of limb;
There are naked arms, with bow and spear,
And furry gauntlets the carbine rear.

There are mothers—and oh how sadly their eyes
    On their children's white brows rest!
There are youthful lovers—the maiden lies,
    In a seeming sleep, on the chosen breast;
There are fair wan women with moonstruck air,
The snow-stars flecking their long loose hair.

They eye him not as they pass along,
    But his hair stands up with dread,
When he feels that he moves with that phantom throng.
    Till those icy turrets are over his head,
And the torrent's roar as they enter seems
Like a drowsy murmur heard in dreams.

The glittering threshold is scarcely passed,
    When there gathers and wraps him round
A thick white twilight, sullen and vast,
    In which there is neither form nor sound;
The phantoms, the glory, vanish all,
With the dying voice of the waterfall.

Slow passes the darkness of that trance,
    And the youth now faintly sees
Huge shadows and gushes of light that dance
    On a rugged ceiling of unhewn trees,
And walls where the skins of beasts are hung,
And rifles glitter on antlers strung.

On a couch of shaggy skins he lies;
    As he strives to raise his head,
Hard-featured woodmen, with kindly eyes,
    Come round him and smooth his furry bed,
And bid him rest, for the evening star
Is scarcely set and the day is far.

They had found at eve the dreaming one
    By the base of that icy steep,
When over his stiffening limbs begun
    The deadly slumber of frost to creep,
And they cherished the pale and breathless form,
Till the stagnant blood ran free and warm.

Bryant was one of the few people to visit the falls in winter and chose to stress this somewhat unfamiliar aspect. Bryant also wrote the text for a large two-volume picture book entitled *Picturesque America*, with engravings by Harry Fenn (1872). This books gives considerable attention to South Mountain and Kaaterskill Clove.

THOREAU, BENJAMIN, MARTINEAU, COLE

The Catskills were visited by Henry David Thoreau in 1844, prior to his residence at Walden Pond. He stayed near Scribner's at the top of Kaaterskill Falls west of South Lake.

> I lodged at the house of a saw-miller last summer on the Catskill Mountains, high up at Pine Orchard, in the blueberry and raspberry region, where the quiet and cleanliness and coolness seemed to be all one . . . which had their ambrosial character. . . . The house seemed high-placed, airy, and perfumed, fit to entertain a travelling god. It was so high, indeed, that all the music, the broken strain, the waifs and accompaniments of tunes, that swept over the ridge of the Catskills, passed through its aisles. Could not a man be a man in such an abode?

The saw-miller's house stood at the junction of Spruce and Lake Creeks, and his host was probably Ira Scribner.

We have already discussed the writing of Henry Abbey, Lionel De Lisser and Eugene Bouton. However, some other extracts from popular writers of the day will be of interest.

The journalist and lecturer Park Benjamin (1809–1864) made the following rather interesting comments after visiting the Catskill Mountain House:

SCENIC EFFECTS FROM LOFTY HEIGHTS

> It is pleasant, for a while, to leave the heated pavements and the garbaged atmosphere of our ever bustling noisy city; to bid adieu to the continued rumbling and rattling of all the various vehicles that the worried horses are destined to drag in merciless labor to and fro the city's length; the cries of the newspaper urchins, more varied in tone than the gamut's self; to flee from patients, clients, patrons and all the constant, never-varying avocations, that tend to harass and perplex the lives of toiling citizens, and perch one's self upon some mountainous elevation, where nature's calmness changes the current of our thoughts, and turns them from the real and artificial miseries of humanity. On such a spot we can enjoy an inward elevation, partaking of the beauty and serenity of the scene, and indulge the mind in instructive reflections upon the past, the present and the future.
> It would seem that the great creator of the universe had built up this mighty eminence that man might know his power, and feeling his own insignificance, despise and shun the vanities and hollow-heartedness of life.

Here the belief is taught that there is but one religion and one great family of mankind. Station yourself upon the projecting rock that hangs in such terrible altitude over the immense space beneath, but attempt not to give utterance to your feeling—language could not express them. Have you ever stood upon a vessel's deck, lashed to her for security, amid the howling tempest's rage, the winds driving her into the sea's deep chasms, and suspending her on the lofty pinnacle of the waves, the lightning flashes brightening the surrounding horrors, and showing by its vivid glares the peril of your situation? Have you ever known the mightiness of the tempest's angry mood at such a moment, and felt how utterly inadequate is speech? If so, then stand upon this high-poised rock and learn that it is not the awfully sublime alone that seals the lips, but that Nature in her calmest mood can subdue the mind to silence.

Henry David Thoreau. Artist unknown. Author's collection

The checkered scene below lies like the lovliest meadow, in variegated patchwork. Hills have disappeared. Here and there, apparently within a narrow lane, a mite is seen. It is the vehicle of some sturdy farmer, drawn by his well-fed span, measuring with rapid pace the broad highway leading to the distant village, whose diminished spires decorate the landscape. Observe that quiet stream attenuated to a brook. One bound would carry you to its opposite bank, were it what it seems, and by that bound you would leap the noble Hudson. See that tiny cloud—smaller than the puff just issuing from your Havana—as it rises from the river's surface. That speck beneath is speeding on its way with a velocity that gladdens its living freight of anxious travelers, and yet to the eye it moves not. Those far-off mountains, rising from the horizon in varied obscure shapes and heights belong to other States. The fleeting clouds in graceful movement pass beneath you, dragging their lengthened shadows over the colored plain, until Nature's curtain, being drawn, shuts out the view. And now the whole becomes one vast fictitious sea, placing you in feeling near the ocean's level, and relieving for a moment the nervous throbs the dizzy height occasioned. Soon the clouds disperse, and, separating, in changing forms, the quiet region underneath lies again before you in all its beautiful and glorious sublimity. Such is nature's tableau. Why was creation formed with features so imposing but for man's great benefit, that he might learn the power and majesty of the Omnipotent?

Come, then, ye multitudes of uneducated mortals, and from this great book store your minds with deep reflections, leading to wisdom and happiness.

And come they did indeed! Among them the deaf lady philosopher Harriet Martineau (1802–1876), an Englishwoman. She wrote the following after a visit to the Catskill Mountain House in 1834:

PHILOSOPHY OF NATURE IN THE CATSKILLS

However widely travelers have differed about other things in America, all seem to agree in their love for the Hudson. The pens of all tourists dwell on its scenery, and their affections linger about it like the magic lights which seem to have this river in their peculiar charge. Yet very few travelers have seen its noblest wonder. I may be singular, but I own that I was more moved by what I saw from a mountain house than by Niagara itself.

The mountain laurel conveyed by association the first impression of coolness. Sheep were browsing among the shrubs, apparently enjoying the shelter of the covert. We scrambled through deep shade for three or four miles, heavy showers passing over us, and gusts of wind bowing the treetops, and sending a shiver through us, partly from the sudden chillness and partly from expectation and awe of the breezy solitude.

After another level reach of road, and another scrambling ascent, I saw something on the rocky platform above our heads, like [to compare great things with small] an illuminated fairy palace perched among the clouds in opera scenery; a large building whose numerous window-lights marked out its figure from amid the thunder clouds and black twilight which overshadowed it.

After tea I went out upon the platform in front of the house, having been warned not to go too near the edge, although there was security against stepping over unawares. The stars were bright, and had conquered half the sky, giving promise of what we ardently desired, a fine morrow. Over the other half the mass of thunder clouds was, I supposed, heaped together, for I could at first discern nothing of the campaign which I knew must be stretched below. Suddenly, and from that moment incessantly, gushes of red lightning poured out from the cloudy canopy, revealing not merely the horizon, but the course of the river in all its windings through the valley. This thread of river, thus illuminated, looked like a flash of lightning caught by some strong hand and laid along in the valley. All the principal features in the landscape might, no doubt, have been discerned by the sumptuous light; but my whole attention was absorbed by the river, which seemed to come out of the darkness like an apparition at the summons of my impatient will. It could be borne only for a short time; this dazzling, bewildering alteration of glare and blackness, of vast reality and nothingness. I was soon glad to draw back from the precipice and seek the candlelight within.

The next day was Sunday. I shall never forget if I live to a hundred, how the world lay at my feet one Sunday morning. I rose very early and looked abroad from my window, two stories above the platform. A dense fog, exactly level with my eyes, as it appeared, roofed in the whole plane of the earth; a dusky firmament, in which the stars had hidden themselves for the day. Such is the account which an antediluvian spectator would probably have given of it. This solid firmament had spaces in it, however, through which gushes of sunlight were poured lighting up the spires of white churches and clusters of farm buildings, too small to be otherwise distinguished, and especially the river, with its sloops floating like motes in the sunbeam. The firmament rose and melted, or parted off into the likeness of snowy sky-mountains, and left the cool Sabbath to brook bright over the land. What human interest sanctifies a birds eye view! I suppose this is its peculiar charm, for its charm is found to deepen in proportion to the growth of mind. To an infant, a campaign of a hundred miles is not so much as a yard square of gay carpet. To the rustic it is less bewitching than a paddock with two cows. To the philosopher, what is it not? As he casts his eye over its glittering towns, its scattered hamlets, its secluded homes, its mountain ranges, church spires and untrodden forests, it is a picture of life; an epitome of the human universe, the complete volume of moral philosophy, for which he has sought in vain in all libraries.

It seems strange to him how man should call anything his but the power which is in him, and which can create somewhat more vast and beautiful than all that this horizon encloses. Here he gains the conviction, to be never again shaken, that all that is real is ideal; that the joys and sorrows of men do not spring up out of the ground, or fly abroad on the wings of the wind, or come showered down from the sky; that good can not be hedged in, or evil barred out; even that light does not reach the spirit through the eye alone, nor wisdom through the medium of sound or silence only. He becomes of one mind with the spiritual Berkeley, that the face of nature herself, the very picture of woods and streams and meadows, is a hieroglyphic writing in the spirit itself, of which the retina is no interpreter. The proof is just below him [at least it came under my eye] in the lady [not American] who, after glancing over the landscape, brings her chair into the piazza, and turning her pack to the campaign, and her face to the wooden walls of the hotel, begins the study this Sunday morning, of her lapful of newspapers. What a sermon is preached to him at this moment from a very hackneyed text! To him that hath much—that hath the eye and ear, and wealth of the spirit, shall more be given; even a replenishing of the spiritual life from that which to others is formless and dumb; while from him that hath little, who trusts in that which lies about him, shall be taken away, by natural decline, the power of perceiving and enjoying what is within his own domain. To him who is already enriched with large divine and human revelations, the scene is, for all its stillness, musical with divine and human speech; while one who has been deafened by the din of worldly affairs can hear nothing in this mountain solitude.

On returning, we found dinner awaiting us, and also a party of friends from Massachusetts, with whom we passed the afternoon, climbing higher and higher among the pines, ferns and blueberries of the mountain, to get wider and better views. They told me that I saw Albany. But I was by no means sure of it. This large city lay in the landscape like an ant-hill in the meadow. Long before sunset I was at my window again, watching the gradual lengthening of the shadows and purpling of the landscape. It was more beautiful than the sunrise of the morning, and less so than that of the morrow. Of this last I shall give no description, for I would not weary others with that which was most sacred to me. Suffice it to say that it gave me a vivid idea of the process of creation, from the moment when all was without form and void, to that when light was commanded and all was light.

Thomas Cole, by Horatio Greenough.
Wadsworth Atheneum, Hartford. Bequest of
Florence Cole Vincent.

The English-born painter Thomas Cole (1801–1848), founder of the Hudson River School of landscape painting, and a resident of Catskill, was also a poet. He was similarly impressed with the sunrise from Pine Orchard:

THE WILD

Friends of my heart, lovers of
    Nature's works.
Let me transport you to those
    wild blue mountains
that rear their summits near the
    Hudson's wave
Though not the loftiest that
    begirt the land,
They yet sublimely rise, and on
    their heights
Your souls may have a sweet
    foretaste of heaven
And traverse wide the boundless.

From this rock,
The nearest to the sky, let us
    look out
Upon the earth, as the first swell
    of day
Is bearing back the duskiness of
    night.

But lo! a sea of mist o'er all beneath;
An ocean, shoreless, motionless and mute,
No rolling swell is there, no sounding surf;
Silent and solemn all; the stormy main
To stillness frozen, while the crested waves
Leaped in the whirlwind, and the loosened foam
Flew o'er the angry deep.

See! Now ascends
The Lord of Day, waking with pearly fire
The dormant depths, See how his glowing breath
The rising surges kindles; lo! they heave
Like golden sands upon Sahara's gales.
Those airy forms disporting from the mass,
Like winged ships, sail o'er the wondrous plain.
Beautiful vision! Now the veil is rent,
And the coy earth her virgin bosom bares,
Slowly unfolding to the enraptured gaze
Her thousand charms.

JOHN BURROUGHS

John Burroughs (1837–1921), son of a farmer, was born in Roxbury. He later taught school in Olive Bridge and worked as a Treasury Clerk in Washington and as a journalist. In 1874 he settled on his farm in Esopus and gave himself over to horticulture and pomology and most importantly to the writing of the many nature essays for which he is best known. He built a rustic retreat, which he dubbed "Slabsides," in the Plattekill Hills and maintained another summer home near Clump Mountain west of Roxbury, known as "Woodchuck Lodge." Both remain today and are open to visitors. He was buried

John Burroughs seated on Boyhood Rock. Courtesy John Burroughs Historical Society.

near Boyhood Rock in Roxbury, from which, as a youth, he enjoyed contemplating the landscape and dreaming.

Burroughs was an avid explorer and among the first to make a recorded visit to the summit of Slide Mountain. There is a memorial to him near the summit. Primarily an essayist, he was a close friend of the poet Walt Whitman and himself a fine poet:

WAITING

Serene I fold my hands and wait,
  Nor care for wind, nor tide, nor sea;
I rave no more 'gainst time or fate,
  For lo! my own shall come to me.

I stay my haste, I make delays,
  For what avails this eager pace?
I stand amid the eternal ways.
  And what is mine shall know my face.

Asleep, awake, by night or day,
  The friends I seek are seeking me.
No wind can drive my bark astray,
  Nor change the tide of destiny.

What matter if I stand alone?
  I wait with joy the coming years;
My heart shall reap where it hath sown,
  And garner up its fruit of tears.

The waters know their own, and draw,
  The brook that springs in yonder heights;
So flows the good with equal law
  Unto the soul of pure delights.

The stars come nightly to the sky,
  The tidal wave comes to the sea;
Nor time, nor space, nor deep, nor high,
  Can keep my own away from me.

The mere titles of his essays give a good idea of the scope of his work: *Wake Robin* (1871); *Winter Sunshine* (1875); *Birds and Poets* (1877); *Locusts and Wild Honey* (1879); *Pepacton* (1881); *Fresh Fields* (1884); *Signs and Seasons* (1886); *Riverby* (1894); *Far and Near* (1904); *Ways of Nature* (1905); *Camping and Tramping with Roosevelt* (1907); and *Leaf and Tendril* (1908). Also, an anthology entitled *In The Heart of the Southern Catskills* and a volume of verse entitled *Bird and Bough* (1906).

Artists and the Catskills

The most famous artist to be associated with the Catskills was John Vanderlyn (1775–1852). He was born and grew up in Kingston. Later a student of Gilbert Stuart, he lived in Paris between 1796 and 1815. During this time he was a protégé of Aaron Burr. He worked in the classical style of David and Ingres and his masterpiece, *Marius among the Ruins of Carthage*, attracted the interest of Napoleon. However, upon return home to the United States he found that there was little market for this style of painting. He returned to Kingston and lived in penury. Late in life he received a commission for the gigantic *Landing of Columbus* to hang in the Capitol rotunda in Washington. His health was so undermined by poor living that he had to hire assistants to help him complete his commission. This one job did not help him much and he was eventually found dead of starvation in his apartment in Kingston. Today there are good collections of his work in the Metropolitan Museum in New York and in the Senate House Museum in Kingston.

Although a native of the Catskills, Vanderlyn was little influenced by his home environment. It remained for the English-born Thomas Cole (1801–1848) to immortalize the Catskills on canvas. Born in the Midlands of industrialized England, where the sky was obscured by a pall of factory smoke, he came to America as a youth, settling first in Philadelphia and later in western Pennsylvania and Ohio. He was impressed by the paintings in the Philadelphia Museum and, on one occasion, walked from Pittsburgh to Philadelphia to study there. His first work was as a portraitist in Ohio.

In 1825 he first visited the Catskill area and was enthralled by the scenery along the Hudson and in the vicinity of the village of Catskill. He was soon a frequent visitor and eventually settled there, where his studio and home may still be visited. His landscape paintings soon gained critical acclaim and began to sell well in New York City. He soon became America's foremost landscape painter and is recognized as the founder of the Hudson River School, which dominated the American artistic scene for many decades. He was particularly attracted to the Great Wall of Manitou and North and South Mountains. Artists Rock is named in his honor, as he used to tell visitors that they could see his home in Catskill from this point. Mount Thomas Cole is also named for him. Aside from his paintings, he was an avid hiker and explorer of the wilds and wrote considerable amounts of descriptive material and some poetry of rather high quality, such as *The Wild*, quoted in the previous chapter. His fondness for the region was so great that, during a trip to Europe, he wrote home: "Neither the Alps, nor the Apennines, no, nor Etna itself, have dimmed in my eyes the beauty of our own Catskills. It seems to me that I look on American scenery, if it were possible, with increased pleasure. It has its own peculiar charm—something not found elsewhere." He painted the view from Jefferson Heights, looking towards the Wall of Manitou, over and over in varying moods of atmosphere, and remained remarkably faithful to the scenery of the area so long as he concentrated upon landscapes. However, later in life he began to paint large allegorical paintings in the Romantic manner. Among the more famous series are *Course of Empire* and *The Voyage of Life*. They gained critical acclaim, but failed to sell well, although of late years they have experienced a rebirth of popularity and appreciation.

Perhaps an even greater technician and master, although not so well known, was Asher B. Durand (1796–1886). Born near Newark, N.J., he first worked as an engraver, and for the rest of his life his work showed the fine hand and meticulous craftsmanship associated with this trade. Among his engravings was Vanderlyn's *Ariadne*. After 1835 he devoted himself to painting and studied in Europe. Upon returning home he devoted himself to local scenery, including the then beautiful Hoboken and Weehawken Cliffs, the Hudson valley, the Catskills and White Mountains. His painting

Asher B. Durand. Author's collection

of *Kaaterskill Clove* dates from 1886. In 1849 he had used this same clove as setting for a double portrait of his friends Thomas Cole and William Cullen Bryant, entitled *Kindred Spirits*. It now hangs above the great stairway in the New York Public Library on Fifth Avenue, and perhaps summarizes the spirit of the Hudson River School better than any other single painting. Others of his works hang in the Corcoran Gallery and the Metropolitan Museum. He was one of the founders of the National Academy of Design and its president from 1845 to 1861.

Kindred Spirits. *Oil painting by Asher B. Durand of William Cullen Bryant and Thomas Cole on an excursion in Kaaterskill Clove. Now hanging in the Main Branch of the New York Public Library.*

Frederick E. Church (1826–1900) was the scion of a wealthy family of Hartford, Connecticut. Evincing great talent at an early age, he studied with Thomas Cole at Catskill. His works tend towards giganticism and are both romantic and realistic in detail. He travelled extensively in North, Central and South America, producing great canvases of absorbing power an exotic beauty. His most famous production is a mural-like oil of *Niagara Falls*, which captures the scope and power of the falls on the one hand and individual whitecaps and sprays of foam on the other. It is a work of both delicacy and power and now hangs in the Corcoran Gallery. He devoted himself less to Catskill subjects than other members of the Hudson River School, but so loved the area that he built his Victorian pseudo-Persian mansion "Olana Castle" across the Hudson from Catskill, with a sweeping panoramic view of the entire Catskill escarpment and the Hudson south to the Highlands. The entire conception is in harmony with his paintings. "Olana Castle" is operated as a museum and is being restored in accordance with the artist's wishes.

John Frederick Kensett (1818–1872) was born in Cheshire, Connecticut, and first worked as an engraver. He began to study oil painting and went abroad to study in England, Düsseldorf and Rome. In 1849, back in the United States, he became a member of the National Academy of Design. While concentrating more on the Lake George and Hudson Highland and Ramapo areas, his output was prodigious and he was closely aligned with other members of the Hudson River School.

Jaspar Francis Cropsey (1823–1900) was born on Staten Island and specialized in New York State and New Jersey scenes. In 1855 he produced an oil painting of the Catskill Mountain House from North Mountain. Now in the Minneapolis Institute of Arts, a reproduction in color can be found in Roland Van Zandt's book *The Catskill Mountain House*.

Sanford Robinson Gifford (1828–1880) was born in Kingston, New York. He studied at Brown University and the National Academy of Design. Travelling to Europe, he took up landscape painting, where he produced such works as *Villa Malta* (National Gallery, Washington), *Tivoli* (Metropolitan Museum) and *Valley of Lauterbrunnen* (Brown University). Returning to the United States, he served in the Civil War. A member of the National Academy from 1854, he was strongly influenced by Thomas cole. His great painting of *Kauterskill Falls* is one of the most impressive items in the American Wing of the Metropolitan Museum and one of the most successful treatments of this popular subject.

George Inness (1825–1894) was born in Newburgh, New York. Showing a strong talent for painting, he was apprenticed to an engraver. In 1845 he opened a studio in New York, and soon the bounty of several patrons made it possible for him to study in Rome and Paris. He was influenced by the Barbizon School, with their interest in atmospheric

George Henry Hall in his studio at the foot of Kaaterskill Clove. Photo by Lionel De Lisser, 1893. Author's collection.

effects. Returning to the United States, he settled first in Medford, Massachusetts, and later in Montclair, New Jersey. From here he made many trips up the Hudson and Delaware Valleys and into the Poconos and Catskills. Among his more famous paintings are *Rainbow After a Storm, Peace and Plenty, Delaware Valley, Autumn Oaks, Delaware Water Gap,* and, more specifically Catskillean in subject matter, *Vernooy Falls.* Major collections of his works are in the Chicago Institute of Art, Brooklyn Museum, Newark Museum and Montclair Museum.

A lesser known artist who was devoted to the Catskill region was George Henry Hall (1825–1918). A native of New Hampshire, he later built a studio and home near La Belle Falls in Kaaterskill Clove. He had studied at Düsseldorf and Paris but closely allied himself with the artists of the Hudson River School. His specialty was still lifes, for which he was quite famous. Lionel De Lisser's *Picturesque Catskills: Greene County* has several photographs of the artist and his studio, showing some of his work in progress.

Innumerable other artists have painted in the region and today Woodstock is still a major center of artistic activity, as is Cooperstown to the west. The unusual beauty of the entire area is an irresistible magnet to the landscape artist.

In a somewhat different tradition illustrators, engravers and lithographers have been drawn to the area. Most famous among them are William H. Bartlett (1809–1854), who produced drawings for Willis's *American Scenery*, William James Bennett, J. C. Bentley and J. R. Smith. Bennett worked for Willis's and Paulding's *New Mirror* and Bentley engraved some of Bartlett's work for *American Scenery*.

In 1870 Harry Fenn did a series of drawings and engravings for Bryant's *Picturesque America*. Fritz Meyer did numerous drawings during this period, which often appeared as "composites." In 1872 Winslow Homer made a very interesting and well-known drawing under Kaaterskill Falls. The great newspaper artist Thomas Nast also did a newspaper composite center-page spread for Harper's Weekly in 1866 featuring the Catskill Mountain House—a lighthearted change from his famous Civil War battlefield sketches. Currier and Ives also produced popular unsigned and undated prints of Catskill scenes.

PART IV
GAZETTEER

ACCORD Ulster Co. Small village at junction of Peters Kill and Rondout Creek, on Rte. 209 and Old Mine Road in Township of Rochester. Jacobus DePuy House (c1725).

ACIDALIA Sullivan Co. On East Branch of Basket Creek south of Cooks Falls, north of Long Eddy. Former wood acid plants.

ACRA Greene Co. Elev. 668 ft. Small community on Rte. 23 west of Cairo and east of Kate Hill. Applejack was produced here during prohibition. Hideout of Jack "Legs" Diamond.

ACRA POINT Greene Co. Elev. 3100 ft. North of Blackhead Mtn. on Escarpment Trail on Wall of Manitou.

ADEN Sullivan Co. North of Bradley.

AEOLUS, CAVE OF Ulster Co. On North Lookout Road on Mohonk grounds, near Gate of the Winds. In ancient mythology, as told in Homer's *Odyssey*, Aeolus was a demi-god who kept the winds in bags and released or recalled them at will. He lived in a cave. The Gate of the Winds is a crevice outside the cave. The rustic ladders that were there for many years have been removed. The area can be dangerous.

AFTON Chenango Co. On Susquehanna River, Rte. 7, D&H RR northeast of Nineveh, southwest of Bainbridge.

AGLOE Delaware Co. On Beaverkill north of Rockland and Roscoe, southeast of Downsville.

ALBRIGHTS Greene Co. Southwest of New Baltimore on Rtes. 9W and 144.

ALCOVE RESERVOIR Albany Co. West of Ravena on Rte. 143. Belongs to city of Albany. Covers 1,400 acres. It is manmade by damming Hannacroix Creek. Dickinson Falls are at its head. Closed to the public.

ALDER LAKE Ulster Co. Source of Alder Creek, which flows south 2 miles to the Beaver Kill near Turnwood. It is at southern foot of the Mill Brook Ridge. For many years a famous fishing club, it was later sold to S. D. Coykendall of Kingston.

ALLABEN Ulster Co. Elev. 990 ft. On Rte. 28 and Esopus Creek where the Shandaken Aqueduct Tunnel debouches. West of Phoenicia and east of Shandaken, near Peck, Broadstreet and Fox Hollows, at foot of Garfield Mtn. Formerly called Fox Hollow but was renamed for Dr. Orson M. Allaben (c1890) of Margaretville.

ALLEN BROOK Greene Co. Drains the Tannersville Reservoirs and Leach and Onteora Lakes.

ALLIGATOR ROCK Greene Co. On the former grounds of Catskill Mountain House near shores of South Lake. In profile it resembles an alligator with its jaws

Farmer of Esopus Valley, c1895. Photo by Lionel De Lisser.

open. It is traditional for visitors to place white-painted loose rocks in its mouth to serve as "teeth," and was a favorite snapshot backdrop. It was also known as Whales Mouth.

ALLIGERVILLE Ulster Co. Old D&H Canal town south of High Falls and north of Accord on Rondout Creek at western foot of Shawangunks in Rochester Twp. Formerly known for its "Irish Brawls."

ALSEN Greene Co. On Hudson River, West Shore RR and Rte. 9W south of Catskill. Here is a plant of the Lehigh Portland Cement Co., which quarries the Kalkberg Cliffs.

ALTAMONT Albany Co. on Rtes. 146, 156, 397 and D&H RR west of Albany, east of Schoharie. Malachi Whipple House. Also see Knox.

AMBER LAKE #1 Sullivan Co. Northwest of White Lake.

AMBER LAKE #2 Sullivan Co. Near Joscelyn and Burnt Hill.

AMPHITHEATRE #1 Greene Co. A great bowl in the north wall of Kaaterskill Clove between Indian Head on the east and Inspiration Point on the west on South Mountain. Also known as the Gulf, it is transversed by the old road from Palenville to the Hotel Kaaterskill at the 1600 ft. level. This is now part of the Sleepy Hollow Horse Trail Network. It can be seen from Rte. 23A south of More's Bridge.

AMPHITHEATRE #2 Ulster Co. In Shawangunks on Minnewaska Estate. Immediately below Awosting Falls on the Peters Kill and Rtes. 44-45.

ANAWANA LAKE Sullivan Co. North of Monticello on Rte. 103.

ANCKEROPS Ulster Co. Site near junction of Vernooy Kill and Rondout Creek, near Wawarsing. Site of Indian council "Big Wigwam."

ANDERSON Sullivan Co. On Willowemoc Creek between Debruce to the west and Willowemoc to the east.

ANDES Delaware Co. On Rte. 28 10½ miles west of Margaretville. Settled c1784, it has many attractive old buildings. Both the Catskill and Andes Ski Centers are hear near Mt. Pisgah.

ANDES JUNCTION Delaware Co. Former junction on the Delaware Northern Railroad where Andes Branch left mainline near Dunraven. Now under waters of Pepacton Reservoir.

ANDRUS HOLLOW Delaware Co. In north side of Dry Brook Ridge one mile east of Arkville, between Reservoir and Negro Hollows.

ANGEL'S PEAK Greene Co. Old name of Vly Mountain.

ANGLE CREEK Greene Co. In Lexington Township, it flows west off Balsam Mtn. into Bushnellsville Creek from a spring at 1800 ft. There is a 311 ft. drop in a one-mile distance.

ANTLERS, THE Greene Co. Former popular resort hotel and station on Catskill & Tannersville RR near Haines Corners. Built in 1890 by Butler & Bullock with room for 125 guests. On Mountain House Road.

APEX Delaware Co. On West Branch of Delaware and Former NYO&W south of Cannonsville Reservoir and Walton, north of Cadosia.

ARBUCKLE HOLLOW Delaware Co. East of Delancey.

ARCHING ROCKS Ulster Co. Below Copes Lookout on Mohonk Estate.

ARCTIC Delaware Co. North of Stilesville.

ARDONIA Ulster Co. Orchards in Plattekill Hills east of Modena, south of Clintondale.

ARENA Delaware Co. It no longer exists, as it is under the waters of Pepacton Reservoir near Dunraven. Formerly on route of the Delaware Northern RR. Arena means sand in Latin and it was named for sand quarries once here.

ARGUSVILLE Schoharie Co. North of Sharon.

ARIZONA Greene Co. Elev. 3400 ft. Point on Escarpment Trail between Stoppel Point and Blackhead Mtn. Formerly called Mt. Webster and The Sentinel. Area so called because it is dry—an arid zone.

ARKVILLE Delaware Co. Elev. 1344 ft. On Rte. 28 and Ulster & Delaware at junction of Dry Brook, Bush Kill and East Branch of Delaware. Former junction of U&D with Delaware Northern RR. Kettle Hill to west; Meade Hill to east and Pakatakan Mtn. to south. Formerly there was an artificial cave here with painted hieroglyphics, which was a popular tourist attraction. It is a major travel junction point. Formerly called Dean's Corners, it was settled in 1792. Headquarters of Delaware & Ulster Rail Ride. Erpf Catskill Cultural Center.

Erpf Catskill Cultural Center, Arkville. Photo by Alfred H. Marks.

ARTISTS GROTTO Greene Co. Located in Kaaterskill Clove near Labelle Falls on Kaaterskill Creek. Probably named for landscape and still life artist George Henry Hall (1825–1913), who owned house near here. It is on private property. Do not enter without prior permission.

ARTISTS ROCK Greene Co. Sandstone ledge on Escarpment Trail north of former Catskill Mountain House. Named for artist Thomas Cole, who liked to paint the view from here. Easily reached from North lake parking area. A recommended mini-hike for non-hikers. Fabulous views and the path is well marked.

ASBURY Greene Co. Located on Old Kings Highway north of Katsbaan. Possibly named for Methodist bishop and revivalist preacher Francis Asbury (1745-1816).

ASHLAND Greene Co. On Rte. 23 west of Windham and east of Prattsville on the Batavia Kill at its junction with West Hollow Brook. Huntersfield Mtn. to north; Tower Mtn. and Patterson Ridge to south. Named for Kentucky home of Henry Clay (1777-1852), "The Great Compromiser." The famous Ashland Academy was also located here. Tanning was carried on here from 1798. In 1810 Jairns Munson operated a ropewalk. St. Joseph's Chapel (c1840), oldest Catholic church in the Catskills.

ASHLEY CREEK AND FALLS Greene Co. Flows down Mary's Glen from North Mountain into North Lake, of which it is principal source.

ASHOKAN Ulster Co. On Rte. 28 between Shokan to the west and West Hurley to the East. Ticetonyk Mtn. to the north. Named for Ashokan, an Esopus Indian chief.

ASHOKAN HIGH POINT Ulster Co. Elev. 2900 ft. Overlooks Ashokan Reservoir to the north, it is south of Brodhead and West Shokan. South Mountain to the northwest and Watson Hollow to the west; Mombaccus Mtn. to the southwest.

Homestead Farm, Ashland. Photo by Alfred H. Marks.

ASHOKAN RESERVOIR See Chapter 3.

ASHTON Ulster Co. West of West Hurley.

ATHENS Greene Co. On Hudson River north of Catskill; Rte. 385, West Shore RR, at West Athens. Originally called Looneburg, it was first settled in 1686, but there is evidence that prehistoric Indians mined flint stones at Flint Hill 12,000 years ago at a site now belonging to the New York Archeological Association. The old Indian village of Potick was located a little back from the river. The Looneburg Patent of 17,500 acres, running from Coxsackie to Catskill Creek and embracing the Athens area, was purchased by Adrian Van Loon, a Walloon whose family had come to America in 1581 shortly after Jacques Cartier had first explored the St. Lawrence area in 1534. They had migrated down through the Adirondacks into the Hudson valley about 1598. Jan Van Loan built a house in Athens in 1708, although a previous owner of the patent had acquired an Indian deed from a certain Caniskeek on April 30, 1665.

The Zion Lutheran Church was organized in 1703, and its first pastor, the Rev. Justus Falkner, was the first Lutheran minister ordained in America.

Isaac Northrup is credited with moving for incorporation of the village in 1805. Athens soon became a port for merchant sailing ships and whalers and supported considerable shipbuilding. The natives favored classic style architecture. This all reflects the "Yankee Culture" of the many settlers from New England. A steam ferry to Hudson was established prior to 1836, and in 1867 Athens became the southern terminus of the Saratoga & Hudson River R.R., known as "The White Elephant Line," because it never paid. Its route along Murderer's Creek northwest of town became the Athens Branch of the West Shore Railroad in 1883. It is now abandoned. Other parts survive as bits of the West Shore Main Line, Penn-Central South Bethlehem Branch and Delaware & Hudson. The Van Loan & Magee Co. built steamboats. Steamboats connecting Athens with New York City were the

Awosting Falls, 1960. Photo by author.

"John Taylor" and "Erastus Corning" of the John H. Starin Line. Starin later became prominent in Long Island Sound shipping. The Starin boats carried cattle as well as passengers. In 1873 the Athens steamboat terminal suffered a disasterous fire and the business declined from then on.

The Schoharie Turnpike (roughly Rte. 145) had been completed to Cooksburg and Schoharie in 1802. However, the Susquehanna Turnpike from Catskill, and the short-lived (1840-1842) Canajoharie & Catskill Railroad, offered strong competition to it.

Development of faster steamboats which did not stop at Athens, completion of the West Shore (1883), Hudson River (1851) and Delaware & Hudson (1868) railroads and the Rip Van Winkle Bridge in the 1930s all served to divert traffic from this once important transportation center. Ice harvesting and brickmaking were the last major industries in the area.

During its heyday Athens had cultural pretensions with fine architecture and an Opera House (now known as the Brooks Building) which can still be seen on Second Street. Located west of town are the once popular picnic resorts of Black, Green and Hollister Lakes. Interesting old buildings in the area include:

Jan Van Loon House (1708), 39 Washington St.
Brandow House (1781)
Van Housen House (18th century)
Isaac Northrup House (1803), Federal style. Washington St.
General Nicholls House (1803), Federal style.
Haight-Gantley-Van Loan Mansion (1812), 38 Franklin St. Built by Gen. Samuel
    Haight. Very elegant; oval ballroom
Old Brick Foundry Building (1813)
Morton House (early 19th century)
Albertus Van Loan House (1824), North Washington St.
Greek Revival Mansion (c1840), 117 North Washington St.
Lydia Coffin House (c1840), Federal style, designed by Barnabus Waterman.
Two Greek Revival houses (c1840), 19 and 21 Franklin St. They have full Doric
    entablatures
Zion Lutheran Church (1853), Brick
Clark House (c1865), 10 South Washington St. High Victorian style with glass
    conservatory and tower
Trinity Episcopal Church (mid-19th century), board and batten construction

ATWOOD Ulster Co. On Rte. 213 in Marbletown Township, near Esopus Creek, between Stone Ridge and Olive Bridge.

AUCHMOODY POND Ulster Co. On Swarte Kill west of West Park.

AUNT TRENS LAKE Ulster Co. Now Lake Katrine.

AUSTIN GLEN Greene Co. A scenic small canyon on Catskill Creek west of Catskill and south of Jefferson Heights. Formerly used by Catskill Mountain Railroad. Crossed by Thruway viaduct.

AWOSTING Ulster Co. Village at east foot of Shawangunk Mts. northwest of Dwaarkill.

AWOSTING FALLS Ulster Co. On Minnewaska Estate on Peter's Kill.

AWOSTING LAKE Ulster Co. Elev. 1867 ft. In Minnewaska State Park. One of the sources of the Peter's Kill. Outlet at north end. 80 acres; more than 1 mile long and 90 feet deep.

BADMAN'S CAVE Greene Co. On Escarpment Trail on North Mountain. Supposed lair of 18th-century outlaws.

BAGLEY BROOK Delaware Co. Rises 8 miles east of DeLancey and flows into West Branch of Delaware River.

BAILEY LAKE Sullivan Co. Near Kiamesha Lake.

BAINBRIDGE Chenango Co. On Susquehanna River; Rtes. 7, 206; D&H RR southwest of Sidney, northeast of Afton. Settled before 1790. Neat Victorian flavored town in hilly region. Has village square with bandstand, Civil War memorial, cast iron fountain. A. Keyes of Bainbridge was moving spirit for construction of Albany & Susquehanna RR, now D&H. There are dairy products processing plants and a Borden Chemical Co. plant. Also coal power plant south of town, near which is a roadside rest area with information plaque on the Unadilla region. Old Jericho Tavern (1793). Presbyterian Church and Congregational Church are of architectural interest.

BAKER CREEK Albany Co. An estuary of the Hudson River between Shad and Schermerhorn Islands.

BALANCE ROCK On Overlook Mtn.

BALD MOUNTAIN #1 Sullivan Co. Elev. 2300 ft. South of Debruce and west of Anderson.

BALD MOUNTAIN #2 Greene Co. Elev 2500 ft. South of Ashland.

BALSAM CAP Ulster Co. Elev. 3623 ft. In Slide Mountain Massif. It is southeast of Slide and Cornell Mountains and was a favorite of John Borroughs.

BALSAM LAKE Ulster Co. Nestled between Woodpecker Ridge and the southern spur of Balsam Lake Mtn. in the wildest part of western Ulster County. Its outlet stream flows one mile south into the Beaver Kill. Its north end is swampy.

BALSAM LAKE MOUNTAIN Ulster Co. Also sometimes called Balsam Roundtop. Elev. 3720 ft. Fire observation tower.

BALSAM MOUNTAIN #1 Greene Co. Elev 3340 ft. East of Halcott Mtn., by which it is separated by Deep Notch through which runs Rte. 42. It is south of West Kill and west of Mt. Sherrill.

BALSAM MOUNTAIN #2 Ulster Co. Elev. 3600 ft. West of Big Indian Hollow overlooking Oliverea. Belle Ayre Mtn. to the north and Haynes Mtn. to the south. It is indented on its east by southeast wall by Lost Clove.

BALSAM ROUNDTOP Ulster Co. See Balsam Lake Mountain.

BALSAM SWAMP Ulster Co. At the headwaters of the Vernooy Kill at the foot of Samson Mtn. in Denning Township. It is one half mile above Vernooy Falls. The area abounds with rattlesnakes. It is nowhere near Balsam Mountain or Balsam Lake.

BANGLE HILL Ulster Co. Elev 2350 ft. In Denning Township. It separates the two branches of Rondout Creek near Sundown. Samson Mtn. and Spencers Ledge to the northeast.

BANNER CREEK Otsego Co. Flows south from east of Otsdawa to Susquehanna River at Oneonta.

BARCLAY HEIGHTS Ulster Co. South of Saugerties.

BARKABOOM MOUNTAIN Delaware Co. Elev. 3100 ft. Western termination of Mill Brook Ridge, overlooking Pepacton Reservoir. Mill Brook to north and Barkaboom Stream to south.

BARKABOOM STREAM Delaware Co. Rises between Barkaboom Mtn. and Touchmenot Mtn. and flows northwest to Pepacton Reservoir. Deerlick Brook is a major northern tributary.

BARKLEY'S HILL Greene Co. In West Jewett.

BARNERVILLE Schoharie Co. North of Cobleskill on Rte. 7. Near Howes Caverns.

BARNEY HOLLOW Delaware Co. Southwest of Downsville.

BARNUM Greene Co. On southern slope of Batavia Kill Valley. East of Van Loan Hill. Maple sugar area.

BARREN ISLAND Albany Co. See Bear Island.

BARRYVILLE Sullivan Co. On Delaware River and Rtes. 99 and 55 east of Minisink Ford, north of Handsome Eddy. Headquarters of Indian League of America. Reber's Resort, 914-557-8321.

BARTLETT HOLLOW Delaware Co. South of Oneonta on Ouleout Cr. on Rte. 357. Formerly Pine Kill.

BASHA or BASHER KILL Sullivan and Orange Cos. Tributary of Neversink River that flows along northwestern base of Shawangunk Mtns. from vicinity of Summitville to Valley Junction. They form important wetlands south of Wurtsboro and are a wildlife refuge.

BASHASVILLE Old name of Westerbrookville.

BASHER KILL See Basha Kill.

BASHERKILL CAVES Sullivan Co. On southeast side of Basher Kill marshes, in Shawangunks. Extensive limestone caves, stalactites, stalagmites, flowstone, drapery and deltas—all very delicate. Closed to the public.

BASIC CREEK AND RESERVOIR Greene Co. On Rte. 32. A northern tributary of Catskill Creek rising near Dormansville and flowing south through the man-made Basic Reservoir (City of Albany) to Catskill Creek near Freehold. Reservoir closed to public.

BASIN CLOVE BROOK Delaware Co. Rises south of DeLancey and flows 4 miles south to Pepacton Reservoir.

BASKET Sullivan Co. At junction of Delaware River and Basket Creek on Rtes. 97 and 17B north of Hankins, south of Long Eddy.

BASKET CREEK Sullivan Co. There are two branches: North Branch rises in Basket Pond south of Burnwood in Delaware Co. and flows southwest to junction with South Branch at Hawks Nest. South Branch rises in Basket Lake, west of Tennanah Lake in Sullivan Co. and flows southwest to Delaware River at Basket.

BASTION FALLS Greene Co. On Lake Creek in Kaaterskill Clove, just below Kaaterskill Falls, near the bridge on the Horshoe Curve on Rte. 23A. Easily seen from road. Trail to Kaaterskill Falls starts here.

BATAVIA KILL #1 Greene Co. Rises between Windham High Peak and Mt. Thomas Cole and flows generally westward past Maplecrest, Hensonville, Windham, Ashland and Red Falls to Schoharie Creek near Prattsville. Followed by Rte. 23 for a long distance.

BATAVIA KILL #2 Delaware Co. Rises near Denver and flows 12 miles southwest to East Branch of Delaware at Kelly Corners.

BATES Schoharie Co. In Potter Hollow.

BATES HOLLOW Schoharie Co. Northwest of Potter Hollow. Congregational Christian Church (1859; original building 1842).

BATTLEMENT TERRACE Ulster Co. Elev. 2200 ft. Atop Castle Point in Shawangunk Mtns. on Minnewaska grounds. Faces west.

BAXTER BROOK Delaware Co. Rises on south slope of Rock Rift Mtn. and flows 7 miles south to East Branch of Delaware River at Harvard.

BAXTER MOUNTAIN Delaware Co. Elev. 2410 ft. At western end of Cherry Ridge at junction of Beaver Kill and the East Branch of the Delaware.

BEACH HILL Delaware Co. Elev. 2285 ft. South of Hunt Hill, north of Mary Smith Hill and south of Pepacton Reservoir.

BEACH RIDGE Greene Co. Separates the West Kill Valley from Halcott area. Vly Mtn. at north end; Halcott Mtn. to south.

BEACH'S CORNER Greene Co. Between Hunter and Hensonville on Rte. 296; northwest end of East Jewett Range.

BEACON HILL Ulster Co. At Minnewaska.

BEAR HILL Ulster Co. At Cragsmoor in Shawangunk Mtns. on Rte. 52.

BEAR HOLE Ulster Co. West of Van Wyck Mtn., north of Bull Run.

BEAR HOLE BROOK Ulster Co. Rises between Van Wyck and Peekamoose

Mountains and flows 2.5 miles south to West Branch of Rondout Creek between Bull Run and Peekamoose Lodge.

BEAR ISLAND Albany Co. Now called Barren Island, a corruption of the Dutch "Bearn." Now joined to the mainland. North of junction of Hannacroix Creek and Hudson River. South of Coeymans. In his *Knickerbocker History of New York*, Washington Irving recounts an interesting episode in the history of Bearn Island:

About this time the testy little governor of the New Netherlands appears to have had his hands full, and with one annoyance and the other to have been kept continually on the bounce. He was on the very point of following up the expedition of Jan Jansen Alpendam by some belligerent measures against the marauders of Merryland, when his attention was suddenly called away by belligerent troubles springing up in another quarter, the seeds of which had been sown in the tranquil days of Walter the Doubter.

The reader will recollect the deep doubt into which that most pacific governor was thrown on Killian Van Rensellaer's taking possession of Bearn Island by wapen recht. While the governor doubted and did nothing, the lordly Killian went on to complete his sturdy little castellum of Rensellaerstein, and to garrison it with a number of his tenants from the Helderberg, a mountain region famous for the hardest heads and the hardest fists in the province. Nicholas Koorn, a faithful squire of the patroon, accustomed to strut at his heels, wear his cast-off clothes, and imitate his lofty bearing, was established in this post as wacht-meester. His duty it was to keep an eye on the river, and oblige every vessel that passed, unless on the service of their High Mightinesses, to strike its flag, lower its peak, and pay toll to the lord of Rensellaerstein.

This assumption of sovereign authority within the territories of the Lords States General, which might have been tolerated by Walter the Doubter, had been sharply contested by William the Testy on coming into office; and many written remonstrances had been addressed by him to Killian Van Rensellaer, to which the latter never deigned reply. Thus, by degrees, a sore place, or, in Hibernian parlance, a raw, had been established in the irritable soul of the little governor, insomuch that he winced at the very name of Rensellaerstein.

Now it came to pass that, on a fine sunny day, the Company's yacht, the Half-Moon, having been on one of its slated visits to Fort Aurania, was quietly tiding it down the Hudson. The commander, Govert Lockerman, a veteran Dutch skipper of few words but great bottom, was seated on the high poop, quietly smoking his pipe under the shadow of the proud flag of Orange, when, on arriving abreast of Bearn Island, he was saluted by a stentorian voice from the shore, "Lower thy flag, and be d—d to thee!"

Govert Lockerman, without taking his pipe out of his mouth, turned up his eye from under his broad-brimmed hat to see who had hailed him thus discourteously. There, on the ramparts of the fort, stood Nicholas Koorn, armed to the teeth, flourishing a brass-hilted sword, while a steeple-crowned hat and cocks tail-feather, formerly worn by Killian Van Rensellaer himself, gave an inexpressible loftiness to his demeanor.

Govert Lockerman eyed the warrior from top to toe, but was not to be dismayed. Taking the pipe slowly out of his mouth, "To whom should I lower my flag?" demanded he. "To the high and mighty Killian Van Rensellaer, the lord of Rensellaerstein!" was the reply. "I lower it to none but the Prince of Orange and my masters the Lords States General." So saying, he resumed his pipe and smoked with an air of dogged determination.

Bang! went a gun from the fortress; the ball cut both sail and rigging. Govert Lockerman said nothing, but smoked the more doggedly.

Bang! went another gun; the shot whistled close astern.

"Fire, and be d—d," cried Govert Lockerman, cramming a new charge of tobacco into his pipe, and smoking with still increasing vehemence.

"Bang! went a third gun. The shot passed over his head, tearing a hole in the "princely flag of Orange."

This was the hardest trial of all for the pride and patience of Govert Lockerman. He maintained a stubborn, though swelling silence; but his smothered rage might be perceived by the short vehement puffs of smoke emitted from his pipe, by which he might be tracked for miles, as he slowly floated out of shot and out of sight of Bearn Island. In fact, he never gave vent to his passion until he got fairly among the Highlands of the Hudson; when he let fly whole volleys of Dutch oaths, which are said to linger to this very day among the echoes of the Dunderberg, and to give particular effect to the thunder-storms in that neighborhood.

It was the sudden apparition of Govert Lockerman at Dog's Misery, bearing in his hand the tattered flag of Orange, that arrested the attention of William the Testy, just as he was devising a new expedition against the marauders of Merryland. I will not pretend to describe the passion of the little man when he heard of the outrage of Rensellaerstein. Suffice it to say, in the first transports of his fury, he turned Dog's Misery topsy-turvy; kicked every cur out of doors, and threw the cats out of the window; after which, his spleen being in some measure relieved, he went into a council of war with Govert Lockerman, the skipper, assisted by Antony Van Corlear, the Trumpeter.

The eyes of all New Amsterdam were now turned to see what would be the end of this direful feud between William the Testy and the patron of Rensellaerwick; and some, observing the consultations of the governor with the skipper and the trumpeter, predicted warlike measures by sea and land. The wrath of William Kieft, however, though quick to rise, was quick to evaporate. He was a perfect brush-heap in a blaze, snapping and crackling for a time, and then ending in smoke. Like many other valiant potentates, his first thoughts were all for war, his sober second thoughts for diplomacy.

Accordingly, Govert Lockerman was once more despatched up the river in the Company's yacht, the Goed Hoop, bearing Antony the Trumpeter as ambassador, to treat with the belligerent powers of Rensellaerstein. In the fullness of time the yacht arrived before Bearn Island, and Antony the Trumpeter, mounting the poop, sounded a parley to the fortress. In a little while the steeple-crowned hat of Nicholas Koor, the wacht-meester, rose above the battlements, followed by his iron visage, and ultimately his whole person armed as before, to the very teeth; while, one by one, a whole row of Helderbergers reared their round burly heads above the wall, and beside each pumpkin-head peered the end of a rusty musket. Nothing daunted by this formidable array, Antony Van Corlear drew forth and read with audible voice a missive from William the Testy, protesting against the usurpation of Bearn Island, and ordering the garrison to quite the premises, bag and baggage, on pain of the vengence of the potentate of the Manhattoes.

In reply, the wacht-meester applied the thumb of his right hand to the end of his nose, and the thumb of his left hand to the little finger of the right, and spreading each hand like a fan, made an aerial flourish with his fingers. Antony Van Corlear was sorely perplexed to understand this sign, which seemed to him something mysterious and masonic. Not liking to betray his ignorance, he again read with a loud voice the missive of William the Testy, and again Nicholas Koorn applied the thumb of his right hand to the end of his nose, and the thumb of his left hand to the little finger of the right, and repeated this kind of nasal weather-cock. Antony Van Corlear now persuaded himself that this was some short-hand sign or symbol, current in diplomacy, which, though unintelligible to a new diplomat like himself, would speak volumes to the experienced intellect of William the Testy; considering his embassy therefore at an end, he sounded his trumpet with great complacency, and set sail on his return down the river, every now and then practicing this mysterious sign of the wacht-meester, to keep it accurately in mind.

Arrived at New Amsterdam he made a faithful report of his embassy to the governor, accompanied by a manual exhibition of the response of Nicholas Koorn. The governor was equally perplexed with his ambassador. He was deeply versed in the mysteries of freemasonry; but they threw no light on the matter. He knew every variety of windmill and weather-cock, but was not a whit the wiser as to the aerial sign in question. He had even dabbled in Egyptian hieroglyphics and the mystic symbols of the obelisks, but none furnished a key to the reply of Nicholas Koorn. He called a meeting of his council. Antony Van Corlear stood forth in the midst, and putting the thumb of his right hand to his nose, and the thumb of his left hand to the finger of the right he gave a faithful facsimile of the portentous sign. Having a nose of unusual dimensions, it was as if the reply had been put in capitals; but all in vain: the worthy burgomasters were equally perplexed with the governor. Each one put his thumb to the end of his nose, spread his fingers like a fan, imitated the motion of Antony Van Corlear, and then smoked in dubious silence. Several times was Antony obliged to stand forth like a fugleman and repeat the sign, and each time a circle of nasal weather-cocks might be seen in the council-chamber.

Perplexed in the extreme, William the Testy sent for all the soothsayers and fortune-tellers and wise men of the Manhattoes, but none could interpret the mysterious reply of Nicholas Koorn. The council broke up in sore perplexity. The matter got abroad, and Antony Van Corlear was stopped at every corner to repeat the signal to a knot of anxious newsmongers, each of whom departed with his thumb to his nose and his fingers in the air, to carry the story home to his family. For several days all business was neglected in New Amsterdam; nothing was talked of but the diplomatic mission of Antony Van Corlear the Trumpeter,—nothing was to be seen but knots of politicians with their thumbs to their noses. In the meantime the fierce feud between William the Testy and Killian Van Rensellaer, which at first had menaced deadly warfare, gradually cooled off, like many other war-questions, in the prolonged delays of diplomacy.

Still to this early affair of Rensellaerstein may be traced the remote origin of those windy wars in modern days which rage in the bowels of the Helderberg, and have well-nigh shaken the great patroonship of the Van Rensellaers to its foundation; for we are told that the bully boys of the

Helderberg, who served under Nicholas Koorn the wacht-meester, carried back to their mountains the hieroglyphic sign which had so sorely puzzled Antony Van Corlear and the sages of the Manhattoes; so that to the present day the thumb to the nose and the fingers in the air is apt to be the reply of the Helderbergers whenever called upon for any long arrears in rent.

BEARN ISLAND See Bear Island.

BEARPEN MOUNTAIN Greene Co. Elev. 3600 ft. East of Roxbury and north of Vega. Site of Big Bear Ski Bowl.

BEARS DEN Greene Co. Area of tumbled boulders and small caves at foot of Sunset Rock on Escarpment Trail. Former Jacob's Ladder was located here.

BEAR SPRING FOREST PRESERVE Delaware Co. Between Downsville and Walton between the forks of the Delaware. On Rte. 206. A game management area.

BEAR SWAMP Albany Co. 2½ miles south of Westerlo on Rte. 404. 316 acres belonging to the Nature Conservancy with swamp, woods and bogs.

BEARSVILLE Ulster Co. On Sawkill two miles west of Woodstock, and on south slopes of Mt. Guardian. Named for the first settler, Christian Baehr. On Rte. 212.

BEATYSBURG Now Summitville.

BEAVER BROOK Sullivan Co. Rises near Yulan and flows 4 miles South to Delaware River east of Minisink Ford.

BEAVER CREEK Ulster Co. On northwest slope of Shawangunks. Runs from below High Point through Louis Ravine to Napanoch and Rondout Creek.

BEAVER DAM Albany Co. Between Berne and West Berne on Rte. 443. Now called Berneville.

BEAVERDAM CREEK Ulster Co. Rises on south slope of Ashokan High Point and flows 4 miles south to junction with Mettacohonts Creek to form Rochester Creek at Liebhardt. Formerly Mombaccus Kill.

BEAVER KILL #1 Ulster and Sullivan Co. See Chapter 3.

BEAVER KILL #2 Ulster Co. A northern tributary to the Esopus at Mt. Pleasant; it has two branches. The West Branch rises on the southern flank of Mt. Tremper, two miles from Mt. Pleasant. The much longer East Branch rises in Pecoy Notch and flows south to Lake Hill and thence southwest, paralleled by Rte. 212, to Mt. Pleasant.

BEAVERKILL Sullivan Co. On the Beaver Kill and Rte. 152 between Waneta Lake and Lewbeach. Site of Public Campsite, covered bridge and state trout hatchery.

BEAVER KILL RANGE Ulster Co. Range of average 3200 ft. elevation separating the Neversink and Beaver Kill watersheds. It runs southwest from Doubletop Mtn. to Mongaup Mtn.

BEAVER MEADOW POND Delaware Co. Northwest of Readburn and Southeast of Piersons.

BECKER HOLLOW Greene Co. South of Hunter Mtn. west off Stoney Clove south of Notch Lake. A difficult trail to top of Hunter Mtn. starts here. Not for novices.

BEDELL Delaware Co. East of Denver.

BEECH HILL Delaware Co. Elev. 2844 ft. West of Touchmenot Mtn. and north of the Beaver Kill.

BEECH HILL BROOK Delaware Co. Rises between Hunt Hill on north and Beech Hill and flows west to Pepacton Reservoir.

BEECH RIDGE Greene Co. See Beach Ridge.

BEECH RIDGE BROOK Greene Co. Flows east off South Vly Mtn. into the West Kill.

BEECHFORD Ulster Co. Small community on the Esopus Creek and old Rte. 28 between Phoenicia and Boiceville.

BEECHWOOD Sullivan Co. On Jones Brook east of Callicoon on Rte. 164.

BEECHER BROOK Ulster Co. Outlet of Beecher Lake. Flows south for 1.5 miles into Beaver Kill.

BEECHER LAKE Ulster Co. Artificial lake south of Mill Brook Ridge in western Ulster County. A famous trout pond. For many years James and Thomas Beecher, brothers of Rev. Henry Ward Beecher and Harriet Beecher Stowe, lived here.

BEE LINE MOUNTAIN Greene Co. Old name for Evergreen Mtn.

BEER KILL Ulster Co. Two branches flow east into Sandburg Creek at Ellenville. The East Branch rises near Ulster Heights and flows through Cape Pond. The West Branch rises near Woodbourne and flows east past Dairyland and Greenfield Park.

BEERS BROOK Delaware Co. Flows 4 miles into West Branch near Beerston.

BEERSTON Delaware Co. On West Branch of Delaware River, Rte. 10, NYO&W RR South of Walton, north of Rock Rift.

BELLE AYRE MOUNTAIN Ulster Co. Elev. 3420 ft. On Rte. 28 at Highmount. There is a major state-operated ski center here. The chair lift operates year around and offers good views.

BELLEVUE Greene Co. Viewpoint on South Mountain Escarpment Trail overlooking Kaaterskill Clove. On grounds of former Hotel Kaaterskill. Popular in 19th century.

BEN GRAY HOLLOW Delaware Co. North of Chiloway.

BENNETT BROOK Greene Co. Flows north off North Dome into the West Kill.

BENNETTSVILLE Chenango Co. On Rte. 206. East of Bainbridge and west of Masonville.

BENTON CORNERS Ulster Co. At base of Shawangunks on Rte. 44 north of Brunswyck, west of Tuthilltown.

St. Paul's Lutheran Church, Berne. Built 1845.

BERNE Albany Co. In Helderbergs on Rte. 443. Settled in 1750 by Palatinates. The first anti-rent meeting was held in St. Paul's Lutheran Church in 1845 (see Irving quotation in article on Bear Island). Possibly named after Berne, Switzerland by early Swiss settlers, the Zeh family. Zeh House (1795), Rte. 443 west of village. Picher's Mill (c1800), still operative till 1970. White Sulphur Springs House (now Pentecostal Campground), typical primitive spa hotel (c1820), Rte. 443 east of town. Former Indian Stockade area, Rte. 443. Corporation Inn, Rte. 443. Old Town Hall. Partridge Run State Game Management Area.

BERNEVILLE See Beaver Dam.

BERRY BROOK Delaware Co. Rises in Hendricks Hollow south of Mary Smith Hill and flows 4 miles south to Beaver Kill near Clear Lake in Sullivan County.

BESSIE'S LAND See Westerbrookville.

BETHEL Sullivan Co. Community originally settled by Moravians in 18th century and more recently site of Woodstock Festival in 1969, held on the farm of Max Yasgur. On Rte. 17B west of White Lake.

BETHEL RIDGE Greene Co. Foothill ridge about 500 ft. elevation between Kaaterskill Creek and Wall of Manitou. Red sandstone.

BIGGER HOLLOW Delaware Co. South of Lake Delaware.

BIG HOLLOW Greene Co. At headwaters of Batavia Kill near Maplecrest. Site of flood control dam and reservoir.

BIG INDIAN Ulster Co. On Esopus Creek and junction with Birch Creek and on Rte. 28 and U & D RR. Formerly known as Big Injin. Supposedly a physically large Indian named Winnisook lived in the area in colonial times. There are many legends surrounding him. Some concern his prowess as a hunter and others as a lover of white women whom he either abducted or seduced to live with him. Some legends have him run down by wolves or bears and others by jealous white lovers. In any case, they all claim that his body was stuffed into a large hollow tree near the railroad station. Still other legends paint Winnisook as an Indian patriot leader. Nothing is clear. Today the area is a major access point for Slide Mountain.

BIG INDIAN HOLLOW Ulster Co. South of Big Indian on Esopus Creek. Many German resorts in the neighborhood. Panther Mtn. to the east and Belle Ayre and Balsam Mtns. to the west.

BIG INDIAN MOUNTAIN Ulster Co. Elev. 3700 ft. South of Eagle Mountain and west of Fir Mtn. near Frost Valley on the West Branch of the Neversink.

BIG POND Delaware Co. South of Barkaboom Mtn. and east of Touchmenot Mtn.

BIG ROSY BONE KNOB Ulster Co. Elev. 2100 ft. Southerly protuberance between Mombaccus Mtn. to the east and Samson Mtn. to the west. South of Spencers Ledge and Little Rocky. Mettacahonts Creek rises on its slopes.

BIG TONCHE Ulster Co. See Tonshi Mtn.

BIG WEST KILL MOUNTAIN Greene Co. Former name of West Kill Mtn.

BINNEWATER LAKE Ulster Co. Not one of the Five Binnewater Lakes in the Shawangunks. This one is source of Stony Hollow Brook near West Hurley and west of Jockey Hill. Binnewater is Dutch term for a back water or inland pool.

Lodge near Big Indian. Note rustic bracketing. Photo by Alfred H. Marks.

BIRCH CREEK Ulster Co. Rises on south slopes of Halcott Mtn. and flows south around Rose Mtn., then turns east to Esopus Creek at Big Indian. Followed by Rte. 28 and U&D RR between there and Pine Hill.

BISCUIT BROOK Ulster Co. Rises between Fir and Big Indian Mtns. and flows 7 miles south to West Branch of Neversink at Frost Valley.

BISHOP FALLS Ulster Co. Formerly on Esopus Creek. Now site of dam of Ashokan Reservoir.

BLACK BROOK Ulster Co. Rises at 3200 ft. level on south slope of Balsam Lake Mtn. and flows south 2 miles to Beaver Kill near Quaker Clearing.

BLACK CHASM Greene Co. Near Plattekill Falls at head of clove.

BLACK CROOK FALLS Greene Co. Near Palenville.

BLACK DOME MOUNTAIN Greene Co. Elev. 3980 ft. Between Mt. Thomas Cole and Blackhead Mtn. in Blackhead Range. Third highest peak in Catskills.

BLACKHEAD MOUNTAIN Greene Co. Elev. 3940 ft. Easternmost peak of Blackhead Range at junction with Wall of Manitou. Fourth highest in Catskills. On Escarpment Trail.

Bailey Beers, native of the Esopus valley, c1895. Photo by Lionel De Lisser.

BLACKHEAD RANGE Greene Co. Includes, from west to east: Mt. Thomas Cole, Black Dome, and Blackhead Mountain. Runs east and west south of headwaters of Batavia Kill. Terminates at east above Purling area.

BLACK LAKE #1 Greene Co. Near Athens.

BLACK LAKE #2 Sullivan Co. Lake and village south of Bethel and on Rte. 55 south of White Lake. Forestine is on its southeastern shore.

BLACK POND Ulster Co. See Chodikee Lake.

BLACK SNAKE BRIDGE Greene Co. On old Mountain Road from Saxe's Farm to Pine Orchard. Crosses a small northern tributary to Stony Creek below bend at Rip Van Winkle House. Recently reconstructed by DEC. Now on horse trail. No record of how it got its name.

BLACK TOM Greene Co. Old name for Mt. Thomas Cole.

BLENHEIM Schoharie Co. On Schoharie River and Rte. 30 south of Breakabeen and north of Gilboa Mine. Mine Kill State Park, site of Blenheim-Gilboa Pumped Storage Facility of the Power Authority of the State of New York. On August 13, 1704, the Duke of Marlborough and Prince Eugene of Savoy defeated the French and Bavarians under Marshal Tallard at Blenheim, Swabia, West Bavaria. Blenheim Bridge (1855) by Nicholas Powers, longest (228 ft.) single wooden covered span in world.

BLIVINVILLE Greene Co. On Kaaterskill Creek south of Cauterskill on Kings Highway.

BLOOMINGBURG Sullivan Co. At the east portal of the former NYO&W tunnel (caution: roof unstable!) under the Shawangunks on Rte. 17M. Old Dutch Reformed Church, Old O&W depot.

BLOOMINGTON Ulster Co. On Rondout Creek and D&H Canal south of Eddyville, east of Rosendale.

BLOOMVILLE Delaware Co. On West Branch of Delaware River and Rte. 10 East of Delhi, west of Hobart. Former western terminus of U&D RR.

BLOSSOM FALLS Ulster Co. South of village of Slide Mtn. On the headwaters of Esopus Creek near Winnisook Lake.

BLUE BELL MOUNTAIN Greene Co. Old name for North Dome.

BLUE HILL Sullivan Co. Elev. 2755 Ft. West of Claryville.

BLUE MOUNTAIN Ulster Co. Near West Saugerties.

BLUE POINT Ulster Co. On Hudson River south of Highland, north of Milton. Opposite Poughkeepsie. Champagne Vineyards, Hudson Valley Wine Co. and winery owned by Monsieur Henri—open to public. Off Rte. 9W.

BODINE LAKE Sullivan Co. At Yulan.

BOICEVILLE Ulster Co. At northwest end of Ashokan Reservoir and junction of Rtes. 28 and 28A, east of Samuels Point.

BOLTON Ulster Co. See Rondout.

BONANZA FALLS Greene Co. At Freehold.

BONTICOU CONSERVANCY Ulster Co. In Shawangunks near Rosendale. Features include ice caves and Table Rocks.

BONTICOU CRAG In Shawangunks northwest of New Paltz on Mohonk property. Elev. 1180 ft. New York Catskill Aqueduct passes underneath. Word means "spotted cow" in Dutch. Possibly named for the ship "Bontecou," which brought Huguenot immigrants from Holland to New Amsterdam in 1663.

BOTSFORD BROOK Ulster Co. Tributary of the Beer Kill near Upper Ulster Lake.

BOUCKS FALLS Schoharie Co. See Middleburg.

BOUCKS ISLAND Schoharie Co. South of Middleburg. On Rte. 30.

BOULDER Greene Co. A large erratic boulder on the Escarpment Trail on south

Mountain above Palenville Overlook. Fine views. Near Fat Mans Delight and south of Eagle Rock. It used to be crowned by a wooden gazebo reached by a rustic stairway when grounds belonged to Catskill Mountain House.

BOVINA Delaware Co. West of Plattekill Mtn. and east of Bramley Mtn. Settled in 1792. Town was named in honor of "The Cow" upon which dairy industry was based.

BOVINA CENTER Delaware Co. West of Bovina at junction of Coulter and Brush Creeks.

BOWERY CREEK Greene Co. At South Durham. Marie Falls are main attraction here. Also Stead's Twin Falls. Bowery means leafy or shady.

BOYHOOD ROCK Delaware Co. Large boulder near childhood home of John Burroughs west of Roxbury and overlooking Old Clump Mtn. Burroughs used to like to sit here and dream. He is buried nearby and it is now a place of pilgrimage. Woodchuck Lodge is nearby.

BOZENKILL GORGE Albany Co. In towns of Knox and Guilderland. 100 ft. deep and 4 miles long. Railroad runs through it.

BRACE HILL Delaware Co. Elev. 2480 ft. North of Downsville.

BRADLEY Sullivan Co. On Neversink River and Rte. 55 northest of Liberty.

BRADSTREET HOLLOW Ulster Co. See Broadstreet Hollow.

BRAGG HOLLOW AND BRAGG HOLLOW CENTER Delaware Co. West of Halcottsville.

BRAMANVILLE Schoharie Co. At Sharon Springs.

BRAMLEY MOUNTAIN Delaware Co. Elev. 2825 ft. East of Delhi Tower.

BRANCH Ulster Co. On West Branch of Neversink River southeast of Spruce and Hemlock and west of Wildcat Mountains.

BRANDOW POINT Greene Co. On Hudson River south of Athens and above Corlaer Kill.

BRANDY BROOK Ulster Co. Rises near Ulster Heights in a swamp and flows 2 miles to Rondout Creek near Lackawack.

BREAKABEEN Schoharie Co. On Rte. 30 and Schoharie Creek north of Gilboa and south of Middleburg. Fertile bottom lands. Toe Path Mountain State Park to north.

BREAKFAST BROOK Near Wurtsboro.

BREATH HILL Ulster Co. Elev. 2568 ft. West of Little Rocky and north of Peekamoose Lake.

BRIDGEVILLE Sullivan Co. East of Monticello and west of Rock Hill on Rte. 17 where it crosses Neversink River. Named for famous early (1807 to 1923) covered bridge here—160 ft. span—built by Major Salmon Wheat of Orange County. Now on county seal.

BRISCOE Sullivan Co. On Rte. 144 and East Branch of Callicoon Creek. East of Jeffersonville, west of Segar Pond.

BRISTOL Old name of Shady.

BRISTOL BEACH Ulster Co. At Malden-on-Hudson. 73 acres with 22-acre sandy beach in protected cove. You can wade out 600 ft. before reaching the main channel. Clean water. Undeveloped.

BRITTS CORNERS Green Co. In Durham area.

BRITTS FALLS Greene Co. On Dwaskill. Formerly known as Patrons Falls.

BROADSTREET HOLLOW AND KILL Ulster Co. South of North Dome and west of Sheridan Mtn. North of Allaben. Nannette Falls are here and Jay Hand Hollow shoots off it to the northwest. Possibly a corruption of Bradstreet Hollow—possibly named in honor of British Major General John Bradstreet, who contested land titles in the vicinity. Also called Forest Valley. Kill flows south to Esopus Creek.

BROCK MOUNTAIN Delaware Co. Elev. 2700 ft. South of Sugarloaf Mtn. near Cat Hollow.

BRODHEAD Ulster Co. Southwest of Ashokan Reservoir on Rte. 28A, southeast of West Shokan. Formerly Brodhead's Bridge.

BRONCKS LAKE Greene Co. West of Coxsackie and south of Climax.

BRONK ISLAND Greene Co. In Hudson River opposite Otter Hook north of Coxsackie, south of New Baltimore. Channel between Island and mainland now silted up.

BROOKSBURG Greene Co. On Rte. 23 and Batavia Kill 2 miles east of Windham.

BROOME CENTER Schoharie Co. West of Livingstonville and northeast of Gilboa.

BROWNS LAKE Sullivan Co. Near Liberty.

BROWN'S STATION Ulster Co. Formerly on U&D RR. Now beneath waters of Ashokan Reservior.

BROWNSVILLE Ulster Co. On Vernooy Kill east of Lackawack.

BRUCEVILLE Ulster Co. On Rondout Creek east of High Falls and west of Lawrenceville.

BRUIN CAUSEWAY Ulster Co. Ten-foot-wide ridge betwen Wittenberg and Cornell Mountains. No place for people with vertigo.

BRUSH BROOK Delaware Co. Flows south from west side of Mt. Warren to Coulter Brook and Bovina Center.

BRUYNSWICK Ulster Co. On Shawangunk Kill north of Pine Bush and south of Canahgote. Name means Bruyn's Place. Settled by a Norwegian, Jacobus Bruyn, before 1700. Johannes Decker House (c1787).

BRYDEN LAKE Delaware Co. East of DeLancey. Flows south into Fall Clove.

BUCKBROOK Sullivan Co. East of Obernburg.

BULLET HOLE #1 Ulster Co. Small hollow in north wall of the Beaver Kill Range near Tunis Pond.

Greek Revival house, Route 213 near Bruceville. Photo by Alfred H. Marks.

BULLET HOLE #2 Delaware Co. Off Tremper Kill south of Andes.

BULL RUN Delaware Co. A stream in Margaretville.

BULL RUN Ulster Co. Location northeast of Sundown on Peekamoose Road and West Branch of Rondout Creek north of Bangle Hill. At food of Bear Hole.

BURGETT CREEK Greene Co. Drains marshes to south of Catskill, east of the Kalkberg. Ramshorn Brook to north and Mineral Spring Brook to west. Near Kykuit.

BURLINGHAM Sullivan Co. On Rte. 61 east of Roosa Gap and north of Bloomingburg. East slope of Shawangunks. On Shawangunk Kill.

BURLINGTON Otsego Co. On Rte. 80 west of Cooperstown, east of Edmeston on Butternut Creek.

BURLINGTON FLATS Otsego Co. On Rte. 51 northeast of Edmeston.

BURNT ACRES Greene Co. On North Mountain Escarpment Trail between Badman's Cave and Profile Rock. Distinguishing feature is small cave called The Cellar.

BURNT HILL Sullivan Co. Near Amber Lake at Joscelyn.

BURNT KNOB Greene Co. Elev. 3180 ft. On Escarpment Trail north of Acra Point and south of Windham High Peak.

BURNWOOD Delaware Co. On Trout Brook south of Peakville on Rte. 17.

BUSH KILL CLOVE Greene Co. See Deep Notch.

BUSH KILL CREEK Delaware Co. Flows west from Fleischmanns to East Branch at Arkville.

BUSHNELLSVILLE Ulster Co. East of Rose Mtn. on Rte. 42. Named for Aaron Bushnell, early tanner. Formerly Millville.

BUSHNELLSVILLE CREEK Greene and Ulster Cos. Flows south 6 miles from Deep Notch to Esopus Creek at Shandaken.

BUTCHER CREEK Greene Co. Rises on south slopes of Stoppel Point and flows south 2 miles to Kaaterskill Creek at Haines Falls.

BUTTERFIELDS Old name for Stone Ridge.

BUTTERMILK FALLS #1 Greene Co. On south wall of Kaaterskill Clove beneath High Peak between Santa Cruz and Wildcat Ravines.

BUTTERMILK FALLS #2 Ulster Co. Near Peekamoose Lodge and Bull Run, on Peekamoose Road to Sundown. Located on Buttermilk Falls Brook, which runs underground for a short distance above the falls. Water spurts out of a hole in the ground into a moss-lined pool. Pretty and spectacular. Easily seen from the road. Private property. Do not trespass or litter here.

BUTTERMILK FALLS #3 Orange Co. Near Highland Falls.

BUTTERMILKK FALLS BROOK Ulster Co. Flows south of Peekamoose Mountain for 2 miles to West Branch of Rondout Creek east of Bull Run. Unusual waterfall; See above (#2).

BUTTERNUT BROOK Ulster-Sullivan Co. Flows south from Mongaup Mtn. to Willowemoc Creek.

BUTTERNUT CREEK #1 Ulster Co. Flows from slopes of Tonshi and Ticetonyk Mtns. for 3 miles to Ashokan Reservoir near Shokan.

BUTTERNUT CREEK #2 Otsego Co. Rises midway between Cooperstown and Edmeston and flows south through Garrattsville, Morris, and Gilbertsville to Unadilla River at Mt. Upton. Launching site and camping ground at Cope's Corner near Gilbertsville.

BUTTERNUT GROVE Delaware Co. On Rte. 17 and O&W RR at junction of Beaverkill and Russell Brook, west of Cooks Falls, east of Horton.

BUTTERNUT MOUNTAIN Delaware Co. See Red Kill Ridge.

BUTTERVILLE Ulster Co. East of Mohonk, west of New Paltz.

BYRDCLIFFE Ulster Co. Artists colony near Woodstock on south slopes of Mt. Guardian. Founded in 1902 by Ralph Radcliffe Whitehead to perpetuate philosophy of William Morris and John Ruskin. Furniture was hand crafted and an art school operated. Bolton Coit Brown and Hervey White are the best known people who have been associated with the colony.

CABLE HOLLOW Delaware Co. East of Beerston.

CABLES LAKE Delaware Co. Northwest of Morton Hill and north of Russell Brook. Now called Trout Pond. Lean-to at each end. Elev. 2100 ft.

CADOSIA Delaware Co. On Rte. 17 and NYO&W RR north of Hancock on East Branch of Delaware River. Former junction of main line and Scranton branch of O&W. Turreted depot still visible from Rte. 17. Former site of wood acid plant of Keery Chemical Company.

CADOSIA CREEK Delaware Co. Rises near Piersons and flows south to junction with East Branch of Delaware River at Cadosia. Formerly followed by Mainline of O&W RR. Seven miles long.

CAHOONZIE Orange Co. On Rte. 42 south of Forestburg, north of Sparrow Bush.

CAIRO Greene Co. West of Catskill and north of Purling on Rtes. 23, 32 and 145, which intersect here. Name changed from Canton in 1808, in honor of Cairo, Egypt. Pronounced Karo. Once a popular summer boarding town at terminus of a branch of the Catskill Mountain RR. Many waterfalls in the vicinity. Catskill Game Farm and "Old Wild West Town" are near here off Rte. 32.

CAIRO ROUNDTOP Greene Co. Elev. 1400 ft. Formerly called Wawantepachook. Also called Round Head.

CALDERBERGHS, THE Greene Co. See The Kalkberg.

CALKINS CREEK Sullivan Co. Northern tributary of North Branch of Callicoon Creek.

CALLABARRACHS, THE Greene Co. See The Kalkberg.

CALLICOON Sullivan Co. On Delaware River at mouth of Callicoon Creek. On Rtes. 97 and 17B and Erie-Lackawanna RR. St. Joseph's Franciscan Friary, with beautiful grounds, is west of town.

CALLICOON CENTER Sullivan Co. On Rtes. 122 and 123 northeast of Callicoon on North Branch of Callicoon Creek.

CALLICOON CREEK Sullivan Co. North branch flows ten miles southwest from Sand Pond to junction with East Branch at Hortonville. East Branch flows 16 miles west from Swan Lake to Callicoon on the Delaware.

CAMPBELL BROOK Delaware Co. Two branches flow west off Campbell Mountain to the East Branch of the Delaware.

CAMPBELL MOUNTAIN Delaware Co. Elev. 2549 ft. North of Cables Lake and west of Brook Mountain and southwest of Sugarloaf Mtn. Northeast of Cherry Ridge.

CANADARAGO LAKE Otsego Co. West of Otsego Lake, south of Richfield Springs, north of Schuyler Lake. Drained at south end by Oaks Creek. Lake is light greenish aqua color. Cottage colonies along Rte. 28 on west shore. State launching site on Rte. 28 3 miles south of Richfield Springs; hard surface ramp and parking for 40 cars and trailers: large and small mouth bass, walleyed pike, northern pike, brown trout, muskies, crappies, bullheads. Norman R. Baker Octagon House (1882), 2 miles south of Richfield Springs.

CANAHGOTE Ulster Co. On Rte. 44 at junction of Shawangunk Kill and Wallkill River. Formerly Tuthilltown. Old Tuthilltown Gristmill on Shawangunk River built 1788 by Selah Tuthill. Still actively using water power and stone millstones. Eleanor and George Smith purchased in 1941. Various meals and flours available at retail.

CANNONSVILLE RESERVOIR Delaware Co. On Rte. 10. At midpoint on north shore of Cannonsville Reservoir, west of Walton, east of Deposit.

Gristmill at Tuthilltown or Canahgote.
Photo by Alfred H. Marks.

CANOE POND Greene Co. North of Leeds.

CAPE, THE Ulster Co. Small community named for a peculiar rock formation at the eastern end of Cape Pond on the Beer Kill above Hanging Rock Falls.

CAPE HORN Greene Co. Famous sharp bend on the old Mountain House Turnpike on the Wall of Manitou. Above Dead Ox Hill and below Short Level.

CAPE POND Ulster Co. Two miles long on the Beer Kill above Hanging Rock Falls. Southeast of Ulster Heights.

CARL BROOK Ulster Co. Named for early settler John Carl. Flows south off Carl Mtn. to Beaver Kill.

CARLISLE Schoharie Co. On Rte. 20. Panoramic Views of Catskill Mtns. to south and southeast.

CARL MOUNTAIN Ulster Co. Elev. 2880 ft. East of Mt. Tremper and southwest of Little Rocky.

CARMANS NOTCH Delaware Co. South of South Kortright.

CARPENTERS POINT Orange Co. Between Neversink and Delaware Rivers in Deerpark Township southeast of Port Jervis. Tri-State Rock is located here and tip of point is in New Jersey. Cemetery property. No entry allowed.

CARRS CREEK Delaware Co. Rises at Franklin Depot and flows west to Susquehanna River at Unadilla. Formerly followed by O&W RR.

CARSON CITY Greene Co. Wild West amusement area near Cairo.

CASCADE BROOK See Joe's Brook.

CASTLE HOLLOW Delaware Co. On south side of Fleischmann Mtn., between Mapledale and Arkville on the Dry Brook.

CASTLE POINT Ulster Co. Elev. 2200 ft. In Shawangunks in Minnewaska State Park. Limestone cliffs overlooking Hamilton Point and Palmaghatt Ravine to southeast. Battlement Terrace on west face.

CASTLES, THE Ulster Co. Elev. 2080 ft. In Minnewaska State Park and grounds of Lake Minnewaska Mountain Houses. On west side of Palmaghatt Ravine. Limestone ledges. Castle Point to south, Kempton Ledge to north. In Shawangunks.

CATHEDRAL GLEN Ulster Co. Small clove on north wall of Belle Ayre Mountain.

CATHEDRAL GORGE Ulster Co. Formerly on Esopus Creek near Brown's Station. Now under waters of Ashokan Reservoir.

CATHEDRAL ROCKS Ulster Co. Below and west of Cope's Lookout on Mohonk Grounds in Shawangunks.

CAT HOLLOW Delaware Co. Between Campbell Mtn. to the west and Sugarloaf and Brock Mtns. to the east. Traversed by the Downsville-Roscoe Road.

CATSKILL Greene Co. County Seat. On Hudson River. Thruway Exit 21, Rtes. 9W and 23, West Shore RR. Catskill is one of the alleged homes of Rip Van Winkle, and was the actual home of Samuel Wilson, who, as a sutler in the War of 1812, became known as Uncle Sam. He resided in a house on West Main Street from 1817 till 1824, in which Martin Van Buren (later eighth president of the United States and a native of Kinderhook across the river) had married Hannah Hoes in 1807. Sam Wilson is fondly remembered and the road bridge across Catskill Creek near downtown is called the Uncle Sam Bridge.

Flour miller, c1895. Photo by Lionel De Lisser. Same timeless methods are still used at Tuthilltown Gristmill at Canahgote.

The first recorded visit of white men to Catskill was by Henry Hudson in 1609, where he found "a very loving people." He traded with the local Mahican Indians, who had recently been ignominiously defeated by the neighboring warlike Mohawks in a battle on Rodgers Island just above the mouth of Catskill Creek. After this the Mohawks claimed hegemony over the Mahicans who shortly thereafter dispersed.

The first recorded settlement is that of Claes Uylenspiegel, a fur trader who before 1650 had a cabin at the foot of the east slope of Hop-O-Nose or Hopp's-Nose, a rock formation projecting into the west bank of Catskill Creek and allegedly named after the prominent proboscis of a local red man named Hopp. This rock later proved an obstruction to navigation and caused numerous steamboat accidents.

Also prior to 1650 Hans Vos, after whom is named the Vosenkill, or Hans Vos Kill, established a mill on the stream named after him. Jan Jansen van Bremen also built on the present site of the Van Veighten House beneath Jefferson Heights at the ford on the King's Highway (end of Suburban Way). Also in the 17th century Marte Gerritse Van Bergen settled in the neighborhood of Leeds, which was the original Old Kaaterskill. (See Leeds, Jefferson, Jefferson Heights). In 1677 Captain Sylvester Salisbury, an officer of the British troops that took over New Netherlands from the Dutch, acquired many thousands of acres along Catskill Creek. In 1705 Francis Salisbury erected a handsome two-story mansion at Leeds.

With development of river commerce the center of activity shifted down the hill to Het Strand or the Landing on the present site of Catskill village. The town was incorporated in 1806. Impetus for this was given by completion of the Susquehanna Turnpike (c1800) to Wattle's Ferry (Unadilla) on the Susquehanna River. Large parts of this Turnpike are utilized today by Route 23. An eastern segment extended from Salisbury, Connecticut to Greendale, across the Hudson from Catskill. This made Catskill the natural ferry place for westward migration as well as for shipping the produce of the interior down river. In 1838 the steamboat *Frank* began plying regularly between Catskill and New York City. The ferry also soon came under steam. The *Frank* was soon followed by the *Utica, Washington, Thomas Powell, New Champion, Andrew Harder, Kaaterskill, Charlotte Vanderbilt, City of Catskill, Catskill, William C. Redfield, Thomas McManus,* and *Onteora.*

As if all this road and river activity wasn't enough to assure prosperity the Canajoharie & Catskill RR was built and operated between Catskill and Cooksburg from 1840 until 1842 when it was closed down after an accident. The tanning industry in the mountains made Catskill a busy deepwater port for receipt of raw hides for tanning and shipment of tanned hides. As the tanning business declined the Catskill Mountain House (1824) began to attract many travellers. Prior to 1824 Erastus Beach of Catskill had been operating stage coach lines up and down the Hudson valley and into the interior. Charles L. Beach eventually assumed control over these operations and also of the Catskill Mountain House itself. He soon turned it into the "Yankee Palace" and improved the Old Mountain Turnpike starting from Catskill. The work of the landscape painter Thomas Cole (1801–1848), who settled in Catskill shortly after his first visit in 1825, and Washington Irving's tale of Rip Van Winkle and William Cullen Bryant's poem "Catterskill Falls" focused interest on the northern Catskills—halfway between the metropolis and the pleasure meccas of Saratoga Springs and Ballston Spa. Catskill became the natural gateway to the Catskills; Catskill Point, where through steamers stopped, was developed. This was an important landing for both Night and Day Line boats until the last Day Line sailing in 1953. The Catskill Evening Line, eventually controlled by Beach interests, sailed right up Catskill Creek into the village. Completion of the Hudson River Railroad on the East Bank of the Hudson in 1851 made Greendale, sometimes called Catskill Ferry, an important station.

To complete the complex, in 1882 Beach interests completed the narrow-gauge Catskill Mountain Railroad from Catskill Point to Palenville, with a branch to Cairo and eventually connections to the top of the Mountains. There were three stations in Catskill: The Point, The Village and a station near the West Shore RR depot, which was up above on a hill. The Catskill Mountain RR ran until 1918. In 1883 the West Shore Railroad, with its high trestle over Catskill Creek, came through town. Changing vacation patterns and the automobile killed the resorts and the little railroads and steamers that served them. Later, the New York Thruway passed outside of town, leaving Catskill off the beaten path after so many years of activity.

Around the turn of the century the shale brick industry was extensive and also provided paving materials for New York City. As early as 1808 there was an iron foundry. Today liqueurs and cement products are manufactured. At the turn of the century Catskill could boast of its own fine resort. The Prospect Park Hotel stood on a bluff north of the village commanding a fine view of the Hudson River and distant Berkshires. Today recreational interests focus on several marinas and the falls on Lampman's Creek are as attractive as ever. Interesting old buildings are:

Van Veighton House (1690), Old Snake Road or Suburban Way.
Francis Salisbury House (1705), Leeds.
"Uncle Sam-Van Buren" House (c1800), West Main Street.
Foundry Building (c1808). 3½-story front and cupola.
Bogardus House (early 19th century). Federal mansion.
First Court House (c1812). 2 story Palladian. Now a Masonic temple.
DuBois House (c1820).
Dr. Albuisson House (c1825). Stepped gables.
Thomas Cole House and Studio and "Cole's Grove," 218 Spring Street. Cole
  resided here between 1836 and 1848.
Shale Brick Company Office (c1840).
Cemorelli House (c1840). Ionic Greek Revival.
Mrs. McCormicks Store (c1844). 2-story brick.
Union Cotton Mills (c1860).
Two DuBois Houses (c1875), 281 West Main St.
Christ Presbyterian Church (remodeled 1870). Charles L. Beach made a gift of
  six Corinthian columns from the same batch used on the Catskill Mountain
  House.
B.B.G. Stone House, 45 Liberty Street.
Octagon House, Cherry Hill.
Presbyterian and Irving School Slides. Steep pedestrian walkways.

CATSKILL CREEK Greene Co. See Chapter 3.

CATSKILL GAME FARM Greene Co. Near Purling off Rte. 32. Large zoo,
childrens amusement area and picnic grounds. Open April 15 to November 15.

CATSKILL MOUNTAIN HOUSE Greene Co. Former large resort hotel at Pine
Orchard atop Wall of Manitou above Palenville on South Mountain. See history
section for full details. All remains have been obliterated. Property now part of
North Lake State Park. Historic marker near site. Fantastic view.

CATSKILL POINT Greene Co. On north side of Catskill Creek at confluence
with Hudson River east of Catskill. Now given over to industry, it formerly was
an important transfer point for steamer, ferry and railroad travel.

CAUDEBEC See Cuddebackville.

CAUTERSKILL Greene Co. Small community at junction of Kaaterskill Creek
and Catskill Creek. Former woodcarving industry.

CAVE MOUNTAIN Greene Co. Elev. 3100 ft. West of Hensonville and south of
Windham.

CAVE POINT Ulster Co. On Hudson River at Ulster Park. Esopus Meadows
Point to north.

CEDAR SWAMP Ulster Co. At headwaters of the Fantine Kill. West of Napanoch.

CELLAR, THE Greene Co. A deep hole in the ground on the Escarpment trail
on North Mountain between Badman's Cave and Profile Rock.

CEMENTON Greene Co. Formerly Smith Landing on the Hudson. It is the
southern section of Alsen. On Rte. 9W and the West Shore RR. Named for
cement plants here.

CENTER BROOK Delaware Co. Rises near Harpersfield and flows west to Middle Brook and North Kortright.

CENTER VILLAGE Broome Co. On Rte. 79. West bank of Susquehanna River. South of Harpursville and north of Ouaquaga.

CENTERVILLE Sullivan Co. Now Woodbridge.

CENTRAL BRIDGE Schoharie Co. On Rtes. 7 and 30A, Schoharie Creek, D&H RR. Howes Cave to west, Delanson to east. Birthplace of George Westinghouse, inventor of the air brake. Secret Caverns nearby.

CENTREVILLE Ulster Co. On Central New England RR. See Lloyd.

CHAMBERS HOLLOW Delaware Co. North of Hawley.

CHARLOTTE CREEK Rises south of Richmondsville in Schoharie Co. and flows southwest past Lutheranville Charlotteville, South Worcester, Davenport, Davenport Center and West Davenport to Susquehanna River at Emmons.

CHARLOTTEVILLE Schoharie Co. On Charlotte Creek southeast of Worcester.

CHASE BROOK Delaware Co. Three miles long. Flows into West Branch of Delaware.

CHEHOCTON Delaware Co. On Rte. 17 and Erie RR south of Deposit, north of Hancock. On West Branch of Delaware River.

CHERRY RIDGE Delaware Co. Separates East Branch of Delaware from the Beaver Kill. Elev. 2620 ft. Baxter Mtn. at west end, Campbell Mtn. at east end.

CHERRYTOWN Ulster Co. Northwest of Mombaccus. Reached from Pine Bush.

CHERRY VALLEY Otsego Co. On Rte. 166 3 miles south of Rte. 20. Elev. 1,326 ft. Lt. Gov. George Clark secured the Cherry Valley Patent in 1738 and in 1740 seven Scotch-Irish Presbyterian families from New Hampshire, under the leadership of Rev. Samuel Dunlop, settled there. This was the first major settlement in western New York, and for many years remained the largest. With the development of the Cherry Valley Turnpike (now Route 20, which today bypasses the town to the north), the village became an important stagecoach stop. Many gunsmiths, including the famous Amasa Belknap, who developed the Balknap rifle, set up shop here to supply the western immigrants on their way to the wilderness.

Cherry Valley is best known for the Cherry Valley Massacre, which occurred during the Revolution on November 11, 1778 at midday. A force of 800 men consisting of 600 Indians and 200 white men, of whom 150 were Tories, attacked the village. The attackers were unable to invest the fort, which stood on the site of the present cemetery and which was commanded by Colonel Ichabod Alden. However, fifteen of the men stationed at the fort, including Colonel Alden, were killed before the attackers were repulsed. The main devastation was wreaked upon the inhabitants of the village. The attackers slaughtered and mutilated their victims, burnt the town and drove off the livestock. They killed thirty persons right off and took a number of prisoners. As they headed south along Cherry Valley Creek, through the snow, they treated them barbarously, killing two mothers and their children. They finally released the remainder, who struggled back through the snow to find the remaining garrison, and some who had escaped into the snowy woods and now returned, burying the dead. As this was going on Colonel Klock, who had been ordered there by General Hand, who was in charge of the patriot forces in Albany, reached the village. He had come from the Mohawk Valley, twenty miles to the north, and had been ordered there to reinforce Col. Alden's men. General Hand had received intelligence of a meeting at Tioga Point on the Susquehanna where it had been decided that Cherry Valley was to be attacked by a force led by Joseph Brant, the Indian leader, and the Tory captain Walter Butler. It is to Brant's credit that it is recorded that he did not approve of the slaughter of the civilians and only accompanied the expedition upon orders and did not actively participate in the massacre. The intelligence of the planned attack came from an Oneida Indian. A monument to the victims is in the local cemetery.

Site of Fort Alden (1778), Cherry Valley. Photo by Alfred H. Marks.

The Cherry Valley Massacre was responsible for the famous punitive expedition down the Susquehanna under General Clinton and also for reprisals under General Sullivan in the Elmira area. These reprisals and the Battle of Oriskany finally broke the strength of the Iroquois Confederation.

An attack by Seneca Indians took place in April of 1780. This time the carnage was less extensive.

After the Revolution the town grew rapidly to over several thousand population as the population tide moved westward over the Cherry Valley Turnpike. From the late 1700s till the Civil War the famous Cherry Valley Academy, a girls finishing school, operated. The Fea Organ Factory added to the prosperity of the town. Eventually, with the coming of the Erie Canal and the New York Central Railroad to the north, the Cherry Valley Turnpike lost importance and the town's population decreased.

Samuel F. B. Morse, while residing in Cherry Valley with his cousin James Morse, and with the assistance of him and Amos Swan, developed the first working telegraphic machine. Swan later revised and improved the Morse Code.

The Cherry Valley & Mohawk Railroad Co. was chartered in 1868 and construction started by the parent Albany & Susquehanna RR. It was completed in 1870 by the Delaware & Hudson, who had leased the Albany & Susquehanna. It ran 23 miles from the main line at Cobleskill by way of Hyndsville, Seward and Sharon Springs. It operated under the name of Delaware & Hudson Cherry Valley Branch until it was abandoned in 1954. The bridge across Route 20 north of town never had tracks layed on it.

Today Cherry Valley is a quiet town and farm center. The Cherry Valley Museum on Main Street has antique furniture, glass, china, and paintings on display.

A natural feature of the area is Judd Falls, formerly called Tekaharawa Falls, near the junction of Routes 166 and 20 and is just 50 ft. back (out of view of the road) from an unpaved parking area.

CHERRY VALLEY CREEK Otsego Co. Rises near Cherry Valley and flows southwest to Susquehanna River at Milford.

CHERRY VALLEY TURNPIKE Chartered in 1799 from Albany to Cherry Valley. It was extended to Manlius in 1803 and work was completed by 1811. It was built to unusually high standards for the time and followed high ridge lines, providing good drainage as well as the bonus of excellent views. It is followed generally by Rte. 20 today, which, however, bypasses Cherry Valley to the north. It was an important route for western migration and later on for shipping farm products to the Hudson. Later it was a principal route to the spas at Sharon and Richfield Springs and also for traffic to Cooperstown.

CHESTNUT CREEK Sullivan Co. Rises on northwest slopes of Thunder Hill and flows east to Rondout Reservoir. Followed by Rte. 55.

CHICHESTER Ulster Co. North of Phoenicia on Rte. 214 and Stony Clove Creek. Named for Samuel Chichester, owner of an early chair factory located here. See Tiskilwa Park.

CHILOWAY Delaware Co. On Beaver Kill and Rte. 17 between Horton and Peakville.

CHIMNEY HOLLOW Ulster Co. Near Mapledale in north wall of Dry Brook Ridge west of Hiram's Knob.

CHINA Delaware Co. North of Stilesville.

CHODIKEE LAKE Ulster Co. Formerly Black Pond. On Black Creek in Plattekill Hills southwest of West Park and northeast of Centreville.

CHURCHILL MOUNTAIN Delaware Co. Elev. 3060 ft. South of Stamford and Mt. Utsayantha and west of Mt. McGregor. Named for Dr. S. E. Churchill, 19th-century physician and resort hotel owner of Stamford.

CITY BROOK Delaware Co. East of Hancock Mountain.

CLAPPER LAKE Delaware Co. East of Fergusonville.

CLARKSVILLE Albany Co. Off Rte. 443 southeast of foot of Helderbergs. Hannacroix Ravine, Onesquethaw Creek are southeast of village. Sinkholes on Bennett Hill Road. Massachusetts, Vermont and Albany can be seen from Clarksville Hill.

CLARYVILLE Sullivan Co. Small village near junction of the East and West Branches of the Neversink River. Famous fishing spot. Halls Mills, covered bridge and large chimney of ruined Snyder & Bushell tannery southwest of town.

CLEAR LAKE Sullivan Co. Flows north into the Beaver Kill near Cragie Clair.

CLIFF LAKE Sullivan Co. West of Swinging Bridge Reservoir.

CLIFFSIDE Otesgo Co. On east shore of goodyear Lake. C&CV RR.

CLIMAX Greene Co. On Rte. 81 east of Greenville, west of Coxsackie. Limited kame and kettlehole area. Quaker farmhouse constructed by Edward Powell (c1790), now owned by George H. Peters. Van Bergen House (18th century), 1½ story. Vandenburg House (18th century).

CLINTONDALE Ulster Co. On Rte. 44, Penn-Central RR, NYNH&H RR and CNE RR east of Modena and west of Highland. Orchards. Mandia Winery and Champagne Cellar on Bedell Ave.

CLOVE Definition (from Dutch "kloof"): A ravine, hollow or notch in the wall of a mountain or ridge. Usually slopes from a valley floor to a plateau. Usually caused by erosion. Many cloves served as travel routes in the Catskills.

CLUM HILL Greene Co. South of Tannersville and northwest of Roundtop Mtn. Elev. 2300 ft.

CLUMP MOUNTAIN Delaware Co. See Old Clump Mountain.

COB CREEK Greene Co. A western tributary of Potic Creek. Flows south from East Greenville.

COBBLE, THE Delaware Co. West of Fraser.

COBBLESKILL Schoharie Co. On Rte. 7 and D&H RR. Settled 1752, incorporated 1868. Elev. 950 ft. Howes Caverns nearby. Central Bridge to east, Richmondville to west. State Agricultural School and Experimental Farm. In 1778 Joseph Brant, leading Indians and Tories, ambushed American force here. First packaged pancake mix concocted here in 1890. Today pancake flour and refrigeration equipment are manufactured here.

COCHECTON Sullivan Co. Village on Delaware River north of Narrowsburg and South of Callicoon on Rtes. 97 and 114 and the Erie-Lackawanna RR. Former western terminus of Cochecton Turnpike. Was important in lumbering days. Indians played lacrosse here and celebrated their dog festivals and green corn dances. Cochecton is a corruption of Kasighton, or Cushetunk—"place of red stone hills." Settled 1757. Octagon barn on Rte. 97.

COCHECTON CENTER Sullivan Co. On Rte. 115. On Ten Mile River southeast of Cochecton.

COCKBURN Ulster Co. Old name for area around West Shore RR depot for Saugerties.

CODFISH STREAM Sullivan Co. Flows west into Neversink River south of Woodridge.

COEYMANS Albany Co. On Rte. 114. On Hudson River east of Ravena, North of New Baltimore. Pronounced "Queemans." Settled by Barent Pieterse Coeymans in 1673. Coeymans is a typical sleepy old Dutch river town. The neighborhood is described in Chapter II of Cooper's *Miles Wallingford*, where it is given the name of Willow Cove:

> The spot where we landed was a small but lovely, gravelly cove, (now enclosed by concrete dikes) that was shaded by three or four enormous weeping-willows, and presented the very picture of peace and repose. It was altogether a retired and rural bit, there being near it no regular landing, no reels for seines, nor any of those signs that denote a place of resort. A single cottage stood on a small natural terrace, elevated some ten or twelve feet above the rich bottom that sustained the willows. This cottage was the very beau ideal of rustic neatness and home comfort. It was of stone, one story in height, with high-pointed roof, and had a Dutch-looking gable that faced

the river, and which contained the porch and outer door. The stones were white as the driven snow, having been washed a few weeks before. The windows had the charm of irregularity, and everything about the dwelling proclaimed a former century, and a regime different from that under which we were then living. In fact, the figures 1698, let in as iron braces to the wall of the gable, announced that the house was quite as old as the second structure at Clawbonny.

The garden of this cottage was not large, but it was in admirable order. It lay entirely in the rear of the dwelling; and behind it, again, a small orchard, containing about a hundred trees, on which the fruit began to show itself in abundance, lay against the sort of amphitheatre that almost enclosed this little nook against the intrusion and sight of the rest of the world. There were also half a dozen huge cherry-trees, from which the fruit had not yet altogether disappeared, near the house, to which they served the double purpose of ornament and shade. The out-houses seemed to be as old as the dwelling, and were in quite as good order.

The Coeymans and New Baltimore areas have always been, and still are, a favorite retirement place for sailors and retired captains.

Places of interest:

Ariaante Coeymans' house (1716), known as Coeymans' Castle; Stone House Road.

Niles House (c1745), built by Charlotte Amelia Coeymans and her husband, Jan Jonas Bronck. Rte. 144.

Van Derzee House (c1775), Van Derzee Road, ½ mile south of Rte. 143.

Blaisdell (c1875), Victorian farm and barn.

Acton Civil Polytechnic Institute (1873), red brick Victorian Mansard school with tower.

COEYMANS CREEK Albany Co. Rises near South Bethlehem and flows southeast to Hudson River at Coeymans.

COEYMANS HOLLOW Albany Co. On Rte. 143 west of Ravena. On Hannacroix Creek. Collins Farm (19th century), brick Federal. Whitbeck Farm (18th century), with Victorian additions. Count's Farm (c1800), brick Federal.

COEYMANS JUNCTION On West Shore Railroad. Now called Ravena.

COHOHATATIA The Indian name of that portion of the Hudson River from Poughkeepsie to Catskill. Means: Place to catch salmon or shad, the name Coho being applied to both types of fish.

COLCHESTER #1 Delaware Co. On the East Branch of the Delaware and Rte. 30, between Shinhopple and Downsville. Founded in 1766 by Russel Gregory.

COLCHESTER #2 Green Co.

COLCHESTER MOUNTAIN. Delaware Co. Elev. 2500 ft. Northwest of Downsville.

COLDBROOK Ulster Co. Small village between Boiceville and Beechford on Esopus Creek, Rte. 28 and the Ulster & Delaware RR. At eastern foot of Mt. Pleasant.

COLD KILL Greene Co. Flows north from col between Indian Head Mtn. and Plattekill Mtn. into Plattekill Creek near head of Plattekill Clove.

COLD SPRING CREEK Delaware Co. Flows south from China to West Branch of Delaware at Stilesville.

COLD SPRING HOLLOW Delaware Co. At head of Huckleberry Brook on south side of Dry Brook Ridge.

COLE LAKE Ulster Co. At Frost Valley.

COLES CLOVE Delaware Co. North of Midpoint of Pepacton Reservoir. Conklin Hill to west.

COLGATE LAKE Greene Co. Between Star Rock and Blackhead Range at headwaters of the East Kill near Jewett.

COLLAR BACK, THE Greene Co. See The Kalkberg.

COLLIERSVILLE Otsego Co. On Rtes. 7 and 28, C&CV RR, D&H RR 5 miles northeast of Oneonta. On Susquehanna River. Preston House (1827), built by Col. Alfred Mumford.

COLONELS CHAIR Greene Co. Elev. 3200 ft. A northern protuberance of Hunter Mountain overlooking town of Hunter. Allegedly looks like a giant armchair. Named for Col. William W. Edwards, an early tanner.

COLUMBIA LAKE Delaware Co. Southeast of Deposit, east of Crystal Lake.

COLUMBUS POINT See Kingston Point.

CONDON HOLLOW Greene Co. Between Halcott and Vly Mountains south of Lexington.

CONESVILLE Schoharie Co. On Manorkill southeast of Gilboa, west of Manorkill.

CONKLIN HILL Delaware Co. Elev. 2380 ft. North of Pepacton Reservoir, east of Downsville and Round Hill.

CONNELLY Ulster Co. On Rondout Creek and Rte. 9W. South of Rondout boat yards.

COOK BROOK Greene Co. Flows north off Plateau Mtn. along west boundary of Elka Park into Grill Lake and Schoharie Creek. Northwest of Spruce Mountain.

COOKSBURG Albany Co. On Rtes. 145 and 81. Formerly on Schoharie Tpke. and Canajoharie & Catskill RR—western end. Railroad closed and never completed after accident near Durham at High Rock. Cooksburg Hotel (1839), now private residence. Flour Mill (1850). Durham to south, Livingstonville to north. On Catskill Creek.

COOKS FALLS Delaware Co. Community on the Beaver Kill and Rte. 17 west of Roscoe and east of Horton. Former wood acid plants. Holcomb Plant.

COOLEY Sullivan Co. On Rtes. 84 and 85 north of Parksville, south of Willowemoc. On the Little Beaver Kill.

COOPER LAKE Ulster Co. Southeast of Lake Hill on Rte. 212. It is now a reservoir for the City of Kingston. Trespassing is forbidden. It was formerly called Shandaken Lake and flowed west into the Beaver Kill. It was artificially raised and now flows east into the Saw Kill. There was anti-rent action in the neighborhood.

Kingfisher Tower on Otsego Lake near Cooperstown. Author's collection.

COOPERSTOWN Otsego Co. County seat. On Rtes. 28, 80 and 31, Cooperstown & Charlotte Valley RR. Elev. 1200 ft. At the south end of Otsego Lake where it debouches into the Susquehanna River, of which it is the principal source. It is 21 miles northeast of Oneonta and 30 miles southeast of Utica.

In 1769 an Irishman named George Groghan, along with 100 associated partners, was granted a patent running from Cherry Valley on the north to Lake Otsego. He built ten buildings, cleared four fields, built a bridge across the Susquehanna River and built a bateau on the lake, but he soon abandoned these improvements and moved west. Possibly he served James Fenimore Cooper, at least in part, as a prototype of Tom Hutter in *The Deerslayer*, one of the Leatherstocking novels.

Prior to 1769 agents of Sir William Johnson (1715–1774) and his son Sir John Johnson (1742–1830), British loyalist leaders living in baronial splendor at Johnstown in the Mohawk Valley, had regularly entered the Otsego area to purchase pelts for the Johnson's extensive fur trade, and also to perform their duties as deputies of the Johnsons in their capacity of Indian commissioners. George Groghan was an associate of the Johnsons. The Johnsons managed to retain the allegiance of the Mohawks and other tribes of the Iroquois Confederation, with Joseph Brant acting as their chief liaison man. Consequently the Otsego area was under Iroquois domination and unfriendly to both the Mohicans and Delawares. This explains much of the action in *The Deerslayer* as Chingachgook, a Mohican, is visiting Lake Otsego to rescue Wah-Ta!-Wah, his beloved, a Delaware maiden who has been abducted by the Iroquois. Tom Hutter the trapper, "owner of the lake," has a house built on piles at a place called "sunken island." Natty Bumppo, or Leatherstocking, the Deerslayer, is a frontiersman and a friend of Chingachgook's and friendly to the Americans, Mohicans and Delawares. It is not our purpose to describe the plot of the novel as the plot is somewhat overstrained, but the historical context and personality types are accurate and true to life. It was published in 1841 from Cooper's recollections of early life at Cooperstown. The story takes place in 1740. Cooper says in the introduction:

> As for the scene of this tale, it is intended for and believed to be a close description of the Otsego, prior to the year 1760, when the first rude settlement was commenced on its banks, at that time only an insignificant clearing near the outlet, with a small hut of squared logs, for the temporary

dwelling of the Deputy Superintendent of Indian affairs. The recollections of the writer carry him back distinctly to a time when nine tenths of the shores of this lake were in the virgin forest, a peculiarity that was owing to the circumstance of the roads running through the first range of valleys removed from the water side. The woods and the mountains have ever formed a principal source of beauty with this charming sheet of water, enough of the former remaining to this day to relieve the open grounds from monotony and tameness.

In most respects the descriptions of scenery in the tale are reasonably accurate. The rock appointed for the rendezvous between Deerslayer and his friend the Delaware, still remains, bearing the name of Otsego Rock. The shoal on which Hutter is represented as having built his "Castle" is a little misplaced, lying, in fact, nearer to the northern end of the lake, as well as to the eastern shore, than is stated in this book. Such a shoal, however, exists, surrounded on all sides by deep water. In the dryest seasons a few rocks are seen above the surface of the lake, and rushes, at most periods of the year, mark its locality.

With respect to the primeval name of the lake Cooper gives the following dialogue in Chapter II:

"I'm glad it has no name," resumed Deerslayer, "or at least, no pale-face name; for their christenings always fortell waste and destruction. No doubt, however, the redskins have their modes of knowing it, and the hunters and trappers, too; they are likely to call the place by something reasonable and resembling."

"As for the tribes, each has its own tongue, and its own way of calling things; and they treat this part of the world just as they treat all others. Among ourselves, we've got to calling the place the "Glimmerglass," seeing that its whole basin is so often fringed with lines, cast upward from its face; as if it would throw back the hills that hang over it."

"There is an outlet, I know, for all lakes have outlets, and the rock at which I am to meet Chingachgook stands near an outlet. Has *that* no colony-name yet?"

"In that particular they've got the advantage of us, having one end, and that the biggest, in their own keeping: they've given it a name which has found its way up to its source; names naturally working up stream. No doubt, Deerslayer, you've seen the Susquehannah, down in the Delaware country?"

During the Revolution, in 1779, James Clinton mounted a punitive expedition down the Susquehanna, which is more fully described in the article on the Susquehanna River. In the introduction to his novel *The Pioneers, or The Sources of the Susquehanna* of 1823 Cooper states:

"Soon after the close of the war, Washington, accompanied by many distinguished men, visited the scene of this tale, it is said, with a view to examine the facilities for opening a communication by water with other points of the country. He stayed but a few hours."

Shortly after the Revolution, in 1785, William Cooper from Burlington, New Jersey, later known as "Judge" Cooper, the father of James Fenimore Cooper, an "enlightened" land promoter, visited the spot. His "enlightenment" consisted in the fact that he purchased large tracts, sub-divided and sold in fee simple, rather than attempting to rent on the manorial system, which led to so many difficulties

Indian Hunter *by John Quincy Adams Ward, Lake Front Park, Cooperstown. Photo by Alfred H. Marks.*

in the Hudson valley. William Cooper acquired title from Groghan and, in 1786, founded the town of Cooperstown on the present site. In 1790 he brought his family there from New Jersey, including the infant James Fenimore (1789–1851). The lad grew up to love the region and made it the setting of several of his most popular novels. In his books he refers to the town as Templeton and his father and/or himself as Judge Temple. The name Templeton is perpetuated in the name of the cabaret of the present Hotel Otesaga, "The Templeton Lounge." Again in the introduction of *The Pioneers*, Cooper says:

[T]he author was brought an infant into this valley, and all his first impressions were here obtained. He has inhabited it ever since, at intervals; and he thinks he can answer for the faithfulness of the picture he has drawn. . . .

Otsego, in common with most of the interior of the province of New York, was included in the county of Albany previous to the war of the separation. It then became, in a subsequent division of territory, a part of Montgomery; and, finally, having obtained a sufficient population of its own, it was set apart as a county by itself, shortly after the peace of 1783. It lies among those low spurs of the Alleghanies which cover the midland counties of New York; and it is a little east of a meridional line drawn through the centre of the State. As the waters of New York either flow southerly into the Atlantic or northerly into Ontario and its outlet, Otsego Lake, being the source of the Susquehanna, is, of necessity, among its highest lands. The face of the country, the climate as it was found by the whites, and the manners of the settlers, are described with a minuteness for which the author has no other apology than the force of his own recollections.

Otsego is said to be a word compounded of Ot, a place of meeting, and Sego, or Sago, the ordinary term of salutation used by the Indians of this region. There is a tradition which says that the neighboring tribes were accustomed to meet on the banks of the lake to make their treaties, and otherwise to strengthen their alliances, and which refers the name to this practice. As the Indian Agent of New York had a log dwelling at the foot of the lake, however, it is not impossible that the appellation grew out of the meetings that were held at his council fires; the war drove off the agent, in common with the other officers of the crown; and his rude dwelling was soon abandoned. The author remembers it a few years later, reduced to the humble office of a smoke-house.

In Chapter I Cooper gives a general description of the surrounding area:

Near the centre of the State of New York lies an extensive district of country, whose surface is a succession of hills and dales, or, to speak with greater deference to the geographical definitions, of mountains and valleys.

It is among these hills that the Delaware takes its rise; and flowing from the limpid lakes and thousand springs of this region, the numerous sources of the Susquehanna meander through the valleys, until, uniting their streams, they form one of the proudest rivers of the United States. The mountains are generally arable to the tops, although instances are not wanting where the sides are jutted with rocks, that aid greatly in giving to the country that romantic and picturesque character which it so eminently possesses. The vales are narrow, rich, and cultivated; with a stream uniformly winding through each. Beautiful and thriving villages are found interspersed along the margains of the small lakes, or situated at those points of the streams which are favorable to manufacturing; and neat and comfortable farms, with every indication of wealth about them, are scattered profusely through the vales, and even to the mountain tops. Roads diverge in every direction, from the even and graceful bottoms of the valleys, to the most rugged and intricate passes of the hills. Academies, and minor edifices of learning, meet the eye of the stranger at every few miles, as he winds his way through this uneven territory; and places for the worship of God abound with that frequency which characterizes a moral and reflecting people, and with that variety of exterior and canonical government which flows from unfettered liberty of conscience. In short, the whole district is hourly exhibiting how much can be done, in even a rugged country, and with a severe climate, under the dominion of mild laws, and where every man feels a direct interest in the prosperity of a commonwealth, of which he knows himself to form a part. The expedients of the pioneers who first broke ground in the settlement of this country are succeeded by the permanent improvements of the yeoman, who intends to leave his remains to moulder under the sod which he tills, or perhaps of the son, who, born in the land, piously wishes to linger around the grave of his father. Only forty years have passed since this territory was a wilderness.

New York State Historical Association, Cooperstown. Photo by Alfred H. Marks.

The above was written in 1823. This is followed by a description of how the
village looked around 1793 and of the circumstances which shaped the architectural bias of the town:

Immediately on the bank of the lake at its foot, stood the village.

It consisted of some fifty buildings, including those of every description,
chiefly built of wood, and which, in their architecture bore no great marks
of taste, but which also, by the unfinished appearance of most of the
dwellings, indicated the hasty manner of their construction. To the eye, they
presented a variety of colors. A few where white in both front and rear, but
more bore that expensive color on their fronts only, while their economical
but ambitious owners had covered the remaining sides of the edifices with a
dingy red. One or two were slowly assuming the russet of age; while the
uncovered beams that were to be seen through the broken windows of their
second stories, showed that either the taste or the vanity of their proprietors
had led them to undertake a task which they were unable to accomplish.
The whole were grouped in a manner that shaped the streets of a city, and
were evidently so arranged by the direction of one who looked to the wants
of posterity rather than the convenience of the present incumbents. Some
three or four of the better sort of buildings, in addition to the uniformity
of their color, were fitted with green blinds, which, at that season at least,
were rather strangely contrasted to the chill aspect of the lake . . . before the
door of these pretending dwellings were placed a few saplings, either
without branches or possessing only the feeble shoots of one or two
summers growth, that looked not unlike tall grenadiers on post near the
threshold of princes.

. . . He had commenced his labors, in the first year of his residence, by
erecting a tall, gaunt edifice of wood, with its gable toward the highway. In
this shelter, for it was little more, the family resided three years. By the end
of that period he had completed his design. He had availed himself, in this
heavy undertaking, of the experience of a certain wandering eastern mechanic, who by exhibiting a few soiled plates of English architecture, and
talking learnedly of friezes, entablatures, and particularly of the "composite
order", had obtained a very undue influence over his tastes, in everything
that had pertained to that branch of the fine arts. Not that Mr. Jones did
not affect to consider Hiram Doolittle a perfect empiric in his profession,
being in constant habit of listening to his treatises on architecture with a
kind of indulgent smile; yet, either from an inability to oppose them by
anything plausible from his own stores of learning, or from secret admira-
tion, he generally submitted to the arguments of his coadjutor. Together
they had not only erected a dwelling, but they had given a fashion to the
architecture of the whole county. The composite order, Mr. Doolittle would
contend, was an order composed of many others, and was intended to be
the most useful of all, for it admitted into its construction such alterations
as convenience of circumstances might require.

Thus Cooper shows how the itinerent Yankee carpenter-architect with his copies
of Palladio, Minard Lefever and Asher Benjamin spread the Greek Revival gospel
in the wilderness of upstate New York.

Today the saplings in the dooryard are graceful mature trees and the classic
architecture has mellowed. In 1793 it simply looked pretentious and ridiculous.

William Cooper was a Federalist and of aristocratic temperament. In 1791
Otsego County was organized with Cooper as judge and Cooperstown as county

Hotel O-te-sa-ga, Cooperstown. Photo by Alfred H. Marks.

seat. The early settlers produced maize, wheat, maple sugar and potash. Judge Cooper was very popular with the settlers. In 1800 he erected Otsego Hall on the present site of Fenimore House. James Fenimore remodelled it in "Gothic" style and added crenelations in 1834 after a long period of travel and residence in Europe. It burned down in 1853. Judge Cooper lost his early popularity after prosecuting Jedediah Peak under the Alien and Sedition Act. A few years later he was hit on the head and killed by an unidentified assailant after leaving a political meeting in Albany.

Shortly after his return from abroad in 1834 James Fenimore Cooper wrote his novel *Home as Found*, sequel to his *Homeward Bound*, which had contrasted European and American city manners and described an adventurous sea voyage from Europe to New York, life in Manhattan and a trip up the Hudson River. The following description of Cooperstown appears in Chapter IX of *Home as Found* when the long-absent natives come over the hill from Cherry Valley and get their first view of the village:

> "Now, do I know where we are," exclaimed Eve, clasping her hands in rapture; "this is the 'Vision,' and yonder indeed, is our blessed home."
> It is known that they were in a small open spot in a forest, and on the verge of a precipitous mountain. The trees encircled them on every side but one, and on that lay the panorama, although the tops of tall pines, that grew

in lines almost parallel to the declivity, rose nearly to a level with the eye. Hundreds of feet beneath them, directly in front, and stretching leagues to the right, was a lake embedded in woods and hills. On the side next the travellers a fringe of forest broke the line of water; tree-tops that intercepted the view of the shores; and on the other, high broken hills, or low mountains rather, that were covered with farms, beautifully relieved by patches of wood, in a way to resemble the scenery of a vast park or a royal pleasure-ground, limited the landscape. High valleys lay among these uplands, and in every direction comfortable dwellings dotted the fields. The dark hues of the evergreens, with which all the heights near the water were shaded, were in soft contrast to the livlier green of the other foliage, while the meadows and pastures were luxuriant with a verdure unsurpassed by that of England.

Bays and points added to the exquisite outline of the glassy lake on this shore, while one of the former withdrew towards the northwest, in a way to leave the eye doubtful whether it was the termination of the transparent sheet or not. Towards the south, bold, varied, but cultivated hills, also bounded the view, all teeming with the fruits of human labor, and yet all relieved by pieces of wood in the way already mentioned, so as to give the entire region the character of park scenery. A wide, deep, even valley commenced at the southern end of the lake, or nearly opposite to the stand of our travellers, and stretched away south until concealed by a curvature in the ranges of the mountains. Like all the mountain-tops, this valley was verdant, peopled, wooded in places, though less abundant than the hills, and teeming with the signs of life. Roads wound through its peaceful retreats, and might be traced working their way along the glens, and up the weary ascents of the mountains, for miles in every direction.

At the northern termination of this lovely valley, and immediately on the margin of the lake, lay the village of Templeton, immediately under the eyes of the party. The Dwellings could not be much less than a mile, but the air was so pure, and the day so calm, that it did not seem so far. The children and even the dogs were seen running about the streets, while the shrill cries of boys at their gambols ascended distinctly to the ear.

As this was the Templeton of "The Pioneers," and the progress of society during half a century is connected with the circumstance, we shall give the reader a more accurate notion of its present state than can be obtained from incidental allusions. We undertake the office more readily because this is not one of those places that shoot up in a day, under the unnatural efforts of speculation, or which favored by peculiar advantages in the way of trade, becomes a precocious city while the stumps still stand in its streets; but a sober country town, that has advanced steadily pari passu with the surrounding country, and offers a fair specimen of the more regular advancement of the whole nation in its progress towards civilization.

The appearance of Templeton, as seen from the height where it is now exhibited to the reader, was generally beautiful and map-like. There might be a dozen streets, principally crossing each other at right angles, though sufficiently relieved from this precise delineation to prevent a starched formality. Perhaps the greater part of the buildings were painted white, as is usual in the smaller American towns; though a better taste was growing in the place, and many of the dwellings had the graver and chaster hues of the gray stones of which they were built. A general air of neatness and comfort pervaded the place, it being as unlike a continental European town, south of the Rhine, in this respect, as possible, if indeed we except the picturesque bourgs of Switzerland. In England, Templeton would be termed a small market-town, so far as size was concerned; in France, a large bourg; while in America it was, in common parlance and legal appellation, styled a village.

Of the dwellings of the place, fully twenty were of a quality that denoted ease in the condition of their occupants, and bespoke the habits of those accustomed to live in a manner superior to the oi polloi of the human race. Of these, some six or eight had small lawns, carriage sweeps, and the other similar appliances of houses that were not deemed unworthy of the honor of bearing names of their own. No less than five little steeples, towers, or belfries, for neither word is exactly suitable to the architectural prodigies we wish to describe, rose above the roofs, denoting the sites of the same number of places of worship; an American village usually exhibiting many of these proofs of liberty of conscience—caprices of conscience would perhaps be a better term—as dollars and cents will by any process render attainable. Several light carriages, such as were suitable to mountainous country, were passing to and fro in the streets; and here and there a single-horse vehicle was fastened before the door of a shop or a lawyer's office, denoting the presence of some customer or client from among the adjacent hills.

Templeton was not sufficiently a thoroughfare to possess one of those monstrosities, a modern American tavern, or a structure whose roof should overtop that of all its neighbors. Still its inns were of respectable size, well piazzed, to use a word of our own invention, and quite enough frequented.

It is obvious that, while retaining an affection for the landscape, Cooper had become an insufferable snob during his foreign sojourn. The rest of the story of the novel is a thinly fictionalized account of an actual dispute which Cooper had with the people of Cooperstown. For many years the citizens had been accustomed to using 3 Mile Point, which belonged to Cooper, as a holiday picnic grove. Upon his return home he forbade continuance of such usage. This made the citizens irate and the controversy went so far as legal contestation. Cooper vindicated his rights, but like his father before him, lost the good will of his neighbors.

The growth of Cooperstown into the present-day "Museum Town" has been gradual and uneventful. The town has always appealed to wealthy, cultured and conservative people and has a well cared for appearance. Elihu Phinney, whose famous and uncannily accurate weather predictions appeared in his Phinney Almanac, lived in Cooperstown. In 1815 the town was developed enough for George Clarke to build the aristocratic "Hyde Hall," a fine example of chaste Greek Revival. In the 19th century many big estates were created in the area. There were excursion steamers on the lake and in 1909 the present great and gracious Otesaga Hotel was erected, the last of the grand hotels of the Catskill region where elegance, dignity and good society are still to be found.

In 1839 Abner Doubleday (1819–1893) wrote down and formalized the rules for the game of baseball, deriving them from the ancient game of One o'Cat. He was then a student at a local military academy. Doubleday was born at Saratoga Springs; after leaving the academy at Cooperstown he attended West Point, where he graduated in 1842. During the Civil War he attained the rank of general and fought at Fredericksburg and Gettysburg. By official decree of the National Baseball Commission in 1908, title to the distinction of having originated the game of baseball went to General Doubleday and to Cooperstown as the Home-town of Baseball.

East end, Hotel O-te-sa-ga, Cooperstown. Photo by Alfred H. Marks.

In 1869 the Cooperstown & Susquehanna Railroad was completed and in 1887 it was leased by the Cooperstown & Charlotte Valley, a line with long-distance pretentions that never developed. The C&CV itself was acquired by the Delaware & Hudson Company in 1903, the C&CV not having gotten any further than East Davenport. The Cooperstown & Charlotte Valley has reverted to independent shortline status, with close cooperation with the D&H Company. Until 1974 it offered steam-powered passenger service with a full-scale dining car. This service was popular and financially successful but had to be terminated owing to new Federal Railroad Administration track safety standards. Service is now freight only. Around the turn of the century Cooperstown was also served by a branch of the Oneonta & Mohawk Valley Electric Interurban Railway, which ran between Oneonta and Richfield Springs.

The Otesaga Hotel was built by Edward Severin Clark in one year in 1909. Mr. Clark's father built the Kingfisher Tower on the lakefront in 1876 and his adjoining home in 1854. They are still private property. The Clark Foundation is still active in many good causes in the Coopertown area. The Mary Imogene Bassett Hospital is the most complete in the area.

Natural scenic attractions include Otsego Lake, Council Rock, the outlet and source of the Susquehanna, Sunken Island, Leatherstocking Falls, The Vision and Natty Bumppo's Cave where, in *The Pioneers*, Chingachgook dies after a forest fire on the mountain. In the 19th century the cave became a popular picnic spot. Today it is on private land above a pasture on the East Shore of the Lake and almost forgotten.

Interesting buildings include:
Hyde Hall, Thomas Hooker, architect. (1883), Greek Revival.
Woodside Hall (1829).
"White House"—Worthington Homestead (1802).
Smithy (1786), oldest building in town, Pioneer St.
Twin Houses, 55 Pioneer St.
Tunnicliff Inn (1802), Pioneer St. 607-547-9860.
Hotel Pratt (1867), Pioneer St. 607-547-2293.
Presbyterian Church (1805–7), oldest church by Cyrus & Cyrenus Clark.
Riverbank House, at outlet of lake
Christ Episcopal Church (1810); J. F. Cooper buried in churchyard.
Otesaga Hotel (1909), Lake Street. 607-547-9931.
Cooper Inn, Main & Chestnut. Part of it is a house lived in by Cooper. 607-547-2567.
Kingfisher Tower, on the lake.

Statues:

James Fenimore Cooper by V. Salvatore, in park on site of former Cooper estate.
Indian Hunter by John Quincy Adams Ward, of Peekamoose Lake (1830–1910), Lake Front Park between Fair & Pioneer Streets.

Museums:

Doubleday Field and Baseball Hall of Fame
Fenimore House Museum and Headquarters, New York State Historical Society. Museum houses Cooper family relics, early American paintings, Shaker furniture, the Van Bergen Overmantel, an extensive collection of life masks of famous Americans by John Henri Isaac Browere (1792–1834), portraits by Gilbert Stuart and Benjamin West, complete documents of the Aaron Burr side of the Burr-Hamilton controversy and an important collection of American folk art.
Art Association Headquarters, 22 Main Street.
Indian Museum, 1 Pioneer Street. Archaeological dioramas; material on New York State Indians.
Carriage & Harness Museum, Elk St. Housed in 1903 Coach House and Stable.
The Farmers Museum, Route 80. Typical colonial and early New York village with restored buildings from all over the state, including farmhouse, smithy, tavern, printing shop, church, doctor's office, drugstore, general store, lawyer's office, schoolhouse. Also, there is the great hoax "Cardiff Giant," presented to the public in 1869 as a petrified prehistoric man, ten feet high, actually a statue. Extremely fine, complete and authentic collection.

Recreational facilities:

Mt. Otsego Ski Area, 7 miles north on Rte. 80. T Bar, 3 rope tows.
Cooperstown Playhouse, Lake Road, 8 miles north on Rte. 80, Broadway plays June-September.
Boat ride on Lake Otsego—Memorial Day to November, daily. 10 Fair Street Dock.
Glimmerglass Opera Theater Summer Festival, July.

Also at the Lakefront there are picnic sites, swimming, boat livery, public dock and launching site (foot of Fair Street), golf, fishing, square dances.

Each summer the New York State Historical Association sponsors seminars on American Culture & Civilization.

Cooperstown Municipal Band plays weekly concerts on the lake front at Hotel Otesaga—raindates: plays in ballroom.

COPE'S LOOKOUT Ulster Co. On Mohonk grounds in Shawangunks. On southwest slope of Eagle Cliff.

CORBETT Delaware Co. Community on the East Branch of the Delaware, between Gregorytown to the west and Downsville to the east.

CORLAER KILL Greene Co. Rises in West Athens and flows south to Hudson River north of Hamburg.

CORNELL MOUNTAIN Ulster Co. Elev. 3860 ft. North of Slide Mtn. and south of Wittenberg. Its summit has a "crown" consisting of circular cliffs topped with trees. It was named for local bigwig Thomas B. Cornell, who was owner of the Cornell Steamboat Co. and a director of the Delaware & Hudson Canal Co. and Rondout & Oswego RR., and also president of the Ulster & Delaware RR.

CORNER, THE See Mount Pleasant.

CORNWALLVILLE Greene Co. Small community southeast of Durham. Location of the Hope Farm Press and Book Shop, prime source for Catskilliana.

COTTEKILL Ulster Co. North of High Falls, east of Stone Ridge and west of Rosendale. Former station on NYO&W RR.

COULTER BROOK Delaware Co. Rises near Bovina Center and flows 3 miles into West Branch of Delaware River.

COUNCIL HILL Sullivan Co. 2 miles north of Wurtsboro.

COUNCIL ROCK Otsego Co. In Otsego Lake near its outlet into the Susquehanna River near Cooperstown. It is an important scene of action in Cooper's novel *The Deerslayer*.

The rock was not large, being merely some five or six feet high, only half of which elevation rose above the lake. The incessant washing of the water for centuries had so rounded its summit, that it resembled a large beehive in shape, its form being more than usually regular and even . . .

This rock, which was a favorite place of rendezvous throughout all that region, and where Deerslayer now expected to meet his friend, stood near this outlet, and at no great distance from the shore. It was a large isolated stone that rested on the bottom of the lake, apparently left there when the waters tore away the earth from around it, in forcing for themselves a passage down the river, and which had obtained its shape from the action of the elements, during the slow progress of the centuries. The height of this rock could scarcely equal six feet, and, as has been said, its shape was not unlike that which is usually given to beehives or to a haycock. The latter, indeed, gives the best idea not only of its form but of its dimensions. It stood, and still stands, for we are writing of real scenes, within fifty feet of the bank, and in water that was only two feet in depth, though there were seasons in which its rounded apex, if such a term can properly be used, was covered by the lake. Many of the trees stretched so far forward as almost to blend the rock with the shore, when seen from a little distance; and one tall pine in particular overhung it in a way to form a noble and appropriate canopy to a seat that had held many a forest chieftain during the long succession of unknown ages, in which America and all it contained existed apart, in mysterious solitude, a world by itself; equally without a familiar history, and without an origin that the annals of man can reach.

The immediate area around the junction of Lake Otsego and the Susquehanna River had long been a site for Indian councils. At a later date the Indian agent had a cabin nearby. A small park on the shore today affords a magnificent view up the lake.

COUNTRYMAN KILL Greene Co. Flows north from Stoppel Point to Dutcher Creek and Kiskatom Brook.

COVERT HOLLOW Delaware Co. North of Delancey.

COVESVILLE Delaware Co. At junction of Red Kill and Bush Kill. West of Fleischmanns on Rte. 28.

COWAN MOUNTAIN Delaware Co. Elev. 2910 ft. South of Hobart.

COXING KILL Ulster Co. On West slope of Shawangunks. Flows north

Council Rock. Photo by author, 1975.

from Lake Minnewaska at east end and continues north and northwest to Rondout Creek at Lawrenceville, traversing properties of Lake Minnewaska Mountain Houses and the Mohonk Trust. There is a former millsite at the split rock and pool (good swimming) at Coxing Camp on the Mohonk Trust grounds. Day use only. Fee.

COXSACKIE Greene Co. On Hudson River, West Shore Railroad, Rtes. 385 and 9W 9 miles north of Catskill, 7 miles south of New Baltimore. Pronounced "Cook-sackie." The name Coxsackie is Indian. However, authorities are divided on the meaning of the name and give it variously as: cut banks, place where geese gather and place of owls or Koeksrackie, meaning "Cooks Little Reach." Take your choice.

Coxsackie was settled in 1661 by Pieter Bronck of Albany, who built house presently used as a museum about 1663. It was incorporated in 1867.

On May 17, 1775, 225 men gathered in the house of Leendert Bronck, who was a member of the Committee of Correspondence and Safety, to sign what has been called the "Coxsackie Declaration," prior to the signing of the national Declaration of Independence on July 4, 1776. They proclaimed that "Americans would not consent to be ruled, save by themselves," and "never to become slaves," and to oppose the "arbitrary and oppressive Acts of the British Parliament."

About 1824 the Robert Owen-inspired Forestville Commonwealth communal socio-religious community was established here.

Today there are granite works and valves are manufactured.

Points of interest:
Haswell's Ravine with its "Hole in the Ground" underground river.
Pieter Bronck House (c1663). Now Bronck House Museum and Home of Greene County Historical Society, which acquired the property in 1939. On Rte. 9W. Thirteen-sided "Freedom Barn," adjacent to Bronck House Museum. Also on display is scale-model replica of Catskill Mtn. House.

Van Bergen House, Coxsackie. Photo by Alfred H. Marks.

Leendert Bronck House (1738).
Klinkenberg House (early 18th century), near Fourmile Point.
Lampman House (c1800).
Hoyer House (c1825), near Fitche's Wharf.
Groesbeck House (19th century), Rte. 385.
Musial Mansion (c1870); Victorian.
Tuesdell House
Briggs House
Van DerBurgh House

COXSACKIE CREEK Greene Co. Rises in West Coxsackie and flows northeast to Hudson River opposite Stuyvesant in Columbia Co.

COXSACKIE ISLAND Greene Co. In Hudson River north of Coxsackie.

CRADLE ROCK RIDGE Ulster Co. Elev. 3160 ft. South of Mill Brook Range and north of Hardenburg and the Beaver Kill.

CRAFTS GLEN Greene Co. In South Durham.

CRAGIE CLAIR Sullivan Co. On Beaverkill east of Rockland and west of Beaverkill.

CRAGSMOOR Ulster Co. In Shawangunks. On Rte. 52 east of Ellenville. Village and art colony. Site of former Cragsmoor Inn. Sam's Point to north. Local features include: Losees Hill, Bear Hill, South Gully, Sun-Ray Springs, Sunken Valley.

CRANE'S POND Sullivan Co. Near Hartwood. Edmund Crane (brother of Stephen Crane, author of *The Red Badge of Courage*) had a home here.

CRAWFORD Ulster Co. North of Ulsterville and east of Sam's Point.

Cragsmoor Free Library, Cragsmoor. Note natural timbers used as columns. Photo by Alfred H. Marks.

CREEKLOCKS Ulster Co. On Rondout Creek and former D&H Canal. South of Bloomington and north of Lefever Falls. Formerly called Wagen Dal. Jacob Aertsen Van Wagenen House (1699).

CREVICE, THE Ulster Co. Rock cleft on south face of Skytop Mtn. on Mohonk grounds. Path goes up through it. Also called Lemon Squeezer and Orange Squeezer.

CROSS MOUNTAIN #1 Ulster Co. Elev. 2500 ft. South of Mt. Pleasant and north of Wittenberg. Traver Hollow to east and Cross Mtn. Hollow to west; at head of Woodland Valley.

CROSS MOUNTAIN #2 Delaware Co. Elev. 2410 ft. Near Grant Mills on Mill Brook east of Pepacton Reservoir and Barkaboom Mtn.

CROSS MOUNTAIN HOLLOW Ulster Co. West of Cross Mtn.

CRUIKSHANK CAVE Ulster Co. On Mohonk grounds.

CRUM ELBOW Ulster Co. Also called Krumm Elbow. Ledges on west bank of Hudson River above Lange Rack and below West Park. Original Dutch name was Kromme Hoek, or "rounded point." Father Divine once owned summer home and boathouse here, built c1850.

CRUMHORN LAKE Otsego Co. Northwest of Maryland.

CRYSTAL LAKE #1 Delaware Co. Southeast of Deposit.

CRYSTAL LAKE #2 Otsego Co. 1 mile north of Garrattsville on Rte. 51. Boating, fishing: perch, bullheads, pickerel.

CRYSTAL LAKE #3 Sullivan Co. On Rte. 26 and East Branch of Ten Mile River.

CUDDEBACKVILLE Orange Co. On Neversink River, D&H Canal and Rte. 209. Formerly on NYO&W RR. Formerly Caudebec. Named for Jacob Cuddeback.

CULVERTOWN Sullivan Co. On Pine Kill west of Haven.

CURRY Sullivan Co. Village midway between Neversink and Rondout Reservoirs on Rte. 55. Turnoff for upper Neversink River points.

DAHLIA Sullivan Co. On Rte. 145 north of White Sulphur Springs and south of Livingston Manor.

DAIRYLAND Ulster Co. Rte. 52 east of Woodbourne, west of Ellenville.

DAISY Ulster Co. Small community at foot of Overlook Mtn. in Lewis Hollow northeast of Woodstock. Near Glasco Tpke. Bluestone was formerly quarried here.

DALLAS POOL Ulster Co. In Shawangunks in Minnewaska area. Pool on Peters Kill above (south of) Awosting Falls. Name possibly derived from French (Huguenot) name for large flat stones. Similar derivation gave names to the Dallas on Columbia River in Oregon and Wisconsin Dells on Wisconsin River.

DAMASCUS Broome Co. On Rte. 17 and D&H RR's Wilkes-Barre line. East of Windsor and west of Deposit, on east bank of Susquehanna River. Formerly Tuscarora. Biblical names are common in this area. St. Paul was miraculously converted on the road to Damascus, Syria.

DANNY'S LOOKOUT Greene Co. Near Orchard Point on Plateau Mtn. Elev. 3700 ft. Named for Danny Showers, who was with the Conservation Department for many years as assistant of survey crew, observer on Hunter Mtn. and forest ranger at Tannersville.

DASHVILLE Ulster Co. On Wallkill River. South of Rifton and southeast of Tillson on Rte. 213.

DAUNESBURG Schenectady Co. On Rtes. 20 and 7. East of Quaker Street and Delanson and west of Schenectady. Named for James Duane (1733–1797), member of Continental Congress and 1st Mayer of New York City, who in his last years settled here. Featherstonaugh House (c1811–1812), designed by J. J. Ramee. Christ Episcopal Church (c1770).

DAVENPORT Delaware Co. On Rte. 23. On Charlotte Creek east of Oneonta and west of Stamford. John Davenport (1597–1670) was a Puritan clergyman very influential in New Haven, Conn. area, whence many settlers came to Delaware County.

DAVENPORT CENTER Delaware Co. On Rte. 23, Charlotte Creek, U&D RR. East of Oneonta, west of Stamford.

DAVIS CORNERS Ulster Co. Locality near Olive Bridge at junction of roads to the Vly and Atwood.

DEAD OX HILL Greene Co. Steep section of old Mountain House Road between Sleepy Hollow and Little Pine Orchard.

DEANS MILL Greene Co. On Rte. 9W north of Albrights, south of Ravena.

DEBRUCE Sullivan Co. Community at junction of Mongaup Creek and Willow-emoc Creek, on Rte. 82 north of Livingston Manor. Hunter Lake and Hunter Lake Falls Catskill State Fish Hatchery (open 8:00 AM to 4:30 PM).

DECATUR Otsego Co. North of Worcester. Stephen Decatur (1779–1820) was American naval hero in War of 1812.

DECKERTOWN Sullivan Co. Community on Willowemec Creek north of Livingston Manor.

DEEP NOTCH Greene Co. Elev. 1901 ft. Between Halcott Mtn. on the west and Mt. Sherrill on the east. Serves as divide between waters of the West Kill to the north and Bushnellsville Creek to the south. Cliffs rise over 1000 ft. immediately adjacent to both sides of Rte. 42. Also known as Bush Kill Clove and Echo Notch.

DEER LAUREL SWAMP Greene Co. Small marsh on northeastern corner of Kaaterskill High Peak at 2000-ft. level.

DEERLICK BROOK Delaware Co. Flows west off Barkaboom Mtn. into Barkaboom Stream.

DEERPARK TOWNSHIP Orange Co. Near confluence of Neversink and Delaware Rivers.

DEER SHANTY BROOK Ulster Co. Arises on southwest slope of Slide Mtn. and flows southwest into East Branch of Neversink River 3.5 miles above Denning.

DELANCEY Delaware Co. On Rte. 10 west of Delhi and east of Walton. The DeLancey family were political leaders, soldiers and merchants prominent in colonial New York.

DELANSON Schenectady Co. On Rtes. 395 and 37, D&H RR. West of Daunesburg and east of Cobleskill. Goyer Airport.

DELAWARE RIVER See Chapter 3.

DELHI Delaware Co. On West Branch of Delaware north of Walton and south of Stamford, on Rtes. 10 and 28. County seat. First meeting of Board of Supervisors was held here on May 30, 1797. Courthouse Square has notable examples of both Greek and Gothic Revival architecture. Fitche's covered bridge and Delaware County Historical Museum are local attractions. Gideon Frisbee House (1797). Husted Hollow Schoolhouse (1850). Charles Evans Hughes, Chief Justice of the United States Supreme Court, studied law here (1881–1882) with Judge William Gleason while teaching at Delaware Academy (now Delhi State College).

DELONG MOUNTAIN Greene Co. See Round Hill.

DENMAN MOUNTAIN Sullivan Co.

Church on Courthouse Square, Delhi. Photo by Alfred H. Marks.

Church on Courthouse Square, Delhi. Photo by Alfred H. Marks.

Elev. 3053 ft. North of Curry and south of Claryville. Highest and only mountain over 3000 ft. in Sullivan Co.

DENNING Ulster Co. West of Woodhull Mtn. on East Branch of the Neversink River. Famous fishing spot.

DENTON FALLS Sullivan Co. On Neversink River south of Bridgeville in the Turner Brook Preserve.

DENVER Delaware Co. On Batavia Kill northeast of Kelly Corners on road to Vega. Area of large dairy farms and beautiful rolling pastureland.

DEPOSIT Delaware Co. On West Branch of Delaware River northwest of Hancock and southwest of Walton. On mainline of Erie RR, which crosses river here. At junction of Rtes. 10 and 17. Settled in 1785; incorporated 1811. On November 7, 1835, ground was broken here for the Erie RR. Was early lumbering town where rafts were made up. Today has light manufacturing and pressed board plant. Many old houses.

DEVASEGO FALLS Greene Co. Now under the waters of Schoharie Reservoir. Because of its horseshoe shape it was considered a "miniature of Niagara."

DEVIL'S BACKBONE Delaware Co. East of Delancey.

DEVIL'S KITCHEN Greene Co. Area of tumbled boulders and fissures on Plattekill Creek near head of Plattekill Clove. Once a popular picnic area with rustic ladders, walkways, etc., it is now a very difficult and dangerous area to visit.

DEVIL'S LAKE Ulster Co. In East Kingston.

DEVILS PATH Greene Co. A 24-mile-long, very difficult, scenic foot trail from the head of Plattekill Clove to West Kill Mountain. It traverses 5 peaks over 3500 ft. Not for novices.

DEVILS PORTAL Greene Co. Rock formation in Stony Clove on the Devil's Path.

DEVILS PULPIT Greene Co. A natural rock pulpit in the side of the Stony Clove.

DEVILS TOMBSTONE Greene Co. Large erratic boulder in Stony Clove just below Notch Lake at a state campsite.

DE WITT LAKE Ulster Co. At Whiteport.

DEWITT POINT Greene Co. On Hudson River near Alsen, north of Duck Cove and south of Inbocht Bay.

DE WITTVILLE Ulster Co. On East Branch of Neversink, north of Claryville, in Denning Township. Abandoned bark-peeling and tanning community. Settled by Baily Beers in 1818.

DIAMOND NOTCH Greene Co. Between Hunter and West Kill Mtns. Elev. 2600 ft.

DIAMOND NOTCH HOLLOW Greene Co. Hollow beneath Diamond Notch through which flows Hollow Tree Brook.

DIANA'S WELL Greene Co. Waterfall and deep pool near the forge section of Purling. Diana was virgin goddess of the chase, the hunt and the moon and used to frequent such spots to bathe. To see her bathing was to be struck dead, or like Actaeon, be turned into a stag.

Bandstand on Courthouse Square, Delhi. Photo by Alfred H. Marks.

DICKIE BARRE Ulster Co. Elev. 1386 ft. In Shawangunks north off Rte. 44 southeast of the Peters Kill and northwest of Coxing Kill. Quartz conglomerate cliffs.

DICKINSON FALLS Albany Co. A 30-ft. fall on Hannacroix Creek above Alcove Reservoir in town of Westerlo. Jonathan Dickinson (1688–1747) was Presbyterian clergyman second only to Jonathan Edwards in sparking the Great Awakening.

DINGLE HILL Delaware Co. On Tremper Kill between Wolf Hollow and Andes. Elev. 2840 ft. A dingle is a shady wooded valley.

DINSMORE POINT Ulster Co. On Hudson River at Ulster Park. Cave Point to the south.

DIVINE CORNERS Sullivan Co. On Rte. 105 north of Lock Sheldrake.

DIXIE LAKE Sullivan Co. East of Liberty and north of Ferndale.

DOG HEAD COVE POINT Ulster Co. On Lange Rack on Hudson River.

DOG'S HOLE Greene Co. A deep pool on Kaaterskill Creek in Palenville. Since 1975 it has been silting up with gravel from an avalanche upstream.

DOLAN'S LAKE Greene Co. Near Hunter ski center. Formerly Top's Lake.

DONOVAN'S BROOK Ulster Co. Flows northwest off Table Mtn. into East Branch of Neversink River.

DOONAN CORNERS Delaware Co. West of Kortright Center.

DORAVILLE Broome Co. On east bank of Susquehanna River opposite Center Village. Dyer Flats on the East Windsor Road are very fertile bottomlands.

DORLOO Schoharie Co. On Rte. 165 west of Cobleskill.

Courthouse Square, Delhi. Photo by Alfred H. Marks.

DORMANSVILLE Albany Co. On Rte. 143 east of Westerlo, west of Ravena.

DOUBLETOP MOUNTAIN Ulster Co. Elev. 3860 Ft. (east peak) and 3800 ft. (west peak). At north end of Beaver Kill Range. Northwest of Frost Valley and southeast of Graham Mtn.

DOUGHERTY BROOK Ulster Co. Flows east by southeast for one mile off southeast slope of Panther Mtn. and Fork Ridge into Woodland Creek.

DOVER KILL Ulster Co. Flows northwest into Rondout Creek below High Falls. In Dutch, doove kill means sluggish stream.

DOWNS BROOK Delaware Co. Rises south of DeLancey and flows 8 miles south through Gregory Hollow to East Branch of Delaware River at Downsville.

DOWNSVILLE Delaware Co. Village at west end of Pepacton Reservoir. Dam is here. Campbell Mtn. to the east and Trout Brook Mtn. to the west. At junction of Rtes. 30 and 206.

DRUID ROCKS Greene Co. Large Puddingstone conglomerate rocks on slopes of South Mtn. on grounds of former Catskill Mountain House. Known as The

Devasego Falls. Now under waters of Schoharie Reservoir. Photo by Lionel De Lisser, 1893.

Toad, The Bear and The Rabbit from fancied resemblance. They are immediately to the west of the foot of Puddingstone Hall and east of Elfin Pass. Druids were ancient Celtic priests. Their monoliths, such as Stonehenge, were places of religious ceremonies and sometimes human sacrifice. An early visitor familiar with Vincenzo Bellini's romantic opera *Norma*, popular in the early 1800s, and dealing with Druidism, may have bestowed the name because of their similarity to Druidical monoliths.

DRUMMOND FALLS Greene Co. Near Palenville.

DRURY HOLLOW Ulster Co. South of Dry Brook, east of Seager. East of Turner Hollow and west of Flatiron Brook, on north slope of Graham Mtn.

DRY BROOK Ulster and Delaware Co. Flows northwest from west slope of Big Indian Mtn. through Seager and Mapledale to Bush Kill at Arkville. Possibly named from German "Drei Brucke" for three covered bridges which cross it.

DRY BROOK RIDGE Ulster and Delaware Co. Parallel to Dry Brook to the north. Elev. 3460 ft.

DRYDEN CREEK Delaware Co. Flows 5 miles south from Loomis to West Branch of Delaware River at Cannonsville Reservoir.

DU BOIS CREEK Greene Co. South of Catskill, it flows north into Catskill Creek near its outlet into Hudson River.

DUCK COVE Greene Co. Bay in Hudson River at Alsen between Silver Point to south and DeWitt Point and Inbocht Bay to north.

DUNBAR HOLLOW Albany Co. Wild scenic valley in northwest corner of Town of Westerlo. Site of infamous murders in 1850.

DUNK HILL Delaware Co. East of Russell Siding.

Dog's Hole, by Thomas Addison Richards. Harper's New Monthly Magazine, *July 1854.*

DUNRAVEN Delaware Co. West of Margaretville on Rtes. 28 and 30 at east end of Pepacton Reservoir.

DURHAM Greene Co. Off Rte. 145 south of Cooksburg on route of old Susquehanna Turnpike. At foot of Mt. Pisgah. There are many waterfalls in the vicinity, including Hultz's Falls, Quarry Falls, Silver Falls in Taylor's Glen, Morrison's Glen, and Shimmering and Rumble-Tumble Falls in Shady Glen. Site of Durham Center Museum. Old Mill Falls, Steads Twin Falls, Crafts Glen, Bowery Creek, Simpsons Falls, Marie Falls.

DURSO CENTER Greene Co. South of Hervey St. (Durso Center).

DUTCHER CREEK Greene Co. Flows northeast off Wall of Manitou north of Stoppel Point to Kiskatom Brook near Round Top.

DUTCHER NOTCH Greene Co. See East Kill Notch.

DUTCHESS FALLS Greene Co. In the Forge section of Purling.

DWAARKILL Ulster Co. Flows east into Shawangunk Kill north of Pine Bush and south of Canahgote. "Dwaars" means "athwart or across" in Dutch and this stream flows across a low flat perpendicular to the Shawangunk Kill.

DWARKILL Ulster Co. On the Shawangunk Kill north of Pine Bush and south of Canahgote. William and Garret Decker House (1776). Thomas Sansen House 1727).

DWASKILL Greene Co. Near Greenville. Has Britt's or Patron's Falls.

DYER FLATS Broome Co. On Susquehanna River in Doraville.

EAGLE CLIFF Ulster Co. Elev. 1412 ft. At southwest end of Mohonk Lake in Shawangunk Mtns. On Mountain House grounds.

EAGLE MOUNTAIN Ulster Co. Elev. 3600 ft. South of Haynes Mtn. and north of Big Indian Mtn. Southwest of Oliverea.

John Bill Rodgers and Dick Misner, hermits of the Dry Brook Valley, c1895. Photo by Lionel De Lisser

EAGLE ROCK Greene Co. On Escarpment Trail on South Mountain on grounds of former Catskill Mountain House. A flat rock above a precipitous drop. Near the Sphinx. Extensive views.

EARLTON Greene Co. On Rte. 81 west of Coxsackie and Climax, east of Greenville.

EAST BERNE Albany Co. On Rtes. 443 and 157A east of Berne, west of Clarksville. Formerly called Werner's Mills and Philadelphia. Warners Lake and Thompson Lake nearby. On Normanskill. There is a shale gorge 200 ft. deep in West Mountain, 1 mile southwest off Rte. 2. Site of 5-story grist mill.

EAST BRANCH See article on Delaware River.

EAST BRANCH Delaware Co. Village at junction of East Branch of the Delaware River and Beaver Kill. On Rtes. 17 and 30.

EAST BROOK Delaware Co. Rises north of Mundale and flows southwest to West Branch of Delaware at Walton.

EAST DURHAM Greene Co. On Rte. 145 northwest of Cairo. Many waterfalls in vicinity. Butterfly Museum.

EAST DURHAM FALLS Greene Co. Near Durham.

EAST JEWETT Greene Co. On the East Kill south of Mt. Thomas Cole and north of Parker Mtn.

EAST JEWETT RANGE Greene Co. North of Tannersville and Hunter and south of East Jewett. Principal peak is Onteora Mtn. Elev. 3220 ft.

EAST KILL Greene Co. Stream rises on west slope of Stoppel Point and flows west south of the Blackhead Range through Colgate Lake to Schoharie Creek at Jewett Center.

EAST KILL MOUNTAIN Greene Co. Alternate name for Onteora Mtn.

EAST KILL NOTCH Greene Co. South of Arizona and north of Stoppel Point. The East Kill drains off to the west and Dutcher Creek to the east. Also known as Dutcher Notch.

EAST KINGSTON Ulster Co. Northeast of Kingston.

EAST MEREDITH Delaware Co. On U&D RR. Northeast of Meredith. Hanford Mills (c1820), now a museum.

EAST MOUNTAIN Ulster Co. Elev. 2200 ft. West of Yagerville.

EAST PANTHER BROOK Delaware Co. Flows 5 miles into West Branch.

EAST SIDNEY Delaware Co. West of Franklin on Ouleout Creek.

EAST SPRINGFIELD Otsego Co. On Rte. 20 east of Richfield Springs, west of Sharon.

EAST TROUT BROOK Delaware Co. Flows 12 miles into West Branch of Delaware.

EAST WILDCAT MOUNTAIN Ulster Co. Elev. 3340 ft. Between branches of the Neversink east of Wildcat Mtn.

Hanford's mill as it appeared in late 1890s. Courtesy Hanford Mills Museum Historic Photograph Collection.

A mill hand turns a barrel top on a vintage 1872 water-powered machine. Courtesy Hanford Mills Museum Historic Photograph Collection.

EAST WINDHAM Greene Co. East of Windham on Rte. 23 atop the Wall of Manitou. Mt. Zoar to the northwest and Kate Hill to the southeast.

EAST WINDSOR Broome Co. On east bank of Susquehanna River opposite Ouaquaga.

EAST WORCESTER Otsego Co. On Rte. 7 and D&H RR. On Schenevus Creek southwest of Cobleskill and northeast of Worcester.

EAVESPORT Ulster Co. Near Eves Point on Hudson River, north of Malden and south of West Camp, on Rte. 9W.

ECHO LAKE #1 Ulster Co. Elev. 2000 ft. On the Greene County line between Overlook Mtn. to the south and Plattekill Mtn. to the north. It is the source of the Saw Kill, which flows out to the west. Formerly called Shue's Pond before echo effect was discovered. It has a shallow, muddy bottom; catfish reported.

ECHO LAKE #2 Sullivan Co. Northwest of Burlingham in Shawangunks. "Sweet Echo, sweetest nymph, that liv'st unseen, Within thy aery shell." ("Comus" by Milton.) Echo was a favorite nymph of Diana.

ECHO LAKE #3 Sullivan Co. East of Forestburg.

ECHO NOTCH Greene Co. See Deep Notch.

ECHO ROCK Ulster Co. Shawangunks. Beneath The Castles on west wall of Palmaghatt Ravine.

EDDYVILLE Ulster Co. On Rte. 213, D&H Canal, Rondout Creek south of Kingston. Last lock to tidewater in good preservation.

EDGEWOOD Greene Co. Small community in Stony Clove south of Devil's Tombstone on Rte. 214.

EDGEWOOD LAKES Sullivan Co. South of Waneta Lake, north of Deckertown and east of Joscelyn.

EDMESTON Otsego Co. On Rte. 80. Formerly terminus of branch of NYO&W RR west of Cooperstown, east of Sherburne. Historical Society Museum, 2nd

Cement kilns, Eddyville. Photo by Alfred H. Marks.

floor of Central National Bank of Canajoharie, Edmeston Office. Open Saturday, 2–6. Free.

EDWARDSVILLE Greene Co. Old name of Hunter.

EIFFERTS POND Sullivan Co. Near Fosterdale.

ELDRED Sullivan Co. On Rtes. 55, 47 and 33. North of Barryville on Halfway Brook. Eldred Preserve.

ELFIN PASS Greene Co. A very narrow defile between Puddingstone Boulders west of Druid Rocks on former grounds of Catskill Mountain House. It is in the third ledge on South Mountain, on the old, now largely overgrown, trail to Fairy Spring.

ELKA PARK Greene Co. A private community of beautiful homes north of Spruce Mtn. between Cook Brook on the west and Roaring Kill on the east, and with Grill Lake to the north. It was founded by Paul Goepel and other members of the Liederkranz Society of New York. Residents are largely German-Americans and there is a large clubhouse and a Memorial Tower. Forest Inn is located here. The grounds are private and patrolled.

ELK BROOK Delaware Co. On Rte. 17 and NYO&W RR. On Beaver Kill west of Horton, east of Peakville.

ELK BUSHKILL Ulster Co. Flows off northwest slope of Fir Mtn. to Esopus Creek between Slide Mountain and Oliverea.

ELK CREEK #1 Greene Co. Rises on west slope of Halcott Mtn. and flows two miles west to Vly Creek north of Halcott Center.

ELK CREEK #2 Delaware Co. South of East Meredith Village.

ELK CREEK #3 Delaware Co. Flows 6 miles south from Elk Creek Village to West Branch of Delaware at Delhi.

ELK CREEK #4 Otsego Co. North of Schenevus.

ELKS BROX PARK Orange Co. A public park on bluffs above Port Jervis offering extensive views over the Delaware and Neversink River valleys and of the Shawangunks and Kittatinnys near High Point, N.J. It is reached by the Kolmar Labs Road, which leaves Rte. 97 just west of Port Jervis, or by a narrow road from the end of Reservoir Avenue in the north part of town.

ELLENVILLE Ulster Co. Located on the Sandburg Creek at the northwestern foot of the Shawangunks near Sams Point. On Rtes. 209 and 52, it is a major trading town and former boarding house center. There are many fine colonial and Greek Revival buildings. The ultramodern Nevele Hotel is south of town. Scenic attractions include North and South Gullys, Ice Caves, Sam's Point and several waterfalls. The

Snubbing post and marker, Ellenville. Photo by Alfred H. Marks.

Women's Christian Temperance Union Headquarters, Ellenville (WCTU). Built 1917. Photo by Alfred H. Marks.

Channelmaster TV plant is located north of town. There are Doll and Antique Automobile museums. Old D&H Canal office building at corner of Berme Road and Canal Street. Also W.C.T.U. Bldg.

ELM RIDGE Greene Co. North of Big Hollow.

EMBOUGHT See Inbocht Bay and Great Embought.

EMMONS Otsego Co. On Rte 7 and D&H RR north of Oneonta, south of Colliersville. Ebenezer Emmons (1799–1863) served on the New York Geological Survey in the period 1838–1842.

EMMONS BOG POND Otsego Co. On Rte. 23 east of Oneonta. Nature sanctuary with unique floating mat of vegetation.

EMORY BROOK Delaware Co. Drains west slopes of Halcott Mtn. and Monka Hill, flowing into Vly Creek at Fleischmanns.

ERTS BROOK Ulster Co. Flows off southeast slope of Wildcat Mtn. to East Branch of Neversink at Denning.

ESCARPMENT Definition: A steep slope or cliff; often made by fracturing or faulting of the earth's crust. The best known escarpment in the Catskills is the Great Wall of Manitou. In the Shawangunks the Traps Area and Millbrook Mtn. form a notable escarpment, as does the Indian Ladder Cliffs section of the Helderbergs.

ESCARPMENT TRAIL Greene Co. A scenic foot trail from Bastion Falls on Rte. 23A in Kaaterskill Clove to Rte. 23 at East Windham. Principal scenic

Fawn's Leap, Palenville.

features include, from south to north: Bastion, Inspiration Point, Belle Vue, Kaaterskill Hotel site, Boulder Rock, Fat Man's Delight, The Sphinx, Eagle Rock, site of Catskill Mountain House, Artist's Rock, Sunrise Rock, Red Hill, Bear's Den, Sunset Rock, Newman's Ledge, Badman's Cave, Burnt Acres, The Cellar, Profile Rock, North Point, Stoppel Point, Black Head, Acra Point and Windham High Peak. Sections of its southern end are easily accessible for shorter hikes. The northern end is less accessible for the casual tourist and requires conditioning. There is considerable exposure at many points with sheer dropoffs. It is highly scenic.

ESOPUS Ulster Co. On Hudson River, Rte. 9W and West Shore RR. South of Ulster Park and north of West Park, at mouth of Black Creek. Indian Rock to north on Hudson.

Formerly called Van Pelts, the town was founded in 1811. This is another likely setting for Cooper's *Clawbonny*. See article on Saugerties.

Mt. St. Alphonsus Seminary (c1900), 4½-story stone Romanesque. Rte. 9W.

Esopus Methodist Church (c1845), clapboard with Greek Revival elements. Rte. 9W.

Saltbox house (early 19th century), clapboard.

"Rosemont," 2-story pre-Revolutionary clapboard on bluff above Hudson River. Formerly home of Alton B. Parker, New York State jurist and 1904 Democratic presidential candidate.

Walter P. Seamon House (1870), 2-story clapboard.

ESOPUS CREEK See Chapter 3.

ESOPUS LAKE Ulster Co. North of Ulster Park and south of Port Ewen. East of Rte. 9W. Mirror Lake immediately to south.

ESOPUS MEADOWS Ulster Co. Shallow area of Hudson River on west side, between Dinsmore Point and Sleightsburg. It is treacherous and often covered with only one or two feet of water and even small craft can easily be wrecked. The main channel here is curved close to the eastern shore and there are sharp reefs. It is protected by Esopus Meadows Light (1872) at the south end on an artificial island. This is not to be confused with the lighthouse at the south end of the natural Esopus Island, located in Dutchess County waters, opposite the outlet of Black Creek in the village of Esopus.

ESPERANCE Schoharie Co. On Rte. 20. Esperance is French for Hope. West of Daunesburg, east of Sloansville. An evergreen tree on the northern end of the village marks the grave of "The Esperance Witch." She was the widow of a Napoleonic War veteran. Unable to speak English and mingle with the villagers, she became an object of suspicion and in a solemn conclave they decided she was a witch and should be put to death. They fired a silver bullet through the window and killed her while she was cooking at an open fire with her children playing around her. A tragic case of fear and ignorance.

Landis Arboretum is here.

EVANS LAKE Sullivan Co. Near Loch Sheldrake.

EVERGREEN FALLS Greene Co. On Plattekill Creek in the Clove below Green Falls and above Rocky Rapids.

EVERGREEN MOUNTAIN Greene Co. Elev. 3360 ft. South of Schoharie Creek and west of Hunter and Rusk Mtns. The West Kill is to the south.

EVES POINT Ulster Co. On Hudson River and West Shore RR. North of Malden, south of Cementon, east of Evesport. Off Rte. 9W. Clapboard saltbox house (c1840).

EVESPORT Greene Co. On Rte. 9W and West Shore RR. On bluff above

Hudson River. West Camp to north, Malden-on-Hudson to south, Eves Point to east.

FAIRY FALLS Ulster Co. In Peekamoose Gorge near headwaters of Rondout Creek.

FAIRY SPRING Greene Co. On grounds of former Catskill Mountain House on South Mountain. It is a moss-covered basin of very cool, clear water off the Escarpment Trail near the Lemon Squeezer. Difficult to precisely identify in dry weather. Charming spot.

FALL BROOK Ulster Co. Flows off east side of Beaver Kill Range south to West Branch of the Neversink between Claryville and Frost Valley.

FALL CLOVE BROOK Delaware Co. Rises in Bryden Lake and flows 5 miles south to Pepacton Reservoir.

FALLING WATERS Greene Co. An old name for the vicinity of Saxe's Farm at foot of Wall of Manitou near Palenville.

FALLSBURGH Sullivan Co. On Rtes. 43 and 53 and Neversink River south of Woodbourne and north of Monticello. Boarding town.

FALLS MILLS Sullivan Co. On Rte. 52A. On East Branch of Callicoon Creek. Southeast of Callicoon.

FANTINE KILL Ulster Co. Drains Cedar Swamp, flowing 3 miles southeast to Sandburg Creek near Ellenville. The name means "fountain brook" or one with rapids, as opposed to Platte Kill or "smooth-flowing brook."

FANTINEKILL Ulster Co. Small community between Mombaccus and Pataukunk in township of Rochester. It is not on the creek of the same name.

FAT MAN'S DELIGHT Greene Co. Near Boulder Rock on South Mountain. It is a very narrow defile on a side trail from Escarpment Trail to Palenville Overlook.

FAWN'S LEAP Greene Co. A narrow canyon with a waterfall on Kaaterskill Creek in the clove north of More's Bridge. Highly scenic, it is on private property and trespassing is forbidden. The sheer rocks can be dangerous. Named for legend of a hunted fawn that leaped across. According to some versions the fawn made it across but the pursuing dog fell in. Other versions have the fawn drown.

FEAGLE LAKE Sullivan Co. At Narrowsburg.

FEAK HOLLOW Delaware Co. South of Mundale.

FEATHERBED HILL Greene Co. The section of the old Mountain House Road on North Mtn. between Short Level and Long Level.

FEATHERBED LANE Greene Co. Old short cut from Hunter Turnpike to Mountain House Road.

FERGUSONVILLE Delaware Co. North of Davenport.

FERNDALE Sullivan Co. South of Liberty on Rte. 17 and the Mongaup River.

FERNDALE FALLS Greene Co. On Kaaterskill Creek in Palenville.

FERNWOOD Sullivan Co. On Basket Creek northeast of Basket.

FEURA BUSH Albany Co. On Rte. 32. South of Albany, north of Dormansville.

FIFTH LAKE Ulster Co. On Wallkill Valley RR. Also known as Williams Lake. It is one of the Binnewater Lakes in northern Shawangunks. Popular resort, Very clear water. North of Rosendale, south of Fourth Lake.

FINGER HILL Ulster Co. In Saugerties with fine views of Esopus Creek and Hudson River.

FIR BROOK Sullivan Co. Joins with Butternut Brook to form Willowemoc Creek near Willowemoc.

FIR MOUNTAIN Ulster Co. Elev. 3620 ft. South of Big Indian and north of Spruce Mtn.

FIRST LAKE Ulster Co. One of the Binnewater Lakes in northern Shawangunks west of Pink Hill. Very clear water.

FISH BROOK Delaware Co. Flows 3 miles south into Cannonsville Reservoir near Rock Rift.

FISH CABIN CREEK Sullivan Co. Flows south from Glen Spey to Delaware west of Knights Eddy.

FISH CREEK Delaware Co. Rises near Luzern and flows 4 miles northwest to Fishs Eddy on East Branch of Delaware River.

FISHS EDDY Delaware Co. On the East Branch of the Delaware between Hancock on the west and East Branch on the east. On Rte. 17.

FITCH'S WHARF Greene Co. On Hudson River south of Coxsackie and Lampman Hill, off Rte. 385. Groesbeck House (19th century). Hoyer House (c1825).

FIVE CASCADES Greene Co. On Kaaterskill Creek below Haines Falls. Formerly there were rustic ladders, etc. Now rather dangerous area.

FIVE STATE LOOKOUT Greene Co. On Rte. 23 on Kate Hill east of East Windham. It is possible to see New York, Vermont, New Hampshire, Massachusetts and Connecticut.

FLAT BROOK #1 Ulster Co. Flows off southeast side of Wildcat Mtn. to East Branch of Neversink above Denning, between Riley and Tray Mill Brooks.

FLAT BROOK #2 Ulster Co. Flows 2 miles south into West Branch of Neversink between Fall Brook and High Falls Brook.

FLATBUSH Ulster Co. On Hudson River and Rte. 32 near Turkey Point. South of Glasco and east of Glenerie Falls. Name derived from Dutch "vlacke bosch" or "level forest" or "flat woodlands." Flatbush Reformed Church (c1808). Benjamin Ten Broeck House (c1751) on River Road.

FLAT HILL Ulster Co. Elev. 1900 ft. West of Steiny Hill and northeast of Vernooy Falls.

FLATIRON BROOK Ulster Co. Flows north off Graham Mtn. to Dry Brook.

FLEISCHMANNS Delaware Co. On Rte. 28 and Ulster & Delaware RR west of Highmount and east of Arkville. Formerly Griffin's Corners and later Fleischmanns Siding. Charles F. Fleischmann of Cincinnati, of yeast and gin fame, who later became a U.S. senator, built a luxurious estate here in 1883 and arrived regularly in his private railroad car at Fleischmann's Siding. He was a great benefactor of the village, as was his relative, Julius Fleischmann. They were of Hungarian Jewish descent and attracted many friends of similar background. Another relative was Louis Fleischmann, "the great Vienna Bread Baker and Restauranteur of Broadway and 10th Street, New York," who invited many of his German friends such as the orchestra conductor Anton Seidel.

FLEISCHMANN MOUNTAIN Ulster Co. Elev. 2900 Ft. Southwest of Fleischmanns. West of Belle Ayre Mtn. and east of Meade Hill. Mine and Castle Hollows in the south slope.

FLINT Ulster Co. East of New Hurley.

FLY BROOK Ulster Co. In Shawangunks. Flows northeast from Mud Pond or Haseco Lake to Peters Kill, passing west of Lake Awosting.

FLY CREEK Otsego Co. West of Cooperstown on Oak Creek.

FLY MOUNTAIN Ulster Co. In Shawangunks north of Whiteport.

FORESTBURG Sullivan Co. On Rtes. 42, 43, 48 south of Monticello, north of Port Jervis.

FOREST GLEN Ulster Co. North of Gardiner, south of New Paltz on Wallkill Valley RR. Abraham LeFevre house (c1742).

FORESTINE Sullivan Co. On Black Lake south of White Lake on Rte. 55.

FOREST LAKE #1 Delaware Co. Northwest of Grooville.

FOREST LAKE #2 Ulster Co. Near Hardenburg.

FOREST RAVINE FALLS Greene Co. In Forge section of Purling.

FOREST VALLEY & CREEK Ulster Co. See Broadstreet Hollow.

FORGE, THE Greene Co. Section of Purling near Shingle Kill and Forest Ravine Falls. The actual forge is now a museum and store. Enoch Hyde and Benjamin Hall built iron forge here in early 19th century. Renamed Purling in 1895 for purling of waters of Shingle Kill. In the vicinity are Millside Falls, Locks Falls, Renny's Falls, Renny's Glen, Glen Falls, Slaters Falls, Diana's Well.

FORGE QUARRY Greene Co. High above Palenville on southeast slopes of South Mtn. Also called High Rock Quarry. Near Palenville Overlook.

FORK RIDGE Ulster Co. Elev. 2200 Ft. On southeast slope of Panther Mtn. It separates Dougherty Brook and Woodland Creek, above Woodland Valley Campgrounds.

FORT DELAWARE Sullivan Co. An on-site recreation at Narrowsburg. Built by The Connecticut Co. in 1754.

FORT HONK Ulster Co. Near Honk Lake north of Napanoch. A pioneer fort.

FOSTERDALE Sullivan Co. On Rtes. 52 and 17B west of Bethel, east of Cochecton on Old Cochecton Turnpike.

FOURMILE POINT Greene Co. On Hudson River north of Athens, south of Fitch's Wharf. Formerly known to river pilots as Chaney Tinker. Klinkenberg House (early 18th century). Stone lighthouse with clapboard wings (early 19th century).

FOUR STATE ROCK Greene Co. Elev. 2575 ft. Another name for Star Rock. North of Onteora Park.

FOURTH LAKE Ulster Co. One of the Binnewater Lakes in Northern Shawangunks south of Whiteport and Third Lake, north of Fifth Lake. Very clear water.

FOWLWOOD BROOK Sullivan Co. Flows southwest into Neversink River near Glen Wild.

FOX CREEK or FOXENKILL Albany Co. Runs parallel to Rte. 433 from Berne area, west past Gallupville to Schoharie River. Falls in town of Berne over limestone ledges.

FOX HOLLOW Ulster Co. Between Garfield and Panther Mtns. near Allaben.

FRANKLIN Delaware Co. On Rte. 357 south of Oneonta on Ouleout Creek.

FRANKLIN DEPOT Delaware Co. Southwest of Bartlett Hollow on NYO&W. RR.

FRANKLINTON Schoharie Co. On Rte. 145 south of Middleburg, north of Livingstonville.

FRASER Delaware Co. On Rte. 10. On West Branch of Delaware southwest of Delhi, northeast of Delancey.

FREEHOLD Greene Co. On Rte. 32 north of Cairo, south of Greenville. Bonanza Falls, Old Freehold Hotel.

FREMONT CENTER Sullivan Co. On Rte. 94 north of North Branch on Hankins Creek.

FRENCH WOODS Delaware Co. On Rte. 97 south of Hancock, north of Long Eddy. This is the turnoff for Lordville-on-the-Delaware.

FRICK POND Sullivan Co. On headwaters of Mongaup Creek, south of Mongaup Mtn. and north of Debruce. West of Mongaup Pond.

FRIDAY MOUNTAIN Ulster Co. Elev. 3694 ft. East of Slide Mtn., south of Cornell and north of Balsam Mtns.

FROG HOLLOW Sullivan Co. North of Debruce.

FROST VALLEY Ulster Co. On West Branch of Neversink south of Slide Mtn. and north of Claryville. Named for extremely cold winters here. Site of former estate of M. R. Cook, now a YMCA camp and conference center. Artificial lake and Camp Wawayanda.

FROTHINGHAM'S DOCK Ulster Co. Dock for West Park.

FULLER HOLLOW Delaware Co. At Gregorytown.

FULTONHAM Schoharie Co. On Rte. 30 and Schoharie Creek. South of Middleburg, north of Breakabeen. Fertile bottom lands for growing vegetables.

Site of old "Upper Fort," one of the three stockaded fortresses in Schoharie Valley. Toe Path Mountain State Park.

FURLOUGH LAKE Ulster Co. On Dry Brook near Mapledale. Estate of the Gould family. Purchased by George J. Gould, oldest son of Jay Gould, in 1893. Originally named Furlow's Pond after a pioneer family. Private patrolled property. Now Residence of Kingdon Gould, Jr., ambassador to the Netherlands.

GALEVILLE Ulster Co. South of Canahgote on Wallkill River.

GALLIS HILL Ulster Co. North of Hurley.

GALLUPSVILLE Schoharie Co. On Rte. 443 east of Schoharie, west of Berne. Becker Stone House.

GARDINER Ulster Co. On Rte. 44, Wallkill River, Wallkill Valley RR. West of Modena, east of Minnewaska. Orchard area.

GARFIELD MOUNTAIN Ulster Co. Elev. 2532 ft. North of Panther Mtn. and east of Fox Hollow.

GARRATTSVILLE Otsego Co. On Rte. 51 and Butternut Creek north of Morris, southeast of Edmeston. Crystal Lake 1 mile to north. Octagon Barn.

GATE OF THE WINDS Ulster Co. in Shawangunk Mtns. on North Lookout Rd. on Lake Mohonk Mtn. House grounds. See Cave of Aeolus.

GAYHEAD Greene Co. North of Cairo.

GERMAN HOLLOW Delaware Co. Southeast of Arkville on the Dry Brook in north flank of Pakatakan Mtn.

GERTRUDE'S NOSE Ulster Co. Elev. 1800 ft. Promontory facing southeast on Eastern escarpment of Shawangunk Mtns. in Minnewaska State Park, to east of Palmaghatt Ravine. South of Millbrook Mountain.

GHOST, THE Greene Co. Another name for Green Falls in Plattekill Clove. At certain angles the spray from the falls resembles a shrouded death's head.

GIANT LEDGE Ulster Co. Elev. 3200 ft. A southern spur of Panther Mtn.

GIANTS INN AND WORKSHOP Ulster Co. On Lake Mohonk Mtn. House grounds. South of Humpty Dumpty Road and southeast Cope's Lookout. Area of tumbled rocks and ledges.

GIFFORD CREEK Otsego Co. Flows south to Susquehanna River east of Oneonta.

GIGGLE HOLLOW Ulster Co. Small hollow on north side of Belle Ayre Mtn. above Pine Hill.

GILBERT LAKE STATE PARK Otsego Co. 12 miles northwest of Oneonta in Laurens Township on Rtes. 51 and 205. Elev. 1500–1800 ft. 1559 acres with 40-ft. deep, 35-acre spring-fed lake with lake trout. A second lake, reached by hiking trails only, has large-mouth bass, bullheads, and pickerel. Also two ponds. Boating, swimming, fishing; 33 cabins and 221 camping sites for tent or trailer. Hot and cold showers, flush toilets, trailer dumping station.

GILBERTSVILLE Otsego Co. On Rte. 51 and Butternut Creek north of Sidney and south of Morris. Gilbertsville Academy (1840).

GILBOA Schoharie Co. On Rte. 30 and Schoharie Creek near Gilboa Dam at north end of Schoharie Reservoir. Named for a ridge in Palestine where Saul was defeated and killed. Fossil giant fern trees were found here—world's oldest living thing. Scientific name for tree ferns is eospermatopteris. They were a seed-bearing tree fern and grew in shore muds of ancient Devonian Sea.

GILL GULLY Ulster Co. On south side of Belle Ayre Mtn. on North Branch of the Dry Brook.

GINSENG MOUNTAIN Greene Co. Elev. 2800 ft. North of Windham, west of Mt. Zoar and east of Mt. Hayden. The roots of the Ginseng plant resemble a little manniken and are believed by many to be both a health food and an aphrodisiac. The gathering of ginseng roots is a traditional Catskill occupation, although illegal on Forest Preserve lands. Formerly Norwood Mtn.

GLADSTONE HOLLOW Delaware Co. Northeast of Andes.

GLASCO Ulster Co. Hamlet on the Hudson River and Rte. 32 between Flatbush and Saugerties at eastern end of the Glasco Turnpike from Woodstock. It is named from a large name originally painted on a wharf warehouse where a Glass Company used to transship their product. The glass was made between 1809 and 1855 at Shady near Woodstock and brought here over the Glasco Turnpike for transfer to boats. The area was originally settled by Palatinates. Shoal waters in the river here are familiar to boatsmen as "The Saddlebags." Numerous old buildings. A typical 19th-century river town.

GLASCO TURNPIKE Ulster Co. Runs from Glasco to Woodstock. A very pretty scenic drive. Originally a toll road.

GLEN ANNA Ulster Co. On Mohonk grounds in Shawangunks between Gatehouse and Hotel on northwest slope. Hemlock ravine.

GLEN BURNIE Delaware Co. Southwest of Bramley Mtn.

GLEN BURNIE BROOK Delaware Co. Flows 3 miles into West Branch of Delaware.

GLENERIE FALLS Ulster Co. Large falls on Esopus Creek near Mt. Marion. Can be seen from Rte. 9W and West Shore RR. Surrounding property is private. Formerly lead works here.

GLEN FALLS Greene Co. On Shingle Kill in Cairo below Shingle Kill Falls. Near The Forge.

GLENFORD Ulster Co. On Rte. 28 west of West Hurley and east of Ashokan. Near Kenozia Lake.

GLEN MARY Greene Co. See Mary's Glen.

GLENNON CREEK Greene Co. Flows from southwest slopes of Stoppel Point to Kaaterskill Creek at Haines Falls.

GLEN PARK Greene Co. Private residential park adjacent to and east of Onteora Park north of Haines Falls. On Saw Mill Creek.

GLEN SPEY Sullivan Co. On Rtes. 42, 41, 32, 31 north of Pond Eddy.

GLEN WILD Sullivan Co. On Rtes. 56 and 57. North of Rock Hill, south of Woodridge. On Fowlwood Brook.

GLIMMERGLASS STATE PARK Otsego Co. At northeast end of Otsego Lake south of East Springfield. Day use only—bathing, picnicing. Open only Saturdays, Sundays, and holidays. Grounds incorporated the Greek Revival mansion Hyde Hall, built by the architect Thomas Hooker in 1833.

Glimmerglass is poetic name given by James Fenimore Cooper to Otsego Lake; see Chapter 3.

GLORY HILL Ulster Co. In Shawangunks on Mohonk grounds east of Skytop.

GOBLIN GULCH Ulster Co. A deep notch immediately east of Ashokan High Point. Possibly it was the outlet for a large lake to the north as there are several fossil waterfalls in the gap. The southern end is on the road from Samsonville to Olive Bridge, at a sharp bend to the east. Also known as Wagon Wheel Gap from an old broken wagon wheel found in a spring here.

GODEFFROY Orange Co. On Rte. 209, Neversink River, old D&H Canal, (locks still visible), Old Mine Road and former NYO&W RR. It is alleged that the old Gumaer dwelling at the west end of Peenpack Flats was the birthplace of Governor DeWitt Clinton (1769–1828), but other sources claim he was born in New Windsor on the Hudson. Formerly called Port Clinton.

GOLDEN HILL Ulster Co. On Rte. 32. Northernmost point in Shawangunks. South of Kingston.

GOODYEAR LAKE Otsego Co. On Rte. 28 and C&CV RR. Formed by damming of the Susquehanna River by a power dam 5 miles northeast of Oneonta. It is south of Milford and north of Colliersville. Cliffside is on east shore. Rest area and informational sign on Rte. 28 just south of dam. There is a launching site at Twin Spruce Trailer Park on Rte. 28 at Portlandville at north end of the lake. Trout, perch, walleyed pike, large and small mouth bass, calico bass. During times of low water in the Susquehanna River water is released only in the early morning.

GOOSEBERRY CREEK Greene Co. Rising in Lake Rip Van Winkle south of Tannersville, it flows west 2 miles to Schoharie Creek.

GRAHAM MOUNTAIN Ulster Co. Elev. 3868 ft. East of Balsam Lake Mtn. and west of Doubletop Mtn.

GRAHAMSVILLE Sullivan Co. On Chestnut Creek at west end of Rondout Reservoir. Junction of Routes 55, 55A and 153. On September 5, 1778 militia led by Lt. John Graham fought Indians in Battle of Chestnut Woods. Graham and two men were killed.

GRAND CANYON Greene Co. Name no longer used. Formerly applied to three separate locations: the Plattekill Clove, the Kaaterskill Clove and the Amphitheatre.

GRAND GORGE Delaware Co. North of Roxbury, east of Stamford and west of Prattsville at junction of Rtes. 23 and 30. On Ulster & Delaware RR. Named for defile at headwaters of East Branch of Delaware between Irish Mtn. on the east and the Moresville Range on the west, through which pass the U&D RR and Rte. 30.

GRAND HOTEL STATION Ulster Co. Former name for Highmount Station on Ulster & Delaware RR. Named for railroad-owned large hotel here.

GRANITE Ulster Co. On former NYO&W RR. On Stony Kill on west slope of Shawangunks near Kerhonkson. Large resort hotel.

GRANTS MILLS Delaware Co. South of Arkville on Mill Brook. North of Cross Mtn. and south of Dry Brook Ridge.

GRAPEVILLE Greene Co. East of Greenville, west of Coxsackie on Grapeville Creek.

GRAPEVILLE CREEK Greene Co. Middle tributary of Potic Creek.

GRASSY SWAMP BROOK Sullivan Co. Rises east of Tusten and flows southwest into Delaware River south of Tusten.

GRAY HILL Sullivan Co. Near Deckertown.

GRAY POND Delaware Co. East of Beerston.

GRAY ROCK FALLS Ulster Co. Immediately below Rocky Rapids at foot of Plattekill Clove in West Saugerties.

GREAT EMBOUGHT Greene Co. Area of marshes and fertile flats south of Catskill, east of the Kalkberg along the Hudson River. Embought (Inbocht) Bay to the south and Kykuit Hill to the north. Drained by Mineral Spring, Ramshorn, Du Bois, and Burget Creeks. See also Inbocht Bay.

GREAT FALLS Greene Co. On Kaaterskill Creek near Kiskatom, east of Palenville. Private property and dangerous.

GREAT VLY Greene and Ulster Co. Large swamp west of the Kalkberg. The Sawyer Kill drains south out of it to Saugerties.

GREAT WALL OF MANITOU Greene Co. The front escarpment of the northern Catskills, running from Overlook Mtn. near Woodstock at the south end to Windham High Peak and Kate Hill at the north end. Elevations range from 2000 to 3000 feet. The former Catskill Mountain House stood atop it at Pine Orchard between South and North Mountains near Palenville. Its northern portion is followed by the Escarpment Trail and it is indented by numerous cloves, the grandest of which are the Kaaterskill and the Plattekill. It is that part of the Catskills observed from the Upper Hudson River.

GREENE POINT Greene Co. East of the Kalkberg at the northern end of Inbocht Bay on the Hudson River below Catskill and above Alsen. Van Arden House (mid 19th century), 2-story clapboard mansion.

GREEN FALLS Greene Co. Also known as The Ghost. Above Evergreen Falls and below Lower Rainbow Falls in Plattekill Clove.

GREENFIELD PARK Ulster Co. Near Ellenville.

GREEN KILL Ulster Co. Flows south into Rondout Creek at Lawrenceville.

GREEN LAKE Greene Co. At West Athens.

GREEN LAKE Greene Co. At West Athens.

GREENVILLE #1 Greene Co. On Rtes. 32 and 81. New England-style village green. Gen. Nathaniel Greene (1742–1786) served in Revolution. County and town were named for him. Prevost Manor House (1793). Episcopal Church (1857).

GREENVILLE #2 Ulster Co. East of Sundown and north of Yagerville at west end of Balsam Swamp on headwaters of East Branch of Rondout Creek.

GREGORY HOLLOW Delaware Co. Northeast of Downsville on Down's Brook.

GREGORYTOWN Delaware Co. On Rte. 30 west of Downsville and east of Shinhopple; near Corbett, on East Branch of Delaware River.

GRIFFIN'S CORNERS Delaware Co. Former name of Fleischmanns.

GRILL LAKE Greene Co. At foot of Plateau Mtn. north of Elka Park. Fed by Cook Brook.

GROOVILLE Sullivan Co. North of Parkston and northwest of Debruce on Sprague Brook.

GROSSINGERS LAKE Sullivan Co. Southeast of Liberty.

GROTE BINNEWATER Ulster Co. On Black Creek west of Highland. Means "Big Pond" in Dutch.

GUARDIAN MOUNTAIN Ulster Co. Elev. 2100 ft. Formerly Saw Kill Head. Between Shady and Woodstock. West of Meads. The Byrdcliffe Colony is on its south slope. Formerly glass works at western foot in Shady.

GUIDERLAND Albany Co. On Rte. 20 northwest of Albany. Case Tavern (1799). Bozenkill Gorge. North House (1784–86) built by Wm. North, aide to Baron Von Steuben during the Revolution. Duane-Featherstonhaugh House (c1816), Georgian colonial.

GULF, THE Greene Co. See The Amphitheatre.

GULF BROOK Delaware Co. Flows west from north of Mary Smith Hill to Holliday Brook.

GULF OF MEXICO BROOK Ulster Co. Flows off south side of Graham Mtn. to Beaver Kill.

GULF ROAD Ulster Co. Old name for road from West Shokan to Sundown. Passes Peekamoose Lake. Buttermilk Falls en route.

GULF SUMMIT Broome Co. On Erie RR mainline, south off Rte. 17 east of Damascus and west of Deposit. The divide between the Susquehanna and Delaware Watersheds on the Erie RR, in the Randolph Hills. From here the waters of McClure's Brook flow east to the Delaware and Cascade Brook flows west to the Susquehanna. This low spot was discovered by Benjamin Wright in 1840. Line was surveyed by John Anderson in 1841. Deep cut is ½ mile long and 200 ft. deep. It required blasting and was a great engineering feat at the time. First train through in 1848. Very cold all year and strong winds blow through.

GUMAER BROOK Sullivan Co. Flows east to Basher Kill between Summitville and Wurtsboro. Not near Gumaer's or Gumaer's Siding in Orange County.

GUMAER FALLS Sullivan Co. On Gumaer Brook north of Wurtsboro.

GUMAER ISLAND Ulster Co. In Rondout Creek between Eddyville and Wilbur.

GUMAER'S Orange Co. Large summer home colony on Erie RR north of Port Jervis in Shawangunks.

GUN HOLLOW Delaware Co. In south side of Hunt Hill.

GURNEYS POND Sullivan Co. Near Harris.

GUYOT HILL Ulster Co. On Mohonk Mountain House golf course in Shawangunks. Elev. 1250 ft. Named for Swiss naturalist and geographer Arnold Henry Guyot (1807–1884). He was a friend of Louis Agassiz. Later, while a professor at Princeton, he did considerable work in the Catskills and visited Mohonk.

HAGADORE BROOK Greene Co. Flows north off North Dome one mile to the West Kill.

HAILES CAVE Albany Co. On Rte. 159. Near Thacher State Park. 2800 ft. long.

HAINES FALLS Greene Co. Second highest waterfall in Catskills, with a single main fall of 160 ft. on Kaaterskill Creek at the head of Kaaterskill Clove. It is on the private grounds of the Twilight Park Association, but may be seen to advantage from the Escarpment Trail between Layman Monument and Inspiration Point. In years past it was owned by Charles W. Haines, who also had a mill on the stream above the falls and a dam with a sluice gate. Around 1860 he built a boarding house named the "Haines Falls House." He also built wooden stairs and ladders to the bottom of the falls. Often he would close the sluice gate on the dam above and build up a considerable head of water. Then, when viewers had assembled at the bottom, he would open the gate and let the water fall with dramatic effect. All these artificial features are now gone and the area, with slippery shale rocks and overhanging precipices, can be quite dangerous. See article on Twilight Park.

Haines Falls. Author's collection.

HAINES FALLS Greene Co. Village at the head of Kaaterskill Clove on Rte. 23A. The Mountain House Road to North Lake branches off to the northeast a short way west of the site of the former Catskill & Tannersvill Rwy. depot, along Butcher Creek. It was once served by two railroads, the C & T and a branch of the Ulster & Delaware, on whose timetables it was called Haines Corners. The present village is located in Great Lot #25 of the Hardenburgh Patent. According to family tradition, Samuel and Elisha Hains (Haines) came to the Tannersville area in 1779, and on April 20, 1780, settled in the area with their wives. Today the village is an active supply and trading center for neighboring summer communities and the North Lake Campsite. Its elevation is 1920 ft. Sunset, Twilight and Santa Cruz Parks, and the Haines Falls waterfall, second highest in the Catskills, are nearby. See separate articles.

HALCOTT CENTER Greene Co. Named for an early settler, George W. Halcott. On Vly Creek at west foot of Halcott Mtn.

HALCOTT MOUNTAIN Greene Co. Elev. 3520 ft. South of Vly Mtn. and north of Rose Mtn.

HALCOTTVILLE Delaware Co. On Rte. 30, U&D RR and East Branch of Delaware River south of Roxbury and north of Kelly Corners. Not near Halcott Mountain or Halcott Center.

HALE EDDY Delaware Co. On Rte. 17 and Erie RR southeast of Deposit, northwest of Hancock on east bank of Delaware River.

HALF WAY BROOK Sullivan Co. Rises in Toronto Reservoir and flows south past Eldred to Delaware River at Barryville.

HALIHAN HILL Ulster Co. Elev. 500 ft. West of Kingston near junction of Saw Kill and Esopus Creek.

HALLENBECK HILL Greene Co. On Rte. 9W west of Athens.

HALLS MILLS Sullivan Co. West of Claryville.

HALSEY BROOK Greene Co. Flows south into East Kill at East Jewett.

HAMBLEVILLE Delaware Co. On Rte. 8. North of Stilesville and Masonville. On Oquaga Creek.

HAMBURG Greene Co. On Rte. 9W, WS RR, Hudson River. North of Catskill and Rip Van Winkle Bridge. 19th-century fishing village. Captain Joseph Allen House (1814), Federal style.

HAMDEN Delaware Co. On Rte. 10, former O&W RR, West Branch of Delaware. East of Walton, west of Delhi and Delancey.

HAMILTON POINT Ulster Co. Elev. 2020 ft. In Shawangunks in Minnewaska State Park. Quartz conglomerate crags overlook Palmaghatt Ravine to southeast.

HANCOCK Delaware Co. At junction of East and West Branch of Delaware River and of Rtes. 17 and 97. On Erie RR and former Scranton branch of O&W Rwy.

HANDSOME EDDY Sullivan Co. On Rte. 97 and D&H Canal. South of Barryville, north of Pond Eddy. Handsome Lake (1735–1815) was Seneca Indian religious prophet.

HANFORD MILLS See East Meredith.

HANGING BIRDS NEST BROOK Ulster Co. Flows north into Esopus Creek from col between Spruce and Hemlock Mtns.

HANGING ROCK FALLS Ulster Co. On Beer Kill near The Cape.

HANKINS Sullivan Co. On Rtes. 97, 17B, and 194; Erie RR; Delaware River and Hankins Creek. South of Basket, north of Callicoon. Former site of large Manny & Ross bluestone yard.

HANKINS CREEK Sullivan Co. Rises in Crystal Lake, northeast of Fremont Center and flows 12 miles southwest to Delaware at Hankins.

HANLEY CORNERS Delaware Co. South of Fleischmanns and north of Mapledale. Access to Belle Ayre Mtn. trails.

HANNACROIX or HANNACROIS Greene Co. On Rtes. 9W, 144, Thruway, WS RR. South of New Baltimore, north of Coxsackie.

HANNACROIX or HANNACROIS CREEK Albany and Greene Co. Rises in Southern Helderbergs and flows through Ravine and over Dickinson Falls first southeast to Alcove Reservoir, then east and northeast to Hudson River. South of Barren Island, Coeymans, near Matthew Point.

HANNACROIX RAVINE Albany Co. In Helderbergs off Cass Hill Road 2 miles west of Clarksville. 3 miles long, 80 ft. deep; waterfalls. 123 acres belong to Nature Conservancy. Creek has cut into shales and sandstone of Hamilton formation.

HANOVER MOUNTAIN Ulster Co. Elev. 2600 ft. East of Balsam Cap, north of Mine Hollow and south of Maltby Hollow. West of Watson Hollow.

HANS VOSEN KILL Greene Co. Also called Vosenkill. Named for pioneer settler who built mill on creek. Rises in Black Lake and flows south to Catskill Creek at Catskill.

HARDENBURGH Ulster Co. On Beaver Kill east of Lew Beach and west of Quaker Clearing.

HARDSCRABBLE Delaware Co. North of Old Clump Mtn.

HARPERSFIELD Delaware Co. On Rte. 23 west of Stamford. Founded by Col. John Harper in 1771. Elev. 1,752 ft. Scene of tory Indian raids during Revolution. In Spring of 1780 Joseph Brant led raid that scalped three residents and took eight captive. Timothy Murphy avenged raid in single-handed attack on a camp of 27 Indians, killing six and chasing away the rest.

HARPURSVILLE Broome Co. On Rte. 79 south of Nineveh, north of Center Village on west bank of Susquehanna River. In 1795 Robert Harpur was granted 30,000 acres and brought in settlers from the Mohawk valley and New England.

HARRIS Sullivan Co. On Rte. 17 south of Liberty, north of Monticello on Spring Brook.

HARTWICK Otesgo Co. On Rte. 205 south of Richfield Springs, north of Oneonta. On Otego Creek.

HARTWICK SEMINARY Otsego Co. On Rte. 80, C&CV RR, Susquehanna River south of Cooperstown, north of Milford. Lutheran Seminary, now College, founded in 1797 by John Christopher Hartwick, an early missionary.

HARTWOOD Sullivan Co. On Bush Kill west of Oakland, east of Forestburg on Rtes. 48, 101 and 49.

HARVARD Delaware Co. West of Shinhopple and east of Centreville on Rte. 30 and East Branch of Delaware River.

HARVEY STREET Greene Co. Falls and stone bridge. See Hervey Street.

HASBROUCK Sullivan Co. On Neversink River, north of Woodbourne. Hasbrouck House (Victorian).

HASECO POND Ulster Co. Also called Mud Pond. In Shawangunk Mtns. Elev. 1845 ft. On private grounds of Awosting Reserve. Outlet is Fly Brook to northwest.

HASWELLS RAVINE Greene Co. In Coxsackie. Known for "Hole in the Ground" underground stream.

HATCHERY HOLLOW Ulster Co. On west slope of Panther Mtn. State Fish Hatchery here.

HATHAWAY POND Delaware Co. North of Kelsey, west of Apex. Source of Sands Creek.

HAUVERPLAUT Greene Co. Area of wooded land near Kykuit in Great Embought south of Catskill.

HAVEN Sullivan Co. On Rte. 209, Mine Road, D&H Canal, NYO&W RR. South of Wurtsboro, north of Westbrookville.

HAWKEYE Greene Co. Ledge high on east face of Kaaterskill High Peak. One alleged site of Natty Bumpo's panegyric.

HAWK MOUNTAIN Delaware Co. Elev. 2040 ft. Near Cadosia at the northeast angle of the junction of Cadosia Creek and East Branch of Delaware. Site of tunnel on former NYO&W RR and large cut on Quickway (Rte. 17). Rattlesnake infested.

HAWKS NEST Sullivan Co. On Rte. 134. On Basket Creek, north of Basket.

HAWKSNEST CLIFFS Sullivan Co. High cliffs on north bank of the Delaware between Mongaup and Barryville. Superb views from Rte. 97 (Hawksnest Drive).

HAWLEY Delaware Co. On Rte. 10, West Branch of Delaware, Delhi Br. NYO&W RR southwest of Hamden, east of Colchester. Hawley Octagon House.

HAWLEY'S LEDGE Greene Co. Near Ashley's Falls in Mary's Glen on North Mtn.

HAYDEN MOUNTAIN Greene Co. South of Mt. Nebo and north of Ginseng Mtn.

HAYNES HOLLOW Ulster Co. Southwest of Haynes Mtn., north of Dry Brook between Seager and Mapledale. Named for early settler Derrick Haynes.

HAYNES MOUNTAIN Ulster Co. Elev. 3420 ft. South of Balsam Mtn. and north of Eagle Mtn.

HAZEL Sullivan Co. On Willowemoc Creek east of Roscoe and west of Livingston Manor. On Rte. 17. Appley's Siding prior to 1902. Former wood acid factories.

HAZEL BROOK Sullivan Co. Flows north into Willowemoc Creek at Hazel.

HEATH Ulster Co. Location near Ulster Landing.

HEATHER CREEK Schoharie Co. Flows 3 miles into Schoharie Creek near Middleburg.

HELDERBERGS Dutch name meaning "clear mountains." They lie generally to the north of the Catskill Mountains proper and geologically, if not historically, are part of them. They have been called the "key to the geology of North America." The Helderberg region was a focal point of the anti-rent movement. Principal attractions include: Thacher State Park, with extensive cliffs and panoramic views running from northwest to southeast. Rtes. 157 and 157A offer scenic lookouts. Indian Ladder Trail and Caves with waterfall. Hailes Cave, Torey Caves.

HELL HOLE Greene Co. Treacherous area at foot of Hell Hole Falls near head of Plattekill Creek Clove.

HELL HOLE CREEK Greene Co. Flows off south side of Kaaterskill High Peak to Plattekill Creek just east of Plaat Clove P.O.

HELL HOLE FALLS Greene Co. On Hell Hole Creek just above junction with Platte Kill Creek. Stone bridge on road to West Saugerties crosses just above falls. Caution—dangerous area

HEMLOCK BROOK Ulster Co. Flows north off Wildcat Mtn. to West Branch of Neversink at Frost Valley.

HEMLOCK GULLY Greene Co. Off Elk Creek on north slope of Halcott Mtn.

HEMLOCK MOUNTAIN Ulster Co. Elev. 3240 ft. Northwest of the West Branch of the Neversink River east of Spruce Mtn.

HEMLOCK POINT Ulster Co. North of Prospect Hill on Hudson River.

HEMP MEADOW BROOK Sullivan Co. Flows south from Smallwood to Mongaup River below Swinging Bridge Reservoir. Hemp was an important crop in colonial times. Its scientific name is "Cannabis sativa," and rope is made from it. It also produces a powerful drug called hashish (today called marijuana), to which early Americans, including George Washington, were strongly addicted. It was grown extensively throughout the colonies.

HENDERSON'S FALLS Ulster Co. On upper Beaverkill near Turnwood. On private property. 25-ft. drop with 15-ft. pool.

HENDRICKS HOLLOW Delaware Co. Flows south from Mary Smith Hill to Berry Brook.

HENSONVILLE Greene Co. On Batavia Kill and Rte. 296 north of Maplecrest and south of Windham.

HERDMAN BROOK Greene Co. Flows south into West Kill from col between Evergreen and Rusk Mtns.

HERSVILLE Sullivan Co. On Rte. 114. Formerly Old Cochecton. West of Fosterdale, east of Cochecton. Home of James C. Curtis, was a station on old Newburgh & Cochecton Turnpike. Built 1830.

HERVEY STREET Greene Co. East of Cornwallville.

HICKORYBUSH Ulster Co. South of Whiteport.

HIDDEN CORNER Ulster Co. West of Gardiner.

HIGGINSVILLE Ulster Co. Northwest section of Kingston, south of Esopus Creek.

HIGH FALLS #1 Greene Co. Community and waterfall east of Palenville on Kaaterskill Creek. The falls are private property, hard to see and dangerous.

HIGH FALLS #2 Ulster Co. West of Rosendale on Rondout Creek and Rte. 213. The falls are the site of a dam and hydro-electric plant. The piers of an old D & H Canal aqueduct may still be seen as well as those of an old lock. The D & H Canal Museum is here. John Burroughs taught school here in his youth. DuPuy's Canal Tavern (1797) now restored as restaurant. George LeFever House (1752) on road south to Mountain Rest. Feather Farm (c1762) opposite LeFever House.

HIGH FALLS #3 Sullivan Co. On Neversink River south of Denton Falls and Bridgeville. In Turner Brook Preserve.

HIGH FALLS BROOK #1 Ulster Co. Tributary of Rondout Creek's West Branch, north of Sundown.

HIGH FALLS BROOK #2 Ulster Co. Flows southeast from slope of Doubletop Mtn. to West Branch of the Neversink south of Frost Valley. Large waterfall one half mile above junction with Neversink.

HIGH FALLS MOUNTAIN Ulster Co. Elev. 3211 ft. South of Doubletop Mtn. High Falls Brook #2 to north.

HIGH KNOB Schoharie Co. Northeast of Conesville.

HIGHLAND Ulster Co. On Rtes. 9W, 44, Mid-Hudson Bridge, WS, former Central New England/ New York, New Haven & Hartford RRs. Railroad bridge across Hudson River from Poughkeepsie to New Paltz. Site of former Hasbrouck's Bellevue Villa Hotel. Area famous for vineyards, wineries and orchards and fruit farms. At Blue Point are Champagne Vineyards and Hudson Valley Wine Co. winery. Open to the public. Wine tastings.

Historic houses:

Col. Jacob Hasbrouck House (1846), sandstone; Vinyard Ave.
Ripper Van Rippoff House (c1690), Flanders Lane.
Presbyterian Church (c1844), elegant Corinthian columns.
Schantz Mill and House (c1800), Vinyard Ave.
Gaffney House (pre-Revolutionary), Vinyard Ave.
Lake House (c1820), clapboard; Rte. 9W circle.
"Sunnycrest" (mid-19th century), home of Civil War General Peter Wanzer at Bluepoint—now a winery.

HIGHLAND LAKE Sullivan Co. East of Eldred. Name of lake and village.

HIGHLAND LANDING Ulster Co. On WS RR and Hudson River opposite Poughkeepsie. Former ferry to Poughkeepsie. Great views from railroad and highway bridges. Davis Place (c1830). Ferryman Inn or "Yelverton House" (18th century), saltbox. Mid-Hudson Hotel (c1850); stepped gables.

HIGHMOUNT Ulster Co. North of Belle Ayre Mtn. and west of Pine Hill on Rte. 28 and Ulster & Delaware RR; the station was formerly known as Grand Hotel Station for their large resort hotel here. Two ski areas nearby. Summit of the U&D route and divide between Hudson and Delaware watersheds. Elev. 1886 ft.

HIGH PEAK Greene Co. Elev. 3655 ft. Now known to be only the 21st Catskill peak in order of height, for many years it was thought the highest. It is known also as Kaaterskill High Peak. In the late 19th century George Harding, owner of the Hotel Kaaterskill, and a strong Republican, almost succeeded in renaming it Mount Lincoln. It is west of Palenville and south of Kaaterskill Clove and north of Plattekill Clove. Roundtop to the west.

HIGH POINT #1 Ulster Co. Elev. 3080 ft. Also known as Ashokan High Point. South of South Mtn. and east of Watson Hollow near West Shokan. There is a spring on it, known as the tidal spring, which ebbs and flows synchronously with the tides of the Hudson River.

HIGH POINT #2 Ulster Co. 2246 ft. In Shawangunks north of Indian Rock and south of Napanoch Point.

HIGH ROCK QUARRY Greene Co. See Forge Quarry.

HIGH VIEW Sullivan Co. West of Bloomingburg and east of Mamakating in Shawangunks. Shawanga Lodge (1895).

HIGHWOODS Ulster Co. Saugerties. Quarryman's Museum.

HILLYER RAVINE Greene Co. On north slope of Kaaterskill High Peak and south wall of Kaaterskill Clove. Site of Viola Falls.

HIRAMS KNOB Ulster Co. Elev. 2800 ft. West of Haynes Mtn., northeast of Dry Brook and east of Mapledale.

HOBART Delaware Co. On Rte. 10, U&D RR and West Branch of Delaware River southwest of Stamford, northeast of Bloomville. Township Methodist Church (1823). St. Peter's Episcopal Church (organized 1794; present building 1801).

HODGE POND Sullivan Co. Southwest of Mongaup Mtn. and west of Mongaup Pond.

HOG MOUNTAIN Delaware Co. East of Kelly Corners.

HOLLIDAY BROOK Delaware Co. Flows north into Pepacton Reservoir from col between Sugarloaf Mtn. to the west and Mary Smith Hill to the east.

HOLLISTER LAKE Greene Co. West of Limestreet.

HOLLOW Definition (as used in the Catskills): a small valley or indentation in the side of a mountain or ridge.

HOLLOW TREE BROOK AND HOLLOW Greene Co. Flows south from east side of West Kill Mtn. into Stony Clove Creek at Lanesville.

HOLLOW TREE MOUNTAIN Greene Co. Former name of spur of West Kill Mtn.

HOLMES HOLLOW Delaware Co. Northeast of Delancey.

HOLMES HOLLOW BROOK Delaware Co. Flows 2 miles into West Branch of Delaware River.

HOMOWACK KILL Sullivan and Ulster Cos. Dividing line between Catskills to the west and Shawangunks to the east. It flows north from the vicinity of Summitville to the Sandburg Creek at Spring Glen. A large lake at Phillipsport was used as a stabilizing basin for former D&H Canal.

HONK FALLS Ulster Co. at Napanoch. 70 ft. Hydroelectric plant. See Rondout Creek.

HONK LAKE Ulster Co. On Rondout Creek below Merriman Dam, near Napanoch. Site of pioneer Fort Honk nearby. On Rte. 55.

HOP-O-NOSE Green Co. Rock formation projecting into west bank of Catskill Creek at Catskill. Caused many steamboat accidents. Named for prominent nose of a local redman named Hopp. Claes Uylenspiegel, a fur trader, had a cabin on its eastern slope prior to 1650. Was later purchased by Frederick Cooke as a site of a family seat.

HOPPS NOSE Greene Co. See Hop-o-nose.

HORSE BROOK Delaware Co. Flows south from Lake Mimi to Beaver Kill west of Roscoe.

St. Peter's Episcopal Church, Hobart. Built 1801. Photo by Alfred H. Marks.

HORSESHOE CURVE Ulster Co. Scenic feature on Ulster & Delaware RR west of Pine Hill and east of Highmount (Grand Hotel Station). It is a double-reverse curve on a 3.2% grade. In early days when surrounding lands were cleared as pasture it provided superb views and was much publicized and illustrated.

HORTON Delaware Co. On Rte. 17 east of East Branch and west of Roscoe at junction of Horton Brook and Beaverkill. Site of Treyz Bros. wood acid plant till 1948.

HORTON BROOK Delaware Co. Flows south into Beaver Kill at Horton.

HORTONVILLE Sullivan Co. East of Callicoon at forks of Callicoon Creek. Tamarack Swamp with sphagnum-tamarack glacial relic marsh, 1 mile east of Delaware River, north of Newburgh Road. Surrounded by native spruce. Contains sundew, pitcher plant, and other tundra species. Home of Dr. Frederick A. Cook, polar explorer with Commodore Robert E. Peary, born in 1865.

HOUGHTALING ISLAND Greene Co. In Hudson River opposite New Baltimore.

HOUSE CREEK Schoharie Co. Flows 5 miles into Schoharie Creek near Breakabeen.

HOWE CAVERNS Schoharie Co. On Rte. 7 near town of Howe's Cave east of Cobleskill and west of Central Bridge. Discovered on May 22, 1842 by Lester Howe, who felt cold air coming up from the ground in his pasture. They have been carved in limestone by an underground river, upon which a boat ride is offered. Features of the caverns are: Flowstone formations, Winding Way, Titan's Temple, The Pipe Organ, The Old Witch, and Bridal Altar. About 1½ miles long and from 160 to 200 ft. deep. Constant year-around temperature of 52°. Reached by electric elevator. Complete tourist facilities at lodge on surface. Open all year, 9 AM to 6 PM daily except Thanksgiving, Christmas and New Years Day.

HOWE'S CAVE Schoharie Co. On Rte. 7 and D&H RR. Elev. 950 ft. East of Cobleskill and west of Central Bridge. Site of Howe Caverns, largest in Northeast.

HUBBEL CORNERS Delaware Co. On Rte. 30, U&D RR and east branch of Delaware north of Roxbury, south of More Settlement.

HUBBELL HILL Delaware Co. Elev. 3000 ft. Northwest of Kettle Hill.

HUBBELL HILL HOLLOW Delaware Co. South of Hubbell Hill and north of Kettle Hill near Kelly Corners.

HUCKLEBERRY BROOK Delaware Co. Also called Cold Spring Brook. Flows west into Pepacton Reservoir south of Pakatakan Mtn.

HUCKLEBERRY LINE Old affectionate name for former Catskill & Tannersville narrow-gauge railroad. Train crews would make unscheduled stops to allow passengers to go berry-picking.

HUDSON RIVER See Chapter 3.

HUGGINS HOLLOW Delaware and Sullivan Cos. South of Huggins Lake, north of Beaver Kill between Beaverkill and Lew Beach.

HUGGINS LAKE Delaware Co. At head of Huggins Hollow.

HUGUENOT Orange Co. On Rte. 209, Neversink River, D&H Canal, O&W RR. South of Godeffroy, north of Port Jervis. Old stone houses. Formerly Peenpack.

HULL POND Sullivan Co. Northwest of Lebanon Lake.

HULTZ'S FALLS Greene Co. In Durham.

HUMPTY DUMPTY Ulster Co. Name of road along cliffs near Lake Mohonk Mountain House in Shawangunks. At southwest and south foot of Eagle Cliff, east of Cope's Lookout and above Giant's Inn and Workshop.

HUNT HILL Delaware Co. Elev. 2380 ft. West of Tomkins Falls, south of Pepacton Reservoir and northwest of Touchmenot Mtn.

HUNTER Greene Co. Village on the Schoharie Creek at the north foot of Hunter Mtn., west of Tannersville and east of Lexington on Rte. 23A. Formerly called Edwardsville in honor of Colonel William W. Edwards, a pioneer tanner who had large works here. The Colonel's Chair (See article) was named for him. This was formerly a terminus of the Stony Clove Branch of the Ulster & Delaware RR and a major boarding town. Red Falls on the Schoharie here.

HUNTER BROOK Greene Co. Flows off south slope of Hunter Mtn. to the West Kill.

HUNTER LAKE AND FALLS Sullivan Co. Near DeBruce.

HUNTER MOUNTAIN Greene Co. Elev. 4040 ft. Second highest peak in the Catskills. Fire observation tower on summit. A mile-long chair-lift to top of Colonel's Chair (see article). Hunter Ski Bowl slopes on north side. Mountain is south of Hunter on Rte. 23A near junction with Rte. 214. View is most impressive from Stony Clove on the east side.

HUNTER NOTCH Greene Co. West of Onteora Mtn., northeast of Hunter. The Red Kill flows through it.

HUNTER POND Sullivan Co. Southwest of White Lake.

HUNTERSFIELD CREEK Greene Co. Flows southwest from west slope of Huntersfield Mtn. to Schoharie Creek at Prattsville.

HUNTERSFIELD MOUNTAIN Greene Co. Elev. 3423 ft. North of Ashland and south of Conesville.

HUNTER SKI BOWL Greene Co. See Hunter and Hunter Mtn.

HUNTERSLAND Schoharie Co. Southeast of Middleburg, northwest of Rensselaerville.

HUNTINGTON RAVINE Ulster Co. Shawangunk Mtns. In Minnewaska State Park. East of Overlook Point and west of Litchfield Ledge.

HUNTLEY HOLLOW BROOK Delaware Co. Flows 2 miles into East Branch of Delaware.

HUNTS CORNER Sullivan Co. On Rtes. 52 and 24 east of Narrowsburg.

HURLEY Ulster Co. On Esopus Creek and Rte. 209. National Historic District. 300 years old. At foot of northernmost Shawangunk Mountains a mile east of Esopus Creek. Numerous early colonial buildings of Huguenot and later British

Old Guardhouse, Hurley. Lt. David Taylor, British spy, was confined here and hanged on apple tree on October 18, 1777. Photo by Alfred H. Marks.

Historic stone houses in Hurley. Van Dusen House (at bottom) was built in 1723 and was temporary capitol of State of New York after burning of Kingston in 1777.

vintage, and a very beautiful church. Hurley is reputedly the largest cluster of privately owned original stone houses in the United States. Originally called Nieuw Dorp or New Village, it was colonized from Wiltwyck, as Kingston was then called, around 1660. The new community was attacked and burned by Indians in 1663. The Hurley Patentee Manor dates from 1696. From November

Historic stone houses in Hurley.

18 to December 17, 1777, Hurley served as the capital of the State of New York when the Committee of Safety of the State of New York sat in the Jan Van Deusen House (1723). The Committee then adjourned to Poughkeepsie. Washington is reputed to have visited Hurley.

Hurley is on the Old Mine Road from Kingston to Pahaquarry, the oldest highway in America. In 1902 the Ellenville & Kingston RR, a subsidiary of the NYO&W, came through; it was abandoned 1957. The new Rte. 209 bypasses the village. On a Saturday each July, known as Stone House Day, the private houses are open to the public and the hosts and hostesses don colonial costumes.

Historic houses:

Jan Van Deusen House (1723), temporary capitol.

Hurley Patentee Manor (1696; remodeled 1747), Rte. 209.

Cornelius Wynkoop Farm (c1667), at corner Hurley Bridge Road and Mountain Road.

Nieuwkirk-McSperit House (date unknown), 2 miles south of corner Hurley Bridge Road and Mountain Road.

Matthew Ten Eyck House (1750), ¾ miles north of corner Hurley Bridge Road and Mountain Road.

Gerret Nieuwkirk House (1769), 1 mile north of corner Hurley Bridge Road and Mountain Road.

Nieuwkirk House (1811), across road from Gerret Nieuwkirk House.

Hurley Reformed Church (c1778).

HURLEYVILLE Sullivan Co. On Rtes. 103 and 104 north of Monticello, south of Loch Sheldrake on East Branch of Mongaup River. Old School Historical and Art Museum.

HURRICANE LEDGE Greene Co. Ledge at 3000 ft. elev. on Kaaterskill High Peak. Overlooks Kaaterskill Clove.

HUSTED HOLLOW Delaware Co. In Kortright.

Historic House, Hurley. Built in English style with "lay-on-your-belly windows". Photo by Alfred H. Marks.

HUSSEY'S MOUNTAIN Ulster Co. Elev. 1005 ft. East of St. Remy and west of Port Ewen.

HUYCK, EDMUND NILES, PRESERVE Albany Co. 1,200 acres near Rensselaerville. It was incorporated in 1931. Includes Lincoln Pond, Lake Myosotis and Rensselaerville Falls.

MOUNT HYMETTUS Ulster Co. South of West Park. John Burroughs named it because of his luck in finding many bees, beehives and wild honey on its slopes. It was near his home. Mt. Hymettus in Greece is famous for its fields of flowers and many bees.

HYNDSVILLE Schoharie Co. On Rte. 10, former D&H RR, Cherry Valley Branch west of Cobleskill.

ICE CAVES MTN. Ulster Co. See Sam's Point.

ILLINOIS MOUNTAIN Ulster Co. Elev. 1129 ft. West of Highland.

INBOCHT BAY Greene Co. Large shallow bay in Hudson River south of Greene Point near Catskill. DeWitt Point to the south. See also Great Embought.

INDEX Otsego Co. On Rte. 28, C&CV RR, Susquehanna River south of Cooperstown, north of Milford. Old mill near Oaks Creek on west side of Rte. 28.

INDIAN HEAD Greene Co. On south side of South Mtn. west of Palenville near foot of Kaaterskill Clove. Rock head said to resemble an Indian. Formerly also known as the Dominie's Face. Top is reached by side trail from Palenville Overlook.

INDIAN HEAD MOUNTAIN Greene Co. Elev. 3573 ft. West of Plattekill Mtn. and east of Twin Mtn. On Devil's Path.

Indian Head from More's Bridge in Kaaterskill Clove. Photo by Alfred H. Marks.

INDIAN LADDER Albany Co. In Thacher State Park on Helderberg Escarpment. In the old days a crude inclined plane was built here and wagons pulled up by cables. Prior to that, it is alleged that Indians put up rustic ladders against the cliffs. The name now applies to a trail along the cliffs.

INDIAN ROCK #1 Ulster Co. On Hudson River above Esopus. Walter Seamon House (1870). "Rosemont", 2-story pre-revolutionary clapboard house. It was the former home of Alton B. Parker, New York jurist and 1904 Democratic presidential candidate.

INDIAN ROCK #2 Ulster Co. Elev. 2160 ft. In Shawangunks north of Lake Maratanza.

INSPIRATION POINT Greene Co. Viewpoint on Escarpment Trail on top of north side of Kaaterskill Clove, east of Sunset Rock. On former grounds of Hotel Kaaterskill. Bellevue to east. Best reached from Scribners.

IRELAND CORNERS Ulster Co. Junction of Rtes. 208 and 44 east of Gardiner and west of Modena.

IRISH MOUNTAIN Delaware Co. Elev. 3060 ft. South of Grand Gorge and north of Shultice Mtn.

IVANHOE Delaware Co. On Rte. 206 east of Masonville. Named for famous novel of Sir Walter Scott.

JACLYN HILL Delaware Co. Elev. 2570 ft. North of Hobart.

JACOBS LADDER #1 Greene Co. In Genesis 29:12 Jacob dreamed that a staircase reached from earth to heaven and he saw angels of God going up and down upon it. Name was applied to a rustic ladder on the old alignment of trail from Catskill Mountain House to North Mtn. Now removed, it was from neighborhood of Bear's Den to top of Sunset Rock. Trail now uses easier route.

JACOBS LADDER #2 Ulster Co. In Shawangunks in Minnewaska State Park. Up Margaret Cliff from Margaret's Stone Parlor.

JAN DE BAKKERS KILL Greene Co. Flows south from Place Corners to Catskill Creek at Cairo.

JAY HAND HOLLOW Greene Co. A northwestern extension of Broadstreet Hollow on south side of North Dome.

JEFFERSON #1 Schoharie Co. On Rte. 10 south of Richmondville, north of Stamford.

JEFFERSON #2 Greene Co. On Rte. 23 west of Catskill, east of Leeds. Sometimes called Jefferson Heights.
    Pioneer Racetrack. Historical marker at end of Suburban Way (formerly Snake Rd.), south of Rte. 23, at Dirck Thunese Van Veghten House, formerly "Mawignack" (1690) and fording place of King's Highway across Catskill Creek. Old fort on hill above fording place. Austin House (19th century), stone 2-story; Rte 23. A. P. Jones House (mid 19th century), 2-story board-and-batten Mansard; Rte. 23.

JEFFERSON HEIGHTS Greene Co. See Jefferson.

JEFFERSON LAKE Sullivan Co. On Callicoon Creek near Jeffersonville.

JEFFERSONVILLE Sullivan Co. On Rte. 52 south of Youngsville and north of Kenoza Lake. On East Branch of Callicoon Creek.

JENKINTOWN Ulster Co. On Rte. 32 north of Modena, south of New Paltz. Orchard area. Evert Terwilliger (Hugo Freer) House (1738–41). Locust Lawn (1814), fine Federal mansion built by Col. Josiah Hasbrouck, who served in House of Representatives.

JERSEY BROOK Sullivan Co. Flows north into Beaver Kill at Beaverkill.

JEWELVILLE Ulster Co. See West Hurley.

JEWETT Greene Co. Southeast of Ashland and north of Jewett Center.

JEWETT CENTER Greene Co. On Rte. 23A west of Hunter and east of Lexington, on the Schoharie Creek south of Jewett.

JIMMY DOLAN NOTCH Greene Co. Twin Mtn. to west and Indian Head to east. Named for early tavern keeper.

JOCKEY HILL Ulster Co. Elev. 600 ft. West of Esopus Creek and north of Stony Hollow. Binnewater Lake to the west and Saw Kill to the north.

JOE'S BROOK Ulster Co. Tributary of Esopus Creek near Slide Mtn.

JOHN CHASE BROOK Greene Co. Small tributary of Schoharie Creek near Lexington.

JOHNNIE BROOK Delaware Co. Flows 2 miles into West Branch of Delaware.

JOHN'S MOUNTAIN Ulster Co. Elev. 1540 ft. South of Cooper Lake and west of Bearsville.

JOHNSON HOLLOW Greene Co. East of Bearpen Mtn. and west of Vly Mtn.

JOHNSON POINT Greene Co. On South wall of Kaaterskill Clove (north slope of Kaaterskill High Peak) east of Santa Cruz Ravine and west of Buttermilk Falls.

JONES GAP Greene Co. See Taylor Hollow.

JOPPENBERG MOUNTAIN Ulster Co. Near Rosendale. Nordic natural Ski jump.

JOSCELYN Sullivan Co. Northeast of Roscoe.

JUDD FALLS Otsego Co. On Rte. 20 at junction of Rte. 166. 50 ft. back from unpaved parking area. Not visible from road. Scenic high falls over limestone ledges. Formerly Tekaharawa Falls.

JUDSON BROOK Sullivan Co. Northern tributary of White Lake.

JUNCTION POOL Sullivan Co. At junction of Beaverkill and Willowemoc Creeks at Roscoe. Famous fishing spot.

KAATERSKILL Poeticized version of Kaatskill or Catskill. Exact derivation is difficult to determine.

KAATERSKILL CLOVE Greene Co. One of the largest and most scenic cloves in the Great Wall of Manitou. It was formed by Kaaterskill and Lake Creeks and has its head near Haines Falls and its foot at Palenville. It is climbed by Rte. 23A, the old Hunter Turnpike alignment being used in many places, particularly at the lower end. Haines Falls, second highest in Catskills, is on Kaaterskill Creek on the private grounds of the Twilight Park Association. Kaaterskill Falls, the highest in New York State, are on Lake Creek in an indentation on the north wall of Kaaterskill Clove and not visible from the highway. The falls near the horseshoe bend on Rte. 23A are Bastion Falls. The yellow-marked side trail from the blue-marked Escarpment Trail is reached most easily from near Bastion Falls. This trail goes to the foot of the bottom part of the two-tiered falls. It is not easy walking without proper footwear. There is limited parking uphill to the west at the site of the former Rip's Lookout gift shop. The south wall of Kaaterskill Clove is formed by Kaaterskill High Peak at the east end and Round Top to the west. There are the remains of an old Tory fort on Round Top from which British and Indian troops used to swoop down and make raids in the Hudson valley. On the south wall are three private residential parks: Santa Cruz, Twilight and Sunset. Santa Cruz is entered through Twilight Park. The streets are restricted and patrolled. Sunset Park has its own separate entrance from Rte. 23A to the west and is open to the public. The former Santa Cruz Inn in Santa Cruz Park and Ledge End Inn in Twilight no longer exist. The large hotel at the head of the clove is the Sunset Springs Hotel, situated at an elevation of 2,600 feet. There are many small torrents on the south wall that tumble down to Kaaterskill Creek. The major three, from east to west, are Hillyer Ravine, Wildcat Ravine and Santa Cruz Ravine. Viola Falls are located in Hillyer Ravine. Other features of the South Wall are Johnson Point and Hurricane Ledge. Most of this side of the Clove is private property and entry is restricted. High Peak and Round Top should be reached by trails from the other side. At highway level the major features, along Kaaterskill Creek, are: More's Bridge, Profile Rock, Mason's cliff, Fawn's Leap, the old tannery ruins (reached by an abandoned road marked "Trail to old fort on Roundtop") and Five Cascades, on Kaaterskill Creek above its junction with Lake Creek. Above this are the remains of a major landslide, and Haines Falls.

Along the creek near the foot of the Clove are the former toll house and home of George H. Hall, the artist. Artists' Grotto and La Belle Falls are nearby, but on private property. Niobe's Cave is also in the vicinity. There are many excellent swimming and fishing holes along the creek and on public land, but camping is restricted and parking is very limited.

The north wall of the clove is formed by South Mountain, with its Palenville Overlook, Indian Head and Boulder Rock lookouts. Prospect Mountain is west of Lake Creek. The Escarpment Trail (marked blue) follows the top of the north wall from the vicinity of Kaaterskill Falls to Boulder Rock, where it turns north. Famous viewpoints include Sunset Rock, Council Bluff, Inspiration Point and Bellevue. The remains of an old carriage road can be seen climbing the north wall of the clove from near Palenville to the site of the former Hotel Kaaterskill. It is now maintained by the DEC as a horseback riding trail. The large indentation in the north wall, west of Indian Head, is known as The Gulf or Amphitheatre. The monument seen northeast of Lake Creek, up on the mountain, is dedicated to Frank D. Layman of Haines Falls, who lost his life fighting a forest fire at that spot on August 10, 1900. It is on the Escarpment Trail. Best access to these Escarpment Trail viewpoints is from either Scribners or Laurel House parking lots.

On Prospect Mountain interesting features include Motorboat Rock, The Sphinx and Prospect Rock. Best reached from Laurel House. The Kaaterskill Falls can be seen from here when foliage is down.

The Clove was popular with painters of the Hudson River School and was the subject of many major works. Perhaps best known is one by Stanford R. Gifford in the Metropolitan Museum of Art in New York. To fully enjoy the beauties of this area be prepared to leave your car and do some walking. The trails are easy if you use the suggested access.

See separate articles for subjects mentioned above.

KAATERSKILL CREEK Green Co. See Chapter 3.

KAATERSKILL FALLS Greene Co. These are the highest waterfalls in New York State—260 ft. in two leaps of 175 ft. and 85 ft. They are located on Lake Creek in the north wall of Kaaterskill Clove, east of Haines Falls. They were highly publicized in the 19th century and became a major tourist attraction. William Cullen Bryant's "Cattserskill Falls" was a major factor in spreading their fame. The poem depicts the great ice cone which sometimes forms in wintertime and was inspired by a winter visit Bryant made to the falls. Bryant is, however, inaccurate in that he says that "Midst greens and shades the Cattserskill leaps." Actually the falls are on Lake Creek.

A famous early hotel, the Laurel House, stood nearby. It was built in 1852 by Peter Schutt. Originally a simple colonial building with accommodations for fifty, after additions in 1881 and 1884, its size was doubled. An impressive Victorian portico adorned its facade. It remained in operation until 1963 but fast decayed thereafter. In 1966 the State purchased it and burned it to clear the site in 1967.

The early owners erected a dam and sluice above the falls to conserve water during dry periods. They would "turn on the water" for a fee when sufficient visitors had assembled at the viewing stations. They also erected rustic stairways and a refreshment stand. All these have long since disappeared. The falls today are on state land and flow with whatever natural volume of water nature provides. Consequently they are at their best during the springtime thaws or after a rainy spell.

There is a large natural amphitheatre behind the upper and higher fall. This is formed by overhanging sandstone ledges and it is possible to walk around behind the falls without getting wet, although the rocks are sometimes slippery and care must be taken not to slip. Also, in recent times, some idiotic visitors have taken up the habit of throwing rocks and other heavy objects from above, which creates a distinct hazard to viewers at the foot of the falls.

The best overall view of the falls is from Prospect Rock near the abandoned right of way of the Ulster & Delaware Railroad branch to the west. Easiest access to the top is on Laurel House Road which turns off the Mountain House Road east of Haines Corners. The bottom is most easily reached by a yellow-marked trail which starts from Rte. 23A, at Bastion Falls. There is limited parking at the former Rip's Lookout a short distance west of Bastion Falls. Comfortable footwear is suggested for the 4/10-mile walk to the foot of the lower fall, from which spot both upper and lower falls may be viewed to best advantage.

Kaaterskill Falls were once as well known as Niagara and were portrayed by innumerable artists, engravers and lithographers, including W. H. Bartlett, Thomas Nast, Fritz Meyer, Jervis McEntee, Thomas Cole, Jaspar F. Cropsey, Currier & Ives and Winslow Homer. They gradually became forgotten until publication of Roland VanZandt's book *The Catskill Mountain House* eulogized them and renewed interest after 1966. While requiring a little effort to view, they are entirely rewarding even during low water, as the setting in itself is extremely picturesque..

KAATERSKILL JUNCTION Greene Co. Just east of Hunter, it was an important railroad junction of the narrow-gauge Kaaterskill Railroad and the Stony Clove Division or the Ulster & Delaware. The U&D originally ran from Phoenicia to Hunter and the Kaaterskill RR from the junction to Kaaterskill Station at the west end of South Lake. When both lines were changed to standard gauge the main line then ran from Phoenicia to Kaaterskill Station and the Hunter Branch ran from Kaaterskill Junction to Hunter.

KAATERSKILL RAILROAD Greene Co. A narrow-gauge line which ran from Kaaterskill Junction to Kaaterskill Station. Eventually it was acquired by the Ulster & Delaware and standard-guaged. It is not to be confused with the parallel Catskill & Tannersville line, which always remained narrow-gauge.

KAATERSKILL STATION Greene Co. This was located at the west end of South Lake and was the depot for the Hotel Kaaterskill. It was served first by the narrow-gauge Kaaterskill Railroad, and subsequently by the narrow-gauge Catskill & Tannersville and the standard-gauge Ulster & Delaware, successor to the Kaater-skill Railroad. Service was continued until 1940 by the successor New York Central Railroad. It was the highest railroad station in the state of New York at 2,145 ft. At one time through coaches, parlor cars and sleepers operated to such distant points as Washington, D.C., Philadelphia, Weehawken, N.J., Saratoga Springs and Montreal. An idea of its onetime activity can be had today at such stations as Interlaken, Zweisimmen or Pontresina in Switzerland.

KABAU LAKE Sullivan Co. Near Cochecton Center.

KALKBERG, THE Greene Co. This is from the Dutch for "chalk rock." The name has also been corrupted to "Callabarrachs," "Collar Back," and "Calder-berghs." It is a long limestone ridge of about 250 ft. elevation parallel to the Hudson from Cementon on the south to Quarry Hill, west of Catskill, at the north. Van Luven Lake sits atop the ridge at 213 ft. Duck Cove, Inbocht Bay and the Great Embought are to the east, as are a number of large cement plants, Rte. 9W and the West Shore Railroad. In the 19th century it was a popular scenic drive from Catskill as good views were obtained of both the Catskills and Berkshires as well as of the Hudson River. Subsequent quarrying for the cement plants has despoiled large areas and placed much of it "off limits." It represents the eastern-most reach of the Catskills.

KANAPE BROOK Ulster Co. Flows northwest into Watson Hollow from col between Ashokan High Point on the north and Mombaccus Mtn. to the south.

KATE HILL Greene Co. Elev. 2300 ft. South of Mt. Zoar and north of Windham High Peak near Rte. 23 and Five State Lookout, on the Great Wall of Manitou.

KATRINA FALLS Sullivan Co. On McKee Brook in Rock Hill.

KATSBAAN Ulster Co. South of Quarryville and north of the Saugerties Exit of the New York Thruway on Rte. 32. "Katsbaan" is Dutch for "tennis court," and it obtained its name because the Indians played lacrosse here. John Jacob Astor had his first fur trading post here. A small stream called the Beaver Kill flows north from there to Kaaterskill Creek and Mt. Airy is to the west. Dutch Reformed Church, stone with tall spire (1862; first church built 1732). Wynkoop House (c1740). Colonial Inn, Rte. 32.

KAUFMANS Delaware Co. South of Andes on Tremper Kill.

KAUNEONGA LAKE Sullivan Co. North of White Lake.

KAZENS POND Sullivan Co. Near Fosterdale.

KELLY CORNERS Delaware Co. At junction of East Branch of Delaware and Batavia Kill on Rte. 30 north Margaretville and south of Halcottville. Extensive dairy farming in this region. On U&D RR.

KELSEY Delaware Co. North of Hancock and south of Cannonsville on Sands Creek.

KEMPTON LEDGE Ulster Co. In Minnewaska Hotel Grounds. In Shawangunks. Elev. 1640 ft. In west wall of Palmaghat Ravine north of The Castles.

KENOZA LAKE Sullivan Co. Village and lake 3.5 miles from Jeffersonville on Rte. 52 and East Branch of Callicoon Creek. Originally Pike Pond. Name changed in 1890 in honor of John Greenleaf Whittier's poem, *Kenoza Lake*. Early hotels included the Kenoza Lake Hotel and the Fern Hotel.

KENOZIA LAKE Ulster Co. Formerly known as Temple Pond, it is at the south foot of Tonshi Mountain between Ashokan and Glenford, just to the north of Rte. 28.

KENROSE SANCTUARY Albany Co. At West Berne. 360-acre wilderness area on Bradt Hollow Road, owned by Nature Conservancy.

KERHONKSON Ulster Co. Formerly Middleport on the old D&H Canal. It is on Rondout Creek at the western foot of the Shawangunks at the junction of Rte. 209 and the Minnewaska Trail (Rt. 55). South of Port Jackson and north of Wawarsing.

KERR BROOK Delaware Co. Formerly followed by NYO & W RR. Rises south of Franklin Depot and flows south to West Branch north of Walton.

KERRYVILLE Delaware Co. South of Piersons and north of Cadosia on Cadosia Creek.

KETCHAM HOLLOW Ulster Co. East of Mts. Wittenberg and Cornell and north of Friday Mtn. Wittenberg Brook flows through it.

KETTLE HILL Delaware Co. Elev. 2100 ft. North of Margaretville.

KEYSERKILL RIVER Schoharie Co. Flows 8 miles into Schoharie Creek near Gilboa.

KIAMESHA CREEK Sullivan Co. Flows east from Kiamesha Lake to Neversink north of Bridgeville.

KIAMESHA LAKE Sullivan Co. North of Monticello on Rte. 42. It is the source of Kiamesha Creek. Formerly known as Pleasant Lake, it was renamed to give it "Indian flavor," as Kiamesha means "clear water." Site of the ultramodern Concord Hotel, designed by noted architect Morris Lapidus.

KILL Dutch word for "creek." The word is also used in the British Isles and appears as Kyle in Scotland.

KIMBALL MTN. Greene Co. Old name for Mt. Thomas Cole.

KINGSTON Ulster Co. seat. On Rtes. 9W, 32, 28, 209, 213 and Exit 19 of

Statue of Henry Hudson by J. Massey Rhind (1898), Kingston. Photo by Alfred H. Marks.

Thruway. On Hudson River and Esopus and Rondout Creeks. On West Shore, Ulster & Delaware, and Wallkill Valley RRs. Formerly on NYO&W Rwy. Although traders had operated from the Rondout area and a small redoubt had been built there earlier, the first permanent settlers came to the area, which was then known as Wiltwyck ("Wild Place"), around 1652. They settled on a high piece of ground overlooking the fertile Esopus Meadowlands, which lie to the west and north. This area had previously been used to grow corn by the Indians and was prime farmland. Although the settlers purchased the land from the Indians, their gradual encroachment caused resentment and in 1659 the First Esopus War broke out and caused the settlers to request a garrison. At this time the settlers were rather thinly spread out. In 1658 Governor Peter Stuyvesant directed that a stockaded town be erected at Wiltwyck, which the English later called Esopustown. The stockaded area was that bounded by the present-day North Front, Green and Main Streets and Clinton Avenue. It contained a guard house, barracks and blockhouse. The stockade consisted of a wooden palisade made of spike-topped logs. There were tunnels running from the basements of the buildings inside to the low-lying meadows.

In 1659 the Dutch Reformed Church was organized and is still considered the seat of the Dutch Reformed Church in America. The present Dutch Reformed Church was built in 1852.

On June 7, 1663, a band of Indians attacked Hurley and Wiltwyck and massacred many inhabitants. This was the outbreak of the Second Esopus War. In November a punitive expedition was mounted which finally broke the power of the Indians.

In 1665 the colony came under English rule. English troops garrisoned at Kingston, as the town was renamed, under a Captain Daniel Brodhead, behaved obnoxiously. When the citizens remonstrated they were accused of causing what was called the Esopus Mutiny. Governor Nicholls intervened and the "mutiny" disolved into legal squabbles and was fogotten.

Dutch rule was restored briefly in 1673, but in 1674 the English regained control until the Revolution. The next century saw peaceful development with Kingston as a sometime base for frontier operations in the French and Indian Wars (1754-1760).

During the Revolution (1775-1781) Kingston served as capital of the State of New York and was the first meeting place of the New York State Senate in 1777. After the defeat of General Burgoyne at Saratoga, General Sir John Vaughan

Governor Clinton Hotel, Kingston. Photo by Alfred H. Marks.

(1738-1795) sailed up the Hudson on a punitive expedition and on October 13, 1777, burned Esopus, as Kingston was still frequently called. This was the last action in the area. The stone-walled buildings were quickly rebuilt and development continued after the war. The present courthouse was built in 1818 on the site of a previous one in which the New York State Constitution was adopted in 1777. In 1812 George Clinton, first governor of New York, was buried in the Dutch Reformed Churchyard.

Senate House (Col. Wessel Ten Broeck House), 1676, Kingston. First capitol of New York. Photo by Alfred H. Marks.

Senate House Museum, Kingston. Photo by Alfred H. Marks.

Fulton's first successful steamboat in 1807 began the development of neighboring Rondout as an important river port and it was for many years the home port of the famous *Mary Powell*. Completion of the Delaware & Hudson Canal in 1828 added to the importance of the port. Kingston developed as transport and finance center for the tanning, ice, brick, and bluestone industries as well as into a farm marketing center.

The coming of the railroads increased Kingston's importance as a transport center. The Wallkill Valley RR was completed to a connection with the Erie in 1872. In 1875 the New York, Kingston & Syracuse (later the Rondout & Oswego and Ulster & Delaware, still later Penn-Central Catskill Branch) was completed from Kingston Point to Stamford. In 1883 the West Shore Railroad from Weehawken to Albany was completed through Kingston and in 1902 the Ellenville & Kingston subsidiary of the New York, Ontario & Western reached Kingston. For many years Kingston boasted a Union Terminal, served by four steam railroads and a local electric traction line.

Kingston was merged with neighboring Rondout in 1878. There was ferry service from Rondout across Rondout Creek to Sleightsburg and across the Hudson to the New York Central depot at Rhinecliff. Steamers of all lines stopped at Kingston Point, where there was a pleasure park and railroad transfer station until 1953. An electric traction line connected old Kingston with the ferries at Rondout, running along Broadway, which linked the two towns. The Union Depot, City Hall and Hospital were built along Broadway and many fine Victorian mansions were built on the heights above Rondout with views across the Rondout Creek and Hudson.

During this era the Cornell and Coykendall families were prominent in business and public improvements. In 1904 the Delaware & Hudson Canal was abandoned, being superseded by the railroads. Ulster & Delaware passenger service ceased in 1954. In 1957 the New York, Ontario & Western was totally abandoned, passenger service having long since ceased, and in 1958 the last West Shore passenger train left town. The Rondout Creek ferry was discontinued upon completion of the Rte. 9W suspension bridge in the 1930s and the Rhinecliff ferry upon completion of the Kingston-Rhinecliff Bridge.

Cordts House, Kingston. Photo by Alfred H. Marks.

All, however, was not negative. The post-World War II era brought the New York Thruway, the light-aggregate industry and IBM to the area and Kingston remains the principal trading center of the west side of the mid-Hudson valley.

The Kingston Model Railroad Club, founded in 1937 as the Hudson Valley Model RR Club, has an annual open house in November.

Miscellaneous interesting buildings and sites:

Senate House (Col. Wessel Ten Broeck House) (1676), Clinton Ave. and North Front St. In 1751 it passed to Abraham Van Gaasbeek and in 1888 it was purchased by State of New York.

Senate House Museum. Regional relics; steamboat relics; collection of John Vanderlyn paintings. Adjacent to Senate House.

Courthouse (1818), Wall St.

Old Dutch Church and Graveyard (1852), Minard Lefever, architect. Gov. George Clinton (1739-1812) buried here.

Fitch Bluestone Dispatch Office (1852), restored and turned into private residence by James Bernardi. On Rondout Creek.

West Strand area, Rondout. On National Register of Historic Places. Classic example of commercial architecture of 1870s.

Old City Hall (19th century), 408 Broadway. Arthur Crooks, architect. Modeled after Palazzio Vecchio in Florence.

John Henry Cordt House (1873), 22-room Victorian mansion; 132 Lindsley Ave.

Clermont Building (19th century), John and Wall Sts.

Fireman's Hall (1857), 267 Fair St.

Kingston Academy (founded 1774), 78 John St.

Octagon House, 603 Broadway.

Gazebo of Cordts House, Kingston. Photo by Alfred H. Marks.

Old City Hall, Broadway, Kingston. Photo by Alfred H. Marks.

Armory, Kingston. Photo by Alfred H. Marks.

Historic Houses in the Stockade area of Kingston.

Old houses in Stockade area:

Pieter Cornelise Louw-Bogardus House (c1668), Converse St. and Frog Alley. Oldest documented house in city.

Van Keuren House, 84 St. James St.

Van Steenbergh House (1700), 97 Wall St.

Cornelius Elmendorf House (before 1777), 225 Wall St.

Tobias Van Buren House, 7 Green St.

Col. Abraham Hasbrouck House, 135 Green St.

Gerrett Van Keuren House, 138 Green St.

Rachel DuMond House (late 18th century), 145 Green St.

Egbert DuMond House, 147 Green St.

Jacobus Coenradt Elmendorf House, 175 Green St.

First Baptist Church, Kingston. Photo by Alfred H. Marks.

John Sudam House (or Van Leuven House) (c1820), 63 Main St.
Tobias Swart House, 74 Main St.
Dr. Elmendorf House, 77 Main St.
Brick House (c1840), 78 Main St.
Cornelius Tappan House, 10 Crown St.; first post office.
Petrus Franciscus Rogan House (or Franz House) (c1750), 42 Crown St.
Matthew Jansen House, 42 Crown St.
Abraham DeWitt Lowe House (c1750), 53 Crown St.
Jacobus S. Bruyn House (c1750), corner of North Front and Crown Sts.
DeWitt House (c1830), 20 John St.
Jan Hendrickse Persen House (18th century), 74 John St.
Luke Kiersted House (18th century), corner of Green and John Sts.
"The Columns" (Reverend Hoes House), Greek Revival, 26 Pearl St.
Cornelius Masten House (1725), 109 Pearl St.
Johannes Masten House, corner of Pearl and Wall Sts.
Coonradt Elmensdorf Tavern, 88 Maiden Lane. Committee of Safety met here.
John McLean House (before 1730), 129 Maiden Lane.
Abraham Masten House, 308 Clinton Ave.
Tremper House (1801), 3 North Front St.
Anthony Freer House, 61 North Front St.
Martinus Hoffman House (or Jan Gacherie House) (1660), corner of Green and
    North Front Sts. Now a restaurant.
Tjerck Claessen DeWitt House (1669), road to Hurley.

KINGSTON POINT Ulster Co. Formerly Columbus Point. On Hudson River east of Kingston, north of Rondout Creek. Formerly important transfer point between Day Line steamers and Ulster & Delaware trains. The Day Line operated a pleasure park here for many years. Now there are oil depots and a public park.

KINNE BROOK AND KINNE-BROOK LAKE Sullivan Co. Flows south from Maplewood to Swinging Bridge Reservoir on Mongaup River.

KIPP HILL Greene Co. Elev. 2000 ft. North of Maben Hill near Mosquito Point at junction of Little West Kill and Schoharie Creek. On Rte. 23A.

Coonradt Elmendorf Tavern (1777), Kingston. Now a private home. Photo by Alfred H. Marks.

KISKATOM Greene Co. In a loop of Kaaterskill Creek atop Bethel Ridge. On Rte. 23A. East of Palenville.

KISKATOM BROOK Greene Co. Flows from Winter Clove past Cairo Round Top and Lawrenceville to Kaaterskill Creek at Kiskatom.

KISKATOM FLATS Greene Co. Extensive fertile flats near Kiskatom. Early settled by the Dutch.

KLEIN KILL Ulster Co. Flows from Palmaghatt Ravine in the Shawangunks to Mara and Shawangunk Kills. Name means Little Brook.

KLEINEKILL LAKE Ulster Co. In Shawangunks beneath Glory Hill on Mohonk grounds.

KNICKERBOCKER POND Sullivan Co. Near Grooville.

KNIGHTS EDDY Sullivan Co. On Rte. 97 and Delaware River and old D&H Canal south of Pond Eddy and north of Mongaup.

KNOB, THE Greene Co. East of Huntersfield Mtn. and west of Richmond Mtn. North of Ashland.

KNOX Albany Co. On Rte. 156 west of Altamont, east of Schoharie. Knox Caves. Bozenkill Gorge. Knoxville Academy (c1830-c1900), now a residence, Rte. 156. Malachi Whipple Farmhouse (c1800) atop Helderberg escarpment, Rte. 156 1.5 miles west of Altamont.

KNOX CAVE Albany Co. On Rte 252 1 mile north of Knox near Thacher Park. Underground caverns 2000 ft. long with 6 levels to depth of 165 ft. in limestone strata. Many fossils, travertine, cave onyx, alabaster formations. "Green Barrel" is 52-ft.-long crawlway. Indians held ceremonies here. Bats and salamanders. Once was officially open to public, but now open only to spelunkers. A large part remains unexplored.

KORTRIGHT Delaware Co. North of Bloomville, southeast of Oneonta on U&D RR. Named for Indian fighter Captain Benjamin Kortright.

Fair Street Dutch Reformed Church (1850), Kingston. Built of local dolomite limestone. Photo by Alfred H. Marks.

Old Dutch Church (1852), Kingston. Minard Lafever, architect. Photo by Alfred H. Marks.

St. James United Methodist Church, Kingston. Photo by Alfred H. Marks.

Ulster County Court House (1818), Wall St., Kingston. Photo by Alfred H. Marks.

KRIPPLEBUSH Ulster Co. Southwest of Stone Ridge. Old home (c1772).

KRUM FALLS Schoharie Co. At Middleburg.

KRUMVILLE Ulster Co. West of Kripplebush and east of Samsonville.

KYKEOUT See Kykuit.

KYKUIT Green Co. Low hill south of Catskill and north of the Great Embought. East of the Kalkberg. Kykuit is roughly translated from the Dutch as "Beacon Hill." The early settlers used it as such to warn of the approach of Indians. John Overbagh settled here in 1722. Clauland House & Barn (c1740).

KYSERIKE Ulster Co. At junction of Peters Kill and Rondout Creek at western foot of Shawangunks. On former D&H Canal. It was center of a millstone industry from colonial times, utilizing the Shawangunk grit, or conglomerate rock. Largest sassafras tree in N. Y. State in Benton Bar Cemetery—50 ft. high with 57-ft. crown, 9'8" circumference at 4 ft. above ground.

LA BELLE FALLS Greene Co. On Kaaterskill Creek near foot of Kaaterskill Clove west of Palenville. Private property.

LABYRINTH, THE Ulster Co. At west base of Skytop on Mohonk Hotel property. Tumbled limestone boulders with a trail running through it.

New housing development in old Dutch style with stepped gables, Mutton Hollow, Kingston. Photo by Alfred H. Marks.

LACKAWACK Ulster Co. West of Napanoch and east of Grahamsville on Rte. 55A. Site of fort at times of Indian raids. The Merriman Dam on Rondout Reservoir is located here.

LACKAWAXEN Pennsylvania. At junction of Lackawaxen Creek and the Delaware River, opposite Minisink Ford in Sullivan County, N.Y. Site of old Indian fort and place where D&H Canal crossed the Delaware on the suspension bridge built by John Roebling in 1848. This bridge is still in use for auto traffic. Toll charged.

LADEW'S CORNERS Ulster Co. Old name for village of Mt. Tremper.

Wall St., Kingston with Pike Plan renovations, 1976. Photo by Alfred H. Marks.

Steamer Washington Irving *at Kingston Point.*

LADLETOWN Ulster Co. On Neversink River south of Denning. Wooden ladles were made here.

LAKE BROOK Delaware Co. Rises in Odel Lake and flows south to West Branch of Delaware at Hobart.

LAKE COMO Ulster Co. At Chichester.

LAKE CREEK Greene Co. Flows west from South Lake past Scribners to Kaaterskill Falls, where it turns south and over Bastion Falls to junction with Kaaterskill Creek in Kaaterskill Clove.

LAKE DELAWARE Delaware Co. On Rte. 28 southeast of Delhi, northwest of Margaretville. Drains into Little Delaware, which flows northwest. Action here in anti-rent war. Norman Gothic home of General Morgan Lewis, related to the Livingstons. St. James Episcopal Church, sandstone.

LAKE HELOISE Greene Co. West of Ginseng Mtn.

LAKE HILL Ulster Co. On Cooper Lake and Rte. 212 west of Bearsville.

LAKE HUNTINGTON Sullivan Co. Village and Lake on Rte. 52, 113, 116 north of Narrowsburg and south of Fosterdale. Popular German ethnic resort around turn of the century.

LAKE KATRINE Ulster Co. Lake and community north of Kingston and south of Ruby. The lake is between Rtes. 9W and 32 but out of sight of both roads. The village is west of Rte. 9W on the West Shore Railroad. Formerly Aunt Trens Lake. Later settled by people of Scottish background, it was named for the beautiful lake in the Trossachs which was the setting for Sir Walter Scott's "Lady of the Lake." Wm. Osterhoudt house (1740) on Neighborhood Road.

LAKE LOUISE-MARIE Sullivan Co. East of Monticello and west of Wurtsboro, immediately to the south of Rte. 17 south of Wanasink Lake.

LAKE MIMI Delaware Co. West of Morton Hill, it is the source of Horse Brook, which flows south to the Beaver Kill west of Roscoe.

LAKE MYOSOTIS Albany Co. Near Rensselaerville in Hyuck Preserve. Myosotis means forget-me-not (flower).

LAKE SUPERIOR Sullivan Co. South of Bethel, southwest of White Lake.

LAKE SWITZERLAND Delaware Co. North of Fleischmanns on Vly Creek.

LAKE UNCAS Sullivan Co. Northwest of Grooville.

LAKEWOOD Sullivan Co. On Rte. 96 east of Tennanah Lake.

LAMBDIN'S GLEN Ulster Co. Near Lake Mohonk Mtn. House on west shore of lake. Picturesque small glen named for early 19th-century painter and print maker John Lambdin.

LAMBS CORNERS Albany Co. East of Medusa.

LAMPMAN HILL Greene Co. Elev. 200 ft. South of Coxsackie on Hudson River.

LANESBORO Pennsylvania. 4 miles east of Susquehanna, Pa. at junction of Susquehanna River and Starrucca Creek, which joins it from the south. D&H RR, Erie RR. Just east of Susquehanna Station on the Erie Railroad is the great masonry Starrucca Viaduct modeled after ancient Roman ones. It has 18 tall, slender, bluestone arches that carry two tracks for 1200 ft. at a height of 110 ft. above the creek and village. Built in 1847 by a Scotsman, James P. Kirkwood, at a cost of $320,000, taking 800 men one year to build. It is very beautiful and well maintained.

LANESVILLE Greene Co. East of Chichester and west of Edgewood on Rte. 214.

LANGE RACK Ulster Co. Cliffs along west bank of Hudson River north of Highland. Name is Dutch for "long reach."

LAPLA Ulster Co. Small location between Olive Bridge and Lomontville.

LATTINTOWN or Lattingtown Ulster Co. Orchard area northwest Marlboro and east of Modena.

LAUNT HOLLOW BROOK Delaware Co. Flows 4 miles into West Branch of Delaware River north of Delancey.

LAUNT POND Delaware Co. In Bear Spring Mountain Game Management Area west of Downsville.

LAUREL CREEK Delaware Co. Flows 4 miles into West Branch of Delaware River near Deposit.

LAUREL HOUSE STATION Greene Co. Actually two closeby but separate stations on the defunct Ulster & Delaware Kaaterskill Branch and Catskill & Tannersville Railroads. Laurel House was located at the top of Kaaterskill Falls.

LAURENS Otsego Co. On Rte. 205 and Otego Creek south of Hartwick and north of Oneonta. Settled in 1790 by Richard Smith of Burlington, N.J.

LAVA Sullivan Co. On Rte. 52 east of Narrowsburg.

LAWRENCEVILLE #1 Greene Co. At north end of Kiskatom Flats on Rte. 32.

Erie Limited *Crossing Starrucca Viaduct westbound in 1947. Erie Railroad photo.*

LAWRENCEVILLE #2 Ulster Co. Near Rosendale. Johnannes DeWitt House (1736), 1 mile west of junction of Green Kill and Rondout Creek.

LAWYERSVILLE Schoharie Co. On Rte. 145 north of Cobleskill, south of Sharon.

LAYMAN MONUMENT Greene Co. On Escarpment Trail ½ mile south of top of Kaaterskill Trail, going towards Inspiration Point. It is on the northern slope of Kaaterskill Clove just east of and above the Horseshoe Curve on Rte. 23A and is visible from the road. It was erected to the memory of Frank D. Layman, a local man who lost his life on the site while fighting a forest fire on August 10, 1900. The monument is a stone cairn with a marble plaque. Fine lookouts over the clove from this location.

LEACH LAKE Greene Co. Small lake east of Tannersville and a tributary of Allen Brook. Supposedly named for unpleasant leaches that make swimming uncomfortable.

LEATHERSTOCKING FALLS Otsego Co. On Rte. 80 2½ miles north of Cooperstown. On private property of Leatherstocking Farm, owned by Mrs. Joseph Campbell, who has layed out a nature trail up the ravine from the highway to the foot of the falls. This is private property and should be respected if the public is to continue to enjoy free access. There is a bridge on a private drive just above the falls and also the remains of an old mill. The falls generally are dry except in very wet seasons.

LEBANON LAKE Sullivan Co. West of Forestburg.

LEDGEWOOD PARK Greene Co. North of Palenville.

Erie RR Starrucca Viaduct at Lanesboro, Pa. Photo by author.

LEEDS Greene Co. On Rte. 23B. Town founded in 1675 by construction of a log cabin near the bridge. Original wooden Leeds Bridge built in 1775. Present beautiful and restored stone bridge built in 1792 after wooden one was washed away by flood. Reformed Church (original bldg. 1732; present bldg. 1817). Johannes Schuneman (1710–1794), known as "Fighting Dominie of the Catskills"

Old stone bridge across Catskill Creek near Leeds. Rebuilt and still in use today. Photo by Lionel De Lisser, 1894.

was pastor. As a patriot, he went about armed even in the pulpit to defend himself against Tories and Indians. Inn of Martin G. Schunemann (1796). House of Francis Salisbury (1705). House of Abraham Salisbury (1730). Van Bergen-Vedder farm (1729).

LEESVILLE Schoharie Co. On Rte. 20 west of Sharon Springs. Settled by Calvin Rich.

LEFEVER FALLS Ulster Co. Small community and falls on Rondout Creek east of Rosendale. Site of small hydro plant and earthworks of Army Corps of Engineers. Ice cave in State Forest Preserve. Must obtain DEC permission to enter.

LEMON SQUEEZER Greene Co. On South Mtn. on former grounds of Catskill Mountain House. A conglomeration of tumbled large flat boulders resembling a present-day "A-frame" dwelling or an old-fashioned fruit press. It is atop the Third Ledge, north of Fairy Spring and south of Elfin Pass and Druid Rocks.

LENAPE LAKE Sullivan Co. South of Morsston.

LEONARD HILL Schoharie Co. South of Broome Center.

LEONTA Delaware Co. On Ouleout Creek north of Franklin.

LEUREN KILL Ulster Co. South of Ellenville, it drains east into Sandburg Creek.

LEWBEACH Sullivan Co. On the Beaver Kill northeast of Beaverkill. On Rte. 152. Shin Creek Falls. Beaverkill Trout Hatchery.

LEWIS CREEK Greene Co. Flows south off Huntersville Mtn. to Batavia Kill between Ashland and Red Falls.

LEWIS HOLLOW Ulster Co. On south flank of Overlook Mtn. near Daisy. Abandoned exploratory coal mines.

LEXINGTON Greene Co. On Rte. 23A between Hunter and Prattsville, at junction with Rte. 42. On Schoharie Creek. St. John the Baptist Ukranian Catholic Church, Rte. 23A, built in 1962 without a nail. Onion domes, Byzantine style. Icons, wood carvings. Constructed of British Columbia red cedar in memory of all Ukranians killed by the Communists. Methodist Church (1820). Lexington House Hotel (1883).

LEXINGTON MOUNTAIN Greene Co. See Packsaddle Mtn.

LIBERTY Sullivan Co. A major junction point of Rtes. 17, 52 and 55. North of Monticello and south of Livingston Manor. On Mongaup River. It was settled around 1793. Later it became, briefly, a fashionable spa and later a T.B. spa. Today it is a trading and entertainment center. The large, half-timbered Grossingers Hotel is just outside town. The former O&W depot is now a restaurant with a collection of railroad artifacts.

LIBERTYILLE Ulster Co. At foot of Shawangunks. Southwest of New Paltz.

LIEBHARDT Ulster Co. On Rochester Creek near Samsomville and Tabasco.

LILY POND Ulster Co. East of New Paltz. Southeast of Plutarch.

LIMESTREET Greene Co. East of Gayhead.

LINCOLN PARK Ulster Co. Suburban area north of Kingston.

LINDEN Delaware Co. On Rte. 30. On East Branch of Delaware. North of East Branch, southwest of Harvard.

LION'S HEAD Greene Co. Eastern peak of Mt. Sherrill.

LITCHFIELD LEDGE Ulster Co. In Minnewaska State Park in Shawangunks. Elev. 2140 ft. North of Castle Point, looking northwest.

LITTLE BEAVER KILL #1 Ulster Co. Flows from Wittenberg Pond to Esopus Creek at Coldbrook.

LITTLE BEAVER KILL #2 Sullivan Co. Flows west from Cooley to Willowemoc Cr. at Livingston Manor.

LITTLE DELAWARE RIVER Delaware Co. Rises near Bovina and flows west to West Branch of Delaware River at Delhi.

LITTLE ESOPUS Old name for Rondout Creek.

LITTLE PECK HOLLOW Ulster Co. On west side of Panther Mtn.

LITTLE PINE ORCHARD Greene Co. Clearing and picnic area at top of Dead Ox Hill and north of Cape Horn on the Old Mountain Road from Saxe's Farm to Catskill Mtn. House area. Beware of rattlesnakes nesting in outhouse.

LITTLE PISGAH Delaware Co. Elev. 3020 ft. Southeast of Mt. Pisgah.

LITTLE ROCKY MOUNTAIN #1 Ulster Co. Elev. 3015 ft. South of Kanape Brook, west of Mombaccus Mtn., east of Spencers Ledge and north of Big Rosy Bone Knob.

LITTLE ROCKY MOUNTAIN #2 Greene Co. Elev. 3060 ft. West of Olderbark Mtn. and east of Warner Creek.

LITTLE SCHOHARIE CREEK Flows 8 miles into Schoharie at Middleburg.

LITTLE SHANDAKEN Ulster Co. Westernmost part of Township of Woodstock, west of Lake Hill.

LITTLE SPRING BROOK Delaware Co. Northeast fork of Spring Brook.

LITTLE WEST KILL Greene Co. Flows northeast off Roundtop Mtn. to Schoharie Creek near Mosquito Point.

LITTLE WEST KILL MOUNTAIN Delaware Co. See Roundtop Mtn.

LIVINGSTON MANOR Sullivan Co. On Rte. 17 north of Liberty and east of Roscoe. On Willowemoc Creek. Named for Dr. Edward Livingston, nephew of Chancellor Robert R. Livingston of Clermont.

LIVINGSTON MARSH AUDUBON SANCTUARY Greene Co. 280 acres south of Catskill on Hudson River. Serves as feeding place for young salt water fish such as striped bass, shad and herring, which spawn in river.

LIVINGSTONVILLE Schoharie Co. On Rte. 145 south of Middleburg and north of Cooksburg. Old Inn.

LIVINGSTONVILLE CREEK Schoharie Co. Flows 6 miles south into Catskill Creek at Livingstonville. Rises west of Rensselaerville.

LLOYD Ulster Co. On Rte. 299 east of New Paltz and west of Highland. Thomas Halstead House, "Glory Land" (1810), on Weeds Mill Road.

LOCH SHELDRAKE Sullivan Co. On Rte. 52 east of Liberty and west of Woodbourne.

LOCKS FALLS Greene Co. On Shingle Kill in Forge section of Purling.

LOMONTVILLE Ulster Co. On Esopus Creek west of Marbletown. Andries DeWitt House (c1753).

LONE MOUNTAIN Ulster Co. Elev. 3721 ft. North of Peekamoose, south of Rocky Mtn. Between Rondout Creek and Neversink River.

LONG EDDY Sullivan Co. On Rte. 97. On Delaware River north of Hankins and south of Hancock at junction of Hoolihan Creek. On Erie RR 4 miles west of Hankins and 6 miles east of Lordsville.

LONG FLAT Delaware Co. On Rte. 30. On East Branch of Delaware River north of East Branch, southwest of Harvard.

LONG LEVEL Greene Co. Stretch of Old Catskill Mountain House Road between Featherbed Hill and Pine Orchard.

LONG PATH More a conception than a fact. It is a projected series of foot-trails following high elevations from the George Washington Bridge to the Adirondacks. Part of it runs through the Catskills and utilizes the Escarpment Trail. Its routing is circuitous and there are several gaps in it. See my *Trail Guide to the Catskills* (New York: Walking News Press, 1975).

LONG POND Sullivan Co. North of Willowemoc on north branch of Fir Brook.

LONGYEAR Ulster Co. See Mount Pleasant.

LOOKOUT ROCK Greene Co. Famous lookout atop Sunset Rock side trail on North Mtn. Albany and Newman's Ledge can be seen.

LOOMIS #1 Delaware Co. On Rte. 206 northwest of Walton.

LOOMIS #2 Sullivan Co. East of Liberty. Dr. Alfred L. Loomis promoted Liberty area as curative for lung diseases.

LOOMIS BROOK Delaware Co. Rises on west side of Loomis Mountain and flows southwest to Cannonsville Reservoir.

LOOMIS MOUNTAIN Delaware Co. Elev. 2260 ft. Northwest of Walton.

LORDS LAKE Sullivan Co. On Rte. 17 west of Mastens; lake to north of Highway. East of Rock Hill, now known as Wanasink Lake. Former D&H Canal reservoir.

LORDVILLE Delaware Co. On Delaware River and Erie RR. Turn south off Rte. 97 at French Woods. South of Hancock and north of Long Eddy. Named for Eleazor Lord of Piermont in Rockland County, who conceived and was first president of Erie Railroad. Very scenic wild river area.

LOSEES HILL Ulster Co. In Shawangunks at Cragsmoor.

LOST CLOVE Ulster Co. In east wall of Balsam Mtn. near col with Belle Ayre Mtn.

LOST CORNERS Ulster Co. At junction of Sandburg and Rondout Creeks.

LOUISA POND Ulster Co. West of Shaupeneak Mtn.

LOUIS RAVINE Ulster Co. At Napanoch in Shawangunks behind prison on Witch's Hole.

LOVER'S RETREAT Greene Co. Formerly was a natural seat formed by intertwined roots of two trees immediately to the south of the former Catskill Mountain House. The trail to it is now closed off as being too narrow and dangerous.

LOWES CORNERS Sullivan Co. Northeast of Grahamsville at northwest end of Rondout Reservoir at junction of Rtes. 55A and 153.

LUCAS KILL Ulster Co. Flows off Kaaterskill High Peak at Manorville to Plattekill Creek.

LUTHERANVILLE Schoharie Co. On West Branch of Charlotte Creek southwest of Richmondville.

LUXTON LAKE Sullivan Co. East of Narrowsburg on Ten Mile River.

LUZERNE Delaware Co. On Fish Creek south of of Fishs Eddy.

LUZON LAKE Sullivan Co. Near Loch Sheldrake.

LYBOLT BROOK Sullivan Co. Near Mongaup Valley.

LYON LAKE Ulster Co. North of Fort Honk.

LYON MOUNTAIN Delaware Co. Elev. 2920 ft. East of South Kortright.

LYONSVILLE Ulster Co. Between Olive Bridge and Kripplebush.

LYONSVILLE POND Ulster Co. North of Lyonsville. Flows into Peters Kill.

MABEN HILL Greene Co. Elev. 1820 ft. South of North Lexington.

MABEN HOLLOW Ulster Co. East of Big Indian Mtn.

MACGOWAN HOLLOW Delaware Co. South of Mundale.

MACKEY Schoharie County. East of North Blenheim.

MACKHACKEMECK Orange Co. Old name for Port Jervis. Also called Maghackemeck.

MAD BROOK Greene Co. Flows south from between Pisgah and Nebo to Batavia Kill at Windham.

MAHACKAMACK Old name for Neversink River.

MAHICCANNITTUCK Indian name for reach of Hudson River between Catskill and Albany. It means "place where the Machicans live."

MALDEN-ON-HUDSON Ulster Co. On Hudson River, West Shore RR and Route 9W, north of Saugerties and south of Eavesport. Staples House (c1837), Bristol Beach and Methodist Church (1867), in bracketed style with tall spire.

MALLORY BROOK Delaware Co. Flows 3 miles into West Branch of Delaware.

MALTBY HOLLOW Ulster Co. Off Watson Hollow west of West Shokan. South of Samuels Point, east of Slide Mtn. and Balsam Cap and north of Hanover Mtn. Site of former Moon Haw Club. Former charcoal burning activity in the area. Formerly Mammy Cotton Holler.

MALTBY HOLLOW FALLS Ulster Co. In 3 tiers on property of Maltby Valley Falls Club, off Moonhaw Road.

MAMAKATING Sullivan Co. On Rte. 17 and O&W RR. On west slope of Shawangunks east of Wurtsboro, west of Bloomingburg at west portal of O&W tunnel.

MANOR KILL Schoharie Co. Flows west from Manorkill to Schoharie Creek at Schoharie Reservoir.

MANOR KILL FALLS Schoharie Co. On Manor Kill just above its outlet into Schoharie Reservoir. Crossed by truss bridge on Prattsville-Gilboa Road. Very beautiful with rock ledges and ferns but difficult and dangerous to see.

MANORKILL Schoharie Co. On Manor Kill. West of Cooksburg and east of Gilboa, in town of Conesville. Incorporated 1836. Richtmyer Tavern (1789), west of village, blend of Garrison Colonial and early Greek Revival.

MANORVILLE Ulster Co. South of Palenville at foot of Wall of Manitou.

MAPLECREST Greene Co. On Batavia Kill southeast of Hensonville. Large resort here. Maple sugar area—good retail buys. Formerly Big Hollow.

MAPLEDALE Ulster Co. On Dry Brook between Arkville and Seager.

MAPLE LAKE Sullivan Co. Near Grooville.

MAPLEWOOD Sullivan Co. On Rte. 17B west of Monticello.

MARA KILL Ulster Co. Flows south into Shawangunk Kill above Canahgote along southeast base of The Traps Cliffs.

MARATANZA LAKE Ulster Co. Elev. 2233 ft. Atop Shawangunks north of Sam's Point. Reservoir for Ellenville.

MARBLETOWN Ulster Co. Laid out in 1670 by committee on which served Captain Henry Pawling. Bevier House (1691), started by Andries Pieterse Van Leuven, who sold to Louis Bevier in 1715. Now a museum and headquarters of Ulster County Historical Society. John Hasbrouck House (1766), served as fort. Leggett Estate, on Rest Place Road. "Pine Farm" (prior to 1750) Dutch Colonial Cottage (1710), also large manorhouse, barns, stables. Davenport or "Olde Lang Syne House" on Leggett Road. Wynkoop-Dixon House (c1763), Rte. 209. Pawling House (c1672–95), west side of Rte. 209 at Hurley town line. Andries De Witt House (c1753), on west bank of Esopus Creek near Lomontville 3½ miles south of Hurley Bridge.

Wynkoop-Dixon House, Marbletown. Photo by Alfred H. Marks.

Ulster County Historical Society Headquarters—Bevier House, Marbletown. Photo by Alfred H. Marks.

MARGARET CLIFF Ulster Co. In Minnewaska State Park in Shawangunks. Elev. 2045 ft. Quartz conglomerate cliffs on southeast escarpment. Wolf's Jaw to north. Slate bank at base. Jacob's Ladder down to Margaret's Stone Parlor.

MARGARET'S STONE PARLOR Ulster Co. In Minnewaska State Park in Shawangunks. At south base of Margaret Cliff near southeast end of Lake Awosting. Tumbled boulders and crevices form a natural "room." Jacob's Ladder up cliff to Margarett Cliff. Murray Hill to south.

MARGARETVILLE Delaware Co. On East Branch of Delaware River at northeastern end of Pepacton Reservoir. At Junction of Rtes. 30 and 28.

MARIE FALLS Greene Co. On Bowery Creek in South Durham.

MARKHAM CREEK AND FALLS Ulster Co. At Samsonville. Old millsite.

MARLBORO Ulster Co. On Rte. 9W, West Shore RR and Hudson River. South of Milton and north of Newburgh. Marlborough Falls are on Maune Kill here. Orchards. Home of Col. Lewis Dubois (1728–1802), of 5th Regiment of the Continental Line. His home (c1763) is believed to be the first clapboard house built in Ulster. Washington visited here. Hotel (1858). McCourt House (c1830). Wineries.

MARLBORO MOUNTAIN Ulster Co. In Plattekill Range. Elev. 1100 ft. Axis runs north to south, between Hudson River on east and Wallkill Valley on west.

MARLBOROUGH See Marlboro.

MARVIN HOLLOW Delaware Co. East of Walton.

MARYLAND Otsego Co. On Rte. 7, D&H RR and Schenevus Creek east of Oneonta and west of Worcester.

MARY'S GLEN Greene Co. Near North Lake. Ashley Creek and Falls are here, as is Hawley's Ledge. Cool shady easy walk.

MARY SMITH BROOK Delaware Co. Flows south into Beaver Kill at Lewbeach.

MARY SMITH HILL Delaware Co. Elev. 2767 ft. South of Beech Hill and north of Huggins Lake.

MASON'S CLIFF Greene Co. Near Profile Rock in Kaaterskill Clove on Rte. 23A just below More's Bridge.

MASON'S RAVINE Ulster Co. Former site of sawmill on the Sawyers Kill north of Seamon's Park in Saugerties.

MASONVILLE Delaware Co. On Rtes. 8 and 206. South of Sidney, north of Deposit, east of Bainbridge and west of Walton.

Mason's Cliff from More's Bridge in Kaaterskill Clove. Photo by Alfred H. Marks.

MASTEN'S LAKE Sullivan Co. North of Yankee Lake on Rte. 17. Site of former exclusive private Sullivan County Club (c1893).

MATAWA LAKE Sullivan Co. South of Livingston Manor.

MATTACAHONTS See Mettacahonts.

MATTHEW POINT Greene Co. On Hudson River. South of New Baltimore and east of Hannacroix.

MAUNE KILL Ulster Co. Flows east into Hudson River at Marlboro.

McCLURE Broome Co. On Rtes. 17 and 41. Turnoff for Oquaga Lake to south. East of Damascus and west of Deposit. On McClure's Brook, which flows east to Delaware.

McDANIEL'S HOLLOW Ulster Co. At Shady.

McGREGOR MOUNTAIN Delaware Co. Elev. 3180 ft. East of Mt. Utsayantha near Stamford.

McKEE BROOK Sullivan Co. In Rock Hill. Katrina Falls.

McKEE'S POND Sullivan Co. Former reservoir for D&H Canal.

McKINLEY HOLLOW Ulster Co. Near Oliverea. Between Balsam Mtn. to the north, Haynes Mtn. to the west and Eagle Mtn. to southwest.

MEADE HILL Delaware Co. Elev. 2200 ft. Western branch of Fleischmann Mtn. East of Arkville.

MEADS Ulster Co. Elev. 1700 ft. Between Overlook Mtn. to east and Mt. Guardian to the west. Named for an early inn, now a Buddhist monastery. Views north to Indian Head Range and south to Hudson Valley and Shawangunks. Near Woodstock. George Mead's inn opened in 1863.

MEDUSA Albany Co. North of Durham. Medusa was one of the three Gorgons; she was a snake-headed female monster, whom to look upon would turn one to stone. She was killed by Perseus. Once a beautiful woman, she offended Athena, who turned her into a monster. Is there possibly a connection here with nearby Athens?

MEDWAY Greene Co. Northwest of Coxsackie. Many Quakers settled here early in the 19th century.

MEEKERS HILL Delaware Co. Elev. 2533 ft. North of Dunraven.

MEEKER HOLLOW CREEK Delaware Co. Rises north of Plattekill Mountain and flows east to East Branch of Delaware River at Stratton Falls.

MELODY LAKE Sullivan Co. On Rte. 102 south of Monticello.

MEREDITH Delaware Co. On Rte. 28 and U&D RR south of Oneonta, north of Delhi.

MERIDALE Delaware Co. On Rte. 28 on Ouleout Creek north of Delhi, south of Oneonta.

MERRICK POND Delaware Co. Southwest of Rock Rift. A source of Read Creek.

MERRIMAN DAM Ulster Co. At eastern end of Rondout Reservoir near Lackawack. Seen from Rtes. 55 and 55A.

MERWIN Delaware Co. On Rte. 17 and Beaver Kill. East of Horton, west of Cooks Falls.

METHOL Delaware Co. On Trout Brook. South of Peakville on Rte. 17. Methol is a type of poisonous wood alcohol obtained by the dry distillation of wood— once a local industry. Plant of Arthur Leighton, the "Acid King."

METTACAHONTS Ulster Co. North of Accord and south of Liebhardt. Not on Mettacahonts Creek.

METTACAHONTS CREEK Ulster Co. Flows southeast from between Big Rosy Bone Knob and Mombaccus Mtn. to Rochester Creek.

MIDDLE BROOK Delaware Co. Rises north of Harpersfield and flows west to Charlotte Creek at Fergusonville.

MIDDLEBURG Schoharie Co. Town was burned in Johnson Raid of 1780. Settled c1712–1714 by Conrad Weiser, a Palatinate, it is alleged to be the oldest town in the Schoharie valley. Weiser moved on to Conestoga, Pa. in 1723, owing to land title problems. It was the site of the Middle of Three Forts in the Valley. Formerly Weiser's Dorf. The Dutch Reformed Church is built of brick and dates from 1786. Krum and Boucks Falls are in the neighborhood and Vroman's Nose has been called "a geological oddity." Octagon House on Rte. 30 west of town.

MIDDLEFIELD Otsego Co. East of Cooperstown and northeast Milford. On Cherry Valley Creek. Schoolhouse Museum.

MIDDLEFIELD CENTER Otsego Co. Northeast of Cooperstown, southwest of Cherry Valley.

MIDDLE MOUNTAIN Delaware Co. Elev. 2975 ft. East of Mary Smith Hill, west of Touchmenot Mtn. and south of Hunt Hill.

MILESES Sullivan Co. North of Hankins on Hankins Creek.

MILFORD Otesgo Co. On Rtes. 28 and 166, C&CV RR and Susquehanna River. North of Oneonta and south of Cooperstown. Railroad shops.

MILL BROOK #1 Ulster Co. Flows southeast from Tabasco to Rochester Creek.

MILL BROOK #2 Delaware and Ulster Co. Rises south of Furlough Lake and north of Balsam Round Top. Flows west to Pepacton Reservoir.

MILL BROOK #3 Sullivan Co. Flows south from neighborhood of Highland Lake to Delaware River at Pond Eddy.

MILLBROOK MOUNTAIN Ulster Co. Elev. 1820 ft. On east face of Shawangunks near Lake Minnewaska, south of The Traps.

MILL BROOK RIDGE Ulster Co. Elev. 3480 ft. Parallel to and south of the Mill Brook near Pepacton.

MILL CREEK Otsego Co. Flows south from West Oneonta to Susquehanna River between Oneonta and Otsego.

MILL HOOK Ulster Co. Locality on Rochester Creek near Port Jackson and Accord.

MILLSIDE FALLS Greene Co. On Shingle Kill near Roundtop. Forge Section.

MILTON Ulster Co. On Rte. 9W, Hudson River, West Shore RR. South of Highland and north of Marlboro. Former home of novelist Mary Hallock Foote.

Points of interest:

Elijah and Micahiah Lewis "Spy House" (before 1760), corner of Indian Rd. and Rte. 9W. Dutch architecture. Washington slept here. Tavern during Revolution. Served as headquarters for Continental Army spies.
Tristram Coffin House, Rte. 9W.
Willow Tree House (c1825), Rte. 9W.
"Rock Cliff" (c1850), once center of a Quaker intellectual colony.
Pieter Jansen House (late 18th century).
Capt. Sherbourn Sears House (mid 18th century; modified in late 19th century), once owned by Father Divine.
Elderhoj Art Colony (early 20th century), stucco Moorish style.
Hepworth Orchards.
Royal Wine Corp. Winery in old West Shore freight station.
Benmarl Winery.

MINE HOLLOW #1 Ulster Co. Between Belle Ayre and Balsam Mtns. at head of North Branch of Dry Brook.

MINE HOLLOW #2 Delaware Co. Between Fleischmann Mtn. and Meade Hill.

MINE HOLLOW #3 Ulster Co. Between Hanover Mtn. and Breath Hill.

MINE HOLLOW BROOK Ulster Co. Runs through Mine Hollow #3.

MINE KILL Schoharie Co. Flows east from South Jefferson to Schoharie Creek at North Blenheim.

MINE KILL STATE PARK Schoharie Co. On Rte. 30. At Blenheim near the Blenheim-Gilboa Pumped Storage Facility.

MINISINK Old name for area around Port Jervis and for Neversink River. From name of local tribe of Delaware Indians.

MINISINK FORD Sullivan Co. On Delaware River and Rte. 97 opposite Lackawaxen, West of Barryville. Site of Indian battle July 22, 1779. Site of Roebling suspension bridge (1848), originally built for D & H Canal.

MINK HOLLOW #1 Greene Co. Notch in Indian Head Range through which ran old Indian trail and early road from Lake Hill to Tannersville area. Roaring Brook flows north and Beaver Kill south. No auto road goes through it now. Easy hiking trail. Near Elka Park. Plateau Mtn. to west and Sugarloaf to east.

MINK HOLLOW #2 Greene Co. Between North Dome on west and West Kill Mtn. on East.

MINK MOUNTAIN Greene Co. See Sugarloaf Mtn.

MINNEWASKA Ulster Co. Name of a ghost town on Rte. 44–55 west of Gardiner and east of Kerhonkson. Millstones were formerly cut here from Shawangunk grit. The former village was located between the present Mohonk Trust lands and those of the Lake Minnewaska Mountain Houses, to the south of the highway. Not much left.

MINNEWASKA, LAKE Ulster Co. South of Lake Mohonk and north of Lake Awosting atop the Shawangunk Ridge, west of Gardiner. Name means "frozen waters." Lake Minnewaska is a glacial lake, oval in shape, with an area of 38 acres at an elevation of 1650 ft. The water is crystal clear, the acidity of the water preventing growth of algae or vegetation. Because of this, and the great depth and hard quartz bottom, the water is a wonderful cerulean blue, similar to Moraine Lake in British Columbia. Quartz conglomerate cliffs, covered with pitch pines, laurel, hemlock and white birch, rise to 145 ft. above the lake. A scenic footpath encircles the lake. There is bathing and canoeing and good scuba diving. The lake empties into Coxing Kill at the east end. Cliff House and Wildmere, the Lake Minnewaska Mountain Houses, formerly over looked the lake from the north and west, respectively. These mountain houses were founded by Alfred H. Smiley, cousin of the Lake Mohonk Smileys, in 1879. Mr. Smiley was a Quaker and maintained a conservative and simple atmosphere in a more rustic manner than that of Lake Mohonk. The estate gradually grew to 10,000 acres, incorporating Lake Awosting to the south. Mr. Smiley's original land purchase was in 1876. In 1970 the owners, the Phillips family, disposed of 7000 acres to the Palisades Interstate Park Commission for formation of the Minnewaska State Park. This now incorporates Lake Awosting and Lake Minnewaska. The park is a wilderness type operation and offers water sports, camping, snow-mobiling, picnicking, rock climbing and cross-country skiing. Mud Pond, or Haseco Lake, is a significant location for the study of ecology.

Cliff house burned in 1978. Wildmere closed as of January 1, 1980, and burned in 1986.

Scenic features in the Minnewaska area (see individual entries) are: Haseco Lake (Mud Pond), Murray Hill, Margarets Stone Parlor, Jacobs Ladder, Margarets Cliff, Wolfs Jaw, Awosting Lake, Hamilton Point, Castle Point, Battlement Terrace, Litchfield Ledge, Huntington Ravine, Overlook Point, Fly Brook, Stony Kill and Falls, Rainbow Falls, Kempton Ledge, Echo Rock, Palmaghatt Ravine, Gertrudes Nose, Millbrook Mtn., Pattersons Pellet, Dallas Pool, Peters Kill Awosting Falls, the Amphitheatre, Beacon Hill, Pine Cliff, Coxing Kill, Sheldon Falls, Dickie Barre, the Traps.

MINNEWASKA STATE PARK Ulster Co. See above article.

MINNEWASKA TRAIL Ulster Co. Name for scenic Rtes. U.S. 44 and N.Y. 55. From Highland on the Hudson near the Mid-Hudson Bridge to Kerhonkson and junction with Rte. 209. Runs via Modena, Ireland Corners, Gardiner, The Traps, Ski Minnie, Minnewaska and Shawangunk Mtns. Superb views to east over Wallkill and Hudson Valleys and to west over Rondout Valley to entire Catskill Range.

MIRROR LAKE Ulster Co. South of Ulster Park and Esopus Lake to east of Rte. 9W.

MITCHELL POND BROOK Sullivan Co. Rises near Fosterdale and flows southwest to Delaware at Skinners Falls.

MITCHELLS STATION Sullivan Co. Now South Fallsburgh. On old O&W Rwy.

MODENA Ulster Co. On Rtes. 44 and 32 and NYNH&H, CNE and PC RRs. East of Gardiner, west of Highland and south of New Paltz. Extensive apple orchards. Modena is a city in Italy, scene of a battle in the Napoleonic Wars.

MOHICAN LAKE Sullivan Co. East of Eldred.

MOHONK, LAKE Ulster Co. West of New Paltz, east of Alligerville, north of Minnewaska and south of Rosendale, atop the Shawangunk Ridge on the grounds of Lake Mohonk Mountain House. Name formerly also applied to the high point immediately east of the lake, now called skytop. This was formerly called Moggonick Point, Mohunk Point and Paltz Point. Lake Mohonk is at an elevation of 1246 ft. and covers 17 acres. It is a glacial lake and of a light green color. The lake supports vegetation and fish life. It is spring fed. There is a foot trail around the lake and sand bathing beaches (open to hotel guests only) on the west shore. The Lake Mohonk Mountain House is at the northwest end, where is also located the boat dock. The outlet of the lake is beneath the hotel! It drains into Mossy Brook. See Lake Mohonk Mountain House in Chapter 11.

From the very beginning formal gardens were laid down and today the floral displays are a famous attraction. There is also an extensive arboretum and experimental garden. The greenhouses are open to the public. There are 60 miles of shale roads, 30 miles of bridle trails, 25 miles of paths and many additional hiking trails and 140 summerhouses on the grounds. Horse-drawn transportation (carriages and sleighs) is still extensively used at Mohonk, and only in recent years have automobiles been allowed to approach the hotel. There is a small "village" near the hotel to house employees, and the residences of the Smiley family are located here.

While the hotel is now owned by a corporation, control of this corporation is vested in the family and they still keep a close interest in the operation of the hotel and estate. In 1963 the Smiley family set up The Mohonk Trust, to which about 6000 acres of Mohonk land were transferred. This land will remain open to both hotel guests and the general public on a nominal fee basis. The land immediately adjacent to the hotel and lake will remain owned by the hotel corporation.

The hotel is open year around and meals are available to day guests, but reservations are mandatory, especially on holidays and weekends. It is usually impossible to get beyond the Mountain Rest Gatehouse unless you are on the "expected arrivals" list. Telephone 914-255-1000 for reservations, ski and other information. Whatever your planned activity it is a good idea to call to avoid possible disappointment. Rock climbing is popular at the Traps and it is usual to find experienced members of the various mountain clubs. This activity is closely supervised and a fee is charged. Inexperienced persons should not attempt this activity and all climbers must sign in with the patrol. Mohonk and Minnewaska are connected by a carriage road but at the present time through vehicle travel is impractical because of obstructions. The road offers attractive hiking and is still useable by carriages as far south as Traps Bridge over Rte. 44. There are also various day-use and overnight camps on the grounds. Check with ranger for locations. Nominal day-use fees are charged on both Trust and Hotel grounds, although day guest are not allowed to use hotel facilities unless taking a meal. Maps are available showing all the various paths and roads and principal points of interest.

See separate entries for the following:

The Traps, Eagle Cliff, Skytop, Cope's Lookout, Arching Rocks, Newlin's Cave, The Labyrinth, Gate of the Winds, Cave of Aeolus, Zaidee's Bower. There are simply too many points of interest to list and the Mohonk grounds will bear many rewarding years of exploration. Dogwood and laurel blossom times are particularly attractive.

MOMBACCUS Ulster Co. Between Fantinekill and Cherrytown.

MOMBASSUS KILL Ulster Co. In town of Rochester. See Beaverdam Creek and Rochester Creek.

MOMBACCUS MOUNTAIN Ulster Co. Elev. 3000 ft. West of High Point, east of Little Rocky, north of Samsonville.

MONESAUING CREEK Ulster Co. Old name of Peters Kill #2.

MONGAUP Sullivan Co. At junction of Mongaup River and Delaware River. Also junction of Rtes. 97 and 31. Near Orange County line.

MONGAUP CREEK Sullivan Co. Flows south from Mongaup Mtn. to Willowemoc Creek at Debruce.

MONGAUP FALLS RESERVOIR Sullivan Co. On Mongaup River, south of Swinging Bridge Reservoir and north of Rio Reservoir. West of Forestburg. Nesting place of bald eagles.

MONGAUP MOUNTAIN Ulster Co. Elev. 3177 ft. South of Hardenburgh and Turnwood.

MONGAUP POND Sullivan Co. At headwaters of Mongaup Creek, south of Mongaup Mountain.

MONGAUP RIVER See Chapter 3.

MONGAUP VALLEY Sullivan Co. On Rte. 17B west of Monticello and east of White Lake on Mongaup River.

MONKA HILL Delaware Co. Elev. 2483 ft. Site of former Grand Hotel near Highmount. Formerly called Monkey Hill. Halcott Mtn. to the north and Rose Mtn. to the east. Good views to southeast.

MONTELA Ulster Co. Name of town that was located in valley now flooded by Rondout Reservoir.

MONTGOMERY HOLLOW Delaware Co. East of Roxbury.

MONTGOMERY HOLLOW CREEK Delaware Co. Flows 5 miles into East Branch of Delaware River.

MONTGOMERY HOLLOW MOUNTAIN Delaware Co. Elev. 3040 ft. Near Montgomery Hollow.

MONTICELLO Sullivan Co. On Rte. 17 south of Liberty and northwest of Wurtsboro, at junction of Rtes. 17B and 42. County seat and trading town. Incorporated in 1830. Monticello Raceway and Airport are nearby.

MONTOMA Ulster Co. North of Glenford, south of Bearsville.

MOON HAW CLUB Ulster Co. Formerly in Maltby Hollow. Property now belongs to Wittenberg Lumber Co. Was fishing and hunting club.

MORE'S BRIDGE Greene Co. Across Kaaterskill Creek in Kaaterskill Clove on Rte. 23A, below Fawn's Leap and above Mason's Cliff. Once popular with artists.

MORE SETTLEMENT Delaware Co. On Rte. 30, U&D RR and East Branch of Delaware north of Roxbury and south of Grand Gorge. Shultice Mountain to the east.

MORESVILLE RANGE Delaware Co. Between branches of the Delaware south of Mt. Utsayantha. Elevations average 3100 ft.

MORGAN HILL Ulster Co. Elev. 550 ft. South of Ashokan Reservoir between Stony Hollow and Esopus Creek.

MORNINGSIDE LAKE Sullivan Co. Near Loch Sheldrake.

MORRIS Otsego Co. On Rtes. 23 and 51 and Butternut Creek west of Oneonta and east of Norwich.

MORRISON'S GLEN Greene Co. In Durham.

MORSSTON Sullivan Co. On Rte. 146 south of Livingston Manor.

MORTON HILL Delaware Co. Elev. 2511 ft. North of the Beaver Kill and south of Pepacton Reservoir. Spring Hollow to the east and Lake Mimi to the west.

MOSES ROCK Greene Co. Spring on face of Wall of Manitou below site of former Catskill Mountain House. Water gushes out of a large rock. Exodus 17:6:

More's Falls from More's Bridge in Kaaterskill Clove. Photo by Alfred H. Marks.

"Moses smote the rock, and the living water gushed forth." There is another similarly named such rock on Kaaterskill High Peak near Twilight Park.

MOSQUITO POINT Greene Co. On Schoharie Creek and Rte. 23A northwest of Lexington between Maben and Vinegar Hills.

MOSSY BROOK #1 Greene Co. The brook in Shanty Hollow.

MOSSY BROOK #2 Ulster Co. Drains Lake Mohonk northwest to Coxing Kill.

MOUNT AIRY Greene Co. Elev. 450 ft. Southeast of Quarryville on Rte. 32. Seen from Thruway.

MOUNT CATHALIA Ulster Co. Formerly called Mt. Meenahga. On Rte. 52 east of Ellenville in Shawangunks. Ski Center. Double chair lift, T-bar, rope tow, school, rentals, patrol, snowmaker, cafeteria, cafe, bar.

MOUNT HYMETTUS Ulster Co. South of West Park. John Burroughs named it because of his luck in finding many bees, beehives and wild honey on its slopes. It was near his home. Mt. Hymettus in Greece is famous for its fields of flowers and many bees.

MOUNT MARION Ulster Co. Village and mountain on Old Glasco Turnpike and West Shore Railroad southwest of Saugerties and west of Glenerie. DeWitt House dates from early 18th century. Mountain can be seen from Thruway and railroad.

MOUNT MEENAHGA Ulster Co. On Rte. 52. On west slope of Shawangunk Ridge east of Ellenville, between North and South Gullies. Mount Meenahga House was here from 1881 to 1963. Meenahga means "huckleberry" in Indian language. See Mount Cathalia.

MOUNTAIN BROOK Delaware Co. Flows 3 miles into West Branch.

MOUNTAIN LAKE Delaware Co. North of Big Pond and Touchmenot Mtn. and south of Barkaboom Mtn.

MOUNTAINDALE Sullivan Co. On Sandburg Creek and Sullivan County Rte. 55 between Spring Glen and Woodridge. Called Sandburgh until 1880. On former O&W Railway mainline. Tomsco Falls.

MOUNT NEBO Greene Co. Elev. 2885 ft. South of Mt. Pisgah and north of Mt. Hayden. In Deuteronomy 32:48 we read, "On that very day the Lord said to Moses, 'Go up on Mount Nebo, here in the Abarim Mountains and view the land of Canaan which I am giving to the Israelites as their possession. Then you shall die on the mountain you have climbed . . .' "

MOUNT PISGAH #1 Delaware Co. Elev. 3345 ft. North of Andes. Site of Catskill Ski Center.

MOUNT PISGAH #2 Greene Co. Elev. 2800 ft. Part of Northwestern Front Range near Windham. North of Mt. Nebo and east of Richmond Mtn. Deuteronomy 3:27: "Go to the top of Mt. Pisgah where you can look out in every direction."

MOUNT PLEASANT Ulster Co. Village on Rte. 28 and U&D RR at junction of Beaver Kill and Esopus Creek. South of Phoenicia and north of Coldbrook. Formerly Longyear.

MOUNT PLEASANT Ulster Co. Mountain west of village of same name. Elev. 2900 ft. South of Romer and east of Crass Mtns. Traver Hollow to the south.

MOUNT SHERIDAN Ulster Co. Elev. 2220 ft. Northwest of Phoenicia between Esopus and Stony Clove Creeks.

MOUNT SHERRILL Greene Co. Elev. 3540 ft. East of Balsam Mtn. and west of North Dome. Named for a Col. Sherrill who owned a large tannery in Shandaken and was killed at Gettysburg.

MOUNT THOMAS COLE Greene Co. Elev. 3940 ft. In Blackhead Range west of Black Dome and east of Maplecrest. Named for famous English-American landscape painter and founder of the Hudson River School. Formerly Black Tom and Mt. Kimball.

MOUNT TOBIAS Ulster Co. Elev. 2540 ft. West of Bearsville and Cooper Lake and Beaver KIll.

MOUNT TREMPER Ulster Co. Elev. 2740 ft. East of Phoenicia and southwest of Carl Mtn. Formerly a fire observation tower. Popular climb. Abandoned mine at 1500 ft. Named for Jacob Tremper. Formerly Timothy Berg. Beware of concentration of rattlesnakes.

MOUNT TREMPER Ulster Co. Village off Rte. 28 and junction with Rte. 212. Formerly Ladews Corners. American Youth Hostel here. North of Cold Brook and south of Phoenicia.

MOUNT UTSAYANTHA Delaware Co. Elev. 3214 ft. South of Stamford. Observation tower and auto road to summit. Picnic grounds. Northeast of Churchill Mtn. and northwest of McGregor Mtn. Named for fictitious Indian princess in a tale by Eugene A. Bouton. See chapter 13 for the Utasayantha Legend.

MOUNT VERNON Sullivan Co. West of Summitville, southeast of Mountaindale.

MOUNT VISION Otsego Co. On Rte. 205. On Otego Creek south of Hartwick, north of Oneonta.

MUDDER KILL Ulster Co. In Town of Rochester.

MUDDY BROOK Ulster Co. Flows east to Woodland Creek from col between Garfield and Panther Mtns.

MUD POND #1 Ulster Co. Also called Haseco Lake. Elev. 1845 ft. In privately owned Shawangunk Preserve south of Minnewaska State Park in Shawangunk Mountains. South of Awosting Lake and north of Lake Maratanza. Drains north into Fly Brook, a source of the Peters Kill.

MUD POND #2 Delaware Co. West of Cables Lake. Drains south into Russell Brook.

MUNDALE Delaware Co. South of Franklin, north of Walton, west of Fraser.

MURDERERS CREEK Greene Co. Rises west of Coxsackie and flows southeast to Hudson River opposite Hudson. Former Athens Branch of the West Shore RR (built originally as Hudson & Saratoga) used to follow the creek. Site of controversial Sleepy Hollow residential development and artificial lake. For the story of how creek got its name see article by Pauline Hommel in Summer 1973 *Catskill Quarterly*.

MURRAY HILL Ulster Co. Elev. 2025 ft. In Shawangunks on east slope. South of Margaret Cliff.

MUTTON HOLLOW Ulster Co. Section of Kingston near Esopus Creek. Formerly given to flooding.

MYRTLE BROOK Greene Co. Flows south from Hunter Mtn. to Stony Clove.

NAHANT Old name of Port Jervis.

NAIAD'S BATH Greene Co. Pool and waterfall on Kaaterskill Creek above junction with Lake Creek and below Five Cascades. "Come ye Naiads! to the fountains lead! Propitious maids! the task remains to sing . . . ."—Armstrong.

NANNETTE FALLS Ulster Co. In Broadstreet Hollow. Named for Indian squaw who sold trinkets to tourists in 19th century.

NAPANOCH Ulster Co. At western foot of Shawangunks and at junction of Rondout and Sandburg Creeks. On Rtes. 209 and 55. Honk Falls and Lake nearby. Large Chateau-style State Correctional Facility (former maximum security prison.) Hydroelectric plant and paper mills. Napanoch Point above on Shawangunks. Napanoch was sacked by Indians in August 1781. New York City, Kingston and New York State records were stored here in October 1777 to keep them safe from British, who burned Kingston. There were ten wagon loads! Bureaucracy is nothing new. Coenradt Bevier House (c1778). Johannes G. Hardenbergh House (1762).

NAPANOCH POINT Ulster Co. Elev 1977 ft. Atop northwest side Shawangunks north of High Point.

NARROW FALLS BROOK Sullivan Co. Rises west of Yulan and flows south to Delaware River south of Tusten.

NARROW NOTCH MOUNTAIN Delaware Co. Elev. 3220 ft. Narrow Notch to west, Irish Mtn. to east.

NARROWSBURG Sullivan Co. On Delaware River and Rtes. 97 and 24. Fort Delaware re-creation. Museum of American Frontier. North of Tusten and south of Cochecton. Fort built in 1754 by the Connecticut Co. Later Joseph Skinner and Moses Thomas, proprietors of Delaware Co.

Napanoch State Prison. Photo by Alfred H. Marks.

NEGRO HOLLOW Delaware Co. South of the Dry Brook, east of Arkville.

NEVERSINK Sullivan Co. On Rte. 55, west of Curry, east of Bradley.

NEVERSINK RESERVOIR Sullivan Co. East of Liberty. See Chapter 3.

NEVERSINK RIVER See Chapter 3.

NEW BALTIMORE Greene Co. On Rte. 144 and Hudson River south of Coeymans and north of Coxsackie. Former sloop and barge building industry. Neat white houses and New England atmosphere. Many Quakers settled here early in 19th century. Popular retirement place for sea and river captains. Many Victorian houses. Parsons-Bronck House (18th century), west side of Rte. 9W near Coxsackie line. Anthony Van Bergen House (c1750).

NEWEIDEN Sullivan Co. On Rte. 23 and East Branch of Ten Mile River east of Narrowsburg at south end of Swamp Pond. Home of Tom Quick, where his family was massacred by Indians.

NEW HURLEY Ulster Co. On Rte. 208 north of Wallkill, south of New Paltz. Attractive church.

NEW KINGSTON Delaware Co. On Plattekill River east of Andes, west of Halcottsville, north of Dunraven.

NEWLINS CAVE Ulster Co. On Mohonk grounds.

NEW LISBON Otsego Co. On Rte. 51 on Butternut Creek, north of Morris. The Grist Mill (1790) at Mill Hollow made Myers Buckwheat, which was sold to Pillsbury Co.

NEWMAN'S LEDGE Greene Co. On Escarpment Trail from Pine Orchard to North Mtn., between Sunset Rock and Badman's Cave. It is just above Sleepy Hollow and there is a 100-ft. sheer drop with a steep 2000-ft. slope below. Considerable exposure here. Excellent views. Named for English clergyman Rev. Newman Hall, a guest at the former Catskill Mountain House.

NEW PALTZ Ulster Co. On Wallkill River, Rtes. 32 and 208, Thruway and Wallkill Valley RR. South of Rosendale and west of Highland. Elev. 236 ft. Founded in 1678 by Huguenots, it was originally a French-speaking settlement, until intermarriage with Dutch and later English changed the local speech. The New Paltz Academy, founded in 1828, later became the New Paltz State Teachers College and is now the New Paltz Campus of the State University of New York. The area is famous for its old stone houses. Huguenot Street is reputed to be the oldest street in the United States which still has its original homes. The stone structures date from 1692. They are incorporated into a twelve-acre historical district.
Huguenot Street houses:

Abraham Hasbrouck House (1692-1712).
Jean Hasbrouck House (1692-1712). Now a Memorial House Museum. The Hasbrouck-Innis-Young Memorial Room is furnished in the style of 1714 by the Huguenot Historical Society.
DuBois Fort or Old Fort (1705).
Deyo House (1692).
Bevier-Elting House (1698).

DuBois Fort, New Paltz. Photo by Alfred H. Marks.

Hugo Freer House (1694).
Lefever House (1799).
French Church. An authentic reconstruction in 1972 of original 1717 church. This is the only reconstruction in the area; all the other buildings are original.
Deyo Hall, 6 Brodhead Avenue.
Bonte Koe Farm–Deyo House (1690), Rte. 32. Bonte Koe or Bonticou means, "spotted cow."

NEW SALEM #1 Albany Co. On Rtes. 85, 85A, 157 at foot of Helderbergs near Thacher State Park.

NEW SALEM #2 Ulster Co. On Rte. 213 east of Eddyville and north of St. Remy at end of D&H Canal on Rondout Creek.

NEW SCOTLAND Albany Co. On Rte. 85 west of Slingerlands, east of New Salem. Andrew J. Whitback Memorial Grove, 26-acre Nature Conservancy on Rte. 85 ½ mile west of village. Five Rivers Conservation Center, Game Farm Road. Vly Creek Gorge, Rte. 203.

NEWTON BROOK Greene Co. Flows north off Balsam Mtn. to West Kill.

NINEVEH Broome Co. On west bank of Susquehanna River north of Harpursville and southwest of Afton. On Rte. 7 and D&H RR at junction of the Binghamton and Wilkes-Barre lines.

Josiah DuBois House, New Paltz. Photo by Alfred H. Marks.

NIOBE FALLS Greene Co. Swimming hole on Kaaterskill Creek in town of Palenville. In mythology Niobe was the proud queen of Thebes in Greece. She incurred the wrath of Latona and Apollo, who thereupon took the lives of her children and husband. According to Thomas Bulfinch: "She was changed to stone, within and without. Yet tears continued to flow; and borne on a whirlwind to her native mountain, she still remains, a mass of rock, from which a trickling stream flows, the tribute of her never-ending grief."

NIOBE'S CAVE Greene Co. In Kaaterskill Clove near Artist's Grotto.

NORMANSKILL Albany Co. Rises near East Berne in Helderbergs and flows east through Normanskill Ravine or The Vale of Tawasentha (one supposed setting of Longfellow's *Song of Hiawatha*) to Hudson River near Glenmount. The D&H RR follows the creek through the ravine.

NORTH BLENHEIM Schoharie Co. On Rte. 30. On Schoharie Creek. Elev. 791 ft. South of Middleburg and north of Gilboa. Site of Blenheim-Gilboa Pumped Storage Facility of the Power Authority of the State of New York, and Mine Kill State Park. Lansing Manor House (1819), 840-acre estate of John T. Lansing; now a museum. Old Blenheim Bridge across Schoharie Creek (1855), world's longest single-span covered bridge, 232 ft. long, 26 ft. wide with 2 driveways. Now closed to autos.

NORTH BRANCH Sullivan Co. On Rtes. 95, 121, 122. On North Branch of Callicoon Creek and Buck Brook northwest of Jeffersonville.

NORTH DOME Greene Co. Elev. 3610 ft. West of West Kill Mtn. and east of Mt. Sherrill.

NORTHEAST HALCOTT MOUNTAIN Greene Co. Elev. 3408 ft. West of Deep Notch and Balsam Mtn.

NORTH FRANKLIN Delaware Co. On Rte. 28 on Ouleout Creek south of Oneonta.

NORTHFIELD Delaware Co. Southeast of Sidney, northwest of Walton.

NORTH GULLY Ulster Co. On western face of Shawangunk Ridge above Ellenville. Mt. Meenahga (Cathalia) to south.

NORTH HARPERSFIELD Delaware Co. Northwest of Stamford.

NORTH KORTRIGHT Delaware Co. On Rte. 23 east of Oneonta and west of Stamford.

NORTH LAKE Greene Co. Elev. 2100 ft. Atop Wall of Manitou above Palenville. Reached by Mountain House Road from Haines Falls. Large State Campsite, bathing beach and picnic area. Adjacent to Pine Orchard, former site of Catskill

Mountain House. Now joined to neighboring South Lake by artificial channel. North Mtn. to the north and South Mtn. to the south. Both lakes formerly belonged to Catskill Mountain House. Fed by waters of Ashley Creek. According to legend, it was one of the two eyes of the reclining giant named Onteora.

NORTH LEXINGTON Greene Co. North of Lexington.

NORTH MOUNTAIN Greene Co. On Wall of Manitou and Escarpment Trail. North of South Mtn. and south of Stoppel Point. Elev. 3000 ft. at North

Jamison House, New Paltz. Photo by Alfred H. Marks.

Point and 3422 ft. at Stoppel Point, in the same massif. Many outstanding features. See separate entries: Artist Rock, Ashley Creek, Ashley Falls, Badman's Cave, Bear's Den, Burnt Acres, Newman's Ledge, Prospect Rock, Red Hill, Spruce Creek, Sunrise Rock, Profile Rock, North Point, Stoppel Point. A moderate climb but take caution on ledges. Excellent viewpoints all along the way. Easy parking at North Lake.

NORTH PLATTEKILL MOUNTAIN Delaware Co. Elev. 3340 ft. West of Old Clump Mtn.

NORTH SETTLEMENT Greene Co. Northwest of Windham.

NORTHWEST MORESVILLE RANGE Delaware Co. Elev. 3240 ft. South of Mt. McGregor near Grand Gorge.

NORTON HILL Greene Co. On Rte. 81 west of Greenville, east of Cooksburg.

NORWOOD MOUNTAIN Greene Co. See Ginseng Mtn.

NOTCH LAKE Greene Co. Formerly Stygian Lake. In Stony Clove and source of Stony Clove Creek. Hunter Mtn. to west; Plateau Mtn. to east.

NUDEBACK RIDGE Schoharie Co. East of Jefferson.

NUMBER TEN HOLLOW Greene Co. Near headwaters of Beaver Kill between Bullet Hole and Quaker Clearing.

OAKES Ulster Co. On WS RR. Name for south end of Highland.

OAK HILL Greene Co. On Rte. 81 and Catskill Creek, north of Durham. There are flat ledges around and above rapids on Catskill Creek. Icicle House (c1800).

OAKLAND Sullivan Co. At junction of Bush Kill and Neversink River. On Rte. 49 west of Paradise and east of Hartwood.

OAKLAND VALLEY Sullivan Co. On Neversink River and former Monticello Branch of O&W RR east of Forestburg and west of Cuddebackville.

OAKSVILLE Otsego Co. West of Cooperstown and south of Canadarago.

OBERNBURG Sullivan Co. On Rte. 95 and Hankins Creek southwest of Livingston Manor.

ODELL Sullivan Co. On Rte. 115 southeast of Bethel.

ODELL LAKE Delaware Co. South of West Harpersfield.

O'HARA CORNERS Greene Co. Northeast of East Durham.

OHIO MOUNTAIN Ulster Co. Elev. 1310 ft. Ohayo is Indian for "stream." Also spelled Ohayo Mtn. Formerly called Beaverkill Mtn. East of Tonshi Mtn., near Glenford.

OHIOVILLE Ulster Co. On Rte. 299 and Thruway east of New Paltz, west of Highland. See Pine Hole Bog.

OLD CATSKILL Greene Co. On Rte. 23. Pieter Souser's Inn—political meetings held here prior to 1797. See Jefferson; Leeds.

OLD CHICHESTER Schoharie Co. North of Livingstonville, south of Rensselaerville.

OLD CLUMP MOUNTAIN Delaware Co. Elev. 3000 ft. Also called simply Clump Mtn. West of Roxbury. John Burroughs home and grave nearby.

OLDERBARK MOUNTAIN Greene Co. Elev. 3440 ft. Southern extension of Plateau Mtn., west of Mink Hollow. East of Little Rocky Mtn. Summit is flat. Formerly known as Oldberg, Oleberg or Oelberg Mtn., all meaning "oil" in Dutch. Possibly early settlers pressed cooking oil from butternuts which grow there. Other possible derivation is Biblical: in Dutch Oelberg also means "Mount of Olives." This would be in line with such other names as Mt. Nebo, Mt. Pisgah and Mt. Zoar.

OLD MILL FALLS #1 Greene Co. On Plattekill Creek near head of clove.

OLD MILL FALLS #2 Greene Co. At Durham.

OLD NICK'S FALLS Greene Co. To south of Palenville. Named for an old native—not the devil.

OLD SENTINEL Greene Co. Elev. 3200 ft. On Wall of Manitou between Dutcher Notch and Arizona. On Escarpment Trail.

OLIVE BRIDGE Ulster Co. South of Ashokan Reservoir on Rte. 213. The original site is under waters of Ashokan Reservoir. John Burroughs taught school here and married local girl. Formerly Tongora or Tongore. Named for former Esopus Indian chief.

OLIVEREA Ulster Co. On Esopus Creek south of Big Indian. Area of German boarding houses and Waldschlosses.

ONDERDONCK LAKE Albany Co. North of Westerlo.

ONEONTA Otsego Co. On Susquehanna River, D&H RR, Rtes. 7, 28, 205. Formerly terminus of U&D RR., now Delaware & Otsego. Southern New York Railroad. Elev. 1,120 ft. Population 1971: 15,693. Largest city and trading town of western Catskill area. Settled in 1780. In 1883 eight railroad workers met in a caboose and organized the Brotherhood of Railroad Trainmen. Site of: State University College, formerly Oneonta Normal School and Oneonta State Teachers College, founded 1889; located at northeast edge of the city. Hartwick College, Oyaron Hill; founded in 1928; Lutheran. The library houses Burroughs, Cooper, and John Christopher Hartwick collections. The Hall of Science has an extensive display of fresh and salt water shells. Yager Museum contains over 20,000 Indian artifacts and relics. Neahwa City Park, Main St. and Neahwa Place. Wilber City Park, Spruce St. Bull Octagon House, corner of Grand and Division Sts. Upper Susquehanna Historical Society Museum, Wilber Mansion, Ford Avenue. Seeley's Nature Museum, 9 River Street.

ONEONTA CREEK Otsego Co. Flows south to Susquehanna River through Oneonta.

ONESQUETHAW CREEK AND CAVES Albany Co. See Clarksville.

ONTEORA Definition: One is that it means "Land in the sky." Another is that it is the name of a monster turned into the Catskill Mountains by Manitou, the Great Spirit.

ONTEORA LAKE Greene Co. Elev. 2200 ft. Between Onteora and Parker Mtns. Fed by Allen Brook.

ONTEORA MOUNTAIN Greene Co. Elev. 3200 ft. East of Hunter and northwest of Tannersville. West of Parker Mtn. Formerly called East Kill Mtn. Name "Onteora" coined in 1843 by Henry Rowe Schoolcraft.

ONTEORA PARK Greene Co. On southeastern slopes of Onteora and Parker Mtns. Private residential park of large rustic homes. Entry is controlled and area is patrolled. The park was founded by Francis B. Thurber in 1883. His sister, Mrs.

Chapel at Onteora Park. Photo by Alfred H. Marks.

THE CATSKILLS

Candace Wheeler, was a patroness of the arts and encouraged such famous people as Maude Adams, Mark Twain and Antonin Dvorak to summer here. She was a founder of the Society of Decorative Arts. The park was originally called Lotus Land and its club house was "The Bear & Fox Inn."

ONTEORA TRAIL Rte. 28.

ONTIORA MOUNTAIN Delaware Co. See Roundtop Mtn.

OQUAGA CREEK STATE PARK Delaware Co. Undeveloped. On Oquaga Creek north of Deposit and south of Masonville. Bisected by Rte. 8 from north to south.

OQUAGA LAKE Broome Co. South of McClure on Rte. 17 between Deposit to east and Damascus to west. Resort area. Formerly served by Erie-Lackawanna RR. Scotts and Hansons are older family resorts (c1870) with casinos, soda fountains, paddle fans, recreation halls, etc. Representative of a quieter era.

ORANGE SQUEEZER Ulster Co. See Crevice, the.

ORCHARD LAKE Sullivan Co. North of Grooville.

ORCHARD PARK Ulster Co. North of East Kingston and South of Flatbush.

ORCHARD POINT Greene Co. Elev. 3600 ft. Northern end of Plateau Mtn. near Danny's Lookout.

OTEGO Otsego Co. On Rte. 7, D&H RR, Susquehanna River. South of Oneonta and north of Wells Bridge. Attractive old homes.

OTEGO CREEK Otsego Co. Rises between Burlington and Oaksville and flows south past Hartwick, South Hartwick, Mt. Vision, and Laurens to junction with Susquehanna River between Otego and Oneonta.

OTIS ELEVATING RAILROAD Greene Co. See Chapter 10.

OTISVILLE Orange Co. On Erie RR & Rte. 211 west of Middletown, in Shawangunk Mtns.

OTSDAWA Otsego Co. West of Oneonta.

OTSEGO LAKE See Chapter 3.

OTTER HOOK Greene Co. On Hudson River opposite Bronk Island north of Coxsackie and south of New Baltimore.

OUAQUAGA Broome Co. On Rte. 79. On west bank of Susquehanna River north of Windsor and south of Center Village.

OULEOUT CREEK Delaware Co. Rises in township of Meredith and flows west past Franklin to Susquehanna River near Unadilla.

OVERLOOK MOUNTAIN Ulster Co. Elev. 3140 ft. Southern terminus of Wall of Manitou, above Woodstock. Southeastern bastion of the Northern Catskills. Commands extensive views. Fire tower. Trail from Meads. Site of former Overlook Mountain House. Echo Lake on its northern slope at 2000 ft. elevation is source of the Saw Kill, which drains to the west. In 19th century bluestone was quarried from its base at Daisy in Lewis Hollow. There have been persistent searches for buried treasure, gold and silver and other minerals. There is no good reason to expect success in such search. From July to September there is a heavy concentration of rattlesnakes, which favor its ledges. In past years natives would hunt them each spring when they emerged from their dens sluggish and heavy with oil. Rattlesnake oil was considered a sovereign remedy for many ills, and the oil commanded a good price. Yager's Cave on north slope.

OVERLOOK POINT Ulster Co. In Shawangunks in Minnewaska State Park. Above northeast end of Awosting Lake.

OWLSVILLE Schoharie Co. East of North Blenheim.

OX CLOVE Greene & Ulster Cos. North of Chichester. Site of Tiskilwa Park.

PACAMA Ulster Co. North of Lapla.

PACKSADDLE MOUNTAIN Greene Co. Elev. 3100 ft. West of Evergreen and Pine Island Mtns.

PAGE'S BROOK Sullivan Co. South of Wurtsboro. Old Saddler's Hell morass on Old Mine Road.

PAKATAKAN MOUNTAIN Delaware Co. Elev. 3100 ft. At Arkville where Dry Brook joins East Branch of Delaware.

PALENTOWN Ulster Co. North of Riggsville, southwest of Samsonville. Named for early tanner Gilbert Palen.

PALENVILLE Greene Co. Village at foot of Kaaterskill Clove on Kaaterskill Creek on Rtes. 32 and 23A. Many attractive waterfalls and rapids within the town.

Rowena Memorial School, Palenville. Photo by Alfred H. Marks.

Episcopal Church, Palenville. Photo by Alfred H. Marks.

These attracted mills at an early date because of the water power they provided. Hezekiah Wynkoop settled in the area in early 18th century. Rapid growth came with establishment of Gilbert Palen's tannery in mid 19th century. Later became a major tourist resort and laid claim to being native village of Rip Van Winkle. Many artists, including George H. Hall, had homes here. Major scenic features include Niobe, Ferndale, Black Crook, Drummond and Old Nick's Falls, the Dog's Hole and Stony Brook Falls.

PALENVILLE OVERLOOK Greene Co. On South Mountain above Palenville. Reached by side trail from Sleepy Hollow Horse Trail.

PALMAGHATT RAVINE Ulster Co. In Shawangunks in Minnewaska State Park and grounds of Lake Minnewaska Mountain Houses. Deep ravine between Hamilton Point and Gertrudes Nose in the east wall of the ridge. It runs from northeast to southwest. Formerly held a notable virgin hemlock stand and other rare plants. Kleine Kill and falls flow from it.

PALMERS ISLAND Greene Co. In Catskill Creek at its junction with Kaaterskill Creek, between Cauterskill to south and Jefferson Flats and Heights to north.

PANTHER CREEK Schoharie Co. Rises east of Summit, flows east to Schoharie Creek at Fultonham.

PANTHER KILL Ulster Co. Flows from spring at 2600 ft. elevation on east side of Panther Mtn. to Woodland Creek.

PANTHER MOUNTAIN Ulster Co. Elev. 3720 ft. South of Garfield Mtn. and north of Giant Ledge and Slide Mtn.

PANTHER ROCK BROOK Sullivan Co. Northern tributary of East Branch of Callicoon Creek.

PARADISE LAKE Sullivan Co. East of Neversink. Source of Wynkoop Brook.

PARKER MOUNTAIN Greene Co. Elev. 2900 ft. In Onteora Park, east of Onteora Mtn. Named for Parker family who owned farm here.

PARKSTON Sullivan Co. On Willowemoc Creek west of Debruce and east of Livingston Manor. On Rte. 81.

PARKSVILLE Sullivan Co. On Rte. 17 and O&W RR north of Liberty, south of Livingston Manor.

PARTRIDGE RUN STATE GAME MANAGEMENT AREA Albany Co. At Berne between Rtes. 6 and 13. Operated by DEC and open to public. 2000-plus acres. Views, hiking, picnicking, hunting.

PATRONS FALLS Greene Co. See Britts Falls. On Dwaskill.

PATAUKUNK Ulster Co. Between Kerhonkson and Fantinekill.

PATTERSON RIDGE Greene Co. Between Schoharie Creek and Batavia Kill.

PEAK BROOK Delaware Co. Rises west of Delhi and flows 3 miles south to West Branch of Delaware west of Delhi.

PEAKVILLE Delaware Co. On Beaver Kill east of East Branch and west of Elk Brook and Horton. On Rte. 17 and former O&W Rwy.

PEAS EDDY AND BROOK Delaware Co. Rises near French Woods in Pierce Pond and flows 4 miles west to East Branch of Delaware at Peas Eddy east of Hancock.

PECK HOLLOW Ulster Co. North of Allaben. Four abandoned mines.

PECOY NOTCH Greene Co. Between Sugarloaf on west and Twin Mtn. on the east.

PEEKAMOOSE FALLS Ulster Co. 0.7 miles west of Peekamoose Lake. It is 50 ft. high. On private property.

PEEKAMOOSE LAKE Ulster Co. Elev. 1415 ft. Near headwaters of West Branch of Rondout Creek. Between Breath Hill to northeast, Peekamoose Mtn. to northwest and Spencers Ledge to the south. Long, narrow and picturesque.

PEEKAMOOSE LODGE Ulster Co. NOT where shown on government map. Actual lodge, owned formerly by Anderson family and where Teddy Roosevelt once visited, is slightly to the northwest. Building shown on government map as Peekamoose Lodge is actually caretaker's house on estate of Mr. Howard Pack.

PEEKAMOOSE MOUNTAIN Ulster Co. Elev. 3843 ft. South of Table Mtn., west of Breath Hill, east of Van Wyck Mtn. and north of Samson Mtn. between West Branch of Rondout Creek and East Branch of Neversink River.

PEENPACK See Huguenot.

PEGGS POINT Ulster Co. On Hudson north of Marlboro and south of Milton.

PELHAM DOCK Ulster Co. On Hudson above Indian Rock in Esopus. Former immense orchard of R. L. Pell (over 25,000 trees), who shipped apples to Queen Victoria, as well as large quantities of table grapes, currants and small fruits. Old stone warehouse.

PELHAM'S LEDGE Greene Co. On Prospect Mtn. Offers good view of Kaaterskill Falls. Near abandoned U&D RR line.

PELNOR HOLLOW Delaware Co. North of Craigie Clair.

PEPACTON Poetic name for East Branch of Delaware River.

PEPACTON Delaware Co. Village covered now by waters of Pepacton Reservoir. Was between Downsville and Shavertown.

PEPACTON BROOK Sullivan Co. Flows south from Denman Mtn. to Chestnut Creek.

PEPACTON RESERVOIR Delaware Co. See article in waterways section.

PERCH LAKE Delaware Co. West of Dunraven, southwest of Wolf Hollow.

PERKINS POND Delaware Co. East of Apex.

PERRY POND AND BROOK Sullivan Co. West of Cochecton Center.

PETERS KILL #1 Ulster Co. Flows down the northwest slopes of the Shawangunks. Flows out of northeast end of Lake Awosting, joined by waters of Fly Brook from southwest, through Dallas Pool, over Awosting Falls to Rondout Creek at Kyserike.

PETERS KILL #2 Ulster Co. Flows south from Lyonsville Pond to Rondout Creek at Accord. Formerly called Monesauing Creek.

PETERS KILL CLIFFS Ulster Co. In Minnewaska State Park in Shawangunks north of Peters Kill and Rte. 44.

PETERS KILL FALLS Ulster Co. In Shawangunks on Peters Kill adjacent to north side of Rte. 44.

PETTIS BROOK Delaware Co. Flows 4 miles into West Branch of Delaware.

PHILLIPSPORT Sullivan Co. Old D&H Canal port named in honor of Phillip Hone, company president and mayor of New York City. On Rte. 209 and Homowack Creek at western foot of Shawangunks south of Ellenville and north of Summitville.

PHOENICIA Ulster Co. At junction of Rtes. 28 and 214 and of Stony Clove Creek and Esopus Creek. Romer Mtn. to the south, Mt. Sheridan to the west and Mr. Tremper to the east. Named for former Phoenix Tannery. Newkirk & Simpson was largest here. A good grade of bluestone was also quarried. Mt. Tremper House located east of town. Many boarding houses in past years. Trading center. Simpson Memorial Ski Center. On U&D RR.

PICKETT BROOK Ulster Co. Flows south off Balsam Cap to Rondout Creek.

PIERSONS Delaware Co. On Cadosia Creek and former O&W RR south of Apex and north of Cadosia.

PIGEON CREEK Ulster Co. Flows south off Doubletop Mtn. to Biscuit Brook at Frost Valley.

PIKE POND Sullivan Co. Now called Kenoza Lake.

PINE BUSH Ulster Co. On Rondout Creek and Rte. 209. North of Kerhonkson and west of Accord. Hoornbeck House (c1766), at end of lane on southeast side of Rt. 209.

PINE CLIFF Ulster Co. Northeast of Cliff House location on grounds of Lake Minnewaska Mountain Houses in Shawangunks.

PINE HILL Ulster Co. On Birch Creek, Rte. 28 and Ulster & Delaware RR. West of Big Indian and east of Highmount. First tannery here was founded by A. M. Guigou, who had served in Napoleon's army and learned tanning in France. He also opened a large boarding house. Originally popular with Christian clergymen, it later became a center of Jewish culture. The Weingart Institute was located here.

PINE HOLE BOG Ulster Co. In Ohioville. Tamarack sphagnum open water marsh.

PINE ISLAND MOUNTAIN Greene Co. Elev. 3140 ft. West of Evergreen Mtn.

PINE KILL Sullivan Co. Flows south from Yankee Lake to Basher Kill at Westbrookville.

PINE ORCHARD Greene Co. Plateau atop Great Wall of Manitou between North and South Mtns. It was the site of the former Catskill Mountain House. It is near North and South Lakes. It was visited by the naturalist John Bartram in 1741. Later area became famous for its "Balm of Gilead" (balsam fir) trees, which were cut for use as Christmas trees and dug up for landscape planting in the 19th century. There are no pine trees here today. Early deeds refer to the area also as "The Little Pine Orchard," but this is not to be confused with what today is called Little Pine Orchard.

PINK HILL Ulster Co. In northernmost Shawangunks south of Hurley and west of Eddyville.

PITTSFIELD Otsego Co. On Rte. 80 and NYO&W RR east of New Berlin and south of Edmeston.

PLAAT CLOVE P.O. Greene Co. Formerly at head of Plattekill Clove.

PLACE CORNERS Greene Co. Southeast of Greenville, northwest of Gayhead.

PLATNER BROOK Delaware Co. Rises west of West Delhi and flows southeast to West Branch of Delaware at Fraser.

PLATTE KILL Definition: In Dutch, a smoothly flowing stream.

PLATTE KILL #1 Greene Co. Rises east of Freehold and flows south to Catskill Creek north of Cairo.

PLATTE KILL #2 Ulster Co. In Shawangunks. Flows southeast from Bear Hill into Shawangunk Kill at Burlingham. It serves as the Ulster-Sullivan line.

PLATTEKILL Ulster Co. On Rte. 32 south of Modena and north of Newburgh. Orchard area.

Silas and Harm Hummel, "Champion coon hunters of the Plattekill Clove," c1893. Photo by Lionel De Lisser

PLATTEKILL CLOVE Greene and Ulster Cos. West of West Saugerties. In Great Wall of Manitou and carved by the waters of Plattekill Creek. (See Chapter 3.) Possibly the most rugged and grand in the entire Catskills. Entirely unspoiled, with only a narrow and dangerous road climbing the north wall. Kaaterskill High Peak to the north and Plattekill Mtn. to the south. Waters of Hell Hole Creek and Cold Kill join those of Plattekill Creek near the head of clove at location known as Hell Hole. Devil's Kitchen is also at head of clove. Mountains on either side rise to 3100 ft. and 3655 ft. The clove is less than one mile long and the elevation rises from 800 ft. at the base to 2000 ft. at the head. There are many sheer precipices and waterfalls. Climbing here can be extremely dangerous. The road is NOT recommended for vehicular use, but makes an interesting walk. Suggest that you carry a canteen with water. Not for the weak or fainthearted. Grand!

PLATTEKILL CREEK Greene and Ulster Cos. See Chapter 3.

PLATTEKILL MOUNTAIN #1 Greene Co. Elev. 3135 ft. On Wall of Manitou south of Plattekill Clove. Indian Head to west and Overlook to the south.

PLATTEKILL MOUNTAIN #2 Delaware Co. Elev. 3260 ft. North of Mt. Pisgah and south of Old Clump Mtn., between Bovina and Roxbury. Ski Center.

PLATTEKILL RIVER Delaware Co. Rises south of Plattekill Mountain and flows 12 miles south to East Branch of Delaware at Dunraven.

PLATTER KILL Schoharie Co. Flows southwest to Schoharie Creek at Gilboa.

PLATT HOLLOW Ulster Co. On the Dry Brook.

PLEASANT BROOK Otsego Co. On Rte. 165 south of Cherry Valley and east of Cooperstown.

PLEASANT LAKE Sullivan Co. See Kiamesha Lake.

PLEASURE LAKE Sullivan Co. On Sheldrake Stream south of South Fallsburgh. Formerly D&H Canal reservoir.

PLOW HOLLOW Delaware Co. East of Beerston.

PLUTARCH Ulster Co. On Swarte Kill, northeast of New Paltz. Plutarch (c46–120 A.D.), Greek essayist and biographer. His *Lives* were popular reading in 18th and early 19th century America.

The big curve on Erie RR along Delaware River at Pond Eddy, Pa. Photo shows a refrigerator train, about 1946. Erie Railroad Co. photo.

POET'S LEDGE Greene Co. Overlooks Palenville from south wall to Kaaterskill Clove. Between Viola Falls in Hillyer Ravine and Hawkeye.

POINT LOOKOUT Greene Co. See Five State Lookout.

POLLY'S MILL STREAM Ulster Co. In Minnewaska area in the Shawangunks. Flows west from atop Kempton Ledge to Peters Kill below junction with Fly Brook.

POMEROY FALLS Greene Co. On Plattekill Creek in Clove.

PONCKHOCKIE Ulster Co. East of Rondout section of Kingston. Limestone cliffs and caves once used for mushroom growing. Name in Indian language means "burial grounds." There are boatyards here. Ponk Hockie Union Congregation Church, on Abruyn Street, is interesting cast concrete Hudson River Gothic structure from late 19th century. Formerly known as "Children's Church." Abandoned cement mine called Glory Hole.

POND EDDY Sullivan Co. On Rte. 97 and Delaware River east of Barryville and west of Mongaup. Across from mouth of Pond Eddy Creek in Pennsylvania. Erie RR crosses Delaware here.

POND HOLLOW Delaware Co. East of Gregorytown.

POPLAR ISLAND Albany Co. In Hudson River east of Selkirk and west of Castleton.

POPLE HILL Ulster Co. Elev. 1972 ft. East of Balsam Swamp.

PORK ISLAND HOLLOW Delaware Co. North of Peakville.

PORT BENJAMIN Ulster Co. On old D&H Canal north of Napanoch and east of Wawarsing.

PORT CLINTON Orange Co. On old D&H Canal near Cuddebackville.

Ponckhockie Cliffs. Photo by Alfred H. Marks.

Old cement mine and kilns, Ponckhockie. Entrance to caverns penetrating under much of Kingston. Photo by Alfred H. Marks.

PORT EWEN Ulster Co. On Rte. 9W and West Shore RR. Bounded on west by Rondout Creek and east by Hudson River. South of Kingston and north of Ulster Park. Gideon Van Aken House (c1708).

PORT HIXON Ulster Co. On old D&H Canal south of Kerhonkson and north of Port Benjamin.

PORT JACKSON Ulster Co. On Rondout Creek near Accord. Old D&H Canal town.

PORT JERVIS Orange Co. At junction of Neversink and Delaware Rivers. On Erie Railroad and Rtes. 209 and 97. Originally called Mackhackemeck, Nahant, and later Minisink, from Indian tribe that had major settlement here. It was settled before 1700 and incorporated in 1907. It was the seat of the Leni-Lenape Confederation of Delaware Indians. Tri-State Rock, where New York, New Jersey and Pennsylvania come together, is on Carpenter's Point south of town. See articles on Tri-State Rock and Carpenter's Point. There are extensive views of Kittatinny, Shawagunk and Catskill Mtns. and the Neversink and Delaware Valleys from Elks Brox Park (see article). Town was named in honor of John Bloomfield Jervis, principal engineer of the Delaware and Hudson Canal. Former Erie Railroad steam locomotive repair shops here. Now an important local trading town. Plated silverware, concrete blocks and textiles are manufactured here. It is the terminus of Erie-Lackawanna Rwy. suburban service, 91 miles from Hoboken, operated by New Jersey Transit.

Ponk Hockie Union Congregational Church, Ponckhockie.

PORTLANDVILLE Otsego Co. On Rte. 80, C&CV RR and Susquehanna River. At north end of Goodyear Lake, north of Oneonta and south of Milford. There is a boat launching site at Twin Spruce Trailer Park on Rte. 28. Count Casimir Pulaski was stationed here in Revolution. Raided by Joseph Brant July 20, 1779. Octagon House, east side of Susquehanna River, 1 mile northeast of village.

PORT ORANGE Orange Co. On Rte. 209, Old Mine Road, O&W RR, D&H Canal south of Westbrookville and north of Cuddebackville. Old canal port.

POSSESSION HOLLOW Delaware Co. North of Shinhopple.

POST CREEK Greene Co. Flows off Kalberg east to Hudson River north of DeWitt Point.

POTIC or POTUCK CREEK Greene Co. A principal northern tributary of Catskill Creek, receiving the waters of Cob, Grapeville and West Medway Creeks. Enters Catskill Creek above Leeds.

POTIC MOUNTAIN Greene Co. Between Potic Creek to the west and Murderers Creek to the east.

POTTER HOLLOW Albany Co. West of Cooksburg and east of Manorkill. Old steepled one-room schoolhouse. Beall Farm, fine Garrison Colonial home.

POTTERVILLE Ulster Co. On Vernooy Kill north of Brownville.

POUCKHOCKIE Ulster Co. See Ponckhockie.

PRATT'S ROCKS Greene Co. On Rte. 23 east of Prattsville and above Schoharie Creek. They are white painted bas-relief carvings on the face of the living rock. They were done by an itinerent stonecutter around 1865 at the order of Zadock Pratt to memorialize his family, possessions, and accomplishments; they include his favorite horse and his son. There is a picnic area and paths to the base of the carvings. See articles on Prattsville and Zadock Pratt in Chapter 12.

PRATTSVILLE Greene Co. West of Ashland and Lexington and east of Grand Gorge on Rte. 23 at south end of Schoharie Reservoir on Schoharie Creek. It was settled by Palatinates and formerly known as Schohariekill. Later renamed in honor of its leading citizen, Zadock Pratt (1790–1871), a tanner who advocated many local improvements and later served in Congress. It is an attractive town with fine shade trees and white painted homes. Pratt's home is now a museum.

PRESTON HOLLOW Albany Co. On Rte. 145 and Catskill Creek. Settled 1730. South of Livingstonville, north of Cooksburg. Old Baptist Church. A whipping post was located on the farm of Lawrence Faulk.

Pratt's Rocks in 1975. Author's son Christopher in foreground. Photo by author.

PRIMROSE BROOK Sullivan Co. The north branch of Gumaers Brook.

PROFILE ROCK #1 Greene Co. On south wall of Kaaterskill Creek Clove on Rte. 23A near More's Bridge. Natural rock formations form many profiles. Some grotesque and some quite natural-looking.

PROFILE ROCK #2 Greene Co. On south side of North Mountain as seen from Escarpment Trail. Supposed to look like George Washington.

PROSPECT HILL Ulster Co. Overlooks Hudson at Ulster Park.

PROSPECT MOUNTAIN Greene Co. A western shoulder of South Mountain west of Kaaterskill Falls towards Haines Falls.

PROSPECT ROCK #1 Greene Co. Ledge on Prospect Mtn. along old Ulster & Delaware Railroad line. Railroad used to keep the trees cut down so passengers could see the Kaaterskill Falls from here. To the west of old Laurel House Station.

PROSPECT ROCK #2 Greene Co. At about 2300 ft. elevation on Escarpment Trail atop Wall of Manitou north of Red Hill and south of Bear's Den. Fine views.

PUDDINGSTONE HALL Greene Co. A narrow fissure in Puddingstone con-glomerate rock in the third ledge on South Mtn. on the old trail from the former Catskill Mountain House to Eagle Rock (now much overgrown). The trail led

Zadock Pratt House, Prattsville. Photo by Alfred H. Marks.

through the fissure and it was much noted for its picturesque cool mossy beauty and illustrated in Bryant and Fenn's *Picturesque America*.

PUMPKIN HOLLOW Delaware Co. Southwest of Davenport Center.

PURLING Greene Co. On Shingle Kill south of Cairo. Scenic features include Shingle Kill Falls, Dutchess, and Forest Ravine Falls. Many German and Austrian resorts. Given present name in 1895 for purling of waters in Shingle Kill.

PUT CORNERS Ulster Co. East of New Paltz.

QUAKER CLEARING Ulster Co. East of Hardenburg on the Beaver Kill. Quaker Cove is to the south and Woodpecker Ridge to the northwest. Junction of several important hiking trails and access parking area. It was a favorite spot of John Burroughs, who described it in his *Locusts and Wild Honey*.

QUAKER COVE Ulster Co. South of Quaker Clearing.

QUAKER STREET Schenectady Co. On Rtes. 7 and 395 west of Duanesburg and east of Central Bridge. Friends Meeting House (1780).

QUARRY FALLS Greene Co. Near Durham.

QUARRY HILL Greene Co. Northern end of the Kalkberg southwest of Catskill. At junction of Rtes. 9W and 23A.

QUARRYVILLE Ulster Co. North of Katsbaan and south of Palenville on Rte. 32. Mt. Airy to the south.

QUICK LAKE Sullivan Co. South of Lewbeach.

QUIERY HILL Schoharie Co. Southwest of North Blenheim.

RAINBOW FALLS #1 Greene Co. On Plattekill Creek in the Clove below Pomeroy and above Green Falls. There are an upper and lower Rainbow Falls; the lower is at the junction of Hell Hole Creek.

RAINBOW FALLS #2 Ulster Co. In Minnewaska State Park in Shawangunks. On Peters Kill north of and below Lake Awosting. Water flows over several ledges for total drop of 75 ft.

RAMSHORN CREEK Greene Co. Crooked creek through marshes east of Kykuit and south of Catskill and DuBois Creek. Empties into Hudson.

RANDOLPH HILLS Broome and Delaware Co. A ridge running north to south, forming the divide between the West Branch of the Delaware River and the Susquehanna River. It is crossed by Rte. 17 and by the Erie Railroad at Gulf Summit.

Gothic Renaissance cottage, Prattsville. Photo by Alfred H. Marks.

RATTLE HILL Ulster Co. Elev. 2905 ft. South of Turnwood.

RATTLESNAKE ISLAND Greene Co. In Hudson River north of Coxsackie Island.

RAVENA Albany Co. On Rte. 9W and West Shore RR, west of Coeyman's. Formerly named Coeyman's Junction. Here Albany Branch of West Shore Railroad struck straight north while mainline veered to northwest. There are limestone swamps 2½ miles northwest of village. Ravena in northeastern Italy was the Western Capital of the Roman Empire after the fall of Rome to the barbarians. Tobias Ten Eyck House (1791), Pictuary Road. Two-story Greek Revival Farmhouse (c1830), southwest of Ten Eyck House. Cider and vinegar are produced locally, and there are quarries.

READBURN Delaware Co. West of Linden, north of East Branch.

READ CREEK Delaware Co. Rises in Merrick Pond south of Rock Rift and flows 8 miles south past Readburn to East Branch of Delaware between Fishs Eddy and East Branch.

RED FALLS #1 Greene Co. On Rte. 23 east of Prattsville and west of Ashland on Batavia Kill.

RED FALLS #2 Greene Co. On Schoharie Creek in town of Hunter. Former site of Col. William W. Edwards' New York Tannery.

RED HILL #1 Greene Co. Steep section of Escarpment Trail in red shale rock and clay north of Sunrise and south of Prospect Rock. On Wall of Manitou.

RED HILL #2 Ulster Co. Elev. 2970 ft. East of Claryville and south of Ladletown. Fire observation tower.

RED KILL #1 Greene Co. Flows south from Hunter Notch to Schoharie Creek.

RED KILL #2 Delaware Co. Flows south from Bearpen Mtn. to the Bush Kill near Covesville.

RED KILL RIDGE Delaware Co. Elev. 3100 ft. West of Red Kill and northeast of Denver. Known locally as Butternut Mtn.

RED LODGE Ulster Co. On East Branch of Neversink north of Denning.

RENARD HILL Delaware Co. Elev. 2260 ft. East of Downsville. Renard is a French name for a fox.

RENNYS GLEN AND FALLS Greene Co. In Forge area of Purling.

RENSSELAERVILLE Albany Co. On Rtes. 85 and 20 southwest of Albany behind the Helderberg Range. Kiliaen Van Rensselaer, the Patroon (c1585–1644), was an Amsterdam diamond and pearl merchant. He was one of the founders and directors of the Dutch West India Company in 1621. He acquired title to a vast tract near Albany which was called Rensselaerwyck, in which was included the site of Rensselaerville. He sent his cousin Arent Van Curler or Van Corlaer (1619–1667), who founded Schenectady, to manage his estates in New Netherlands. Van Curler maintained good relations with the Indians, which may partly account for the willingness to build a village so far from the protection afforded by proximity to the Hudson River, as was Schenectady. Rensselaerville is of much later date, having been founded in 1788 after the American Revolution, when the threat of Indian attack was diminished.

Samuel Jenkins, the "Father of Rensselaerville," first visited the site in 1787. Located here in 1788 and built house and gristmill in 1789. Town was known as Jenkins Mills from 1795 to 1806.

Points of interest:

Edward Niles Huyck Preserve, 1200 acres of unspoiled forest and woodland incorporated into a preservation trust in 1931. It includes Rensselaerville Falls, Lincoln Pond and Lake Myosostis, where swimming and picnicking are allowed.

Trinity Episcopal Church (1815), Ephraim Russ, architect.

"Locust Place" (1812), home of Jonathan Jenkins, early mill owner; Ephraim Russ, architect.

Bank Houses and old library (early 19th century), Main St.

Grist Mill (1880), built by Francis C. Huyck to replace one built in 1789 by Samuel Jenkins. Ran until 1938.

Stevens House (1809); Palladian door and windows; Ephraim Russ, architect.

James Rider House (1823), Ephraim Russ, architect.

Sployd House (1825); has 1-story, 2-bay pedimental porch; detail of gem-like delicacy.

Presbyterian Church 1844–48), Ephraim Russ, architect.

RESERVOIR HOLLOW Delaware Co. North of Pakatakan Mtn. on the Dry Brook. East of German Hollow and west of Andrus Hollow.

RESULT Greene County. West of Coxsackie.

REVONAH LAKE Sullivan Co. North of Liberty.

REXMERE Delaware Co. Large old hotel, now used for other purposes, near Stamford. See Chapter 11.

RICHFIELD Otsego Co. On Rte. 20 to northwest of Richfield Springs.

RICHFIELD SPRINGS Otsego Co. On Rte. 20 and Central NY RR. Elev. 1270 ft. Former spa resort, presently trading town. In 1757 Indians led British Army forces to the Great Sulphur Spring. Village was settled in 1791 and first spa established in 1820. The last active bath house, on Gould Ave., closed in 1972 and is now used as a nursing home. Water may still be obtained from the spring at

Views of Rensselaerville. Photos by Alfred H. Marks.

Views of Rensselaerville. Photos by Alfred H. Marks.

Views of Rensselaerville. Photos by Alfred H. Marks.

the DAR Memorial Fountain on Main Street (Rte. 20), opposite the Post Office. There is an historical marker at the fountain. The actual spring area is above in the park about 50 ft. in from the north side of the road and is enclosed by an iron fence. This park is quite extensive and features a fountain and Victorian bandstand. The town was originally served by a branch of the Delaware, Lackawanna &

Western Railroad and an interurban electric line from Cooperstown (now abandoned.) The railroad was later operated as the Central New York Railroad, and in November 1974 was acquired for operation by the Cooperstown & Charlotte Valley Co. On a hill just east of town on Rte. 20 is Allens Lake with an aereation fountain. It is part of the Municipal Water System. Tunnicliff Mill, Rte. 20 at west end of town. First Presbyterian Church (1877; first building 1803). Bible Church. Baker Octagon Barn, 2 miles south of town on west side of Lake Canadarago.

RICHMOND MOUNTAINS Greene Co. Elev. 3220 ft. West of Mt. Pisgah, east of The Knob and north of Windham.

RICHMONDVILLE Schoharie Co. On Rtes. 7 and 10 and D&H RR west of Cobleskill and northeast of Worcester. Boughton Octagon House.

RICHTMYER PEAK Greene Co. Western extension of Mt. Pisgah.

RIDER HOLLOW Ulster Co. The valley of the North Branch of the Dry Brook. South of Belle Ayre Mtn. and north of Hiram's Knob. West of Balsam Mtn. and Mine Hollow.

RIFTON Ulster Co. On Wallkill River and Rte. 213. At junction of Wallkill and Swarte Kill. Sturgeon Pool to northwest. South of St. Remy and north of New Paltz. Hendrick Smit House (c1715).

RIGGSVILLE Ulster Co. East of Flat Hill on Cherrytown Road.

RILEY BROOK Ulster Co. Flows off southeast side of Wildcat Mtn. into the East Branch of the Neversink River north of Denning. South of Flat Brook and north of Erts Brook.

Perrine's Bridge across Wallkill River near Dashville. On Route 213 near Thruway. Photo by Alfred H. Marks.

Interior, Perrine's Bridge, showing arch and truss construction. Photo by Alfred H. Marks.

RIO Orange Co. On Rte. 42 south of Forestburg, north of Sparrow Bush.

RIO RESERVOIR Sullivan Co. On Mongaup River south of Swinging Bridge Reservoir. Northwest of Rio, southwest of Forestburg. Nesting area for bald eagles.

RIP'S BOULDER Greene Co. A flat-sided mossy boulder in Sleepy Hollow, behind the site of the former Rip Van Winkle House on the Old Mountain Turnpike. Alleged location of Rip's nap. Formerly pointed out to all tourists while horses were rested. A pleasant hike on a hot day.

RIP'S LEDGE Greene Co. Above Sleepy Hollow and Rip's Boulder.

RIP'S LOOKOUT Greene Co. Now site of access parking on Rte. 23A west of Bastion Falls and east of Haines Falls. Formerly a restaurant and gift shop. Good view down Kaaterskill Clove.

RIP'S RETREAT Greene Co. Former commercial amusement development at North Lake. Now picnic area. North of Pine Orchard. Near North Lake Beach.

RIP VAN WINKLE BROOK Greene Co. See Sleepy Hollow Brook.

RIP VAN WINKLE HOUSE Greene Co. Former small inn and refreshment establishment at 1275 ft. level of North Mountain in Sleepy Hollow on Old Mountain Turnpike to Catskill Mountain House. Near Rip's Boulder. Horses were rested here before climbing Dead Ox Hill. Foundations still visible. Appeared in many illustrations and post cards.

RIP VAN WINKLE LAKE Greene Co. Source of Gooseberry Creek south of Tannersville. Formerly Voss Lake.

ROAH HOOK Albany Co. On Hudson River north of Coeymans between Coeymans Creek and Hudson River proper.

ROARBACK BROOK Greene Co. Flows east off Vly Mountain to the West Kill.

ROARINGBROOK or KILL Greene Co. Flows north from Mink Hollow to Schoharie Creek near Elka Park.

ROBERTS HILL Greene Co. On Rte. 9W north of Coxsackie. Single-story Georgian Mansion with dormers (c1750), Rte. 9W north of town. Anthony Van Bergen House (c1750), Rte. 9W south of town.

ROBERTSONVILLE Sullivan Co. Now renamed White Sulphur Springs.

ROBINSON HILL Greene Co. North of West Coxsackie near Thruway.

ROBINSON LAKE Delaware Co. At head of Steele Brook north of Delhi.

ROCHESTER Ulster Co. On Rondout Creek.

ROCHESTER CREEK Ulster Co. Flows south from junction of Beaverdam and Mettacahonts Creeks at Liebhardt to Rondout Creek at Accord.

ROCHESTER HOLLOW Ulster Co. In southern flank of Rose Mtn. between Big Indian and Pine Hill.

ROCK CITY Ulster Co. At foot of Overlook Mtn. north of Woodstock. Named for former bluestone quarrying.

ROCK HILL Sullivan Co. On Rte. 17 west of Wurtsboro and east of Monticello. Wanasink Lake, Katrina Falls on McKee Brook.

ROCKLAND Sullivan Co. North of Roscoe, south of Agloe. On Beaverkill. Old Grist Mill.

ROCK PASS Ulster Co. In Shawangunks on Laurel Ledge Road on Mohonk grounds. To north of hairpin turn. Road does not go through it.

ROCK RIFT #1 Ulster Co. In Shawangunks on Mohonk grounds. Crevices.

ROCK RIFT #2 Delaware Co. Rte. 10 and O&W RR. On West Branch of Delaware south of Walton.

ROCK RIFT MOUNTAIN Delaware Co. Elev. 2420 ft. Near Rock Rift.

ROCKROYAL Delaware Co. On Trout Creek north of Cannonsville.

ROCK VALLEY Delaware Co. On Rte. 134 south of Peakville, north of Long Eddy on North Branch of Basket Creek.

ROCKY MOUNTAIN Ulster Co. Elev. 3508 ft. South of Slide Mtn. and northeast of Lone Mtn. West of Balsam Cap.

ROCKY RAPIDS Greene Co. In Plattekill Clove on Plattekill Creek. Near bottom of clove. Above Gray Rock Falls.

ROME Sullivan Co. Old name for Wurtsboro.

ROMER MOUNTAIN Ulster Co. West and south of Esopus Creek and east of Woodland Creek near Phoenicia. Elev. 2160 ft. Named for William C. Romer, Hudson River steamboat operator and partner in former nearby Mount Tremper House.

RONDOUT Definition: redoubt, from Dutch *ronduit*, subsequently corrupted to Redoubt, Rundoubt, Roundout and Rondout.

RONDOUT Ulster Co. Formerly Bolton. Originally a separate city at the junction of Rondout Creek (formerly called the Wallkill River at this place) with the Hudson River, opposite Rhinecliff. It was merged into the City of Kingston in 1878. Neighboring Wilbur and Ponckhockie, now also part of Kingston, were major steamboat centers. Rondout was home port to the famous *Mary Powell* and paddlewheel towboats *Norwich* and *Austin*, which used to pull long tows of coal barges from the outlet of the Delaware & Hudson Canal here to New York City.

The Strand, Rondout, c1890. Photo by Lionel De Lisser.

The Strand, Rondout, 1975. Photo by Alfred H. Marks.

Rondout ferry house, c1890. Photo by Lionel De Lisser.

Kingston-Rhinecliff ferryboat Transport. *Courtesy of the Steamship Historical Society Library, University of Baltimore.*

There were also ferries to Rhinecliff, Sleightsburg and Connelly. Today Rte. 9W crosses the creek on a high suspension bridge. The former waterfront was called "The Strand." Ulster & Delaware passenger trains used to originate both at Kingston Point and Rondout before climbing the steep hill to the Union Depot in upper Kingston. Urban renewal is fast clearing away the typical old river town commercial buildings. There are quite a few fine older churches and homes on the slopes above town. See articles on Kingston, Wilbur, Kingston Point and Ponckhockie.

RONDOUT CREEK See Chapter 3.

RONDOUT RESERVOIR Sullivan and Ulster Co. See Chapter 3.

ROOD CREEK Delaware Co. Flows 3 miles north into West Branch of Delaware at Hale Eddy.

ROOM, THE Greene Co. Rock formation of tumbled boulders on north face of South Mountain on former grounds of Catskill Mountain House. It is in the first ledge.

ROOSA GAP Sullivan Co. In Shawangunk Mtns. southeast of Summitville.

ROOSA POND Ulster Co. West of Lyonsville Pond in Marbletown Township.

ROSCOE Sullivan Co. At junction of Beaver Kill and Willowemoc Creek and also of Rtes. 17, 91, 92 and 124. East of Cooks Falls and west of Livingston Manor. Former terminus of summer passenger service on O&W Rwy. Junction Pool here is famous fishing spot and Antrim Lodge is a famous meeting place for fishermen. Excellent food and charming atmosphere, but in author's opinion greedy in their pricing. Trading town. Formerly Westfield Flats.

Sloop Clearwater *moored at Rondout, with Route 9W suspension bridge in background. Photo by Alfred H. Marks.*

ROSEBOOM Otsego Co. On Rte. 166 south of Cherry Valley and north of Milford. On Cherry Valley Creek.

ROSE BROOK Delaware Co. Flows 6 miles northwest from Old Clump Mountain to West Branch of Delaware River at South Kortright.

ROSE MOUNTAIN Ulster Co. Elev. 3090 ft. South of Halcott Mtn. and east of Pine Hill and Highmount. Although the mountain is covered with wild roses, it takes its name from a local family.

ROSENDALE Ulster Co. At the gap which Rondout Creek makes in the Shawangunk Mtns. South of Kingston and north of New Paltz at junction of Rtes. 32 and 213. In 1828 it was discovered that the local limestone made an excellent hydraulic cement. An active cement industry once flourished in the area, but it was superseded by "Portland" cement. Some Rosendale cement is still produced for underwater work. Rosendale cement was used for the Brooklyn Bridge foundations and towers, and its fame spread rapidly thereafter. There is a high trestle of the Wallkill Valley Railroad, built in 1872. It was on the route of the former D & H Canal. See articles on Rondout Creek in Chapter 3 and Wallkill Valley RR in Chapter 10.

ROSE'S POINT Orange Co. On Rte. 209. D&H Canal crossed Neversink River here on aqueduct. William Rose of Connecticut built an early gristmill here before the Revolution. It served as a fort.

Wallkill Valley RR bridge near Rosendale. 150 ft. high. Photo by Alfred H. Marks.

Snyder House, built c1820, Route 213 west of Rosendale. Note variegated color glazed bricks in otherwise formal Georgian facade. Photo by Alfred H. Marks.

ROUMAKER'S HEL See Page's Brook and Saddler's Hell.

ROUND HEAD Greene Co. See Cairo Round Top.

ROUND HILL Greene Co. Elev. 2585 ft. South of Hensonville and west of Maplecrest. West of Van Loan Hill and east of Cave Mtn. Formerly called Delong Mtn.

ROUNDOUT See Rondout.

ROUND TOP #1 Greene Co. Village south of Cairo and Purling. Many German resorts. See also Cairo Round Top.

ROUNDTOP #2 Delaware Co. Elev. 3440 ft. East of Roxbury and north of Bearpen Mtn.

ROUNDTOP MOUNTAIN Greene Co. Between Kaaterskill Clove to the north and Plattekill Clove to the south. West of Kaaterskill High Peak. Santa Cruz, Twilight and Sunset Parks on northern slopes. Elev. 3440 ft. There was a Tory and Indian Fort near its summit, the site of which was unknown for many years. In 1975 it was discovered by Mr. Edward G. West, a local historian and surveyor who was formerly with the New York State Conservation Department. It was from this fort that Joseph Brant and others made raids into the Hudson Valley for hostages and to wreak havoc along the frontier. In 1975 Edward G. West discovered ruins of Joseph Brant's Tory Fort near top on Platterkill Clove side.

Old cement kilns near Rosendale. Photo by Alfred H. Marks.

ROXBURY Delaware Co. Between Grand Gorge to the north and Halcottsville to the south on the East Branch of the Delaware River, Rte. 30 and the U & D RR. It was the hometown and birthplace of two famous individuals: John Burroughs, the naturalist, and Jay Gould, the financier and railroad magnate. They both frequently visited their old hometown throughout their lives and Burroughs had a summer home here called Woodchuck Lodge. Jay Gould built a beautiful Memorial Church and his daughter Helen spent much time here and was the town's philanthropist. Many Gould family retainers and servants retired to this clean little town of wide shady streets and white painted houses. John Burroughs is buried nearby. See biographies of both men in Chapter 12. Also see Boyhood Rock.

Woodchuck Lodge, summer home of John Burroughs, Roxbury. Photo by Alfred H. Marks.

Gould house, Roxbury. Photo by Alfred H. Marks.

Jay Gould Memorial Reformed Church, Roxbury. Photo by Alfred H. Marks.

Greek Revival farmhouse (built c1820), Roxbury. Photo by Alfred H. Marks.

RUBY Ulster Co. Near Zena

RUMBLE-TUMBLE FALLS Greene Co. In Shady Glen near Durham.

RUSK MOUNTAIN Greene Co. Elev. 3680 ft. Between Schoharie Creek to north and West Kill to the south. West of Hunter Mtn. and east of Evergreen Mtn.

RUSSELL BROOK Delaware Co. Flows south from Cables Lake to Beaver Kill at Butternut Grove.

RUSSELL LAKE Delaware Co. North of Kelsey. A source of Sands Creek.

RUTH Schoharie Co. East of South Jefferson.

RUTSONVILLE Ulster Co. North of Dwaarkill. Col. Johannes Jansen House (1771).

ST. ANN'S PEAK Greene Co. West of West Kill Mtn. and east of North Dome.

ST. ELMO Ulster Co. On CNE, NYNH&H and PC RRs. East of Wallkill. St. Elmo was a 4th-century martyr and patron saint of sailors.

ST. JOSEN Ulster Co. At northwestern foot of Shawangunks on Rondout Creek. East of Port Jackson and south of Accord. On former D&H Canal.

ST. JOSEPHS Sullivan Co. Location of Catholic retreat houses and summer camps. South of Monticello near junction of Rtes. 42 and 108. On former O&W Rwy., Monticello Branch.

ST. JOSEPHS LAKE Sullivan Co. At St. Josephs.

ST. REMY Ulster Co. On Rte. 213 southeast of Eddyville. St. Remigius, born c439, was Archbishop of Rheims and converted King Clovis.

SACKETT LAKE Sullivan Co. On Rte. 45 southwest of Monticello.

SADDLER'S HELL See Page's Brook.

SAMSON MOUNTAIN Ulster Co. Elev. 2812 ft. East of Bangle Hill and west

of Spencers Ledge. Between the two branches of Rondout Creek. Named for
Henry A. Samson, pioneer tanner.

SAMSONVILLE Ulster Co. Village on Mettacahonts Creek at the south foot of
Mombaccus Mtn. West of Krumville and north of Liebhardt. Once the largest
town in the Catskills. Former site of large tannery built by Henry A. Samson.
Gilbert Palen and Zadock Pratt also had tanneries here. Markham Falls was
important for water power. Local attractions include a fossil waterfall north of the
village and the Samson House.

SAM'S POINT Ulster Co. Elev. 2255 ft. Highest point in the Shawangunks. Also
called Ice Cave Mtn. for several such near here. It is east of Ellenville and north of
Cragsmoor and Walker Valley. Haseco Lake (Mud Pond) and Napanoch Point to
the north. Lake Maratanza is a clear shallow pond atop Sam's Point, immediately
to the north of the "Point" and lookout place. It is reached off Rte. 52 ten miles
south of Ellenville. The auto road which climbs to the top encircles the lake. The
summit is a broad, flat plateau, with much dwarf or stunted vegetation. Views are
extensive in all directions. Admission fee is charged. Huckleberries grow in
profusion and may be picked for a fee in season. In past years many berry pickers
lived in tar-paper shacks in the vicinity. The mountain is named for Sam Gonzalez,
who when pursued by Indians jumped from the point. He was not killed but
landed in the branches of a tree and escaped. Formerly called "Big Nose of
Aioskawasting."

SAMUEL'S POINT Ulster Co. Elev. 2674 ft. In the Catskills at the west end of
Ashokan Reservoir. South of Traver Hollow and Cross and Wittenberg Mtns.
Maltby Hollow to the west.

Great Nose of Aiowasting and Rock Crevice, Sam's Point. Photo by Alfred H. Marks.

Rock Crevice at Sam's Point, Ice Caves Mtn. Photo by Alfred H. Marks.

SANDBURG CREEK Sullivan and Ulster Cos. Flows east from Silver Lake near Woodridge to Spring Glen, where it turns north along the western foot of the Shawangunks past Ellenville to the Rondout Creek at Napanoch. Major tributaries are the Leuren, Beer and Fantine Kills. Its valley was followed by the former O&W Rwy. and D&H Canal. Also called Sandburg Kill.

SANDBURGH Sullivan Co. Now called Mountaindale.

SANDERS KILL Ulster Co. On west slope of Shawangunks. Flows northeast from between Stony and Peters Kills from northeast of Lake Awosting to Stony Kill near its debouchment into Rondout Creek south of Accord.

SAND LAKE Sullivan Co. North of Callicoon Center. Headwaters of North Branch of Callicoon Creek.

SAND POND Ulster Co. South of Hardenburg and north of Willowemoc. Source of Butternut Brook.

SAND POND MOUNTAIN Ulster Co. Elev. 3062 ft. North of Sand Pond and southwest of Willowemoc Mtn.

SANDS CREEK Delaware Co. Flows 11 miles south from Kelsey to West Branch of Delaware River at Hancock.

SANFORD AND NORTH SANFORD Broome Co. On Rte. 41 north of McClure, south of Vallonia Springs and Afton.

SANFORD CORNERS Greene Co. On Rte. 81 southeast of Greenville, west of Surprise.

SANFORD HOLLOW Delaware Co. North of New Kingston.

SANTA CRUZ PARK Greene Co. Adjacent to Twilight Park. This private residential community is entered through Twilight Park, with which it was incorporated in 1935. The scenic Santa Cruz Ravine is immediately east and the former Santa Cruz Inn, now a private residence, was located on its western edge. The park was popular with Philadelphians around the turn of the century. William P. Houston was prominent among them. See Twilight Park.

SANTA CRUZ RAVINE Greene Co. On north face of Roundtop Mtn. in south wall of Kaaterskill Clove. Johnson Point to the east.

SAPBUSH CREEK Ulster Co. Tributary of Mill Creek near Cherrytown.

Trinity Episcopal Church, Barclay Heights, Saugerties. Photo by Alfred H. Marks.

SAUGERTIES Ulster Co. On Rte. 9W, Thruway Exit 20, West Shore RR. At junction of Esopus Creek and Hudson River, midway between Kingston and Catskill.

The name derives from "saw mills"— *Zaagertjis* in Dutch—which were built on the Esopus Creek prior to 1663. The remains of one can be seen in process of restoration at Seamon Memorial Park on Rte. 9W at north end of town. Settled by the Dutch, it was developed by the Livingstons. It once had an extensive lumbering and paper industry (Cantine Coated Paper Co.), and shipped much bluestone.

Saugerties in around 1800 is well described by Cooper in his novel *Afloat and Ashore.* The following description can fit only one spot in Ulster County on the Hudson—the confluence of the Esopus and Hudson at Saugerties. Even the description of the house seems to generally fit the Mynderse House of 1690 with its "new" wings of 1743.

My father died on the farm on which he was born, and which descended to him from his great-grandfather, an English emigrant that had purchased it of the Dutch colonist who had originally cleared it from the woods. The place was called Clawbonny, which some said was good Dutch, others bad Dutch; and now and then a person ventured a conjecture that it might be Indian. Bonny it was, in one sense at least, for a lovelier farm is not on the whole of the wide surface of the Empire State. What does not always happen in this wicked world, it was as good as it was handsome. It consisted of three hundred and seventy-two acres of first-rate land, either arable or of rich river bottom in meadows, and of more than a hundred of rocky mountain side, that was very tolerably covered with wood. The first of our family who owned the place had built a substantial one-story stone house, that bears the date of 1707 on one of its gables; and to which each of his successors had added a little, until the whole structure got to resemble a cluster of cottages thrown together without the least attention to order or regularity. There were a porch, a front door, and a lawn, however; the latter containing half a dozen acres of a soil as black as one's hat, and nourishing eight or ten elms that were scattered about as if their seeds had been sown broadcast. In addition to the trees and a suitable garniture of shrubbery, this lawn was coated with a sward that, in the proper seasons, rivalled all I have read or imagined of the emerald and shorn slopes of the Swiss valleys.

Clawbonny, while it had all the appearance of being the residence of an affluent agriculturist, had none of the pretension of these later times. The house had an air of substantial comfort without, an appearance that its interior in no manner contradicted. The ceilings were low, it is true, nor were the rooms particularly large; but the latter were warm in winter, cool in summer, and tidy, neat, and respectable all the year round. Both the parlors had carpets as had the passages and all the better bedrooms; and there were an old-fashioned chintz settee, well stuffed and cushioned, and curtains in the "big parlor," as we called the best apartment—the pretending name of drawing-room not hav-

Restoration of old sawmill, Saugerties. Photo by Alfred H. Marks.

ing reached our valley as far back as the year 1796 or that in which my recollections of the place, as it then existed, are the most vivid and distinct.

We had orchards, meadows, and ploughed fields all around us; while the barns, granaries, stiles, and other buildings of the farm were of solid stone, like the dwelling, and all in capital condition.

There was a mill, just where the stream that runs through our valley rumbles down to a level below that on which the farm lies, and empties itself into a small tributary of the Hudson. This mill was on our property, and was a source of great convenience and of some profit to my father. There he ground all the grain that was consumed for domestic purposes for several miles around; and the tolls enabled him to fatten his porkers and beeves, in a way to give both a sort of established character. In a word, the mill was the concentrating point for all the products of the farm, there being a little landing on the margin of the creek that put up from the Hudson, whence a sloop sailed weekly for town. My father passed half his time about the mill and landing, superintending his workmen, and particularly giving directions about the fitting of the sloop, which was his property also, and about the gear of the mill.

We were all four of us seated on a rude bench that my mother had caused to be placed under the shade of an enormous oak that stood on the most picturesque spot, perhaps, on the whole farm, and which commanded a distant view of one of the loveliest reaches of the Hudson. Our side of the river, in general does not possess as fine views as the eastern, for the reason that all our own broken, and in some instances magnificent, background of mountains, fills up the landscape for our neighbors, while we are obliged to receive the picture as it is set in a humbler frame; but there are exquisite bits to be found on the western bank, and this was one of the very best of them. The water was as placid as molten silver, and the sails of every vessel in sight were hanging in listless idleness from their several spars, representing commerce asleep.

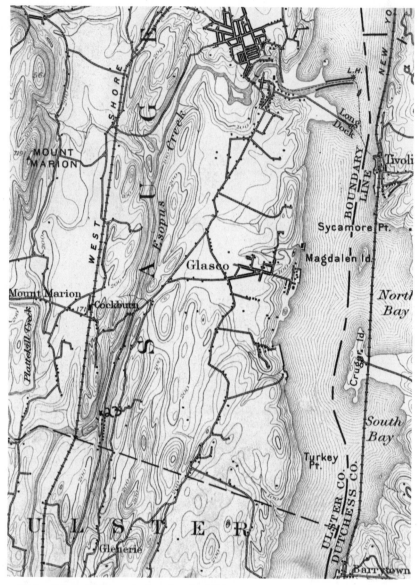

Hudson River near Saugerties (top of map), c1900.

We have given such a long description of Clawbonny as it could well fit any prosperous West Shore Ulster County farmstead of the era. Most likely Cooper had a composite in mind when he wrote the above, but Saugerties brings it particularly to mind.

Points of interest:

Barclay and Finger Hills—fine views of both Hudson and Catskills.

Saugerties-Tivoli ferryboat Air Line. *Photo by Lionel De Lisser.*

Washburns Point at confluence of Esopus Creek and Hudson.
Mason's Ravine and old gristmill, known as "Falling Waters."
Lighthouse (1869), two-story brick, replacing earlier light of 1838.
Mynderse House (1690, with 1743 additions), believed oldest in Saugerties; on
  bluff over Hudson and Esopus.
Cornelius Lamberts Brink House (1701).
Christian Myer House (1724), Old Kings Highway.
DuBois-Kierstede House (1727), Main Street.
Samuel Schoonmaker House (1727), Main and Malden Streets. Captain John
  Field House (c1840), Greek Revival mansion with fluted Doric columns.
Henry (?) Brink House (1743), Kings Highway.

At the south end of town on Rte. 9W there are several sharp bends in the road
and bluestone walls layed up along them. Several old houses and churches in this
neighborhood are reminescent of the following short extract from Cooper's *Miles
Wallingford*.

"St. Michael's churchyard is beautifully ornamented with flourishing cedars.
These trees had been cultivated with care, and formed an appropriate ornament
for the place. A fine cluster of them shaded the graves of my family, and a rustic
seat had been placed beneath their branches, by order of my mother, who had
been in the habit of passing hours of meditation at the grave of her husband".
This scene describes the grave of Grace Wallingford, "The Lily of Clawbonny," a
character quite obviously patterned after Cooper's own beloved sister who had
died young.

This particular description might equally well fit the Church of the Ascension
(1842) on Rte. 9W in West Park, but the rest of the story description does not fit
the Esopus area as well.

Our Lady of the Valley RC Church, Saugerties. Photo by Alfred H. Marks.

The old commercial neighborhood, Cantine paper mill, and falls of the Esopus are also worth a visit. There are many fine homes and churches in the town besides those listed above. Seamon's Park has extensive floral displays and an annual Chrysanthemum Festival in the autumn. Wede Marine Museum. Several marinas.

SAUNDERS KILL Ulster Co. See Sanders Kill.

SAW KILL Ulster Co. Flows west from Echo Lake between Plattekill and Overlook Mtns. Thence turns south at Shady and circles back east around Mt. Guardian (formerly Saw Kill Head) past Bearsville and Woodstock to vicinity of Halihan Hill and village of Sawkill, where it flows into Esopus Creek.

SAW KILL HEAD Ulster Co. See Guardian Mountain.

SAWKILL Ulster Co. At junction of the Saw Kill and Esopus Creek. South of Halihan Hill and north of Jockey Hill.

SAW MILL CREEK Greene Co. Flows south off Onteora Mtn. near Glen Park to Gooseberry Creek southwest of Tannersville.

SAWYER KILL Ulster Co. Flows south from the Great Vly swamp southwest of the Kalkberg to the Hudson River north of Saugerties. Named for saw mills along its side.

SAXE'S FARM Greene Co. Name of location of tollgate at foot of Old Mountain Turnpike up North Mountain to Pine Orchard in the days of the Catskill Mountain House. At foot of Sleepy Hollow. In 1914 it was known as "Mt. View Farm—Frederick Saxe, Prop." Today it is access point to Sleepy Hollow Horse Trail

Samuel Schoonmaker House and Smokehouse, Main and Malden Streets, Saugerties. Photo by Alfred H. Marks.

Network, but parking is severely limited and adjacent property owners discourage it. There is today in operation another nearby farm known as Saxe's Farm on Saxe's Road over on Bethel Ridge.

SAXEVILLE Ulster Co. On Rte. 209 south of Hurley and north of Marbletown.

SAXTON Ulster Co. Location at junction of Rtes. 32 and 32A south of Palenville.

SCHENEVUS Otsego Co. On Rte. 7, D&H RR. Schenevus Creek west of Worcester and east of Oneonta.

SCHENEVUS CREEK Otsego Co. Rises southwest of West Richmondville and flows generally southwest, past East Worcester, Worcester, Schenevus, and Maryland to junction with Susquehanna River near Colliersville.

SCHERMERHORN FALLS Greene Co. Near Cairo.

SCHERMERHORN ISLAND Albany Co. In Hudson River east of Selkirk.

SCHOHARIE Seat of Schoharie Co. 1971 pop. 1,106. On Rte. 30 and 443. Elev. 611 ft. South of junction of Schoharie Creek with Fox Creek.

Originally named Brunnen Dorf (Spring Village) by German Palatinate religious refugees in period just before Revolution (c1760), although there were Dutch settlers as far back as 1724 when the first Dutch Reformed Church was erected. Growth was sufficient to require a replacement church in 1737. It is alleged that Schoharie is the third oldest upstate village.

In 1778 the Reformed Dutch Church, built in 1772 to replace that of 1737, was fortified by construction of a palisade around it and block houses immediately to the northeast and southwest as well as shelters for refugees. The building itself is of lime and sandstone and massively built. It stands at the southeast corner of the junction of Fox and Schoharie Creeks. Rev. Johannes Schuyler was pastor at the time of its construction and the mason work was directed by his brother John.

Old Stone Fort Museum, Schoharie. At right: grave of David Williams, captor of Major Andre.
Alfred H. Marks.

This became known as Lower Fort. Middle Fort was at Middleburg and Upper Fort at Fultonham. This is the only one remaining.

The principal attack upon this lower fort was in the late afternoon of October 17, 1780, when a force of 800 men led by Joseph Brant, the Indian leader, and Sir John Johnson attacked. They were repulsed by sharpshooters stationed in the steeple, which was removed in 1830.

The stockade was removed in 1785. In 1844 the Dutch Reformed Church Society erected a new church of brick in the village and sold the old fortress church to the State of New York for use as an arsenal. It was so used until 1873 when it was presented to Schoharie County for preservation. The Schoharie County Historical Society was formed in 1889 and took over its maintenance. Today it houses a museum with a collection of Indian land deeds, colonial documents, early tools, vehicles, furniture, household items of the arts and crafts etc. Adjoining it is the William W. Badgley Historical Museum with similar exhibits.

The museums are open May 1 through October 31 from 10 AM till 5 PM. Closed Mondays in May, September and October.

The grave of David Williams, one of the captors of Major Andre, is located in the graveyard, marked by a marble shaft.

In 1865 the Schoharie Valley Railroad was built from Schoharie Jct. near Central Bridge to Schoharie, a distance of 4.3 miles. It was acquired by the Delaware & Hudson in 1906. The Middleburgh & Schoharie Railroad ran 5 miles further to Middleburgh. It was built in 1867 and also acquired by the Delaware &

Hudson. The entire combined line had been abandoned by 1942. At the Schoharie Valley Railroad Center, on Depot Lane at the north end of the town west off Rte. 30 is an old combination passenger and baggage coach from the Middleburgh & Schoharie RR, in service from 1891 to 1936. It was built by the Gilbert Car Co. of Troy and is presently undergoing restoration. There is also an old brick station house which has been restored, a cast iron fountain and craft shop.

Points of interest:

Old Courthouse, Main St.

Parrott House Hotel (c1820), adjacent to Courthouse. Main dining room has gallery of portraits of governors of New York.

Johannes Ingold House (1795), southwest end of village.

Jacobus Stein House, Rte. 443.

George Mann Tory Tavern, Rtes. 30 and 443.

Simon Larrabee Mill, Rte. 443 1 mile east of Rte. 30.

Swats Tavern (c1772), Rte 30 ½ mile north of village. Duel between Phillip Schuyler 2nd and Josiah Clark was fought behind building in 1820.

Schwartz Octagon House, Grand St.

SCHOHARIE CREEK See Chapter 3.

SCHOHARIEKILL Greene Co. See Prattsville.

SCHOHARIE MANOR Greene Co. Private residential park near Elka Park. Colonial-styled buildings and club house.

SCHOHARIE RESERVOIR See article under Waterways.

SCHOHARIE TURNPIKE Built in 1802 between Athens and Schoharie. Roughly same as Rte. 145 from Cooksburg to Schoharie.

SCHOHARIE VALLEY The lower valley at the north end was settled by Dutch in late 1600s, and the central portion, between Central Bridge and Gilboa, by Palatinates in the period 1712–13. There were seven villages and three forts: Lower Fort at Schoharie, Middle Fort at Middleburgh and Upper fort at Fultonham. Only the Lower Fort survives. It was attacked by Joseph Brant and Sir John Johnson on Oct. 17, 1780. The central Schoharie Valley is very fertile farm land and raises vegetables. It is followed by Rte. 30 for most of its course below Gilboa Dam on Schoharie Reservoir. Tow Path Mountain State Park is at Fultonham. There is a pumped storage facility and recreation area at North Blenheim.

SCHOOLHOUSE BROOK Greene Co. Flows south from Evergreen Mtn. to West Kill.

SCHUMACHER POND Sullivan Co. Southwest of Yulan.

SCHUYLER LAKE Otsego Co. On Rte. 28. At south end of Canadarago Lake. Old Stone Church built by George Herkimer (1839–1840), now Universalist Church. Herkimer farm on west side of Rte 28 just north of village.

SCRIBNERS Greene Co. Location on Lake Creek east of its junction with Spruce Creek. Named for a boarding house once run by Silas Scribner; Thoreau stayed here. Apparently Scribner also owned a saw mill. Scribners is within easy reach of the Kataterskill Falls and old Laurel House and Hotel Kaaterskill sites and is a major access point for all these and the Escarpment Trail. It is reached by Scutt Road, which runs south from Mountain House Road just west of the gatehouse for the North Lake Campsite. Parking is limited. There is a horse corral to serve the needs of the Sleepy Hollow Horse Trail network which starts here. The modern Scribner Hollow motel is on Rte. 23A between Tannersville and Hunter.

SCUDDER BROOK Ulster Co. Tributary of Beaver Kill near Turnwood.

SEAGER Ulster Co. Location along the Dry Brook near Turner Hollow south of Mapledale. Named for Hiram Seager, who settled here in 1800. Covered bridge. Access parking.

SEAMON'S PARK Ulster Co. See Saugerties and Mason's Ravine.

SECOND LAKE Ulster Co. A Binnewater Lake in Northern Shawangunks west of First Lake. Very clear water.

SECRET CAVERNS Schoharie Co. 35 miles west of Albany near Central Bridge and Howes Caverns. Commercially operated, offering a 45-minute tour. Caverns have a natural entrance and are rich in stalactites, stalagmites and golden flowstone formations. There is an underground waterfall which falls 100 ft. from surface. Fossilized sea life

SEGAR POND Sullivan Co. On Rte. 114 east of Kenoza Lake. Near Briscoe.

SELKIRK Albany Co. On Rte. 9W and Thruway. Major railroad junction on New York Central and West Shore Railroads. Site of large modern Alfred E. Perlman Yard and other railroad facilities. Now operated by Conrail.

SENECA HOLLOW Ulster Co. On south side of Rose Mtn.

SEWARD Schoharie Co. On Rte. 165 west of Cobleskill. There is a lake here.

SEXSMITH LAKE Delaware Co. Near Davenport.

SHACKPORT Delaware Co. Northeast of Meridale.

SHAD ISLAND Albany Co. In Hudson River north of Coeymans and South of Selkirk. It is beneath both railway and Thruway bridges.

SHADY Ulster Co. On the Saw Kill at west foot of Mt. Guardian, north of Bearsville. Former glass industry. Formerly called Bristol.

SHADY BROOK Greene Co. In Windham.

SHADY GLEN Greene Co. Near Durham. Rumble-Tumble and Shimmering Falls.

SHANDAKEN Name means "rapid waters" in Indian language.

SHANDAKEN Ulster Co. Village on Esopus Creek at junction with Bushnells-ville Creek. North of Panther Mtn. and east of Rose Mtn. At junction of Rtes. 28 and 42, and on U & D RR. Big Indian to the west and Allaben to the east. Site of former Palace Hotel.

SHANDAKEN CREEK Ulster Co. Easternmost tributary of Dry Brook, south of Belle Ayre Mtn. near Seager.

SHANDAKEN LAKE Ulster Co. See Cooper Lake.

SHANDAKEN MOUNTAINS Ulster Co. Name formerly applied to the central Catskill Mountains.

SHANDELEE LAKE Sullivan Co. South of Livingston Manor. Drains north to Willowemoc Creek. Named in honor of French friend of Dr. Edward Livingston named DeChandla c1825.

SHANTY HOLLOW Greene Co. In north side of Hunter Mtn. Mossy Brook flows through it.

SHARON Schohrie Co. On Rte. 20 north of Cobleskill and east of Sharon Springs.

SHARON SPRINGS Schoharie Co. On Rte. 20 west of Sharon and east of Leesville. A spa in a valley on a hill. Elev. 1,320 ft. Fine views to the north over Mohawk valley. There are medicinal white sulphur springs here. A permanent Indian village occupied the site and the Indians made use of the springs. This spa was popular during the 19th century and is now in some decline. The Imperial Baths have 6 buildings and cover 500 acres. There are 132 bathrooms offering sulphur and magnesia waters for cure of arthritis, rheumatism and nervous disorders. European inhalation facilities, Nauheim baths, etc. There are still a number of large old spa hotels in operation with walks, groves, verandahs, etc., most in Greek Revival or Victorian styles. The old Sharon Springs Hotel was a notable Greek Revival structure, 3 stories high and with long pillared portico. At present the resort is frequented mostly by Orthodox Jewish people who mostly arrive by bus; there is direct service to New York City. Many older hotels and boarding houses are closed up and fast going to ruin.

SHAUPENEAK MOUNTAIN Ulster Co. Elev. 910 ft. West of Esopus, north of Plattekill Hills.

SHAVERTOWN Delaware Co. Former village under waters of Pepacton Reservoir near where Rte. 30 crosses at midpoint.

SHAVERTOWN BRIDGE Delaware Co. See above.

SHAWANGUNK KILL Sullivan and Ulster Cos. Flows northeast from New Vernon, past Pinebush to Canahgote along eastern base of Shawangunk Mountains. Empties into Wallkill River.

SHAWANGUNK MOUNTAINS See Chapter 2.

SHAWANOESBERG See Council Hill.

SHELDON FALLS Ulster Co. On Peterskill north of Rte. 55.

SHELDRAKE POND AND STREAM Sullivan Co. Flows south from vicinity of Loch Sheldrake through Pleasure Lake and past South Fallsburgh to Neversink River at Glen Wild. A sheldrake is a merganser duck.

SHERWOODS CORNERS Ulster Co. East of Wallkill.

SHIMMERING FALLS Greene Co. In Shady Glen near Durham.

SHIN CREEK Ulster and Sullivan Co. Flows west from Mongaup Mtn. to Beaver Kill near Lewbeach.

SHIN CREEK FALLS Sullivan Co. Near Lewbeach on private property. Multi-tier falls—some of 20 ft.

SHINGLE GULLY Ulster Co. In west slope of Shawangunks north of Ellenville. Ice caves at top.

SHINGLE KILL #1 Orange Co. Rises north of Cahoonzie and flows 4 miles south to Delaware at Sparrow Bush.

SHINGLE KILL #2 Greene Co. Flows northeast from Blackhead Mtn. to Forge section of Purling, where there are falls. Thence north to Catskill Creek near Cairo.

SHINGLE KILL FALLS Greene Co. Near Forge in Purling.

SHIN HOLLOW Orange Co. ¾-mile-long, 40-ft. deep cut near Gumaers in Shawangunks. Site of bloody labor confrontation.

SHINHOPPLE Delaware Co. On Rte. 30 and East Branch of Delaware River. East of Harvard and west of Downsville.

Olive and Hurley Baptist Meeting House, Route 28, Shokan. Photo by Alfred H. Marks.

SHOKAN Ulster Co. On Rte. 28 and U&D RR north of Ashokan Reservoir, west of Ashokan and east of Boiceville. Road to dam runs south from here. Ticetonyk Mtn. to the north. Was relocated here when reservoir was built.

SHOLAM Ulster Co. Northwest of Brownville, northeast of Lackawack and south of Yagerville. In Township of Wawarsing. It was founded in 1837 by Jewish families and was the site of the first synagogue in the Catskills. Owing to poor soil, farming proved to be impractical and they turned to mending old clothing which they purchased in the city and peddled throughout the mountains. There is an airstrip here.

SHUE'S POND Ulster Co. See Echo lake.

SHULTICE MOUNTAIN Delaware Co. Elev. 3280 ft. South of Grand Gorge and Irish Mtn. West of Roundtop and north of Bearpen Mtns. Northeast of Roxbury.

SICKLES CREEK Green Co. Rises south of Hannacroix and flows southeast into Coxsackie Creek.

SIDNEY Delaware Co. Elev. 900 ft. on Susquehanna River. On Rte. 8, across river from Rte. 7, west of Unadilla, east of Bainbridge. On former NYO&W and D&H RRs. Pioneer cemetery dates from 1787. Bluestone is quarried. Magneto manufacturing. Bendix plant.

SIDNEY CENTER Delaware Co. On Carrs Creek. East of South Unadilla.

SILVER CREEK Otsego Co. Flows south to Susquehanna River in Oneonta.

SILVER FALLS Greene Co. In Taylor's Glen near Durham.

SILVER HOLLOW #1 Ulster Co. Between Mt. Tremper and Carl Mtn. west of Willow. Off Rte. 212.

SILVER HOLLOW #2 Ulster and Greene Cos. Southwest of Little Rocky Mtn. and west of Carl Mtn. near Warner Creek.

Views of Sharon Springs, including Magnesia Spring . Photos by Alfred H. Marks.

SILVER HOLLOW MOUNTAIN Greene Co. Elev. 3000 ft. North of Silver Hollow.

SILVER HOLLOW NOTCH Greene Co. Between Silver Hollow and Edgewood.

SILVER LAKE #1 Delaware Co. Rte. 28. East of Lake Delaware.

SILVER LAKE #2 Delaware Co. North of Hale Eddy, southeast of Deposit.

SILVER LAKE #3 Sullivan Co. Source of Sandburg Creek. East of Woodbridge.

SILVER LAKE #4 Greene Co. In East Windham. South of Mt. Zoar and west of Kate Hill. Empties west to Batavia Kill at Hensonville.

SILVER POINT Greene Co. On Hudson River at south end of Duck Cove near Alsen. Large cement loading dock here.

Pavillion Hotel, Sharon Springs. Photo by Alfred H. Marks.

SI MEADE HOLLOW Greene Co. Between Vly and South Vly Mtns. Off Johnson Hollow.

SIMPSON FALLS Greene Co. Near Durham.

SIMPSONVILLE Delaware Co. North of Davenport.

SKINNERS FALLS Sullivan Co. On Rte. 97 and Delaware River at junction of Mitchell Pond Brook. Named for Daniel Skinner, "Admiral of the Delaware," believed to have been first man to guide a raft down the Delaware. Subsequent raftsmen were expected to pay him alcoholic tribute. Settled c1764.

SKYTOP Ulster Co. On Mohonk Mountain House grounds in Shawangunks. Elev. 1542 ft. For a long time believed highest point in range. Formerly called Mohonk Mountain. It is crowned by the Albert K. Smiley Memorial Tower, built in 1923. It is built of Shawangunk grit, which is quarried at its base. Funds were contributed by 875 Mohonk guests. There is a beacon light and lookout cabin for a fire ranger. Five states can be seen from the tower and its location is at the junction of three townships: Marbletown, Rochester and New Paltz. There are several reservoirs on Skytop and numerous paths and an excellent carriage drive, with extensive views. The cliffs are high and rugged. Features of the mountain are: The Crevice (also called Lemon or Orange Squeezer), Staircliff and Washington's Profile, seen from across the Lake. Day use fee to enter area.

SLABSIDES Ulster Co. The rustic retreat of John Burroughs near West Park in the Plattekill Mtns. It is a National Historic Landmark and is surrounded by a 175-acre wildlife refuge. One mile west off Rte. 9W. Write caretaker for appointment.

SLATERS FALLS Greene Co. On Shingle Kill in Cairo Township. Forge section.

SLAWSON MOUNTAIN Sullivan Co. Elev. 2494 ft. East of Willowemoc.

SLEEPY HOLLOW #1 Greene Co. Not to be confused with the Sleepy Hollow of the Pocantico River at North Tarrytown in Westchester County, where is located the Headless Horseman Bridge mentioned in Washington Irving's *Legend of Sleepy Hollow*. This Sleepy Hollow is where Rip Van Winkle is alleged to have taken his long nap. It is in the eastern flank of North Mountain and the Old Mountain Turnpike climbs up through it from Saxe's Farm to Pine Orchard. The name of the brook flowing through it is properly Stony Brook, although it is also called Rip Van Winkle Brook and Sleepy Hollow Brook. It is best seen from the Old Mountain Turnpike, now the Sleepy Hollow Horse Trail.

SLEEPY HOLLOW #2 Ulster Co. On Mohonk grounds in Shawangunks. A glen in the east face of the ridge near Rhododendron Bridge on Oak Drive north of Undercliff Road.

Views of Sharon Springs. Photos by Alfred H. Marks.

SLEEPY HOLLOW LAKE Greene Co. On Rte. 385 north of Athens on Murderers Creek. Site of controversial residential development. Many ecological and zoning questions raised.

SLEIGHTSBURG Ulster Co. At southwest corner of junction of Rondout Creek and Hudson River opposite Rondout. Formerly a chain ferry to Rondout. Popular retirement town for rivermen.

SLIDE MOUNTAIN Ulster Co. Elev. 4180 ft. Highest in Catskills and in New York State south of the Adirondacks. It is located south of Oliverea and north of Frost Valley. The Esopus, Rondout and Neversink streams all take their rise off its massif. Hemlock Mtn. is to the west, Giant Ledge to the northwest, Mt. Cornell to the northeast, Friday Mtn. to the east, Rocky Mtn. to the southeast, Lone Mtn. to the south and the valley of the Neversink to the southwest. The Winnisook

Sleightsburg, c1890. Photo by Lionel De Lisser.

Sleightsburg-Rondout chain ferry, c1890. Photo by Lionel De Lisser.

Lake and Club are on its western slope, where it is approached by the Big Indian-Claryville Road. The shortest, safest and easiest trail departs from near the Winnisook Club to the summit. However, it is very rocky and eroded and miserable underfoot and affords few good views until near the top. It is a grind. A more scenic route is via the ridge line of Wittenberg and Cornell, but this is much longer and more difficult—not for a novice or unaccompanied climber. The Curtis Trail on its south slope, while scenic, had best be left to the experienced climber. Another, and the oldest, trail was laid out in the last century by James W. Dutcher, a mountain guide who owned a boarding house nearby. He built some stone stairs and found a scenic and easy route. However, most of his route is now on the private lands of the Winnisook Club. The view from the top of slide is superb and you can see all the highest peaks in the Catskills, as well as much of the Shawangunks and Berkshires. There used to be a fire observation tower here, but it has been

James W. Dutcher leads a party of young ladies down Slide Mountain, c1895, using rustic stairway he constructed. Photo by Lionel De Lisser.

removed. There are several leantos, but they are almost always crowded and it is best not to count on spending the night here. The mountain is named for the scars of a landslide on its northwestern slope in 1820. It was first recognized as the highest peak in the Catskills by Princeton University geologist Arnold Henry Guyot. It was explored and publicized by John Burroughs and there is a memorial plaque near the summit which reads: "In Memoriam, John Burroughs who, in his early writings, introduced Slide Mountain to the World. He made many visits to this peak and slept several nights beneath this rock. This region is the scene of many of his essays. Here the works of man dwindle in the Heart of the Southern Catskills."

SLIDE MOUNTAIN Ulster Co. Location in Esopus Valley northwest of Slide Mtn. between Winnisook Club and Oliverea. German Alpine resorts in the area. Very beautiful.

SLINGERLANDS Albany Co. South of Albany on Rtes. 43 and 85.

SLOANVILLE Schoharie Co. On Rtes. 20 and 30A north of Central Bridge. Site of Joseph Brant Encampment on Rte. 30A south of village.

SMALLWOOD Sullivan Co. South of White Lake on Mountain Lake and White Brook.

SMITH LANDING Greene Co. On Hudson River near Alsen and Cementon.

SNYDER HOLLOW Ulster Co. Old name for Woodland Valley.

Big Indian Valley near village of Slide Mountain. Photo by Alfred H. Marks.

SOCCANISSING See Wawarsing.

SOMERSET LAKE Delaware Co. On Rte. 97 north of Lordville, west of French Woods.

SOUTH BEARPEN MOUNTAIN Greene Co. Elev. 3410 ft. South of Bearpen and west of Vly Mtns.

SOUTH BERNE Albany Co. Northeast of Rensselaerville. Near Onderdonk Lake.

SOUTH BETHLEHEM Albany Co. On Rte. 396 north of Ravena.

SOUTH BROOK #1 Ulster Co. In South Hollow.

SOUTH BROOK #2 Sullivan Co. South Branch of Gumaers Brook.

SOUTH CAIRO Greene Co. On Rte. 23 and Catskill Creek.

SOUTH DURHAM Greene Co. On Rte. 23 between Cairo and East Windham. Site of Bowery Creek, Marie Falls and Stead's Twin Falls.

SOUTHEAST WARREN MOUNTAIN Delaware Co. Elev. 3020 ft. Northwest of North Plattekill Mtn. and north of Round Top.

SOUTH FALLSBURGH Sullivan Co. On Neversink River and Rte. 42 north of Monticello. Resort town. Site of former O&W high trestle. Formerly Mitchells Station.

SOUTH GILBOA Schoharie Co. On U&D RR west of Gilboa and east of Stamford.

SOUTH GULLY Ulster Co. Clove in west side of Shawangunk Mtns. Southeast of Ellenville and northwest of Cragsmoor. There is a poor road up the gully from

Rte. 52 to Cragsmoor. The author ripped the oil pan off his car driving it. Mt. Cathalia (alias Meenagha) to north.

SOUTH HARTWICK Otsego Co. On Rte. 205 and Otego Creek south of Hartwick and north of Oneonta.

SOUTH HOLLOW Ulster Co. Off Watson Hollow. South of South Mtn. and north of Ashokan High Point. South Hollow Brook flows through.

SOUTH JEWETT Greene Co. On Rte. 23A between Hunter to the east and Jewett Center to the west. On Schoharie Creek.

SOUTH KORTRIGHT Delaware Co. On U&D RR off Rte. 10. On West Branch of Delaware River southwest of Hobart, northeast of Bloomville. Old stone walls and houses give area a manorial aspect.

SOUTH LAKE Greene Co. One of twin lakes atop the Wall of Manitou west of Pine Orchard. They are in a saddle between North Mtn. and South Mtn. Formerly separate, they have been artificially joined since 1974 by the cutting of a channel. South Lake receives the flow from North Lake and in turn empties into Lake Creek near the former Kaaterskill Station. There is a new sand bathing beach and extensive parking lots on the south shore. Under the ownership of the former Catskill Mountain House, boat houses were located here. The lake was known as Sylvan Lake and used for evening festivities and canoe parties, frequently illuminated by Japanese lanterns. The lake was painted by Thomas Cole a number of times. The most famous treatments are entitled "Lake With Dead Trees" and "Catskill Lake." It was also the subject of a winter scene by William H. Barlett. Now part of the gounds of the North Lake Campsite.

SOUTH MOUNTAIN #1 Greene Co. Elev. 2480 ft. On Great Wall of Manitou overlooking Palenville at the foot of Kaaterskill Clove. North Mtn. to the north and Prospect Mtn. to the west. Kaaterskill Clove to the south. Pine Orchard sat in the saddle between it and North Mountain. In the last century much of South Mtn., as far south as Boulder Rock, belonged to the Catskill Mountain House. From there west the mountain belonged to the Hotel Kaaterskill. Today the entire mountain belongs to the State of New York. Probably no other single mountain in the Catskills had as dense a network of trails and as many named features, most of which are described by separate articles in this section. Famous features include: Alligator Rock, The Amphitheatre, Druid Rocks, Eagle Rock, Elfin Pass, Fat Man's Delight, Fairy Spring, the Gulf, Indian Head, Inspiration Point, Kaaterskill Falls, Lemon Squeezer, Lover's Retreat, Moses Spring, Palenville Overlook, Puddingston Hall, The Room, Sphinx Rock, Star Rock and Sunset Rock. On the northern side there are three distinct ledges. The summit is somewhat flat and there is a small swamp. The Escarpment Trail runs around the south and east sides at about 2200 ft. Many excellent viewpoints. Probably the most accessible and rewarding mountain in return for a modest hiking effort.

SOUTH MOUNTAIN #2 Ulster Co. Elev. 2180 ft. West of Ashokan Reservoir, south of Samuel's Point and West Shokan, east of Hanover Mtn. and north of High Point.

SOUTH PLATTEKILL MOUNTAIN Delaware Co. Elev. 3260 ft. North of Hubbell Hill and south of North Plattekill Mtn.

SOUTH UNADILLA Delaware Co. On Carrs Creek east of Sidney.

SOUTH VALLEY Otsego Co. On Rte. 165 west of Cobleskill, east of Coopers-town.

SOUTH VLY MOUNTAIN Greene Co. Elev. 3360 ft. South of Vly Mtn., west of Beech Ridge and east of Johnson Hollow.

SOUTH WESTERLO Albany Co. On Rte. 32 north of Greenville. Originally Smiths Corners. Palmer House (1807), now "The Blue Churn," on Rennselaerville Turnpike. Jared Reynolds House (1807), now "Colonial Manor," on Rte. 405. Asher Morse House (1838), Main Street.

SOUTHWEST HUNTER MOUNTAIN Greene Co. Elev. 3740 ft. Southwest of Hunter Mountain and east of West Kill Mtn. near Diamond Notch.

SOUTHWEST MORESVILLE RANGE Delaware Co. Elev. 3040 ft. Northwest of Irish Mtn. and southeast of Northwest Moresville Range.

SPANISH MINE Ulster Co. At Ellenville. 500-ft. tunnel; marble wishing well.

SPARROW BUSH Orange Co. On Rte. 97. Erie RR trestle across Delaware here. North of Port Jervis, south of Mongaup. Golf course. Railroad classification yards.

SPENCERS LEDGE Ulster Co. Elev. 2700 ft. West of Little Rocky and east of Samson Mtn. South of Peekamoose Lake, between the branches of Rondout Creek.

SPHINX, THE Greene Co. On Prospect Mtn. overlooking Rip's Lookout.

SPHINX ROCK Greene Co. On Escarpment Trail on South Mtn. south of Eagle Rock overlooking the valley, below the trail.

SPOONER BROOK Delaware Co. Flows south into the Beaver Kill at Horton.

SPRAGUE BROOK Sullivan Co. Near Livingston Manor.

SPRING BROOK #1 Delaware Co. Flows south from Brook Mtn. to the Beaver Kill.

SPRING BROOK #2 Delaware Co. Flows 6 miles into East Branch of Delaware.

SPRINGFIELD Otsego Co. On Rte. 20 east of Richfield Springs, west of Sharon Springs. Town established 1797.

SPRINGFIELD CENTER Otsego Co. On Rte. 80 9 miles north of Cooperstown at north end Otsego Lake. Near Glimmerglass State Park. Denny's Toy Museum—dolls, trains, books, games, antique toys. Picnic grounds. Magic lantern shows. Open daily, May 15 to Oct. 15. Weekends from Easter.

SPRING GLEN Ulster Co. On Homowack Creek and Rte. 209 south of Ellenville and north of Phillipsport.

SPRING LAKE Delaware Co. South of West Meredith. Drained by Steele Brook.

SPRINGTOWN Ulster Co. On Rte. 32 north of New Paltz, south of Tillson.

SPRUCE CREEK Greene Co. Flows south from North Mtn. to Lake Creek between Scribner's and Kaaterskill Falls.

SPRUCE GLEN Ulster Co. In Shawangunk Mountains north of Murray Hill and south of Margarets Cliff.

SPRUCE MOUNTAIN Ulster Co. Elev. 3380 ft. Southeast of Fir Mtn. and northwest of Hemlock Mtn. Formerly called Spruce Top.

SPRUCETON Greene Co. East of West Kill and south of Evergreen Mtn. where Herdman Brook enters the West Kill.

SPRUCE TOP MOUNTAIN Greene Co. Elev. 3380 ft. North of Plateau Mtn. and south of Elka Park.

SQUIRMER VALLEY Albany Co. North of Oak Hill.

STAIRCLIFF Ulster Co. On east face of Skytop at Mohonk.

STAMFORD Delaware Co. Near headwaters of West Branch of Delaware River on Rtes. 23 and 10 and U&D RR west of Grand Gorge and northwest of Hobart. Mt. Utsayantha to the south. Settled by people from Stamford, Connecticut. Attractive colonial village. On June 26, 1883, Theodore Roosevelt stayed at the Delaware Valley Inn, where his signature may still be examined in the guest register. Location of the former large and luxurious Churchill Hall and Rexmere Hotels.

STANTON HOLLOW Greene Co. At head of Elk Creek west of Northeast Halcott Mtn.

STAR ROCK #1 Greene Co. Elev. 2575 ft. Also called Four State Rock. North of Onteora Park and east of Parker Mtn.

STAR ROCK #2 Greene Co. Location on South Mtn. between Fairy Spring and Eagle Rock on "cutoff" red-marked trail parallel to the Escarpment Trail near Boulder Rock.

STARRUCCA CREEK Entirely in Pennsylvania. It flows north into the Susquehanna River at Lanesboro. For much of its length it is followed by the Wilkes-Barre Div. of the Delaware & Hudson RR. However, its main interest is the famous Starrucca Viaduct at Lanesboro. See Lanesboro.

STEAD'S TWIN FALLS Greene Co. Near South Durham.

STEELE BROOK Delaware Co. Rises in Spring Lake and flows south to West Branch of Delaware River at Delhi.

STEINY HILL Ulster Co. Elev. 1400 ft. East of Flat Hill and north of Riggsville.

STEPHEN CRANE LAKE Sullivan Co. On Bush Kill at Hartwood. Stephen Crane (1871–1900), American novelist, famous for his novel *The Red Badge of Courage*. *The Sullivan County Sketches of Stephen Crane* were edited by Melvin Schoberlin in 1949.

STEVENSVILLE Sullivan Co. Between Liberty and White Lake. Named for Stevens Bros., early tanners.

STILESVILLE Delaware Co. On Rte. 10. Below Cannonsville on West Branch of Delaware River north of Deposit, at junction of Cold Spring Brook.

STOCKPORT Delaware Co. South of Hancock on Delaware River and Erie RR.

STONE CABIN BROOK Ulster Co. Flows off Van Wyck Mtn. to West Branch of Rondout Creek at Bull Run.

Greek Revival house, Stone Ridge. Photo by Alfred H. Marks.

Stone Ridge Library, formerly Edward Lounsberry and Cornelius Hasbrouck House. Photo by Alfred H. Marks.

STONE RIDGE Ulster Co. On Rte. 209 south of Marbletown. Formerly Butterfields. Site of Ulster Community College. Many stone houses, some with attractive iron work. Stone Ridge Library (1770), formerly Edward Lounsberry and Cornelius Hasbrouck House. Major Cornelius E. Wynkoop–Wm. Lounsberry House (1772); Washington slept here November 15, 1782. Johannes and Sarah (Sally) Tack Tavern (c1727–1772); Washington dined here while staying at Wynkoop House, across the street (Rte. 209). Ulster County Court met here in 1777 after burning of Kingston.

STONY BROOK #1 Greene Co. Correct name of brook in Sleepy Hollow.

STONY BROOK #2 Ulster Co. In Shawangunks. Flows south from Losees Hill into Platte Kill.

STONY BROOK FALLS Greene Co. On Stony Brook.

STONY CLOVE Greene Co. Runs between Lanesville and Kaaterskill Junction. Utilized by Rte. 214 and formerly by Ulster & Delaware RR. Most dramatic part between Hunter and Plateau Mtns. near the north end.

STONY CLOVE CREEK Greene and Ulster Co. Flows south from Notch Lake to Esopus Creek at Phoenicia.

STONY CREEK Ulster Co. Rises in swamp atop Morgan Hill north of Lapla and flows south to Esopus Creek near Lomontville.

STONY HOLLOW Ulster Co. Hollow and village on Stony Hollow Creek. On Rte. 28 and U&D RR between Kingston and West Hurley. Former bluestone quarrying center. Millstones once made here.

STONY HOLLOW CREEK Ulster Co. Flows from Stony Hollow east to Esopus Creek at Kingston.

STONY KILL Ulster Co. In Shawangunks. Flows north down west slope from High Point, past Granite, to Rondout Creek near Accord.

STONY KILL FALLS Ulster Co. In Shawangunks. On Stony Kill northwest of Lake Awosting. 87-ft. drop. Off Rock Haven Road, in Minnewaska State Park.

STOPPEL POINT Greene Co. Elev. 3420 ft. On Wall of Manitou and Escarpment Trail north of North Mtn. and south of Black Head.

Major Cornelius E. Wynkoop—Wm. Lounsberry House, Stone Ridge. Photo by Alfred H. Marks.

STOVIC CAVES Ulster Co. On Mohonk grounds.

STRATTON FALLS Delaware Co. On Rte. 30, East Branch of Delaware River and U&D RR north of Halcottville, south of Roxbury.

STRAWBERRY KNOB Greene Co. North of Ashland.

STRYKERSVILLE See West Conesville.

STURGEON POOL Ulster Co. Artificial lake on Wallkill River west of Rifton just above confluence with Rondout Creek.

STYGIAN LAKE Greene Co. See Notch Lake. In the classical mythology, River Styx was in Hades.

Tack Tavern, Stone Ridge. Photo by Alfred H. Marks.

SUCKER BROOK Ulster and Sullivan Co. Flows south from Mongaup Mtn. to Mongaup Pond.

SUGARLOAF BROOK Ulster and Sullivan Co. Flows south from Red Hill to Rondout Reservoir at Lowes Corners.

SUGARLOAF MOUNTAIN #1 Delaware Co. Elev. 2512 ft. South of Pepacton Reservoir and north of Brook Mtn. Cat Hollow to the west and Holiday Brook to the east.

Historic house, Stone Ridge. Photo by Alfred H. Marks.

Marbletown Reformed Church, Stone Ridge. Photo by Alfred H. Marks.

SUGARLOAF MOUNTAIN #2 Greene Co. Elev. 3800 ft. Mink Hollow and Plateau Mountain to the west and Pecoy Notch and Twin Mtn. to the east. Traversed by Devil's Path. Formerly Mink Mtn.

SUMMIT Schoharie Co. On Rte. 10 south of Richmondville, north of Jefferson.

SUMMIT MOUNTAIN Ulster Co. Village on Birch Creek between Monka Hill and Rose Mtn. Near Pine Hill.

SUMMITVILLE Sullivan Co. On Rte. 209 and former D&H Canal. It is at western foot of Shawangunk Mtns. and was high water point in the canal between Delaware and Hudson watersheds. Also formerly an important junction point on O&W Rwy. where mainline met with branches to Port Jervis and Kingston. Passengers changed here for Monticello and Ellenville. Formerly Beatysburg.

SUNDOWN Ulster Co. At junction of East and West Branch of Rondout Creek. Northeast of Lowes Corners and southwest of Peekamoose Lake.

Stygian Lake in Stony Clove. Photo by Alfred H. Marks.

SUNDOWN CREEK Ulster Co. Another name for East Branch of Rondout Creek.

SUNRISE ROCK Greene Co. On Escarpment Trail on Great Wall of Manitou between Artists Rock and Red Hill. Sheer dropoff. Great view.

SUNSET PARK Greene Co. South of Haines Falls and west of Twilight Park. Site of large Sunset Park Hotel built by C. A. Clegg at 2600 ft. elevation. It commands the entire Kaaterskill Clove. Of stone and wood construction, it featured the waters of the Sunset Spring high up on Roundtop Mtn. Now called Sunset Springs Hotel.

SUNSET ROCK #1 Greene Co. Viewpoint on Escarpment Trail on North Mtn. Formerly reached by Jacob's Ladder. Extensive view over North and South Lakes, Pine Orchard, South Mtn. and Kaaterskill High Peak was popularized by William H. Bartlett, Thomas Cole, Sanford Gifford and Currier & Ives. Also fine views north from Lookout Point. Echo effect from North Mtn.

SUNSET ROCK #2 Greene Co. On Escarpment Trail atop north wall of Kaaterskill Clove on South Mtn. between Layman Monument and Inspiration Point. View of Upper Kaaterskill Clove, entire rise of High Peak and Roundtop Mtns., Santa Cruz, Twilight and Sunset Parks and Haines Falls. A favorite of President Ulysses S. Grant.

SUNSET SPRINGS HOTEL Greene Co. See Sunset Park.

SUNSIDE Greene Co. North of South Durham.

SURPRISE Greene Co. On Rte. 81 east of Greenville, west of Coxsackie.

Abandoned Erie Railroad Hotel-Depot, Susquehanna, Pa. Built in 1848 of red brick in Hudson River Gothic style. Upstairs was used as hotel with lunchroom and station facilities on ground floor. Erie RR Mainline and author's son Christopher in foreground. Photo (1975) by author.

SUSQUEHANNA, PA. At the south dip of the Great Bend of the Susquehanna River into Pennsylvania, on south bank, across from Oakland. Former division point of Erie RR, with extensive car shops. Large red brick Gothic passenger depot and hotel, now going into ruin, built 1848. McKune Cemetery on hill above depot has grave of Joseph Smith's son.

SUSQUEHANNA TURNPIKE Ran from Catskill on Hudson River to Wattle's Ferry (Unadilla) on Susquehanna River. It was a major artery of early development. Parts are utilized by present Rtes. 23 and 145, but most sections are now back roads and a few short sections have been abandoned. An excellent monograph by David George Erdmann is in the Winter 1973 *Catskill Quarterly*.

SUTTON HILL Greene Co. West of West Durham.

SWAMP POND Sullivan Co. On Rte. 23 near Neweiden. East of Narrowsburg.

SWAN LAKE Sullivan Co. Lake and village west of Liberty. Source of West Branch of Mongaup River. Once famous for pickerel. Named for Alden S. Swan, early developer.

SWARTE KILL Ulster Co. Flows north into Wallkill at Rifton. Name is Dutch for Dark or Black Kill, from tannin in water in Plattekill Hills.

SWEET MEADOWS Ulster Co. North of Jockey Hill, west of Halihan Hill.

SWINGING BRIDGE RESERVOIR Sullivan Co. On Mongaup River south of Mongaup Valley, north of Rio Reservoir. Nesting place of Bald Eagles.

SYLVA Ulster Co. West of Plattekill, east of New Hurley. Orchard area. In classical mythology, Sylvanus was a woodland demigod.

SYLVAN LAKE Greene Co. See South Lake.

TABASCO Ulster Co. Location south of Samsonville and north of Mombaccus.

TAB HOLLOW Delaware Co. East of Hawk Mountain.

TABLE MOUNTAIN Ulster Co. Elev. 3847 ft. North of Peekamoose and south of Lone Mtns.

TABLE ROCKS Ulster Co. In Northern Shawangunks in property of the Bonticou Conservancy near Rosendale.

TOCOMA Delaware Co. Northwest of Ivanhoe.

Abandoned Erie Railroad Hotel-Depot at Susquehanna, Pa. Note trefoil windows in gable ends and pointed arches. Photo (1975) by author.

TANNERSVILLE Greene Co. Atop Kaaterskill Clove west of Haines Falls and east of Hunter on Rte. 23A. Formerly served by Ulster & Delaware and Catskill & Tannersville Railroads. Once a major boarding house center. On Lake Rip Van Winkle and Gooseberry Creek. Onteora Park to the north. Named for extensive early tanning industry.

TANZMAN LAKE Sullivan Co. Near Parkville.

TAYLOR HOLLOW Greene Co. In north side of Hunter Mtn. between Colonel's Chair and Rusk Mtn. Formerly Jones Gap.

TAYLOR'S GLEN Greene Co. Near Durham. Taylor's and Silver Falls.

TEKAHARAWA FALLS See Judd Falls.

TELFORD HOLLOW Delaware Co. North of Downsville.

TEMPLE POND Ulster Co. See Kenozia Lake.

TEN MILE CREEK Albany Co. Rises south of Rensselaerville and flows 10 miles south to Catskill Creek at Oak Hill. Ten Mile Creek Conservancy has 111 acres on Hale Road 1.7 miles south of Rensselaerville; wooded areas and ravines.

TEN MILE RIVER Sullivan Co. Flows south from Neweiden to Delaware River at Tusten.

TENNANAH LAKE Sullivan Co. Resort community and lake southwest of Roscoe on Rte. 96.

TERPENING POND Ulster Co. West of Esopus.

TERRACE MOUNTAIN Ulster Co. Elev. 2400 ft. Northern extension of Wittenberg Mtn.

TERRY CLOVE BROOK Delaware Co. Rises south of Delancey and flows 5 miles south to Coles Brook and Pepacton Reservoir.

THACHER, JOHN BOYD, STATE PARK Albany Co. In Helderbergs 15 miles west of Albany on Rte. 157 near Knox Cave. Features include: Cliffside overlooks, picknicking facilities, scenic drives, hiking trails, Indian Ladder, Hailes Cave (2800 ft. long), Tory Caves where in 1777 Jacob Salsbury, a British spy for General Burgoyne, hid. Camping. Swimming pool.

THIRD LAKE Ulster Co. Binnewater Lake in Northern Shawangunks north of Whiteport and south of First Lake. Very clear.

THOMPSON HOLLOW Delaware Co. Northwest of New Kingston on Platte Kill River west of Plattekill Mtn.

THOMPSONS LAKE Albany Co. On Rte. 157A. Near Thacher State Park east of East Berne in Northern Helderbergs.

THOMPSONS LAKE CAMPSITE Albany Co. 3 miles west of Thacher State Park on Rte. 157. Swimming, fishing.

THOMPSONVILLE Sullivan Co. On Rte. 161 and Kiamesha Creek north of Bridgeville.

THUNDER HILL Sullivan Co. Elev. 2242 ft. Southwest of Grahamsville.

TICETONYK MOUNTAIN Ulster Co. Elev. 2527 ft. West of Tonshi Mtn. and south of the Little Beaver Kill. North of Ashokan Reservoir and Shokan.

TILLSON Ulster Co. Also called Tillson Flats. On Rte. 32 south of Rosendale, north of New Paltz. The Rosendale Woods and Sandplains are privately owned.

TIMMERMAN HILL Greene Co. Elev. 596 ft. North of High Falls on Kaaterskill Creek. South of Kiskatom.

TISKILWA PARK Ulster Co. Near Chichester in Ox Clove. Formerly private picnic grounds for employees of furniture factory. Ox Clove Canyon and Creek.

TITUS LAKE Delaware Co. north of North Harpersfield.

TODD BROOK Ulster Co. Flows southwest from Belle Ayre Mtn. to Dry Brook near Mapledale. Named for early settler Dyer Todd.

TODDSVILLE Otsego Co. Southeast of Cooperstown on Oak Creek.

TOE PATH MOUNTAIN CAMPSITE Schoharie Co. Four miles south of Middleburg on Rte. 30.

TOMKINS FALLS Delaware Co. On Barkaboom Stream east of Hunt Hill and Barkaboom Mtn. Also Tompkins Falls.

TOMKINS HOLLOW Ulster Co. In Dry Brook Ridge Southeast of Mapledale.

TOMSCO FALLS Sullivan Co. East of Mountaindale on Sandburg Creek. Railings, bridges, hiking trails.

TOMY KILL Ulster Co. In Shawangunks. Flows southwest from south of Walker Valley into Shawangunk Kill.

TONCHE HOOK Ulster Co. Hill west of Ticetonyk Mtn. Near junction of Beaver Kill and Esopus Creek.

TONGORE Ulster Co. Area of Marbletown Township. Near Olive Bridge. No specific center. Also Tongora. Named for Esopus chieftain.

TONSHI MOUNTAIN Ulster Co. Elev. 2000 ft. East of Ticetonyk Mtn. and west of Ohio Mtn. North of Kenozia Lake and Ashokan Reservoir.

TOPATCOKE Ulster Co. Atop Shawangunks east of Louis Ravine and north of Napanoch Point.

TOPATCOKE SPRING Ulster Co. On banks of Rondout Creek at Napanoch.

TOP'S LAKE Greene Co. See Dolan's Lake.

TORONTO LAKE Sullivan Co. West of Toronto Reservoir.

TORONTO RESERVOIR Sullivan Co. On Rte. 13 south of Black Lake.

TORY CAVES Albany Co. See Thacher State Park.

TORY SWAMP Greene Co. On Kaaterskill High Peak above Santa Cruz Ravine and below Hurricane Ledge. See Roundtop Mtn.

TOUCHMENOT MOUNTAIN Delaware Co. Elev. 2760 ft. South of Pepacton Reservoir and Barkaboom Mtn. East of Middle Mtn.

TOWER BROOK Delaware Co. Flows west from Moresville Range to West Branch of Delaware at Hobart.

TOWER MOUNTAIN #1 Greene Co. Elev. 2980 ft. South of Ashland.

TOWER MOUNTAIN #2 Delaware Co. Elev. 2420 ft. North of Rock Rift and Beerston.

TOWNSEND HOLLOW Delaware Co. On Emory Brook north of Monka Hill.

TRAPS, THE Ulster Co. In Shawangunks on Mohonk Trust property. Millbrook Mountain to south and Sleepy Hollow to north, on east face of ridge. Overcliff Road on west side and Undercliff Road on east face—carriages only. Rte. 44 passes through a gap bridged by a steel girder bridge of the old Minnewaska Carriage Road. It is a famous climbing area for rock climbers. Limestone and conglomerate cliffs backed by gentle western slopes—cuesta type formation. Formerly millstones were cut here. Elevations run to 1220 ft., looking out over the Wallkill Valley.

TRAVER HOLLOW Ulster Co. Southwest of Mt. Pleasant, southeast of Cross Mtn., east of Samuel's Point and west of Ashokan Reservoir. Crossed by high viaduct on Rte. 28A.

TRAY MILL BROOK Ulster Co. Flows west off Van Wyck and Peekamoose Mtns. to East Branch of Neversink River east of Denning.

TREADWELL Delaware Co. Northwest of Delhi, south of Oneonta.

Typical 19th-century home in central Catskills, near Mt. Tremper. Photo by Alfred H. Marks.

TREMPERS KILL Delaware Co. Flows south from Andes past Kaufman's to Pepacton Reservoir. Formerly followed by branch of Delaware Northern Railroad.

TRI-STATE ROCK Orange Co. On Carpenter's Point at intersection of N.J., N.Y. and Pa. See Port Jervis.

TRITON CAVE Greene Co. Below Haines Falls, in Kaaterskill Clove.

TROJAN LAKE Sullivan Co. Northeast of Deckertown.

TROTTER'S See Hartwood.

TROUT BROOK #1 Sullivan and Delaware Co. Flows northwest from Tennanah Lake to Beaver Kill at Peakville.

TROUT BROOK #2 Delaware Co. Rises in Launt Pond in Bear Spring Game Management Area and flows 10 miles south to East Branch of Delaware at Shinhopple.

TROUT BROOK #3 Delaware Co. Rises south of Colchester Mountain and flows 7 miles past Trout Brook Mountain through Wilson Hollow to East Branch of Delaware at Downsville.

TROUT BROOK FALLS Ulster Co. 1 mile north of brook junction with Rondout Reservoir. 25 ft. high.

TROUT BROOK MOUNTAIN Delaware Co. Elev. 2420 ft. Near Corbett.

TROUT CREEK #1 Ulster Co. Flows south from Balsam Swamp near Greenville to Rondout Reservoir.

TROUT CREEK #2 Delaware Co. In Town of Tompkins. Flows 10 miles south from Tacoma into Cannonsville Reservoir.

TROUT CREEK Delaware Co. Village on Rte. 206. On Trout Creek north of Rock Royal, east of Masonville and west of Walton.

TROUT POND Ulster Co. See Cable's Lake.

TUCKERS CORNERS Ulster Co. West of Milton and east of Plattekill.

TUNIS LAKE Delaware Co. On Rte. 28 northwest of Mt. Pisgah.

TUNIS POND Ulster Co. South of Graham and Doubletop Mtns. and east of Vly Pond near Bullet Hole at headwaters of Beaver Kill.

TURKEY HILL Ulster Co. at Kerhonkson.

TURKEY POINT Ulster Co. East of Flatbush on Hudson River.

TURK HOLLOW Delaware Co. Between Vly and Halcott Mtns. North of Halcott Center.

TURNER BROOK PRESERVE Sullivan Co. Near Wolf Lake. Includes Denton and High Falls.

TURNER HOLLOW Ulster Co. West of Graham Mtn., south of Dry Brook at Seager. Cascade and falls.

TURNWOOD Ulster Co. On Beaver Kill east of Lewbeach and west of Hardenburgh. At junction with Alder Creek. Site of Salmo Fontinalis Fishing Club.

TUSTEN Sullivan Co. On Rte. 97, Erie RR, Delaware River and junction with Ten Mile River. South of Narrowsburg and north of Minisink Ford. Stone Arch Bridge on Ten Mile River. Baptist Church (1856), named for Colonel Benjamin Tusten of the Goshen Militia, hero of Battle of the Minisink.

TUTHILL Ulster Co. West of Gardiner.

TUTHILLTOWN Ulster Co. On Rte. 44 at junction of Shawangunk Kill and Wallkill River. Old Tuthilltown Gristmill on Shawangunk River, built 1788 by Selah Tuthill; still actively using water power and millstones. Eleanor and George Smith purchased in 1941. Various meals and flours available at retail.

TWAALFSKILL Ulster Co. Flows northeast into Hudson at Highland.

TWADELL MOUNTAIN Delaware Co. Elev. 2290 ft. Fire observation tower. West of Baxter Mtn. between junction of Beaver Kill and East Branch of Delaware River.

TWILIGHT PARK Greene Co. Private residential park located at head of Kaaterskill Clove near village of Haines Falls. Haines Falls, second highest in the Catskills, is on the grounds just below the gatehouse and stone bridge across Kaaterskill Creek. Entry is controlled and the grounds are patrolled. All four inns that once operated in the park are now out of operation and there are no public accommodations in the park.

The Twilight Park Association was formed in 1887 by Charles F. Wingate; the property was purchased that year from Charles W. Haines, who owned a mill on the stream above the falls and the Haines Falls House. He had also constructed wooden stairways to the base of the falls. Much of the property purchased had been Mr. Haines' sheep pasture. Mr. Haines had built a dam with a sluice gate above the falls which allowed the water to be "turned on" or "turned off." Thus

View of Twilight Park from Route 23A in Kaaterskill Clove. Photo by Alfred H. Marks.

he could build up a good head of water and turn them on with dramatic effect once viewers had assembled at the foot of the falls. Mr. Haines was a very religious man and refused to "turn on the falls" on Sunday.

Many of the original cottagers were members of the Twilight Club in New York and came from there and Brooklyn. They included such substantial people as Silas Sadler Packard, an educator who had founded Packard College and pioneered the entrance of women into commerce; I. Reynolds Adriance of Poughkeepsie, owner of Adriance-Platt & Co., which manufactured the famous Buckeye Reaper and line of farm equipment—then the largest industry in Poughkeepsie; Eben Erskine Olcott, a distinguished metallurgical engineer who was also president of the Hudson River Day Line. Charles Frederick Wingate (1847–1909), himself, had impressive credentials as a consulting sanitary engineer, author and editor. His brother, General George Wood Wingate, and his nephew, Brigadier General George Albert Wingate, who was also a distinguished attorney and for many years Surrogate of Kings County, were also leaders in the Association.

Spiritual needs of the members were served by the Episcopal Memorial Church of All Angels, which is affiliated with the Albany Diocese, and by the former Union Chapel, which has been converted into a private residence.

There were four inns in the park. Perhaps the most popular was Twilight Inn, which burned with tragic loss of life in 1926. Ledge End Inn, which opened in 1890, was a rustic building commanding a fine view down Kaaterskill Clove. It was razed on April 23, 1975. The Squirrel Inn was run by Quakers named Pim for many years and subsequently, until the 2nd World War, by Miss Abigail Foulke. It was then closed for good. Santa Cruz Inn, in adjacent Santa Cruz Park, has been converted into a private residence.

TWIN MOUNTAIN Greene Co. Elev. 3640 ft. West of Plattekill Clove, Indian Head Mtn. and Jimmy Dolan Notch. East of Pecoy Notch and Sugarloaf Mtn. Crossed by Devil's Path. This range formerly known as Schoharie Peaks.

TYLER BROOK Sullivan Co. Northern tributary of North Branch of Callicoon Creek.

TYLERTOWN Sullivan Co. Near East Branch of Ten Mile River.

ULSTER HEIGHTS Ulster Co. On Rte. 154 west of Ellenville and Cape Pond, on the Beer Kill.

ULSTER LANDING Ulster Co. On Hudson River 2 miles north of Kingston-Rhinecliff Bridge. 92-Acre County Park with 3000 ft. of unspoiled river frontage. Ravines. Beautifully wooded. Formerly St. George's Camp. "Wrongside" (c1825), name given to estate by Livingstons who thought their relatives should have built on eastern shore instead.

ULSTER PARK Ulster Co. On Rte. 9W, West Shore RR and Hudson River south of Port Ewen and north of Esopus.

ULSTERVILLE Ulster Co. Off Rte. 52 to north of Shawangunk Kill. East of Walker Valley and west of Pinebush.

UNADILLA Otsego Co. On Rte. 7, D&H RR and Susquehanna River south of Wells Bridge and east of Sidney. Settled 1790, incorporated 1827. Formerly called Wattle's Ferry, and was western terminus of Susquehanna Turnpike from Catskill. Silos and farm machinery are manufactured here.
   Points of interest:
Hotel Bishop; unique Victorian style.
St. Matthews Episcopal Church (1809), Gothic Revival.
Georgian colonial house, Main St.; exquisite fan and side lights around front door.
62 Main St.; unique blend of stone and Greek Revival with Victorian cupola.
Unadilla House Hotel (1804).
Mulford & Sivers Hall (1879).
St. Ambrose RC Church; small freestone chapel.
Fancher Octagon House, Watson St.

UNADILLA FORKS Otsego Co. West of Richfield Springs and southwest of Cooperstown near headwaters of Unadilla River. Flowery meadows. Formerly on Unadilla Valley RR. Bucolic village with general store beside meandering river.

UNADILLA RIVER Forms boundary between Otsego County on east and Chenango County on west. Rises in neighborhood of West Winfield, in Herkimer County, and flows south past Unadilla Forks, Leonardsville, West Edmeston, New Berlin, South New Berlin, and Mount Upton to junction with Susquehanna River at Sidney. Principal tributary in Otsego County is Butternut Creek, which flows into it below Mount Upton. In the past its valley was followed by the New York, Ontario & Western and Unadilla Valley railroads, both now abandoned. It is followed on its west bank, in Chenango County, by Rte. 8.
   See also Chapter 3.

UNION CENTER Ulster Co. West of Ulster Park.

UNION GROVE Delaware Co. Now under waters of Pepacton Reservoir. Formerly between Arena and Shavertown.

UNIONVILLE Sullivan Co. On Rte. 55 east of Curry.

UPPER ULSTER LAKE Ulster Co. West of Ulster Heights on Botsford Brook.

VALLEY JUNCTION Orange Co. Where the Basher Kill joins the Neversink River. Former railroad junction where Monticello Branch of O&W RR left the Summitville-to-Port Jervis line.

VALLONIA SPRINGS Broome Co. On Rte. 41 south of Afton, north of Sanford.

VAN HORNESVILLE Herkimer Co. On Rte. 80 northeast of Richfield Springs. Village was founded by Abraham Van Horne (1736–1810), who is buried near Methodist Church. He was a member of the Tryon Committee of Safety in 1775 and fought at the Battle of Oriskany. He was in the State Legislature 1779–1786 and sherriff of Tryon County from 1781 till 1785. Owen D. Young (1874–1962),

Old Gristmill, Van Hornesville. Photo by Alfred H. Marks.

former head of the General Electric Co., was a lifelong resident; he restored several houses and an old gristmill (1791), which is still operative as the Van Hornesville Co-op, Inc., and also donated a park, school and municipal swimming pool. Very attractive town. There is a rustic horse trough still operable in the center of town.

VAN LOAN HILL Greene Co. Elev. 2520 ft. Southwest of Maplecrest. East of Round Hill and west of Mt. Thomas Cole. Possibly named for mapmaker and guidebook writer Walton Van Loan. See Athens for Van Loan family background.

VAN LUVEN LAKE Greene Co. Elev. 213 ft. Atop the Kalkberg.

VAN WYCK MOUNTAIN Ulster Co. Elev. 3206 ft. West of Peekamoose and Table Mtns.

VEDDER HILL Greene Co. Elev. 500 ft. West of Catskill and Kaaterskill Creeks and east of Bethel Ridge.

VERKEERDER KILL AND FALLS Ulster Co. In Shawangunks north of Sam's Point. Flows southeast off High Point to Shawangunk Kill at Ulsterville. The 100-ft.-high scenic falls are on the east face of cliffs.

VERNOOY CREEK Ulster Co. Also called Vernooy Kill. Rises in Balsam Swamp near Greenville and flows south to Rondout Creek near Napanoch. Rattlesnakes abound along this creek.

VERNOOY FALLS Ulster Co. On Vernooy Creek southwest of Flat Hill on Riggsville-Greenville skimobile trail. Painted by George Inness.

VETERAN Ulster Co. On Rte. 212 west of Saugerties. Mt. Airy to the north and Mt. Marion to the south.

VINEGAR HILL Greene Co. Elev. 2069 ft. Near Lexington east of Vly Mtn. Near junction of west Kill and Schoharie Creek. Mosquito Point to the north.

VIOLA FALLS Greene Co. In Hillyer Ravine on south wall of Kaaterskill Clove. Below Poet's Ledge and above Profile Rock. Named for profusion of violets near falls.

VLIGHTBERG See Ponckhockie.

VLY Definition: swamp or bog (Dutch).

VLY, THE Ulster Co. South of Olive Bridge and Davis Corners and northwest of Stone Ridge. West of Atwood.

VLY CREEK Greene Co. Flows south and southwest from southern slopes of Vly Mtn. to Bush Kill at Fleischmanns.

VLY CREEK GORGE Albany Co. On Rte. 203 in New Scotland. Steep falls in shale. Ruin of old mill above falls.

VLY MOUNTAIN Greene Co. Elev. 3529 ft. West of Vinegar Hill, southeast of Bearpen Mtn. Turk Hollow to the south and Little West Kill to the north. Formerly Angel's Peak.

VLY POND Ulster Co. Southwest of Graham Mt. Drains south into the Beaver Kill near Quaker Clearing.

VORHEES BROOK Sullivan Co. Flows northwest to Beaver Kill between Beaverkill and Lewbeach.

VOORHEESVILLE Albany Co. On Rtes. 156 and 85A and D&H, NYC and West Shore RRs. West of Albany, north of Salem.

VOSBURGH SWAMP Greene Co. north of Athens, along Hudson River.

VOSENKILL Greene Co. See Hans Vosen Kill.

VOSS LAKE Greene Co. See Rip Van Winkle Lake.

VROOMAN'S NOSE Schoharie Co. Near Middleburg. Named for local family. Looks like a nose.

WAGEN DAL Ulster Co. On Rondout Creek. See Creeklocks.

WAGON WHEEL GAP Ulster Co. See Goblin Gulch.

WALKER VALLEY Ulster Co. On Rte. 52. Southeast of Ellenville, west of Pine Bush. Attractive small ponds.

WALLKILL Ulster Co. Formerly Shawangunk P.O. On Rte. 208, Wallkill River, Wallkill Valley RR north of Walden and south of New Paltz. Farm and orchard area. General Slicing Machine has a plant here. Falls on River. State Prison and Farm. One contemplated site of Woodstock Festival. Severyn Bruyn House (c1766). Terwilliger Houses (c1730), near Indians' "New Fort."

WALLKILL RIVER See Chapter 3.

WALTON Delaware Co. On Rtes. 10 and 206, NYO&W RR and West Branch of Delaware southwest of Delhi, northeast of Deposit, southeast of Sidney. Incorporated 1851.

WANASINK LAKE Sullivan Co. East of Rock Hill, north of Rte. 17.

WANETA LAKE Sullivan Co. On Rte. 151 south of Beaverkill.

WARNER CREEK Ulster Co. Rises south of Silver Hollow Notch and flows southwest to Stony Clove Creek at Chichester.

WARNERS LAKE Albany Co. On Rte. 43 at East Berne.

WARNERVILLE Schoharie Co. On Rte. 7 west of Cobleskill, east of Richmondville.

WARREN Herkimer Co. On Rte. 20 east of Richfield Springs, west of Sharon Springs. Settled in 1793 by John Tunnicliff, Jr., who was born in 1751 in Derby, England. He came to America in 1772 and was a soldier in the Revolution. Settled in Warren in 1793 and died in 1814. Buried in Tunnicliff Cemetery on Hoke Road, 1 mile south of Rte. 20. Youngs Lake. Petrified Creatures Prehistoric Museum, Rte. 20.

WARREN MOUNTAIN Delaware Co. Elev. 2880 ft. South of South Kortright.

WASHBURNS POINT Ulster Co. At confluence of Esopus Creek and Hudson River in Saugerties.

WASHINGTON LAKE Sullivan Co. North of Yulan.

WASHINGTON'S PROFILE #1 Greene Co. See Profile Rock and North Mountain.

WASHINGTON'S PROFILE #2 Ulster Co. On Skytop at Lake Mohonk. Visible from across the lake.

WATSON HOLLOW Ulster Co. The hollow of the Bush Kill southwest of West Shokan. Hanover Mtn. and Breath Hill to the west and South Mtn. and Ashokan High Peak to the east.

WATSONVILLE Schoharie Co. On Rte. 30 and Schoharie Creek south of Middleburg, north of Breakabeen.

WAWAKA LAKE Delaware Co. On East Branch of Delaware River at Halcottville.

WAWANTAPACHOOK Greene Co. See Cairo Round Top.

WAWARSING Ulster Co. On Rte. 209 and Rondout Creek at west foot of Shawangunks. On D&H Canal, NYO&W RR north of Ellenville and south of Kerhonkson. Abraham Bevier House. Jacobs Bruyn House (c1760). DePuy-DeWitt House ("Soccanissing") (c1750). Johannes G. Hardenbergh House (1762). Vernooy-Bevier House (c1760).

WEAVER HOLLOW Delaware Co. South of New Kingston, northwest of Margaretville, north of Dunraven.

WELCH CORNERS Schoharie Co. Northeast of South Jefferson.

WELLS BRIDGE Otsego Co. On Rte. 7, Susquehanna River, D&H RR east of Unadilla, west of Otego.

WEST ATHENS Greene Co. On Rte. 9W and West Shore RR north of Catskill and south of Coxsackie. West Athens Hill: deepkill flint quarry and paleo-Indian workshop.

WEST BERNE Albany Co. On Rte. 443 east of Schoharie, west of Berne. Kenrose Sanctuary, Bradt Hollow Road.

WEST BRANCHES See Beaver Kill, Delaware River, Neversink River and Rondout Creek.

WEST BROOK Delaware Co. Rises north of Walton and flows south to West Branch of Delaware at Walton.

WESTBROOKVILLE Sullivan Co. On Rte. 209, Old Mine Road, D&H Canal, O&W RR south of Wurtsboro and north of Cuddebackville. Named for Dirck Van Keuren Westbrook, first white settler. Formerly known as Basha's Land, Bessie's Land or Bashaville. Old stone house well preserved, claimed to be oldest in Sullivan County (early 1700s), served as a fort; now a restaurant.

WEST BURLINGTON Otsego Co. On Rtes. 80 and 51 east of Edmeston, west of Cooperstown.

Falls and Mill Race, West Berne. Photo by Alfred H. Marks.

WEST CAMP Ulster Co. On Hudson River, Rte. 9W and West Shore RR. North of Eavesport and south of Cementon. Queen Anne of England sent Palatinate refugees here in 1710 in an unsuccessful attempt to manufacture turpentine.

WEST CAVE MOUNTAIN Greene Co. Elev. 3040 ft. Southwest of Windham and west of Cave Mtn. East of Tower Mtn.

WEST CONESVILLE Schoharie Co. On Manor Kill southwest of Gilboa and west of Manorkill. Formerly Strykersville.

WEST COXSACKIE Greene Co. On Rte. 9W and West Shore RR (Coxsackie depot). New York State Vocational Institution. Cooper, in his novel *Home as Found*, gives the following description of an up-river village which might well apply to West Coxsackie, even today:

"An extraordinary taste is afflicting this country in the way of architecture," said Mr. Effingham, as they stood gazing . . . ; "nothing but a Grecian temple being now deemed a suitable residence for a man in these classical times [1836]. Yonder is a structure, for instance, of beautiful proportions, and at this distance apparently of precious material, and yet it seems better suited to heathen worship than to domestic comfort."

The malady has affected the whole nation," returned his cousin, "like the spirit of speculation. We are passing from one extreme to the other, in this as in other things. One such temple, well placed in a wood, might be a pleasant object enough; but to see a river lined with them, with children trundling hoops before their doors, beef carried into their kitchens, and smoke issuing, moreover, from those unclassical objects, chimneys, is too much even for a high taste; one might as well live in a fever. Mr. Aristabulus Bragg, who is a wag in his way, informs me that there is one town in the interior that has actually a market-house on the plan of the Parthenon!"

This last quip is not so extreme—the Arcade in Providence, R.I., is indeed a Market Building so designed!

Note the preponderance of Greek Revival in the following list:

Sylvestre House (c1840), Ionic Greek. Adjoining house has stepped gables. Abraham Van Dyck House. Unnamed two story Greek Revival Doric Temple House (c1840). #307 Mansion Street—2 story stone, 18th century. One-room schoolhouse (c1800).

The above mix was also apparent in 1836 to Cooper:

"As we recede from the influence of the vulgar architects," he said, "we find imitation taking the place of instruction. Many of these buildings are obviously disproportioned, and then, like vulgar pretension of any sort, Grecian architecture produces less pleasure than even Dutch."

"I am surprised at discovering how little of a Dutch character remains in this State," said the baronet, "I can scarcely trace that people in anything, and yet I believe they had the moulding of your society, having carried the colony through its infancy."

WEST DAVENPORT Delaware Co. On Rte. 23, U&D RR and Charlotte Creek east of Oneonta.

WEST DELHI Delaware Co. Northwest of Fraser, southeast of Treadwell.

WEST DURHAM Greene Co. West of Durham near Mt. Pisgah.

WESTERLO Albany Co. On Rte. 143 east of Rensselaerville, west of Ravena. Chesterville Academy (c1800), by Gabriel Pinney, now a private residence. Moses Smith House, North Road on Basic Creek. Archibald Green House, Main Street. Dunbar Hollow, site of infamous murders in 19th century. Bear Swamp, 2½ miles south.

WEST EXETER Otsego Co. On Rte. 51 northwest of Cooperstown.

WESTFIELD FLATS Sullivan Co. Old name for Roscoe.

WESTFORD Otsego Co. North of Worcester.

WEST FULTON Schoharie Co. South of Cobleskill. Toe Path Mountain.

WEST HARPERSFIELD Delaware Co. On Center Brook west of Harpersfield, east of North Kortright.

WEST HOLLOW Greene Co. North of Ashland between Huntersfield Mtn. and The Knob.

WEST HOLLOW BROOK Greene Co. Flows south from West Hollow to Batavia Kill at Ashland.

WEST HURLEY Ulster Co. On Rte. 28 and U&D RR. Junction with Rte. 375. At northeastern end of Ashokan Reservoir. Formerly Jewelville.

WEST JEWETT Greene Co. Southwest of Jewett.

WEST KILL #1 Greene Co. Rises between Hunter and West Kill Mtns. and flows west past Spruceton and West Kill to Schoharie Creek at Lexington.

WEST KILL #2 Schoharie Co. Rises south of Summit. Flows southeast to Schoharie Creek at North Blenheim.

WEST KILL Greene Co. Village on the West Kill west of Spruceton.

WEST KILL MOUNTAIN Greene Co. Elev. 3880 ft. Also called Big West Kill. Southwest of Diamond Notch and Hunter Mtn. East of North Dome. Traversed by Devil's Path.

WEST LAURENS Otsego Co. On Rte 23 west of Oneonta, east of Morris.

WEST MEDWAY CREEK Greene Co. Eastern tributary of Potic Creek.

WEST MEREDITH Delaware Co. Northwest of Delhi and south of Oneonta.

WEST ONEONTA Otsego Co. On Rte. 23. On Otego Creek.

WEST PARK Ulster Co. On Hudson River, Rte. 9W, West Shore RR south of Esopus and north of Highland. This was the home of John Burroughs in his later years and is well described in many of his essays. His rustic summer retreat, "Slabsides," is also in the town, but not along the river. It is back on the hills off Ackert Road across the railroad, on the southern slopes of Shaupeneak Mountain.

See article on Saugerties for Cooper's descriptions of early life in this general area.

Points of interest:

Marist brothers Novitiate (1910) by Carrere & Hastings of New York, who are best known for the Main Branch of the New York Public Library; French-style chateau of 36 rooms with twelve fireplaces. It makes extensive use of marble and California Tile. It was built for Col. Oliver Hazard Payne, an oil magnate and associate of John D. Rockefeller. Overlooks the Hudson on east side Rte. 9W. Bluestone walls along highway. The extensive and elaborate stables, designed by John Burroughs' son, Julian, who was the estate manager from 1914 till 1918, are to the west of the highway and were developed as a restaurant and shopping complex. Now closed.

Church of the Ascension (1842), Episcopal. Two ogee windows; east side Rte. 9W just south of Marist Novitiate. It could well fit the description of St. Michaels given by Cooper in *Miles Wallingford*. (See Saugerties article.)

It is best identified from the highway by its rustic gateway. Such a gateway was described by Donald G. Mitchell in his 1867 book entitled *Rural Studies:*

"Lastly, there is your hospitable gate, with its little rooflet stretched over it, as if to invite the stranger loiterer to partake at his will of that much of the hospitalities of the home. Even the passing beggar gathers his tattered garments under it in a sudden shower, and blesses the shelter. And I introduce upon the next page a very homely specimen of this class of gates, which I remember to have sketched many years ago somewhere in County Kent, England."

"Either my own pencillings were very bad, or else the engraver has failed to give the character of its rough rooflet; which, if I remember rightly, was but a thatch of broom, or of sedge. Yet who does not see written all over it—plain as it is: Loiter if you like! Come in, if you like! And I love to think that some little maid, under it—in some by-gone year—said her good-night to some parting Leander. Who shall laugh at this, that has ever been young? Are not the little maids and the Leanders always growing up about us? I always felt sure when I found such covered wickets that no curmudgeon lived within."

The actual churchyard gate is almost an exact replica of Mitchell's sketch and verbal description; it is not unlikely that the owner acted upon Mitchell's hint. It must be remembered that this busy highway was at that time but a quiet rural lane. It is interesting to note on old maps that the railroad is shown with a heavy line and the road in light ones. On modern maps just the reverse is true.

Mitchell lived from 1822 till 1908 and was quite involved in architecture and landscaping, although he is better remembered as a novelist. Under the pen name of Ike Marvel he wrote two highly popular sentimental novels—*Reveries of a Bachelor* in 1850 and *Dream Life* in 1851. He was influenced by the work and writing of Newburgh-born Andrew Jackson Downing (1815–1852), whose book *Architecture of Country Houses* of 1850 helped to popularize the Gothic, villa and board-and-batten styles and the concept of giving careful attention to landscaping. These influences should be kept in mind while travelling the mid-Hudson valley.

Riverby—Home of John Burroughs (c1873). Two-story stone, designed and landscaped by Burroughs. South of Church on east side.
Van Benschoten Home, two-story stone and shingle, French Provincial influence.
Wellwaet Weestel van Weetelstoop House (undated).
Greek Revival clapboard—Temple façade (c1835).
House 1½ story clapboard (c1835).
Santa Maria Novitiate (mid 19th century) two-story brick Italianate Victorian Villa style.
Mother Cabrini School (1820), two-story stone with later Carpenter Gothic elements. St. Francis Xavier Cabrini (Mother Cabrini) (1850–1917) was born in Italy and came to the United States in 1889. She founded order of Sisters of the Sacred Heart of Jesus and devoted herself to founding orphanages. Canonized by Pope Pius XII in 1946—the first U.S. citizen to be canonized.
Mill Building (mid 19th century), 2½-story stone, Rte. 9W near Esopus line.

WEST RICHMONDVILLE Schoharie Co. On Rte. 7 west of Cobleskill, northeast of Worcester.

WEST SAUGERTIES Ulster Co. Village at foot of Plattekill Clove. South of Palenville.

WEST SETTLEMENT #1 Delaware Co. West of Roxbury. Methodist Church (1832).

WEST SETTLEMENT #2 Greene Co. Northwest of Ashland.

WEST SETTLEMENT CREEK Greene Co. Near Halcott Center.

WEST SHOKAN Ulster Co. At west end of Ashokan Reservoir near Maltby and Watson Hollows on the Bush Kill. South of Samuel's Point and east of Hanover Mtn. On Rte. 28A and Gulf Road to Sundown.

WEST STOPPEL POINT Greene Co. Elev. 3100 ft. West of Stoppel Point.

WESTVILLE Otsego Co. On Rte. 166 and Cherry Valley Creek. North of Milford, south of Cherry Valley.

WEST WEST KILL MOUNTAIN Greene Co. Elev. 3420 ft. West of West Kill Mtn.

WHALE'S MOUTH Greene Co. See alligator Rock.

WHISKEY POINT Ulster Co. On Hudson River at East Kingston.

WHITE LAKE Sullivan Co. West of Monticello on Rte. 17B. South of Liberty. Settled by Moravians. Woodstock Festival was held on farm of Max Yasgar between here and Bethel to the west.

WHITE MAN MOUNTAIN Delaware Co. Elev. 3140 ft. Northeast of Roxbury.

WHITEPORT Ulster Co. On Wallkill Valley RR south of Eddyville, north of Rosendale. DeWitt Lake is here.

WHITE ROE LAKE Sullivan Co. Southwest of Grooville.

WHITE SULPHUR SPRINGS #1 Sullivan Co. West of Liberty on Rte. 52.

WHITE SULPHUR SPRINGS #2 Albany Co. On Rte. 443 east of Berne. Old (c1800) White Sulphur Springs House with galleries and porticos. Now Pentecostal Campground. Typical early spa hotel. Formerly Robertsonville.

WHITCOMB HOLLOW Delaware Co. South of Middle Mtn., north of Lewbeach.

WHITFIELD Ulster Co. On Peters Kill south of Lyonsville and north of Accord.

WHITMAN Delaware Co. On Rte. 8. South of Masonville, north of Stilesville.

WILBUR Ulster Co. West of Rondout. See Rondout.

White Sulphur Springs Hotel. Photo by Alfred H. Marks.

White Sulphur Springs Hotel with ancient Gazebo. Photo by Alfred H. Marks.

WILDCAT FALLS Greene Co. In Wildcat Ravine.

WILDCAT MOUNTAIN Ulster Co. Elev 3160 ft. East of Frost Valley between the branches of the Neversink River.

WILDCAT RAVINE Greene Co. On north side of Kaaterskill High Peak in south wall of Kaaterskill Clove. Buttermilk Falls to west and Hillyer Ravine to east.

WILLIAMS LAKE Ulster Co. On Wallkill Valley RR north of Rosendale. See Fifth Lake.

WILLOW Ulster Co. On Rte. 212 west of Lake Hill.

WILLOWEMOC Sullivan Co. On Willowemoc Creek east of Debruce. Pronounced Willow-wee-mock.

WILLOWEMOC CREEK See Chapter 3.

WILLOWEMOC MOUNTAIN Ulster Co. Elev. 3224 ft. East of Mongaup Mtn. near headwaters of Willowemoc Creek.

WILLSEY BROOK Sullivan Co. Flows east to Basher Kill at Wurstboro.

WILSON HOLLOW Delaware Co. On Rte. 206 northwest of Downsville. Trout Brook Mountain to west, Brace Hill to northeast.

WILSON, KENNETH L., STATE PARK Ulster Co. At Wittenberg. A new recreational day use park. 18-hole golf course, picnic grounds, athletic fields, 30 acres artificial lake on Beaver Kill.

WILTWYCK Ulster Co. Original name of Kingston. Means "wild place."

WINCHELL Ulster Co. West southwest of Olivebridge.

WINCHELL FALLS Ulster Co. On Esopus Creek 500 ft. above Olive Bridge (covered bridge). On private property.

WINDHAM Greene Co. Resort village. On Rte. 23A west of Hensonville and east of Ashland. On Batavia Kill. Mts. Hayden, Nebo and Richmond to north; Cave Mtn. to south. Many Greek Revival structures. New Englandish appearance. Home of New York State Governors Washington Hunt and Lucius P. Robinson.

WINDHAM HIGH PEAK Greene Co. Elev. 3524 Burnt Knob and Acra Point to southeast. Kate Hill to north. Traversed by Escarpment Trail.

WINDSOR Broome Co. On Rtes. 17 and 79 and west bank of Susquehanna River east of Binghamton, west of Damascus and Deposit. Village green at northwest corner of Old Rte. 17 and Rte. 79.

WINNISOOK Alleged name of the Big Indian of legendary fame. See Chapter 5.

Former Fitch Bluestone Co. office with West Shore RR Wilbur Viaduct. Photo by Alfred H. Marks.

WINNISOOK CLUB & LODGE Ulster Co. On western slopes of Slide Mtn. on Big Indian-Claryville Road. Private Club.

WINNISOOK LAKE Ulster Co. Elev. 2664 ft. On grounds of Winnisook Club. Artificial. Private property. Can be seen from public road.

WINNISOOK LAKE MOUNTAIN Ulster Co. Elev. 3260 ft. Immediately west of Winnisook Lake.

WINTER CLOVE Greene Co. In Wall of Manitou between North Mtn. and Stoppel Point. Resort area with older Mountain House.

WINTER HOLLOW Delaware Co. North of New Kingston.

WINTERTON Sullivan Co. On Rte. 62 and O&W RR. On east side of Shawangunks south of Bloomingburg.

WITCH'S HOLE See Louis Ravine.

WITTENBERG MOUNTAIN Ulster Co. Elev. 3780 ft. North of Cornell, south of Terrace and west of Cross Mtn. in the Slide Mtn. Massif. Traver Hollow to the east; Woodland Valley, shoulder of Slide Mtn., and Giant Ledge to west. Traversed by Slide Mtn.-Woodland Valley trail. Old spellings were: Whittemberg and Wittemberg.

WITTENBERG P.O. Ulster Co. On upper part of Little Beaver Kill north of Tonshi and Ticetonyk Mtns. and south of Bearsville and Mt. Tobias. Formerly Yankeetown. Not near Wittenberg Mtn.

WITTENBERG BROOK Ulster Co. Rises on south slope of Wittenberg and Cornell Mtns. and flows through Ketcham Hollow to Maltby Hollow Brook.

WITTENBERG POND Ulster Co. Near Wittenberg P.O. on Little Beaver Kill.

WOLFF LAKE Sullivan Co. South of Lake Louise-Marie and west of Yankee Lake. Former D&H Canal reservoir.

WOLF HOLLOW Delaware Co. South of Andes and west of Margaretville. On Trempers Kill west of Dunraven.

WOLF'S JAW Ulster Co. In Shawangunks at northeast foot of Margaret Cliff.

WOODBOURNE Sullivan Co. On Rtes. 52 and 42 east of Loch Sheldrake, west of Dairyland, north of Fallsburg. Red brick prison, now narcotics treatment center.

WOODCHUCK LODGE Delaware Co. Former summer home of John Burroughs near Roxbury and Boyhood Rock. Here he entertained such famous people as Henry Ford and Thomas A. Edison. Still in Burroughs family and sometimes open to public when family is in residence.

WOODHULL MOUNTAIN Ulster Co. Elev. 3040 ft. Southeast of Wildcat Mtn. and southwest of Van Wyck Mtn. East of Denning.

WOODLAND CREEK Ulster Co. Flows north from Slide Mtn. to Esopus Creek near Phoenicia.

WOODLAND VALLEY Ulster Co. Valley of Woodland Creek. Panther Mtn. to the west, Romer, Terrace, Wittenberg and Cornell Mtns. to the east and Giant Ledge and Slide Mtn. to the south. Formerly known as Snyder's Hollow. Public campsite here. Major trail access point.

WOODPECKER RIDGE Ulster Co. Elev. 3460 ft. East of Beecher Lake and west of Balsam Lake. It is a southern offshoot to the Mill Brook Range. Beaver Kill and Quaker Clearing to the south.

WOODRIDGE Sullivan Co. At headwaters of Sandburg Creek on Silver Lake. On old O&W RR and Rtes. 53, 54 and 57. Hasidic community here. Formerly called Centerville.

WOODSTOCK Ulster Co. On the Saw Kill at foot of Overlook Mtn. to the east of Bearsville and north of West Hurley. Originally settled by Dutch and Palatinates. Some New Englanders settled here after 1783. Town looks like New England village with central green and white churches and Greek Revival homes. A very pretty town. Early industries included glass making and blowing, bluestone quarrying and charcoal burning. Many bluestone walls remain in the vicinity. The town appeals to artists and early in this century the Byrdcliffe Art Colony (see article) was founded by Ralph Whitehead. It remains active. The town appeals to a Bohemian element that is bemusedly tolerated by the natives and this makes the town a very colorful place. It also has some light industry and is one of the more attractive suburbs of the Kingston Metropolitan Area. It was named for Woodstock in England.

WOODSTOCK FESTIVAL This was originally planned to be held in Woodstock, with its artistic and Bohemian ambiance. However, the town fathers outlawed the event. After attempts to hold it at Wallkill, it was finally held on the farm of Max Yasgur on the road between White Lake and Bethel (Rte. 17B) in Sullivan County, August 14–17, 1969. It was planned as an "Aquarian Exposition," and featured

Church of Christ-on-the-Mount. Woodstock, near Meads. Photo by Alfred H. Marks.

such popular youth entertainers as Creedence Clearwater, Jefferson Airplaine, Joan Baez, The Who, Janis Joplin, Ravi Shankar and Joe Cocker. It was planned that the profits would come from a movie made of the event. While a commercial venture, it was planned to appeal to the ideals of a then very frustrated youth and give them an opportunity to demonstrate and make a peaceful statement. It succeeded very well at this and turned out to have great sociological significance as a protest against established values. Hundreds of thousands of young people came. They camped out in the fields, roosted in trees, got high on pot, skinny dipped, sang, dreamed and had a euphoric good time. Major traffic jams developed and food and sanitation facilities became overtaxed. However, even despite rain, everyone had a great time and it is generally agreed that the younger generation did make a point about their views and philosophy. Possibly it helped lead to a more open society. One thing is certain: it will long be remembered by the natives!

WORCESTER Otsego Co. On Rte. 7, D&H and Schenevus Creek northeast of Oneonto and southwest Cobleskill. 2nd Baptist Church (1841). Worcester Historical Museum, Main Street.

WURTSBORO Sullivan Co. At western foot of the Shawangunks on Rtes. 17 and 209, the Basher Kill and former routes of D&H Canal and O&W Rwy. It came into prominence upon completion of the old Cochecton Turnpike (Rte. 17) as here it crossed the Old Mine Road (Rte. 209), and was a major "jumping off" place for the "wilds" of Sullivan County. Named for the brothers Maurice and William Wurts, who projected and built the D&H Canal. Formerly named Rome.

The Green, Woodstock, with Dutch Reformed Church. Photo by Alfred H. Marks.

WYNCOOP BROOK Sullivan Co. Flows south from Paradise Lake near Curry to Neversink River at Hasbrouck.

YAGERS CAVE Ulster Co. On north slope of Overlook Mountain.

YAGERVILLE Ulster Co. On Trout Creek south of Greenville and north of Sholam.

YANKEE LAKE Sullivan Co. South of Mastens Lake and east of Wolff Lake. Drains into Pine Kill. Built as reservoir for D&H Canal.

YANKEETOWN Ulster Co. See Wittenberg P.O.

YANKEETOWN POND Ulster Co. East of Wittenberg, north of Tonshi Mtn. A source of the Little Beaver Kill.

YORK LAKE Sullivan Co. North of Minisink Ford.

YOUNGS Delaware Co. East of Sidney.

YOUNGS GAP Sullivan Co. North of Liberty and south of Parksville. Elev. 1840 ft.

YOUNGS HOLLOW Ulster Co. South of Balsam Lake and Graham Mtns., near Gulf of Mexico Brook, northeast of Quaker Clearing.

YOUNGS LAKE Herkimer Co. South of Rte. 20 in Warren.

YOUNGSVILLE Sullivan Co. On Rte. 52 west of Liberty, east of Jeffersonville on East Branch of Callicoon Creek and Panther Rock Brook.

YULAN Sullivan Co. On Rtes 21 and 22 north of Barryville. Bodine Lake is here.

William and Maurice Wurts, founders of the D & H. Courtesy of D & H RR.

ZAIDEES BOWER Ulster Co. On Mohonk grounds down from Laurel Ledge Road. A mass of tumbled boulders forming a "Natural Room." Possibly named for Zaidee Price, a farmer's daughter living in the Wallkill Valley, who attempted unsuccessfully to elope with Edward Roblin. Her father imprisoned her at home and had him thrown into jail at Goshen on a false claim of debt. Later Zaidee married another, who proved to be poor, and died of a broken heart. Ultimately Roblin escaped and eloped with the jailer's daughter.

ZENA Ulster Co. On Saw Kill east of Woodstock and north of West Hurley. Waterfalls and City of Kingston Reservoir here.

ZOAR MOUNTAIN Greene Co. Elev. 2700 ft. North of East Windham, west of Kate Hill and east of Ginseng Mtn. In the Holy Land it is to the southwest of Mts. Pisgah and Nebo. According to the Bible, it was the refuge of Lot and the only one of the three cities of the plain which was not destroyed with Sodom and Gomorra. Also spelled Segor.

ZOOM FLUME Greene Co. Artificial waterfall in East Durham.

PART V
APPENDIX

ORIGIN OF COUNTIES IN THE CATSKILL REGION

1683	Albany	Named for Duke of Albany and York, later James II.
	Ulster	Named for Duke of York's earldom (county) in Ireland.
1791	Otsego	"Place of council rock" in Indian language. Taken from Montgomery County.
1795	Schoharie	"Floating driftwood" in Indian language. Taken from Albany and Otsego Counties.
1791	Delaware	Named for the river, which was named for Lord Delaware, governor of the Virginia colony. Taken from Ulster and Otsego Counties.
1800	Greene	Named for General Nathaniel Greene. Taken from Albany and Ulster Counties.
1809	Sullivan	Named for Major General John Sullivan, who served in the French and Indian War and the Revolution. Taken from Ulster County.

POPULATION AND AREA OF CATSKILL COUNTIES AND TOWNS, 1980 CENSUS

ALBANY COUNTY
(Catskill region portion only)

Berne	2,532
Coeymans	7,896
Knox	2,471
New Scotland	8,979
Ravena	3,091
Rensselaerville	1,780
Voorheesville	3,320
Westerlo	2,929

DELAWARE COUNTY

Andes	1,312
Delhi	5,295
Deposit	1,810
Hancock	1,526
Margaretville	755
Roxbury	2,291
Sidney	4,861
Stamford	1,240
Walton	3,329

Area		
(sq. miles)	*Population*	*Per Sq. Mile*
1,440	46,824	32.5

GREENE COUNTY

Athens	3,462
Cairo	4,729
Catskill	11,453
Coxackie	6,018
Durham	2,283
Greenville	2,849
Hunter	2,252
Lexington	819
New Baltimore	3,050
Prattsville	666
Tannersville	685
Windham	1,663

Area		
(sq. miles)	*Population*	*Per Sq. Mile*
648	40,861	63.1

OTSEGO COUNTY

Cherry Valley	1,205
Cooperstown	2,342
Edmeston	1,732
Hartwick	1,796
Laurens	2,101
Maryland	1,690

Middlefield	1,870
Oneonta Twp.	4,655
Oneonta City	14,933
Richfield Springs	1,561
Springfield	1,239
Unadilla	1,367
Worcester	1,993

Area (sq. miles)	Population	Per Sq. Mile
1,004	59,075	58.8

SCHOHARIE COUNTY

Cobleskill	5,272
Esperance Twp.	1,591
Fulton	1,394
Gilboa	1,078
Middleburg	1,358
Richmondville Twp.	2,186
Schoharie Village	1,106
Schoharie Twp.	3,107
Sharon Twp.	1,915
Sharon Springs	514
Wright Twp.	1,302

Area (sq. miles)	Population	Per Sq. Mile
624	24,750	36.2

SULLIVAN COUNTY

Bethel Twp.	3,335
Bloomingburg Village	338
Callicoon	2,998
Cochecton	1,330
Fallsburgh	9,862
Liberty Twp.	9,879
Liberty Village	4,293
Mamakating Twp.	7,717
Monticello	6,306

Neversink Twp.	2,840
Rockland Twp.	4,207
Thompson Twp.	13,550
Tusten Twp.	1,424
Woodridge	809
Wurtsboro	1,128

Area (sq. miles)	Population	Per Sq. Mile
986	65,155	66.8

ULSTER COUNTY

Ellenville	4,405
Esopus Twp.	7,605
Gardiner Twp.	3,552
Hurley	6,992
Kingston City	24,481
Kingston Twp.	924
Lloyd Twp.	7,875
Marbletown	4,956
Marlborough	7,055
New Paltz Twp.	10,183
New Paltz Village	4,938
Olive Twp.	3,924
Plattekill Twp.	7,409
Rochester Twp.	5,344
Rosendale Twp.	5,933
Rosendale Village	1,134
Saugerties Twp.	17,975
Saugerties Village	3,882
Shawangunk Twp.	8,186
Ulster Twp.	12,319
Wawarsing Twp.	12,956
Woodstock	6,823

Area (sq. miles)	Population	Per Sq. Mile
1,131	158,158	139.8